BEN'S MEAT BIBLE

130 classic recipes from around the world

BEN'S MEAT BIBLE

BEN O'DONOGHUE

Foreword by Curtis Stone

hardie grant books

Contents

FOREWORD

If I could have anyone cooking a barbie for me, it's Ben.

We first met more than 15 years ago, while honing our craft (and running amok) in London during the nineties. Even back then, Ben (or, as many of us know him, Bender) was known among our mates as 'the meat freak' because of his tendency to cook and eat tonnes of it. So it is only natural that four out of five of his brilliant cookbooks are meat-centric – this bloke is really fanatical about his protein. Since those London days, we've cooked and travelled together all over Oz, and Bender continues to soak up inspiration from his travels, using new cooking techniques or experimenting with crazy, unique flavour combos. I'm in awe of what an attentive, dedicated learner he is; he's like a sponge.

Luckily for you and me, the culmination of all the meat knowledge Bender has garnered over the many years of his enviable cooking career is shared here in his aptly titled *Meat Bible*. As you would expect from a 'bible', these recipes draw on a huge array of cuisines, cuts of meat and cooking styles, and I just know this is a cookbook that will take pride of place in my collection. A few favourites so far include Japanese braised wagyu short ribs (page 32), Dukkah lamb cutlets (page 52) and finger-lickin' Brazilian cachaça chicken (page 106). How's that for diversity?

Bender, I might not say it to your face, mate, but I'm mega-proud of all you've achieved. You're one of my favourite people to cook with, learn from and teach, not to mention stay up with until 7 am yabbering on about food over a few bottles of vino. I'm looking forward to firing up the barbecue together again soon and tasting a couple more of these bloody delicious recipes first-hand from the creator – and to beating you at the game of backyard cricket that will inevitably follow. Good work, as always, mate.

Cheers guys. Get cooking!

Curtis Stone

Introduction

To put it plainly, this book is a celebration of animals. It's not deliberately the worst vegetarian recipe collection in the world, but it *is* an ode to what I love to do most: prepare and cook savoury recipes based on animal protein.

It may seem a little strange to say that this book 'celebrates' animals and go on to provide 130 recipes in which they feature as the main ingredient, but in using the term 'celebrate' I mean the sheer appreciation of every part of the animal. It would be disingenuous to the animal, and the life it has given us, if we did not make the most of all of it. This is the philosophy of nose-to-tail eating that many chefs around the world, including myself, follow when it comes to eating and cooking with meat.

For me, cooking meat is all about showing respect to the animal's life and welfare by choosing to use well-reared and well-cared-for animals, and, in death, to waste little of the animal by making use of all of it, including those parts that lie beyond the fillet – sweetmeats, offal and, of course, good old fat. Bones can be stored in the freezer for making stock and nourishing broth, and fat can be rendered and used to add flavour in all sorts of dishes. This is a lifestyle of old – and by that I don't mean paleo, I mean frugality. Traditionally, when there was meat in the kitchen, every inch of it was cherished and made use of. I remember, when asking my grandma 'what's for dinner?', the reply was often 'bread and dripping' – and I knew she was serious.

I appreciate that not everyone is on board with this particular style of cooking or eating. When I started writing this book, I also wanted to express my love of meat through recipes that I have eaten and collected from different cultures and cuisines. During my 22 years as a cook, chef and television personality, I've worked in international restaurants and I've shared meals with people from all walks of life in the far reaches of the world. Understanding and respecting cultural sensitivities when it comes to animals and how they are consumed (or in some cases, not consumed) was paramount in my travels as a chef. It is these experiences that drive me; they remind me how rich the world of meat and cooking is and how these animals are central to culinary celebrations and feasts everywhere.

Writing this book while living in Australia made me conscious of the meat available here, and I found myself holding back on some recipes. I felt that because of our climate, choosing to cook some meat, in particular game, would mean compromising on quality due to availability. While living in the UK and Europe, I absolutely loved cooking game birds like grouse, woodcock and grey leg partridge. In Australia, our environmental laws prevent us from eating our own game, with a few exceptions like roo, wallaby and emu. While filming *Surfing the Menu* with my old mate Curtis Stone, I was lucky enough to try one of the best wild birds I've ever eaten when we had a feast of magpie geese with a group of local kids in Kakadu.

For five years, while working at the River Café in London, I didn't cook or eat beef at all. This was during a time when BSE, or mad cow disease, was at its peak. Rose and Ruth (then co-owners of the River Café) flatly refused to cook beef, and they weren't going to cook anything that wasn't British. This commitment to locality impressed on me the point that we should take care when buying meat and make a point of learning about the provenance and husbandry of the animals we eat.

On that note, have a go and buy the best quality meat you can find out of respect for the animal, approach cooking your meat with frugality, use everything and, finally, cook it with love.

Ben O'Donoghue

Chef's Notes

Most ingredients in this book can be bought from good supermarkets or specialist stores. I always try to buy the best ingredients I can afford, and you'll find that there is a big pay-off in flavour when you go the extra mile.

Cheese Cheese, whether parmesan or cheddar, is always freshly grated.

Chicken Chicken is free-range and organic.

Lemons For zesting, lemons are unwaxed.

Cream Cream is generally pouring (single/light) cream with a fat content of 35%.

Eggs Eggs are standard medium 55 g (2 oz) and preferably free-range and organic.

Herbs I generally use fresh herbs, but I've noted where dried herbs are necessary (for example, in rubs and a few sauces). If I have any leftover hard herbs like thyme, sage, rosemary, curry leaves or lime leaves, I like to dry them by simply tying them together with string and hanging them up in a cool, dry place before storing them in airtight containers. When it comes to oregano, I prefer to use the flowering dried variety, sometimes known as wild oregano.

Salt Maldon is the most widely available quality sea salt but any good-quality sea salt flakes are fine. Rock salt is always coarse unless otherwise stated. Crystal salt is the same as sea salt flakes.

Spices If you're using ground spices from jars, make sure that they haven't been sitting around unused for years. Ground spices tend to lose their potency after 6 months, so if you're unsure, pick up a fresh jar – or even better, grind your own from the whole spice.

Tomato sauce Tomato sauce (ketchup) is generally good old Heinz.

BEEF & VEAL

BEEF FAJITA

OSSO BUCO WITH GREMOLATA

CLASSIC MEATLOAF

PHILLY CHEESESTEAK ROLLS

BEEF PHO

CORDON BLEU VEAL SNIZZA WITH SALSA

FRUIT-STUFFED GIANT MEATBALLS IN CRAZY WATER

BEEF RENDANG

CUBAN-STYLE CHEESEBURGER

JAPANESE BRAISED WAGYU SHORT RIBS

CARPETBAG STEAK WITH KATAIFI-WRAPPED OYSTERS

VEAL SWEETBREADS WITH REMOULADE

EASY BIBIMBAP BEEF

PULLED BEEF BURGERS

HERB'S LASAGNE

STEAK, SMASHED POTATOES AND BÉARNAISE

SALT BEEF BAGEL WITH HOT ENGLISH MUSTARD AND PICKLES

STEAK TARTARE

BEEF MASSAMAN CURRY

Beef fajita

SERVES 4–6

1 × 500 g (1 lb 2 oz) wagyu beef skirt or flank steak
8 small corn tortillas
100 g (3½ oz/¾ cup) grated cheddar cheese
1 quantity Guacamole (page 220)
250 g (9 oz/1 cup) sour cream
2 limes, sliced into wedges

MARINADE

2 tinned chipotle chillies in adobo
1 teaspoon smoked paprika
250 ml (8½ fl oz/1 cup) freshly squeezed orange juice
juice of ½ lime
3 tablespoons tomato sauce (ketchup)
2 tablespoons dried oregano
½ teaspoon ground cumin
2 tablespoons white-wine vinegar
2 teaspoons salt
½ teaspoon ground black pepper

QUICK-PICKLED ONIONS

250 ml (8½ fl oz/1 cup) water
½ tablespoon dried oregano
2 bay leaves
½ teaspoon ground cumin
1 habanero or fresh green chilli, sliced
2 red onions, finely sliced and soaked in salted water for 30 minutes
1 garlic clove, crushed
1 tablespoon sherry vinegar

TOMATO SALSA

3 vine-ripened tomatoes, diced
juice of 1 lime
2 tablespoons chopped fresh coriander (cilantro)
salt and pepper, to taste

This Mexican feast will knock your socks off. The quick-pickled onions really liven up your taste buds and the guacamole will blow you away. If you're not up to making the full feast, then keep it simple with either the salsa or the onions and serve alongside grated cheese and sour cream.

First, prepare the marinade by mixing the ingredients in a large bowl. Add the beef, combine thoroughly and allow to marinate for at least 2 hours, preferably overnight.

To make the quick-pickled onions, bring the water, herbs, spices and chilli to the boil in a small saucepan. Drain the onions and place them in a bowl with the garlic. Pour the aromatic liquid over the onions and garlic, then leave to cool for at least 1 hour.

Prepare the tomato salsa by combining the salsa ingredients in a bowl. Adjust the seasoning to taste and set aside.

When ready to cook, remove the beef from the marinade and set it aside on a plate. Pour the marinade into a small saucepan and simmer for 10 minutes, until thickened and reduced.

Heat a chargrill pan over high heat (or crank up the barbecue) and cook the beef for 2–4 minutes on each side, or until cooked to your liking. Remove to a chopping board and slice into fine strips across the grain. Drizzle with the cooked marinade.

Drain the cooled pickled onions and sprinkle with the vinegar before serving.

To enjoy, fill a tortilla with beef, quick-pickled onions and salsa, then add cheese, guacamole, sour cream and fresh lime to your liking. This is great served buffet-style, so everyone can make their fajita to their tastes.

Osso buco with gremolata

SERVES 4

35 g (1¼ oz/¼ cup) plain (all-purpose) flour

salt and freshly ground black pepper

4 × 450 g (1 lb) pieces veal shin on the bone, about 4 cm (1½ in) thick

2 tablespoons olive oil

100 g (3½ oz) salted butter

1 onion, finely chopped

1 carrot, finely chopped

1 celery stalk, finely chopped

375 ml (12½ fl oz/1½ cups) dry white wine

400 g (14 oz) tinned chopped tomatoes

1 garlic bulb, sliced through the centre horizontally

zest of 1 unwaxed lemon

250 ml (8½ fl oz/1 cup) veal or beef stock (see page 216), plus extra if needed

GREMOLATA

3 garlic cloves

1 bunch flat-leaf (Italian) parsley, leaves picked

shredded zest of 2 unwaxed lemons

Preheat the oven to 180°C (350°F).

Season the flour generously with salt and pepper. Lightly dredge the veal pieces in the seasoned flour and shake off the excess flour.

Heat the oil and butter in a large flameproof casserole dish. Working in batches, fry the veal over a high heat for 2–3 minutes on each side, until browned, then transfer to a plate.

Turn the heat down to medium and sauté the onion, carrot and celery for 5–7 minutes, until golden. Pour in the wine and allow it to bubble away for 5 minutes, stirring, until the liquid has reduced by half. Stir in the tomatoes, garlic, lemon zest, stock and season with salt and pepper. Immerse the veal in this sauce – the liquid should come at least halfway up the sides of the dish – then bring to the boil. Cover the pan with a sheet of baking paper and then aluminium foil.

Cook in the preheated oven for 1–1½ hours, or until the veal is very tender and almost falling from the bone. Stir from time to time, gently moving the slices, and if it seems dry, add a little more stock or water.

While the veal is cooking, make the gremolata. Roughly chop the garlic and parsley leaves together. Mix in the shredded zest and pile the gremolata in a bowl.

Once cooked, carefully remove the osso buco from the sauce in whole pieces; it is traditionally served with the delicious bone marrow in the centre of each piece. Taste the sauce for seasoning and use a hand-held blender to whizz until smooth.

Serve the osso buco with a lovely creamy mash or soft polenta (page 182), and top with the sauce and liberal sprinklings of gremolata.

Classic meatloaf

SERVES 6–8

3 slices white bread, crusts removed
1 onion, diced
2 celery stalks, diced
2 carrots, diced
2 garlic cloves, diced
1 rosemary sprig, finely chopped
500 g (1 lb 2 oz) minced (ground) beef
500 g (1 lb 2 oz) minced (ground) veal
2 eggs, beaten
2 teaspoons dijon mustard
125 ml (4 fl oz/½ cup) tomato sauce (ketchup)
1 teaspoon Tabasco sauce
50 g (1¾ oz/⅓ cup) roasted macadamia nuts, roughly chopped
200 g (7 oz) pancetta or bacon slices
3 tablespoons Vanilla bourbon syrup (page 222) or 2 teaspoons maple syrup

Preheat the oven to 180°C (350°F).

Whizz the bread in a food processor to fine crumbs, then transfer to a large bowl and mix together with the diced vegetables, garlic and rosemary. In a separate bowl, mix the beef, veal, eggs, mustard, tomato sauce and Tabasco, then use your hands to knead until thoroughly combined. Mix the meat and breadcrumb mixtures together, along with the nuts. Combine, but don't overmix.

Line a 20 cm × 10 cm × 6 cm (8 in × 4 in × 2½ in) loaf tin with the pancetta, slightly overlapping each piece. Gently brush the pancetta with the vanilla bourbon syrup, making sure you cover the sides as well as the base.

Spoon the meatloaf mixture into the tin and press down so the meat is evenly distributed. Fold over the pancetta ends and flatten the top of the meatloaf. Drizzle with the remaining bourbon syrup and bake in the oven for 45 minutes.

Remove the meatloaf from the oven and set aside for 5 minutes before inverting onto a baking tray lined with non-stick baking paper. Return the meatloaf to the oven and bake for a further 5–10 minutes to colour up the pancetta – it should turn a lovely golden brown. When the meatloaf is done, allow to cool for 5 minutes. Transfer to a chopping board and serve sliced into thick slabs.

Philly cheesesteak rolls

SERVES 4

2 red onions, sliced
1 green capsicum (bell pepper), seeds removed and sliced
2 tablespoons olive oil
4 long, soft bread rolls
salted butter, to spread
1 teaspoon Meat salt (page 225) or sea salt
2 habanero chillies, sliced
150 g (5½ oz/1 cup) grated Monterey Jack or cheddar cheese

BEEF PATTIES

500 g (1 lb 2 oz) minced (ground) beef
4 garlic cloves, finely chopped
1 small green capsicum (bell pepper), seeds removed and diced
1 large red onion, grated
1 teaspoon ground cumin
salt and freshly ground black pepper

It would seem that dude food or American diner food is quite trendy, and I think it has its place. It's not something you want to eat every week, but once in a while it hits the spot. This recipe is my take on the famous steak sandwich and really is the duck's nuts. I have given this a super-charge in the heat department by using habanero chillies. Traditionally, Philly cheesesteak rolls use rib-eye, but burger patties work really well – not to mention they're more economical.

Preheat the barbecue or place a chargrill pan over a medium–high heat.

To make the patties, use your hands to mix the beef with the garlic, capsicum, onion and cumin and season well with salt and pepper. Form into 4 burger-sized patties about 1 cm (½ in) thick and cook on the barbecue or chargrill pan over medium heat for roughly 4 minutes on each side for medium rare. Set aside.

Meanwhile, preheat the grill (broiler) to medium. Place the sliced onions and capsicum on a baking tray under the grill, drizzle over the oil and cook for 5 minutes, until soft.

Slice open the buns and spread them with butter. Use your hands to break the cooked beef patties into pieces and place them on the base of the bun. Next, add the grilled onions and capsicum. Season the buns with the meat salt, layer on the sliced chillies and top generously with cheese.

Place the filled rolls under the grill and cook until the cheese has melted and the buns are golden.

Beef pho

SERVES 4

500 g (1 lb 2 oz) dried rice noodles for pho
500 g (1 lb 2 oz) beef sirloin or blade, sliced very thinly

PHO BROTH

2 kg (4 lb 6 oz) raw beef bones (brisket bones are best)
2 onions, roughly diced
3 cm (1¼ in) piece fresh ginger, peeled and sliced
5 star anise
3 cinnamon sticks or cassia bark pieces
500 g (1 lb 2 oz) beef brisket (optional)

GARNISHES

large handful bean sprouts
large handful Thai basil
red bird's eye chilli, sliced
lime or lemon wedges
Fermented chilli sauce (page 221) or sriracha
hoisin sauce

This is a classic Vietnamese noodle soup, and requires some preparation the day before you want to eat this dish. The broth makes more than you need for this recipe – use the remaining broth for the delicious, dumpling-filled Short soup on page 138 or freeze it for another time.

Prepare the pho broth one day in advance.

Place the bones in a large pan and add enough water to cover. Bring to the boil and cook vigorously for 5 minutes. Drain and rinse the bones in cold water. Wipe out the pan with paper towel and replace the bones. Pour in 6 litres (202 fl oz/24 cups) of fresh cold water. Bring to the boil over high heat, then reduce the heat to a gentle simmer. Skim off any scum that comes to the surface. Add the remaining broth ingredients and the beef brisket (if using) and simmer, partially covered, for 3 hours. Season with salt and a little sugar to taste, if necessary.

Drain the broth into a large container and cool before refrigerating. Skim off any residual fat that comes to the surface once the broth has cooled. Slice the beef brisket and refrigerate.

The next day, soak the rice noodles in a large bowl of boiling water and leave to soften for about 10 minutes, or until the noodles are tender. Drain and set aside.

In a large saucepan, bring 2.5 litres (85 fl oz/10 cups) of the pho broth to a rolling boil over high heat.

Divide the drained rice noodles, raw beef slices and the reserved beef brisket between serving bowls. Ladle over the hot broth (this will cook the raw beef). Serve garnished with bean sprouts and Thai basil. Allow everyone to season their bowl with as much fresh chilli, lime or lemon juice, chilli sauce and hoisin sauce as they like.

Cordon bleu veal snizza with salsa

SERVES 4

8 veal scaloppine, weighing 125 g (4½ oz) each
4 slices leg ham
8 slices provolone cheese or fresh mozzarella
75 g (2¾ oz/½ cup) plain (all-purpose) flour
salt and freshly ground black pepper
3 eggs, lightly beaten
60 g (2 oz/1 cup) Japanese panko breadcrumbs or dried breadcrumbs
125 ml (4 fl oz/½ cup) vegetable oil
2 large knobs salted butter
rocket (arugula) or watercress, to serve

SALSA

2 vine-ripened tomatoes, seeds removed, diced
½ red onion, diced
10 basil leaves, chopped
2 tablespoons red-wine vinegar
2 tablespoons extra-virgin olive oil
salt and freshly ground black pepper

I have a very vivid image of eating this as a young child. Cordon bleu was my go-to dish if and when we had to go out for dinner. Mum and Dad would have a bottle of Black Tower Riesling along with the meal, which I think in the 1970s was par for the course. Veal cordon bleu is pretty much a schnitzel on steroids. The salsa adds a freshness to this dish, but the Blue cheese sauce on page 222 also does the trick.

Sandwich the veal between 2 sheets of plastic wrap and pound with a meat mallet or rolling pin, until about 5 mm (¼ in) thick. Take 2 veal scaloppines of the same size and top one with a slice of ham, leaving a 5 mm (¼ in) border of veal around the edges. The ham should not be overhanging; if it is, just trim it back to fit.

Next, lay a double layer of cheese on top of the ham and place the second scaloppine on top. Lightly pound around the edges with the mallet (or rolling pin) to seal. Repeat to make 3 more veal sandwiches.

In a shallow dish, mix together the flour, salt and pepper. Set up your bench with an assembly line of seasoned flour, beaten eggs and breadcrumbs.

Dredge the sandwiched veal in the flour, knocking off any excess, then dip into the egg, followed by the breadcrumbs. Use your hands to firmly press the breadcrumbs onto the veal. If you have time, transfer the veal to a baking tray lined with baking paper and chill in the refrigerator for 1 hour before cooking. (This will help the crumbs stay intact when cooking.)

Meanwhile, make the salsa. Mix the tomatoes, onion, basil, vinegar, olive oil and salt and pepper in a small bowl.

To cook the veal, heat half the oil and half the butter in a medium-sized non-stick frying pan until the butter is foaming. Add 2 portions of the veal to the pan and cook over high heat for 1 minute. Turn the heat down to medium and continue to cook for a further 3–4 minutes. Flip the veal over and cook for a further 3 minutes. Drain on paper towel and place in a warm oven while you repeat the process with the remaining veal portions. Serve with the salsa on top of the veal with rocket or watercress on the side.

Fruit-stuffed giant meatballs in crazy water

SERVES 4

400 ml (13½ fl oz/1⅔ cups) good-quality chicken stock (see page 216)

100 g (3½ oz/½ cup) yellow split peas, soaked overnight and drained

1 teaspoon sea salt

450 g (1 lb) minced (ground) beef

2 shallots, finely diced

2 eggs

1 tablespoon rice flour

60 g (2 oz/¼ cup) dried apricot halves, diced

6 dried dates, halved, pitted and diced

2 tablespoons currants

2 tablespoons pistachios

2 tablespoons pine nuts

125 g (4½ oz/⅔ cup) short-grain rice, soaked overnight and drained

cooked couscous, to serve

mint and flat-leaf (Italian) parsley, chopped, to garnish

CRAZY WATER

675 g (1½ lb) tomatoes

900 ml (30½ fl oz) cold water

3 large garlic cloves, chopped

2 tablespoons finely chopped flat-leaf (Italian) parsley

½ small fresh red chilli or ½ teaspoon dried chilli flakes

3 tablespoons extra-virgin olive oil

We made this dish for a Persian dinner special at Billykart Kitchen. The recipe is inspired by one of Greg Malouf's – mine is slightly simpler and includes a delicious 'crazy water' sauce.

Prepare the meatballs. In a medium-sized saucepan, bring the stock to the boil. Add the split peas, return to the boil, then lower the heat. Cover and simmer for 20–30 minutes, or until the stock has been completely absorbed. Season with the salt, transfer to a large bowl, then leave to cool completely.

In a separate large bowl, combine the beef with the shallots, eggs, rice flour, dried fruit and nuts. Take a handful of the mixture and throw it against the inside of the bowl in a slapping motion. Continue to grab handfuls of the mixture, slapping it repeatedly. This will help the meatballs hold together. Add the drained rice and split peas and use your hands to combine and slap the mixture again. Repeat this action for about 5 minutes, until the mixture becomes firm and compact (about 20 slaps should do it).

Next, make the 'crazy water' to poach the meatballs in. Place the tomatoes in a large saucepan of boiling water for 1 minute. Drain and rinse under cold water and allow to cool. Remove and discard the skins, scoop out and discard the seeds, then dice the flesh. Return the tomatoes to the saucepan, along with the remaining ingredients for the crazy water, and bring to the boil. Simmer over medium heat for 15–20 minutes to reduce the liquid by about half.

Divide the meatball mixture into 8 equal portions. Using wet hands, roll each portion into a smooth round ball about the size of a tennis ball. Drop the meatballs into the bubbling crazy water, then cover and simmer for 1 hour, turning occasionally to ensure the meatballs cook evenly.

Serve the meatballs and broth with some couscous on the side. Sprinkle over some fresh mint and parsley to finish.

Beef rendang

SERVES 4–6

90 g (3 oz/1 cup) desiccated (dried, shredded) coconut
100 ml (3½ fl oz) coconut oil
60 g (2 oz) *sambal oelek* (see note)
60 g (2 oz) tamarind concentrate
1 heaped tablespoon white (granulated) sugar, plus extra if needed
1 heaped tablespoon palm sugar (jaggery) or soft brown sugar
5 kaffir lime leaves, 1 finely sliced
1 lemongrass stalk, bruised
800 g (1 lb 12 oz) beef skirt steak (I like grass-fed steak), sliced into large chunks
200 ml (7 fl oz) water
800 ml (27 fl oz) coconut milk
juice of 1–2 limes
2 teaspoons fish sauce
steamed rice, to serve

SPICE PASTE

20 g (¾ oz) shallots
20 g (¾ oz) ginger
30 g (¾ oz) galangal
20 g (¾ oz) garlic cloves
90 g (3 oz) lemongrass stalks, white parts only

Toast the coconut in a small frying pan until golden and aromatic. Remove from the heat and allow to cool. Blitz in a food processor until you have fine crumbs and set aside.

Next, make the spice paste. Place the ingredients in a food processor or blender and blitz until you have a fine paste. Add a splash of water if the paste is a little dry.

Heat the coconut oil in a large heavy-based saucepan over medium heat and fry the spice paste for 5 minutes, or until aromatic. Add the sambal oelek and tamarind concentrate, then continue to cook until the oil begins to separate from the mixture. Stir in both the sugars, the whole lime leaves and the bruised lemongrass. Add the beef and allow to cook in the paste for 2–3 minutes. Pour in the water and coconut milk and bring to the boil, then reduce the heat and simmer for about 1 hour, or until the meat is tender.

Season with lime juice to taste, and add the fish sauce and a little more sugar if needed.

Garnish with the reserved finely sliced lime leaf and serve with rice.

NOTE

Sambal oelek *is a spicy Indonesian chilli paste that can be found in Asian supermarkets.*

Cuban-style cheeseburger

SERVES 4

1 tablespoon oil
4 sesame hamburger buns, halved
4 tablespoons dijon mustard
8 slices Swiss cheese
4 slices good-quality smoked leg ham
4 large gherkins or pickles, sliced, plus extra to serve
softened butter, to brush the buns
fries, to serve (optional)

BEEF PATTIES

500 g (1 lb 2 oz) minced (ground) beef or veal
4 garlic cloves, finely diced
1 small green capsicum (bell pepper), finely diced
50 g (1¾ oz/⅓ cup) grated red onion
¾ teaspoon ground cumin
1½ teaspoons sweet Spanish paprika
salt and freshly ground black pepper

To prepare the patties, use your hands to mix the beef with the garlic, capsicum, onion and spices until well combined. Season with salt and pepper. Form the mixture into 4 burger-sized patties.

In a large frying pan, heat the oil. Cook the patties over medium–high heat for 4–6 minutes on each side, until well coloured and medium rare (or cooked to your liking). Remove from the pan and set aside.

Give the pan a wipe with paper towel and place back on the heat. Toast the buns in the pan and spread the tops and bottoms with mustard.

Lay a slice of cheese on the bottom portion of each bun and place a patty on top, followed by a slice of ham, another slice of cheese, and finally the pickle. Top with the other half of the bun and repeat with the remaining burgers. Brush the buns well with butter and cook on a sandwich press until golden and the cheese is melted and oozing. Alternatively, wrap the burgers in foil and cook in a hot frying pan with a heavy-based pan placed on top of the burger to press it down. Cook until golden brown and the cheese is melted.

Serve with extra pickles and French fries if you like.

Japanese braised wagyu short ribs

SERVES 4

4 × 300 g (10½ oz) wagyu beef short ribs
100 ml (3½ fl oz) light soy sauce
3 spring onions (scallions), white parts only, chopped
3 dried shiitake mushrooms
3 garlic cloves
500 ml (17 fl oz/2 cups) veal or beef stock
100 g (3½ oz) unsalted butter, cubed

AJÍ PANCA SAUCE

½ teaspoon dried oregano
1 tablespoon fermented Korean chilli paste (available from Asian supermarkets)
60 ml (2 fl oz/¼ cup) rice vinegar
1 teaspoon sea salt flakes
1 teaspoon finely cracked black pepper
1 tablespoon finely grated garlic
1 teaspoon ground cumin
2 tablespoons sake
2 tablespoons sunflower oil

TO SERVE

cooked short-grain rice
Togarashi salt (page 227)
shiso cress or watercress

Once a month at Billykart Kitchen we do a different Friday night menu that focuses on a particular cuisine from around the world. This braised short rib recipe from our Japanese night was one of our most popular dishes. Having access to a water bath and circulators at the restaurant allows us to cook meat at low temperatures for long periods of time, which helps achieve a lovely soft texture in the meat. However, this oven method is a perfectly good alternative. The *ají panca* sauce is spicy and sharp and helps cut the richness of the beef.

Place the beef and soy sauce in a large zip-lock bag. Transfer to the refrigerator to marinate for at least 3 hours or, ideally, overnight.

Preheat the oven to 110°C (225°F). Remove the ribs from the marinade and place them in a flameproof casserole dish with the spring onion whites, mushrooms, garlic and stock. Cover with a sheet of baking paper, then with aluminium foil and finally seal with the lid. Place in the oven and allow to cook for 4–5 hours, or until the beef is very tender.

Meanwhile, make the *ají panca* sauce. Blend the sauce ingredients together in a food processor and set aside.

Carefully remove the beef to a plate. Strain the cooking liquid into a small saucepan and skim as much fat as possible from the surface. Place the pan with the cooking liquid over a medium heat and simmer, uncovered, to reduce the liquid by about half. Transfer the beef back into the casserole dish, along with the reduced liquor, and heat to a simmer on the stove top. Add the butter and use a spoon to baste the sauce continuously over the beef. The sauce should be thick and evenly glaze the ribs. Stir in the *ají panca* sauce and check the seasoning. Continue to simmer for a further 10 minutes, basting with the glaze frequently.

Serve with steamed rice sprinkled with togarashi salt and shiso cress or watercress.

NOTE

Wagyu short ribs are available from specialty butchers, but if you can't find them, use the more affordable alternative of grass-fed beef short ribs. If you have time, marinate the beef the night before you want to cook it for maximum flavour. Any left-over ají panca *sauce is also excellent served with chargrilled steak.*

Carpetbag steak with kataifi-wrapped oysters

SERVES 4

4 x 200 g (7 oz) pieces beef fillet, middle cut or thick end
16 Pacific oysters, cleaned and grit-free
12 slices prosciutto or bacon
1 tablespoon dried wakame seaweed
1 teaspoon light soy sauce
1 teaspoon rice vinegar
½ teaspoon caster (superfine) sugar
½ teaspoon sesame oil
500 ml (17 fl oz/2 cups) vegetable oil, plus 2 tablespoons
1 knob salted butter
2 tablespoons oyster sauce
100 g (3½ oz) kataifi pastry (see note)
1 tablespoon wasabi paste
sea salt flakes
1 teaspoon toasted sesame seeds

This recipe is a throwback to a golden age of classic club food – the 1950s and 1960s. As a kid, I remember these were on the menu at our local seaman's club in Port Hedland. Here, I've reworked this retro dish, making it a little more modern.

Preheat the oven to 180°C (350°F). Use a sharp paring knife to cut a horizontal pocket in the side of each beef fillet. Fill each pocket with 2 oysters. Wrap the prosciutto around the beef, then use a toothpick to secure the prosciutto to the beef by piercing it through.

Soak the wakame in a small bowl of water for 5 minutes, drain, then squeeze out the excess liquid. In another small bowl, combine the soy sauce, vinegar, sugar and sesame oil, then add the wakame and toss to coat. Set aside while you get on with the rest of the recipe.

Heat 2 tablespoons of the oil and all of the butter in a flameproof casserole dish or frying pan over medium heat and seal the beef, turning often, for 4–5 minutes. Use a brush to baste the beef all over with the oyster sauce, then transfer to the oven and cook for a further 10–15 minutes for medium rare. Remove from the oven and allow to rest for 10 minutes (the beef will continue to cook while it is resting). Brush with the remaining oyster sauce and set aside.

Arrange the kataifi into 8 evenly sized bunches on a dry chopping board or work surface. Dab a touch of wasabi paste on an oyster, lay it on the edge of a kataifi bunch and gently roll up to enclose. Repeat with the remaining oysters.

Heat the oil in a small saucepan and fry the kataifi-wrapped oysters for 1 minute, until lightly golden brown. Drain on paper towel and season with sea salt.

Serve each steak with 2 crisp oysters and a small pile of the wakame salad, then top with the sesame seeds.

NOTE

Kataifi pastry is a finely shredded pastry that is typically used in Mediterranean and Middle Eastern cooking. It can be bought from most Greek delis and Lebanese or Turkish stores; there is no real substitute as hand cutting filo just doesn't cut the mustard.

Veal sweetbreads with remoulade

SERVES 4

I started cooking sweetbreads when I was first sous chef in Sydney and I fell in love with them. Most people shy away from eating them but they are wonderful if prepared well. They have a soft texture and nutty flavour. If you like lambs' brains, then these are a step up.

500 g (1 lb 2 oz) veal sweetbreads
1 tablespoon good-quality dijon mustard
salt and freshly ground black pepper
120 g (4½ oz/2 cups) Japanese panko breadcrumbs or fresh white breadcrumbs
125 ml (4 fl oz/½ cup) vegetable oil
100 g (3½ oz) salted butter
lemon wedges, to serve

POACHING LIQUOR

375 ml (12½ fl oz/1½ cups) cold water
125 ml (4 fl oz/½ cup) white wine
1 onion
1 celery stalk
1 teaspoon black peppercorns
4–5 thyme sprigs
1 bay leaf

CELERY REMOULADE

185 g (6½ oz/¾ cup) whole-egg mayonnaise
2 hard-boiled eggs
2 teaspoons dijon mustard
1 teaspoon tarragon vinegar or white-wine vinegar
¼ teaspoon Tabasco sauce
2 teaspoons capers, rinsed and chopped
1 tablespoon chopped flat-leaf (Italian) parsley
1 spring onion (scallion), white part only, chopped finely
½ bunch celery, stalks and leaves
½ bunch mint leaves
dash of extra-virgin olive oil
lemon juice, to taste

Soak your sweetbreads in plenty of cold water for at least 2 hours or, ideally, overnight.

Drain the sweetbreads and combine with all the poaching liquor ingredients in a saucepan. Bring to the boil over high heat and skim off any scum that appears on the surface. Reduce the heat and simmer for 10 minutes. Turn the heat off and allow the sweetbreads to steep for 10 minutes before removing them from the liquor.

Remove the outer membrane from the sweetbreads, being careful not to pick at every little membrane, or you will be left with only small nuggets. Transfer to the refrigerator to cool for 20 minutes.

Meanwhile, make the celery remoulade. In a bowl, mix all the ingredients for the remoulade, except for the celery, mint, olive oil and lemon. Taste and adjust the seasoning if required. Slice the celery stalks finely and stir them into the mixture. Fold in the celery and mint leaves and dress with a dash of olive oil and lemon juice to taste. Set aside.

Pat the sweetbreads dry, spread liberally with mustard and season with salt and pepper. Place the breadcrumbs into a large bowl and dip the sweetbreads in, turning to coat. Gently press to stick the crumbs to the sweetbreads.

Heat half the oil and half the butter in a non-stick frying pan over medium heat until the butter is foaming. Carefully add the sweetbreads one at a time, cooking in batches if necessary to avoid overcrowding the pan. Allow the sweetbreads to brown on one side for 3–4 minutes, basting with the butter in the pan as they cook. Allow them to develop a nice golden crust before flipping over and cooking on the other side for another 3 minutes, until golden brown.

Serve the sweetbreads with the remoulade and a wedge of fresh lemon.

Easy bibimbap beef

SERVES 4

370 g (13 oz/2 cups) short-grain white rice
90 g (3 oz/1 cup) bean sprouts
60 ml (2 fl oz/¼ cup) rice vinegar
2 teaspoons salt
1 tablespoon sugar
3 tablespoons light soy sauce
pinch chilli powder
3 teaspoons sesame oil
1 carrot, sliced into thin matchsticks
2 garlic cloves, finely chopped
salt and freshly ground black pepper
1 zucchini (courgette), sliced into thin matchsticks
400 g (14 oz) beef fillet, thinly sliced
2 egg yolks
60 g (2 oz/¼ cup) Japanese mayonnaise
1 spring onion (scallion), chopped
2 sheets toasted nori, sliced into thin matchsticks
1 tablespoon toasted sesame seeds
kimchi, to serve (optional)

KOREAN HOT SAUCE

80 ml (2½ fl oz/⅓ cup) fermented Korean chilli paste (available from Asian supermarkets)
125 g (4½ oz/½ cup) miso paste
1 tablespoon finely chopped bird's eye chillies
1 tablespoon finely chopped green capsicum (bell pepper)
6 garlic cloves
60 g (2 oz/⅓ cup) sesame seeds
2 tablespoons rice vinegar
1 tablespoon sesame oil

This is a Korean staple and an extremely popular dish. The name 'bibimbap' basically translates as 'mixed rice' and is perfect for a quick and simple weeknight meal. To make life easier, find one of those funky peelers that creates fine, long strands of veg to save on all the knife work; it will be your friend for life. If you don't fancy mixing raw egg into the rice, simply fry some eggs to serve on top of the rice.

To make the Korean hot sauce, place all the ingredients in a food processor and purée until smooth. Set aside 2 tablespoons of the sauce and store the remainder in the refrigerator (see note).

Rinse the rice under cold running water until the water runs clear. Drain and transfer to a saucepan, along with 1 litre (34 fl oz/4 cups) fresh water. Bring to a simmer over medium heat, then reduce the heat to low, cover and cook for 15–20 minutes, or until tender but not mushy. Set aside.

Bring a saucepan of salted water to the boil and blanch the bean sprouts for 30 seconds. Drain and refresh under cold running water. Transfer to a small bowl and set aside.

Combine the vinegar, salt, sugar, 1 tablespoon of the soy sauce and the chilli powder in a small saucepan. Bring to the boil and stir continuously to dissolve the sugar. Remove from the heat and allow to cool. Pour the cooled mixture over the bean sprouts and set aside to pickle.

Meanwhile, heat 1 teaspoon of the sesame oil in a large frying pan over high heat. Add the carrot and half the garlic, and stir-fry for 1 minute. Season to taste with salt and pepper and use a slotted spoon to remove the garlic and carrot. Set aside. Repeat with the zucchini and the remaining garlic.

Heat the remaining sesame oil in the pan over medium–high heat. Add the beef and stir-fry for 1–2 minutes, until browned and just cooked through. Add the remaining soy sauce and set aside.

Divide the cooked rice between serving bowls and arrange the carrot, zucchini, beef, pickled bean sprouts and egg yolks on top. Dollop with a little mayonnaise and scatter over the spring onion, toasted nori and sesame seeds. Serve with the Korean hot sauce and, if you like, a side of kimchi.

NOTE

This recipe makes more Korean hot sauce than you need for the recipe, about 200 g (7 oz). Store the remaining sauce in an airtight container, where it will keep refrigerated for up to 3 weeks. The Korean hot sauce is just like any tasty condiment, but better! It's excellent served alongside barbecued or grilled meat or fish – and in burgers, too.

Pulled beef burgers

SERVES 6

1 × 2 kg (4 lb 6 oz) piece beef brisket, thick end
2 tablespoons Meat salt (page 225)
2 tablespoons soft brown sugar
125 ml (4 fl oz/½ cup) water
250 ml (8½ fl oz/1 cup) Barbecue sauce (page 223)
salt and freshly ground black pepper
6 soft burger or hot-dog buns
salted butter, melted, to brush the buns
habanero chilli sauce, to taste

SLAW

¼ head red cabbage, finely sliced
3 tablespoons sour cream, plus extra to serve
juice of 2 limes
1 red onion, finely sliced
½ bunch tarragon
½ bunch chives, cut into 2 cm (¾ in) lengths

We use brisket a lot at Billykart Kitchen. It's a great cut of meat that's full of flavour and well-marbled with intercostal fat, especially the thick end, which really lends itself to long, slow cooking methods. These pulled beef burgers sell so well and are such a treat to eat. Well worth the effort! Make the barbecue sauce in advance. Don't despair if you have leftovers – I like to use the beef as a filling for pierogi (page 74) and serve simply with sour cream.

The day before you want to eat this, prepare the beef. Mix the meat salt in a small bowl with the sugar. Rub this mixture all over the beef and allow to marinate overnight in the refrigerator.

Preheat the oven to 160°C (320°F). Transfer the beef to a roasting tin, pour in the water and cover tightly with foil. Roast in the oven for 5–6 hours, until meltingly tender and falling apart. Use a fork to shred the beef, stir in enough of the barbecue sauce to moisten, and season with salt and pepper.

Make the slaw. In a large non-reactive bowl, mix the cabbage, sour cream and lime juice with your hands until the cabbage is well-coated. Add the onion and herbs and season well with salt and pepper.

Toast the buns lightly by heating them in the oven for 5 minutes. Brush the tops and bottoms with butter. Fill the buns with pulled beef, a little more barbecue sauce if desired, slaw, extra sour cream and chilli sauce.

Herb's lasagne

SERVES 8

60 ml (2 fl oz/¼ cup) olive oil
2 onions, grated
3 carrots, grated
2 celery stalks, grated
2 zucchini (courgettes), grated
500 g (1 lb 2 oz) minced (ground) beef (preferably grass-fed beef)
2 tablespoons dried oregano
800 g (1 lb 12 oz) tinned chopped tomatoes
250 g (9 oz) dried lasagne sheets
butter, for greasing
250 g (9 oz/2 cups) grated cheddar cheese

WHITE SAUCE

100 g (3½ oz) salted butter
100 g (3½ oz) plain (all-purpose) flour
1 litre (34 fl oz/4 cups) milk
1 teaspoon hot English mustard
salt and freshly ground black pepper

My son Herb absolutely loves lasagne. I've seen him eat three or four portions of this in one go! Herb isn't a huge fan of veg so my wife Dee and I smuggle it into the meaty sauce.

Heat 2 tablespoons of the oil in a large heavy-based saucepan and gently cook the grated vegetables for 5 minutes, until softened. Add the beef and oregano, breaking up the beef with a wooden spoon and allowing it to brown. Add the tomatoes, along with 400 ml (13½ fl oz) water, to the beef. Cover, turn the heat down to medium and cook for 1 hour while you prepare the rest of the lasagne.

Bring a large saucepan of water to the boil and blanch the lasagne sheets a couple at a time until soft but not completely cooked. Remove with a slotted spoon and brush each sheet with a little of the remaining oil to prevent them from sticking to one another. Set aside on a plate.

Preheat the oven to 170°C (340°F) and grease a 30 cm × 25 cm × 6 cm (12 in × 10 in × 2½ in) ovenproof dish with butter.

Make the white sauce by melting the butter in a medium-sized saucepan. Add the flour and stir vigorously with a wooden spoon until it comes together in a smooth paste. Cook over medium heat for 1–2 minutes, then add half the milk, a little at a time, whisking continuously until the sauce thickens. Whisk in the remaining milk; it should be a thick but pourable consistency. Stir in the mustard and season well with salt and pepper.

To assemble the lasagne, spread a layer of white sauce over the base of the greased dish. Top with a layer of the parboiled pasta sheets, followed by a thin layer of beef sauce, making sure to completely cover the pasta. Repeat the layers 4–5 times until you have used all of the pasta and beef sauce, and finish with a final layer of white sauce. Scatter over the cheese and bake for 30–40 minutes, until golden brown and bubbling. Remove from the oven and allow to sit for a few minutes before slicing up to serve.

Steak, smashed potatoes and béarnaise

SERVES 4

500 g (1 lb 2 oz) small potatoes, skin on
2 tablespoons Meat salt (page 225)
2 tablespoons duck fat (see page 229)
4 × bone-in rib-eye (tomahawk) steaks (about 375 g/13 oz each)
1 tablespoon olive oil
salt and freshly ground black pepper

BÉARNAISE SAUCE

3 tablespoons white-wine vinegar
5 black peppercorns
1 bay leaf
1 shallot, finely chopped
1 tarragon sprig, plus 1 teaspoon chopped tarragon
1 large egg yolk
200 g (7 oz) unsalted butter, melted

Place the potatoes in a large saucepan and fill with water. Bring to the boil and simmer for 10–15 minutes, until just tender but still firm. Drain and allow to cool slightly. Use the palm of your hands to squash the potatoes, one by one, and place them in a bowl. Season with the meat salt.

Heat the duck fat in a large non-stick frying pan over high heat until hot and almost smoking. Add the smashed potatoes, turn the heat down to medium and cook, undisturbed, to allow a crust to form on the outside of the potatoes. Try not to stir them, as they will continue to break up as they cook – only turn them over once.

Preheat the barbecue or place a large chargrill pan over medium–high heat.

Rub the steaks with the olive oil and season well with salt and pepper. Cook on the barbecue or chargrill pan over medium–high heat until cooked to your liking (10–12 minutes per side for medium rare). Transfer the steaks to a plate and allow to rest under foil for at least 10 minutes before serving.

Make the béarnaise sauce. Heat the vinegar, peppercorns, bay leaf, shallot and tarragon sprig in a small saucepan and bring to the boil. Simmer for 5 minutes, until reduced to about 1 tablespoon of liquid, then strain the liquid into a small bowl and set aside.

Place a small heatproof bowl over a pan of gently simmering water, making sure the base of the bowl does not touch the water. Add the egg yolk to the bowl with the reserved vinegar reduction and set over a very low heat, whisking until light and fluffy (when you lift the whisk up, the egg should hold its shape). Remove from the heat and gradually whisk in the melted butter, a little at a time, until you have a loose, mayonnaise-like consistency. Mix in the remaining chopped tarragon and season with salt and pepper.

Divide the cooked potatoes between serving plates and arrange the steaks on top. Spoon over the béarnaise sauce and serve immediately.

Salt beef bagel with hot English mustard and pickles

SERVES 4–6

4–6 plain bagels
90 g (3 oz/⅓ cup) mayonnaise
1 tablespoon hot English mustard
6–8 gherkins (pickles), halved (I like McClure's pickles)

SALT BEEF

2 quantities Beer brine (page 231)
1 × 2 kg (4 lb 6 oz) thick end piece beef brisket
1 onion, sliced in half
1 carrot, roughly chopped
1 celery stalk, leaves on, roughly chopped
1 leek, white part only, roughly chopped
½ garlic bulb, cloves separated
2 bay leaves
½ teaspoon black peppercorns
1 tablespoon white vinegar

While living in London, I spent many a weekend morning either walking home through Brick Lane from clubs or strolling through the markets with my wife, shopping and people-watching (and seeing if we could find our stolen bikes at the flea market!). However we spent this time, all roads eventually led to one place: Beigel Bake, the bagel shop towards the north end of Brick Lane. I would always have the salted beef bagel that came with the tang of pickles and a hit of hot mustard – these bagels are probably the best street food in the UK.

Eight days before you plan to cook this, make the brine according to the method on page 231. Allow it to boil for 5 minutes, then remove the pan from the heat and leave the brine to cool to room temperature.

Use a skewer or a sharp knife to pierce the beef all over and place it in a large plastic container. Pour over the cooled brine, ensuring that the beef is completely covered. It may need weighing down; if so, use a couple of saucers. Cover with a lid and store in the refrigerator for 7 days.

One day before cooking, drain off the brine and soak the beef in fresh cold water for a further 24 hours, changing the water at least once.

The next day, transfer the beef to a large saucepan, cover with cold water, put the lid on and bring to the boil. Skim off any scum that rises to the surface and add the onion, carrot, celery, leek, garlic, bay leaves, peppercorns and vinegar. Turn the heat right down to a low simmer and cook for 1½–2 hours, until the meat is completely tender and soft when pierced with a skewer. Keep the beef submerged during cooking, topping up with boiling water if necessary. Remove and set aside. Reserve the cooking liquor and use it as stock for soup or as a base for the Beef pho broth (page 22), or freeze it.

Slice the bagels in half and lightly toast them. In a bowl, mix the mayonnaise with mustard. Liberally spread all over one half of each bagel.

Slice the salt beef into thick slabs and divide between the bagels. Spoon on more mayonnaise, top with the pickles and sandwich with the top half of the bagel.

NOTE

You'll want to plan ahead with this recipe because the beef needs to be brined at least a week in advance. Any left-over salt beef is an excellent cold cut and makes delicious Reuben sandwiches.

Steak tartare

SERVES 2

150 g (5½ oz) grass-fed rump steak
4 shakes Tabasco sauce
3 shakes worcestershire sauce
2 shakes tomato sauce (ketchup)
sea salt and freshly ground black pepper
2 egg yolks
1 hard-boiled egg, whites separated and finely grated on a box grater
2 teaspoons chopped shallots
1 teaspoon capers, rinsed
2 teaspoons finely chopped gherkins (pickles)
½ bunch flat-leaf (Italian) parsley, finely chopped
Melba toast or French fries, to serve (optional)

This is a nice meal to share – not to mention it's protein in its purest form. I love the clean mineral taste of raw meat. Try to buy the best steak you can afford. This tartare makes a nice light lunch or supper dish.

Trim the beef of all the fat and sinew, then chop as finely as possible with a sharp knife. Add the Tabasco, worcestershire and tomato sauces, and season with salt and pepper.

Shape the beef into thick discs, one per person, and arrange on a serving plate. Carefully place an egg yolk on top. Arrange the hard-boiled egg whites, shallots, capers, gherkins and parsley around the steak. This is delicious served with Melba toast or French fries.

Beef massaman curry

SERVES 4

600 g (1 lb 5 oz) blade steak or gravy beef, cut into 4 cm (1½ in) dice
1.6 litres (54 fl oz) coconut milk
1 tablespoon peanut oil
1 tablespoon palm sugar (jaggery) or soft brown sugar
2 tablespoons fish sauce
300 g (10½ oz) potatoes or sweet potatoes, cut into 4 cm (1½ in) dice
10 cocktail white onions
steamed rice, to serve
roasted peanuts, to garnish
coriander (cilantro) leaves, to garnish
lime wedges, to garnish (optional)

CURRY PASTE

1 red onion, diced
5 garlic cloves, crushed
1 lemongrass stalk, white part only, finely sliced
3 cm (1¼ in) piece galangal, peeled and sliced
8 coriander (cilantro) roots, scraped
5 dried long red chillies, seeds removed, soaked in a bowl of water

SPICE MIX

1 teaspoon coriander seeds
1 teaspoon cumin seeds
1 cardamom pod
1 cinnamon stick
2 whole cloves
1 star anise
1 tablespoon sea salt

Bring the beef and the coconut milk to the boil in a large saucepan. Turn the heat down and simmer for 1½ hours, or until the beef is soft and falling apart.

Meanwhile, make the curry paste. Dry-fry the onion, garlic, lemongrass, galangal and coriander roots for 5 minutes in a wok or large frying pan. Stir continuously to stop any of the ingredients catching. Drain the chillies and add them to the pan, along with a splash of water. Cover and allow to cook for 2 minutes, or until the onion is soft, then remove from the heat and cool slightly. Transfer to a blender or food processor and blend to form a smooth paste. Set aside 3 tablespoons of paste and transfer the remainder to an airtight container and store in the freezer for another time.

To make the spice mix, preheat the oven to 150°C (300°F). Arrange all the spices on a baking tray and roast for 10 minutes, or until the spices are fragrant. Allow to cool briefly, then grind in a spice grinder or mortar and pestle, in batches, until you have a fine powder.

Heat the peanut oil in a large, deep frying pan over medium–high heat and fry the spice mix and the curry paste for 5 minutes, until fragrant. Stir continuously with a wooden spoon to prevent the paste from burning as it begins to change colour. Add the palm sugar and continue to cook for 1–2 more minutes, then add the fish sauce and the cooked beef, along with its coconut milk broth. Stir well to combine and bring to the boil. Reduce the heat to medium, add the potatoes and onions, and cook for a further 20–30 minutes, or until the potatoes are cooked.

Taste the curry and adjust the seasoning, if required, with more sugar and fish sauce to balance the flavours.

Serve with steamed rice, top with the roasted peanuts and coriander leaves, and accompany with lime wedges, if desired.

POKKA

LAMB

DUKKAH LAMB CUTLETS

GREEK LAMB IN A BAG

LAMB BURGER

HARIRA

LAMB CROWN ROAST WITH OLIVE SAUCE

LAMB CURRY WITH SPINACH

LAMB RIBS WITH APPLE SLAW

DEVIL'S LAMB'S FRY

HERB-CRUSTED LAMBS' BRAINS AND SPICY TOMATO SAUCE

MONGOLIAN-STYLE LAMB SHANKS

ROAST LAMB SADDLE

LANCASHIRE HOTPOT

LAMB PIEROGI

LAMB SHISH WITH SPICED EGGPLANT AND YOGHURT

MY OLD MAN'S IRISH STEW

SHEARER PIE

LAMB SHANKS WITH CHICKPEAS AND FRIED EGGPLANT

SLOW-COOKED LAMB BELLY

Dukkah lamb cutlets

SERVES 4

2 garlic cloves
salt and freshly ground black pepper
2 tablespoons olive oil
3 bunches heirloom baby carrots, or 4 regular carrots cut into sticks
2 tablespoons molasses
110 g (4 oz/1 cup) dukkah (see note)
1 tablespoon sumac (see note)
30 g (1 oz/½ cup) roughly chopped mixed flat-leaf (Italian) parsley and mint, plus extra for garnish
12 lamb cutlets
200 g (7 oz) hummus
60 g (2 oz/¼ cup) plain yoghurt

These are great on their own as a party snack, but when served with a warm salad of roasted root veg and herbs they make a fuss-free weeknight meal.

Preheat the oven to 180°C (350°F).

In a mortar and pestle, pound the garlic with a pinch of salt into a smooth paste, then stir in the olive oil. Transfer to a bowl and toss with the carrots.

Place the carrots in a single layer on a baking tray lined with baking paper and roast in the oven for 20 minutes, until tender. Remove from the oven, drizzle over the molasses and sprinkle with a good pinch of dukkah. Return to the oven to roast for a further 5 minutes, then transfer to a bowl and toss with the sumac and chopped herbs.

Meanwhile, heat a large non-stick frying pan over medium heat. Season the lamb cutlets with salt and pepper and cook for 3–4 minutes on each side for medium rare. Once cooked to your liking, transfer to a plate lined with paper towel to soak up any juices and fat. Using a butter knife, spread the cutlets with hummus and dip them into the remaining dukkah, ensuring that they are well coated.

Spread the remaining hummus onto a serving plate and arrange the carrots and dukkah lamb cutlets on top. Serve dolloped with the yoghurt and garnished with chopped herbs.

NOTE

Dukkah is an Egyptian blend of nuts, seeds and aromatic spices. It's excellent rubbed on meat or in meat marinades. Sumac is slightly tart and adds a great flavour to salads and meat. Both are available from good supermarkets.

Greek lamb in a bag

SERVES 6–8

6 garlic cloves
1 teaspoon salt
3 tablespoons roughly chopped oregano
1 tablespoon roughly chopped rosemary
grated zest of 1 lemon and juice of 2 lemons
freshly ground black pepper
½ teaspoon ground cinnamon
3 tablespoons olive oil
1 × 2 kg (4 lb 6 oz) leg of lamb
1 kg (2 lb 3 oz) potatoes, halved or quartered
5 bay leaves

MINT YOGHURT

250 g (9 oz) plain Greek-style yoghurt
juice of ½ lemon
1 tablespoon olive oil
handful mint, shredded

Crush the garlic with the salt using a mortar and pestle. Add the herbs, lemon zest, pepper and cinnamon, then crush a little more to make a rough paste. Stir through 2 tablespoons of the oil. Using a sharp knife, spear the lamb all over, and rub in the herb paste, pushing it deep into the holes. Transfer the lamb to a large bowl (or use a zip-lock bag), pour in the lemon juice and marinate overnight.

The next day, take the lamb out of the refrigerator an hour before you want to cook it. Preheat the oven to 160°C (320°F).

Arrange 2 long pieces of aluminium foil – one widthways, the other lengthways – to form a cross inside a roasting tin, then lay 2 long pieces of baking paper on top in the same fashion. Toss the potatoes with the remaining oil and season with salt and pepper, then tip onto the centre of the paper. Bring up the sides of the paper and foil, then pour the marinade from the lamb over the potatoes and throw in the bay leaves. Set the lamb on top of the potatoes and scrunch the foil together to completely enclose and seal in the lamb, leaving enough room for it to steam. Transfer to the oven and cook for 4½ hours, until the lamb is very tender.

Remove from the oven. Turn the oven temperature to 220°C (430°F). Unwrap the parcel and scrunch the foil and paper under the rim of the tin, then baste the lamb with the juices and return to the oven for a further 20 minutes, until browned.

Remove the lamb from the oven. Carefully transfer to a platter, then wrap in foil and allow to rest. Turn the potatoes over and return to the oven for 10 minutes to crisp up, then season with salt to taste, if necessary.

While the potatoes are cooking, stir together all the ingredients for the mint yoghurt. Serve the lamb with the potatoes and meaty juices from the tin, and a dollop of yoghurt on the side.

PRODUCE OF GREECE
ACHAIA CLAUSS
OUZO

Lamb burger

SERVES 4

500 g (1 lb 2 oz) minced (ground) lamb
1 teaspoon salt
1 teaspoon ground black pepper
1 tablespoon dijon mustard
1 tablespoon Meat salt (page 225)
oil for frying
4 Turkish buns, sliced in half
good-quality tzatziki
two large handfuls wild rocket (arugula)
4 tablespoons crumbled feta
2 tablespoons harissa paste (see note)

PICKLED CUCUMBER RELISH

1 telegraph (long) cucumber
½ red onion
1 teaspoon salt
1 teaspoon sugar
white-wine vinegar, to taste

In a bowl, combine the lamb with salt, pepper and mustard. Divide into 4 equal balls, throwing and slapping each one between your hands before pressing out into a patty. Place them in the refrigerator while you get on with the rest of the recipe.

Make the pickled cucumber relish. Slice the cucumber and red onion as finely as possible, using a mandoline or vegetable peeler, and place them in a bowl. Sprinkle with the salt and sugar and allow to macerate for 10 minutes. Squeeze out the excess moisture and sprinkle with vinegar to taste – make it as sharp or as sweet as you like. Set aside.

Sprinkle the patties with a little meat salt just before cooking.

To cook, heat a frying pan or a hotplate over medium–high heat. Lightly oil the surface and lay on the patties. Cook for 5–6 minutes on each side. Allow the patties to form a nice crust before you attempt to turn them; this will both enhance the texture and help prevent them breaking up. Flip the burgers and continue to cook until nicely browned. Once the patties are done, remove them from the heat and allow to rest.

While the meat is resting, toast your bread buns, cut side only, until nicely golden brown.

To serve, spread one half of each bun with some tzatziki. Divide the rocket between the buns, add some pickled cucumber relish and crumble over the feta. Finally, top with the lamb patties and lashings of harissa. Sandwich with the other half of the bread and eat immediately.

NOTE

Harissa paste is a hot red pepper paste from North Africa. It is a mixture of peppers, dried red chillies, garlic and spices. You can buy it from good independent delis or large supermarkets.

Harira

SERVES 4–6

1 tablespoon clarified butter or salted butter
2 large onions, chopped
30 g (1 oz/1 cup) chopped flat-leaf (Italian) parsley
1 tablespoon finely chopped celery leaves
salt and freshly ground black pepper
1 teaspoon turmeric
½ teaspoon ground cinnamon
225 g (8 oz) lamb shoulder, cut into 1 cm (½ in) cubes
6 chicken wings
90 g (3 oz/½ cup) dried green lentils
2 tablespoons coriander (cilantro) leaves
900 g (2 lb) ripe tomatoes, peeled, seeds removed and chopped
1.3 litres (44 fl oz/5 cups) water
90 g (3 oz/½ cup) short vermicelli noodles
3 tablespoons plain (all-purpose) flour mixed with 120 ml (4 fl oz/½ cup) water
lemon wedges, to squeeze

My first taste of this nourishing soup was in Morocco. We were filming a show called *Planet Food* during Ramadan and harira was cooked for me in a family home. Traditionally, Moroccans eat this to break the daily fast during the holy month.

Melt the butter in a large saucepan and add the onions, parsley, celery leaves, 1 teaspoon of pepper and the turmeric. Sauté over low–medium heat for 3–4 minutes. Add the cinnamon, lamb and chicken wings. Cook slowly over a low heat for 15–20 minutes, turning the mixture, until golden but not browned.

Rinse the lentils in cold water and discard any discoloured ones. In a mortar and pestle, pound the coriander with a pinch of salt to form a paste. Add the lentils, coriander paste and tomatoes to the pan and cook for 15 minutes on a low heat. Add the water, bring to the boil and simmer for 45 minutes–1 hour, until the lentils are soft. Season the soup to taste, add the noodles, then bring to the boil once more. Cook for 2 minutes, stir in the flour-water mixture and cook for a further 3 minutes, stirring continuously to prevent lumps from forming. Serve immediately with lemon wedges.

NOTE

If you want to make this gluten-free, leave out the flour.

Lamb crown roast with olive sauce

SERVES 6

1 × 2 kg (4 lb 6 oz) lamb crown roast or 2 × 1 kg (2 lb 3 oz) lamb racks (6–8 chops), French-trimmed
3 garlic cloves
4 rosemary sprigs
salt and freshly ground black pepper
1 tablespoon olive oil
2 onions, thickly sliced
250 ml (8½ oz/1 cup) water

OLIVE SAUCE

100 ml (3½ fl oz) extra-virgin olive oil
125 g (4½ oz/1 cup) mixed pitted olives
2 garlic cloves, thinly sliced
6 anchovy fillets, chopped
1 tablespoon capers, rinsed and drained
100 ml (3½ fl oz) cream
1 tablespoon chopped mint
1 tablespoon chopped flat-leaf (Italian) parsley
juice of 1 lemon

The great thing about going to a butcher to buy your meat is that you can ask them to prepare cuts that are normally not available in supermarkets. Crown roast is the perfect example: a loin rack of lamb consisting of about eight to ten bones, which is French-trimmed and tied so that the loin faces inwards, forming a crown shape. You don't see crown roasts too often in a supermarket, so if you can't get hold of one, then two good-sized lamb racks will do. Just get them French-trimmed and have most of the fat removed.

Preheat your oven to 220°C (430°F).

Take the lamb out of the refrigerator at least 30 minutes prior to cooking.

Using a sharp knife, make small diagonal cuts across the fat of the lamb. If using 2 lamb racks, you will also need to assemble the crown roast. With the fat facing inwards, bend the 2 racks into semicircles. Press the ends of the racks together so they form a whole circle and secure with 2 lengths of kitchen string: one around the base of the roast, and one slightly higher up.

In a mortar and pestle, pound the garlic and rosemary sprigs with salt and pepper until you have a fine paste. Stir in the oil and rub the mixture all over the lamb. Wrap each point of bone in aluminium foil.

Lay the onion slices in a large roasting tin and place the lamb on top, bones up. Pour the water into the tin. Transfer to the oven to cook for 15 minutes, or until nicely coloured and the fat is crisp and golden. Turn the oven down to 180°C (350°F) and cook until the thickest part of the lamb reads 64°C (150°F) on a meat thermometer, approximately 45 minutes. Remove from the oven and rest for 15 minutes.

To make the olive sauce, heat the oil in a small saucepan and gently fry the olives for 1–2 minutes, until fragrant. Add the garlic, anchovies and capers and fry for 2 minutes. Pour in the cream, remove from the heat and stir well. Finally, stir in the chopped herbs and the lemon juice. Serve the lamb on a large platter with the olive sauce spooned around it. I also love this with a simple side of steamed silverbeet (Swiss chard).

Lamb curry with spinach

SERVES 4–6

6 garlic cloves
4 cm (1½ in) piece fresh ginger
60 ml (2 fl oz/¼ cup) vegetable oil
500 ml (17 fl oz/2 cups) plain yoghurt
60 g (2 oz/¼ cup) good-quality masala curry paste
1 kg (2 lb 3 oz) diced lamb shoulder
5 onions, chopped
salt and freshly ground black pepper
2 teaspoons mild chilli powder
3 teaspoons ground coriander
4 cm (1½ in) piece cassia bark
4 vine-ripened tomatoes, roughly chopped
500 g (1 lb 2 oz) spinach
1 bunch coriander (cilantro), finely chopped
steamed rice, to serve

I love farmers' markets and have been to many around the country. Sometimes you find a producer who is making something that just blows your mind. I discovered Raj (www.rajkotwala.com.au) and his array of masalas at the Barossa Farmers' Market. I think this recipe is excellent with his terkari masala paste, which is worth taking the trip to the Barossa for!

The day before you want to eat this, purée the garlic and ginger in a food processor with half of the oil and combine with the yoghurt and curry paste. Mix well, pour over the lamb and place in the refrigerator to marinate for 24 hours.

The next day, preheat the oven to 160°C (320°F).

Heat the remaining oil in a flameproof casserole dish over medium heat and sauté the onions with a pinch of salt until soft and translucent. Add the chilli, ground coriander and cassia bark, followed by the lamb and its marinade, then tip in the tomatoes. Stir well and bring almost to the boil. Place a tight-fitting lid on the dish and cook in the oven for about 1½ hours, or until the lamb is meltingly tender.

Roughly 20 minutes before the lamb is ready, wash the spinach well and steam in a saucepan with only the water clinging to its leaves. Drain and cool. When cool enough to handle, squeeze excess water from the spinach, then purée in a food processor or blender.

Once the lamb is cooked, stir through the puréed spinach and season with salt and pepper. Garnish with chopped coriander and serve with steamed rice.

Lamb ribs with apple slaw

SERVES 4–6

2 kg (4 lb 6 oz) lamb breast ribs
1 tablespoon Fire and smoke salt (page 226) or cajun spice mixture
1 tablespoon soft brown sugar
1 tablespoon sea salt flakes
250 ml (8½ fl oz/1 cup) water
140 g (5 oz/½ cup) Barbecue sauce (page 223)

APPLE SLAW

100 g (3½ oz) red cabbage, finely sliced
100 g (3½ oz) white cabbage, finely sliced
1 red apple, finely shredded
1 medium carrot, finely shredded
1 tablespoon lemon juice
160 g (5½ oz/⅔ cup) sour cream
salt and freshly ground black pepper

Preheat the oven to 160°C (350°F).

Mix the fire and smoke salt, sugar and sea salt together in a bowl and rub the mixture into the lamb ribs. Pour the water into a deep roasting tin, add the ribs and cover with aluminium foil. Cook in the oven for 2½ hours, or until the lamb is very tender.

Meanwhile, make the apple slaw. Mix both cabbages, apple and carrot with the lemon juice in a bowl. Stir in the sour cream and season to taste.

When the ribs are cooked, brush liberally with the barbecue sauce and transfer to the grill (broiler) to char under high heat for 2–3 minutes.

To serve, carve the lamb ribs and dollop some apple slaw on the side.

Devil's lamb's fry

SERVES 4

35 g (1¼ oz/¼ cup) plain (all-purpose) flour
salt and freshly ground black pepper
2 pinches cayenne pepper
500 g (1 lb 2 oz) lamb's liver, cleaned and sliced into 3 cm (1¼ in) scallops (ask your butcher to do this)
30 g (1 oz) salted butter
2 tablespoons olive oil
2 red onions, finely sliced
1 bay leaf
2 tablespoons balsamic vinegar
240 g (8½ oz/1 cup) tomato passata (puréed tomatoes)
4 thick slices sourdough
½ garlic clove, peeled
extra-virgin olive oil, for drizzling

Season the flour well with salt, pepper and cayenne. Dip the liver pieces into the seasoned flour and coat well.

Melt the butter in a heavy-based non-stick frying pan over medium heat until foaming. Fry the floured liver gently for 2 minutes on each side, until browned. Remove from the pan and drain on a plate lined with paper towel while you make the sauce.

Wipe the pan with a paper towel and heat the oil. Sauté the onions and bay leaf over medium heat for 10 minutes, until the onions are soft and translucent. Add the balsamic vinegar and tomato passata and stir. Bring to the boil and lower the heat to simmer for 5 minutes, until it is thick and reduced.

Meanwhile, toast the sourdough. Rub the slices with the garlic clove and drizzle well with extra-virgin olive oil. Season with salt and pepper.

Taste the sauce and adjust the seasoning if necessary. Add the drained livers to the sauce and stir to heat through.

Spoon onto toasted sourdough and serve drizzled with extra-virgin olive oil.

Herb-crusted lambs' brains and spicy tomato sauce

SERVES 4

Lambs' brains are often overlooked and under-rated. They have a beautiful nutty flavour and soft texture that is perfect if coated in a contrasting crispy crumb.

6 lambs' brains
1 carrot, diced
1 celery stalk, diced
1 onion, diced
4 thyme sprigs
1 bay leaf
salt and freshly ground black pepper
2 litres (68 fl oz/8 cups) water
dijon mustard, for brushing
100 ml (3½ fl oz) sunflower oil
100 g (3½ oz) salted butter
red vine sorrel and rocket (arugula) leaves, to garnish
extra-virgin olive oil and balsamic vinegar, to serve

SPICY TOMATO SAUCE

1 kg (2 lb 3 oz) ripe cherry tomatoes
½ bunch thyme sprigs, leaves picked
2 garlic cloves
1 red chilli
100 ml (3½ fl oz) olive oil

HERB CRUMBS

180–240 g (6½–8½ oz/3–4 cups) Japanese panko breadcrumbs or fresh breadcrumbs
15 g (½ oz/½ cup) chopped flat-leaf (Italian) parsley
60 g (2 oz/1 cup) chopped fresh mixed herbs (thyme, basil and tarragon)

Rinse the brains in cold salted water and set aside to drain.

Place the carrot, celery, onion, thyme, bay leaf and 1 teaspoon of pepper in a large saucepan. Fill the pan with the water, set over a high heat and bring to the boil for about 10 minutes. Turn the heat down to a simmer. Season well with salt. Add the drained brains to the vegetable stock and, if needed, top up with more water to cover. Cook very gently for 5 minutes, then remove from the heat.

Using a slotted spoon, remove the lambs' brains from the stock and transfer them to a plate lined with paper towel. Discard the stock. The brains should be just firm. Allow to cool slightly, just enough so you can handle them. Using a sharp knife, split the brains in half. Remove any excess meat from the base so that you have nice uniform-sized brains. Cover and refrigerate while you make the spicy tomato sauce.

Preheat the oven to 160°C (320°F).

To make the tomato sauce, lay the tomatoes on a baking tray with the thyme, garlic, chilli and olive oil, and season with salt and pepper. Roast in the oven for about 20 minutes, until well blistered and soft. Put the tomatoes into a food processor or blender and blitz to a purée. Transfer to a saucepan and simmer gently over low heat for 15–20 minutes, until thick. You will need to stir often to stop the sauce from catching. Season with salt and pepper and keep warm. Rinse out the food processor or blender and dry.

To make the herb crumbs, place 60 g (2 oz/1 cup) of the breadcrumbs in a food processor or blender, along with the herbs and a good pinch of salt. Blend on high speed until the mixture is super-fine. The mixture will be quite moist at this stage. Gradually add the remaining breadcrumbs – you want the mixture to become loose and dry. Tip into a bowl and use your hands to ensure there are no lumps.

Using a pastry brush, generously coat the brains in mustard and gently roll in the herb crumb so that it sticks to the mustard. Remove to a tray and repeat with the remaining lambs' brains.

Heat the sunflower oil and butter in a large frying pan. When the butter begins to foam, gently add the herb-crusted brains. Cook over medium heat for 4–5 minutes, until the crust becomes slightly crispy, then turn and cook for another 4–5 minutes. Avoid cooking with too high a heat, as the herb crust will lose its vibrant colour.

To serve, spoon some spicy tomato sauce onto a serving plate and arrange the brains on top. Garnish with a small delicate salad of red vine sorrel and rocket, simply dressed in extra-virgin olive oil and a drop of balsamic vinegar.

Mongolian-style lamb shanks

SERVES 6

125 ml (4 fl oz/½ cup) hoisin sauce
2 tablespoons oyster sauce
2 tablespoons light soy sauce
1 tablespoon tomato sauce (ketchup)
2 tablespoons dry sherry
1 tablespoon honey
1 tablespoon grated fresh ginger
1 tablespoon crushed garlic
½ teaspoon dried chilli flakes
6 lamb shanks
250 ml (8½ fl oz/1 cup) beef stock
6 spring onions (scallions)
150 g (5½ oz) snow peas (mangetouts)
1 head broccoli, separated into large florets, or 1 bunch broccolini
2 baby bok choy (pak choy), cut in half
steamed rice, to serve

Here I've played around with a Chinese takeaway classic. I think the use of good slow-cooked lamb shank adds a wow factor and takes this old favourite to the next level.

Preheat the oven to 150°C (300°F).

In a large bowl, combine the sauces with the sherry, honey, ginger, garlic and chilli flakes. Add the lamb shanks and, using your hands, mix to coat the lamb well. Cover with plastic wrap and leave to marinate in the refrigerator for at least 4 hours or, ideally, overnight.

Place the lamb in a roasting tin with 150 ml (5 fl oz) of the beef stock. Slice the spring onion bulbs from the stem, trim the stringy bits from the bottom and wash the stems well. Slice them in half and add the white parts to the roasting tin; chop the green tops and set aside.

Cover the shanks with a snug-fitting sheet of baking paper followed by a sheet of aluminium foil over the top of the tin. Transfer to the oven and cook for 3 hours. Remove from the oven and use tongs to turn the lamb shanks. If the meat is already falling from the bones at this point, they are ready; if you have larger shanks they may need more time.

Use a fork to remove the meat from the bones, keeping the meat in large pieces and removing any sinew and fat as you go. Top up the juices from the roasting tin with the remaining beef stock; this will be your sauce.

Bring a large saucepan of water to the boil and add the snow peas, broccoli and bok choy. Reduce the heat to medium and blanch the vegetables for 1 minute – they should be just tender and still crunchy and green. Drain and set aside.

Toss the lamb, blanched vegetables, reserved chopped spring onion greens and sauce together. Serve with steamed rice.

Roast lamb saddle

SERVES 6

1 × 1.2 kg (2 lb 10 oz) boned lamb saddle (see method)
100 g (3½ oz) baby spinach
salt and freshly ground black pepper
500 g (1 lb 2 oz) caul fat
dijon mustard, for spreading
1 quantity Herb crumbs (see page 67)
Estragon sauce (page 218), to serve (optional)
roasted root vegetables, to serve

Ask your butcher to prepare the lamb saddle for you so that the 2 loins can be rolled together and wrapped by about 4–5 cm (1½–2 in) of fat either side of the loins. The fat on the sides of the saddle needs to be trimmed so that it is not too thick. Ask for the tenderloins to be separated and trimmed and for the silver skin to be trimmed off the loins. A good butcher should be able to do this quite easily.

Wash the spinach and place in a saucepan with only the water clinging to its leaves. Place over medium heat, cover, and wilt the spinach for 2 minutes. Drain and allow to cool. Squeeze off any liquid and liberally season. Set aside.

Lay the boned saddle out on a chopping board, loin side up, so that one fat flap is closest to you and the other is furthest from you. Place one of the tenderloins in the gap between the 2 loins on the saddle. Arrange the spinach on top of the tenderloin and place the remaining tenderloin on top. Take the edge of the fat flap closest to you and pull it over the loin furthest from you. Fold over the other fat flap so that you have a rolled saddle stuffed with spinach. Set aside.

Lay the caul fat in a large rectangle on your work surface. Place the rolled saddle on the edge of the caul fat closest to you and carefully but firmly roll the saddle in caul fat, taking care to avoid tearing the fat. Trim the excess fat from the ends of the saddle. Using kitchen string, fasten the saddle by making about 6 firm knots along its length. Allow the meat to rest in the refrigerator for an hour or so, uncovered.

Preheat the oven to 160°C (320°F).

Heat a large frying pan over medium heat. Season the saddle and place in the pan. Cook on all sides, turning gently, until golden brown all over. Remove from the heat and leave to cool completely. (This will allow it to firm up.)

Place the lamb saddle on a foil-lined roasting tin and roast in the oven for 25–30 minutes, or until the lamb reaches 64°C (150°F) on a meat themometer (for medium rare). Remove from the oven and allow to rest for a few minutes, then use a pair of scissors to remove the kitchen string.

Using a palette knife, spread the saddle liberally with mustard. Roll the saddle in the herb crumbs. Slice the saddle into portions and serve with the Estragon sauce, if you like, and roasted vegetables.

Lancashire hotpot

SERVES 4

150 g (5½ oz/1 cup) plain (all-purpose) flour
salt and freshly ground black pepper
8 × 150 g (5½ oz) lamb neck chops
100 ml (3½ fl oz) olive oil
4 onions, thinly sliced
3 garlic cloves, sliced
2 bay leaves
50 g (1¾ oz) unsalted butter, melted
1 tablespoon thyme leaves
700 g (1 lb 9 oz) waxy potatoes, peeled and cut into 1 cm (½ in) slices
200 ml (7 fl oz) chicken stock
gremolata (page 16), to serve

This classic English lamb dish is one of my favourites, as it is such an easy dish to put together – truly comforting on a winter's day. Don't be afraid to play around with root vegetables, substituting the potato for taro, sweet potato or Jerusalem artichoke.

Preheat the oven to 180°C (350°F).

Combine the flour with a good pinch of salt and pepper in a zip-lock bag. Add the lamb chops and shake the bag for 30 seconds to evenly coat the lamb.

Heat 50 ml (1¾ fl oz/¼ cup) of the oil in a large frying pan over medium–high heat. Shake the lamb to remove excess flour, then fry in batches for 2–3 minutes on each side, until golden. Remove from the pan and set aside.

Wipe the pan clean with paper towel and place over medium heat. Add the remaining oil and sauté the onions, stirring, for 10–12 minutes, until they are soft and starting to colour. Stir in the garlic and cook for a further 3 minutes, or until golden brown.

Place the lamb chops in a flameproof casserole dish, then top with the onion mixture and bay leaves. Pour over the melted butter and scatter over the thyme, and season with salt and pepper. Arrange the potatoes over the top of the onions in a circular pattern, overlapping slightly.

Pour the stock over the potatoes, then cover the casserole with a lid. Transfer to the oven and bake for 20 minutes, then reduce the oven temperature to 130°C (240°F) and cook for a further 2½ hours, or until the potatoes and lamb are tender and the sauce has thickened. Remove the lid, then switch the oven to the grill (broiler) function. Grill under high heat for 3 minutes, or until the potatoes are golden. Set aside to rest.

Divide the hotpot between bowls, sprinkle with gremolata and serve.

Lamb pierogi

SERVES 4

2 tablespoons olive oil
1 onion, diced
100 g (3½ oz) celery, diced
2 carrots, diced
300 g (10½ oz) left-over Greek lamb in a bag (page 54), shredded
3–4 tablespoons Barbecue sauce (page 223)
1 litre (34 fl oz/4 cups) vegetable oil, for deep-frying

PIEROGI PASTRY

310 g (11 oz) plain (all-purpose) flour, plus extra for dusting
1 teaspoon salt
2 tablespoons sour cream
1 egg
125 ml (4 fl oz/½ cup) water

MINTED YOGHURT

200 g (7 oz) plain Greek-style yoghurt
½ bunch mint leaves, roughly chopped
1 Lebanese (short) cucumber, unpeeled and diced
sea salt

Pierogi are Polish dumplings not dissimilar to ravioli. We make them at Billykart Kitchen and fill them with a variety of savoury ingredients like shredded beef, duck confit, blue cheese and asparagus. You can either cook them in boiling water, much like ravioli, or, as in this recipe, deep-fry them.

Make the pastry. In a food processor, blitz the flour and salt until well combined. Tip into a large bowl. In a cup with a pouring lip, combine the sour cream and egg. Gradually incorporate the sour cream and egg mixture into the flour mixture. Add the water slowly until the mixture forms small lumps. Turn out the dough onto a floured work surface and knead for 3–5 minutes to form a firm ball. Wrap the dough loosely with plastic wrap and refrigerate for 1 hour.

To make the filling, heat the olive oil in a large non-stick frying pan and add the onion, celery and carrots. Sauté over medium heat for 2 minutes, then turn the heat down to low and cook gently for 8–10 minutes, stirring occasionally, until the vegetables are soft and slightly sweet.

Remove from the heat and add the cooked vegetables to a large bowl with the shredded left-over Greek lamb. Mix well. Add the barbecue sauce and use your hands to work it through thoroughly. Set aside.

Make the minted yoghurt by combining all the ingredients together in a small bowl. Chill in the refrigerator until ready to serve.

Remove the pastry dough from the refrigerator. Set up your pasta machine on a clean work surface (or use a rolling pin). Flour the work surface and divide the dough into 2 portions. Flatten each portion slightly so that it can easily pass though the pasta machine. Roll out the dough, dusting with flour as you go to prevent sticking, until the dough is no thicker than 3 mm (⅛ in) and as wide as the machine. (This will take some folding and shaping.)

Lay the pastry sheet out on the floured work surface. Using an 8 cm (3¼ in) pastry cutter, cut out rounds, wasting as little dough as possible. Place teaspoonfuls of filling in the centre of each round. Dab the edges of one round with a little water and fold the dough over the meat filling, gently pressing the edges to secure. Repeat with the remaining pierogi.

Heat the vegetable oil in a heavy-based saucepan or deep-fat fryer to around 175°C (345°F), or hot enough to make a small piece of bread sizzle in 15 seconds when dropped into the oil. Carefully add the pierogi in batches to prevent overcrowding, and deep-fry for 1–2 minutes, until golden. Serve hot, with the minted yoghurt on the side.

Lamb shish with spiced eggplant and yoghurt

SERVES 4–6

1 garlic clove
2 tablespoons harissa paste (see note)
juice of 1 lemon
1 kg (2 lb 3 oz) lamb backstrap or loin fillet, cut into fairly large dice
salt and freshly ground black pepper
12 bamboo skewers, soaked in water
12 baby Roma (plum) tomatoes
25 g (1 oz/½ cup) chopped mint, to garnish
15 g (½ oz/½ cup) flat-leaf (Italian) parsley, to garnish
green salad leaves, to serve

SPICED EGGPLANT AND YOGHURT

2 eggplants (aubergines)
2 tablespoons salt
125 ml (4 fl oz/½ cup) olive oil
1 brown onion, sliced
½ teaspoon cumin seeds
90 g (3 oz/⅓ cup) plain Greek-style yoghurt
½ teaspoon ground cumin

Slice the eggplants into 5 mm (¼ in) thick slices and sprinkle with the salt. Leave in a colander for 10–15 minutes. Rinse the eggplant slices and pat dry with paper towel.

Heat the oil in a large frying pan until almost smoking and pan-fry the eggplant, in batches, until golden brown on both sides and soft. Transfer to a plate lined with paper towels to drain off the excess oil. Arrange the fried eggplant slices on a serving plate in one layer.

In the same pan, add the sliced onion and cumin seeds and sauté until the onion is tender and lightly coloured. Arrange the onions over the eggplant in a similar fashion. Dollop over the yoghurt and sprinkle with ground cumin. Set aside.

Using a mortar and pestle, pound the garlic to form a smooth paste. Add the harissa and lemon juice and combine to form a loose paste. In a bowl, toss the lamb with the spice mixture and season with salt and pepper. Thread the lamb pieces onto the bamboo skewers, alternating the lamb and tomatoes.

Heat a chargrill pan (or barbecue) over medium–high heat. Cook the lamb shish for about 5–8 minutes on each side. Remove and allow to rest for 5 minutes before serving with the chopped herbs and a crisp green salad.

NOTE

Harissa paste is a hot red pepper paste from North Africa. It is a mixture of peppers, dried red chillies, garlic and spices. You can buy it from good independent delis or large supermarkets.

My old man's Irish stew

SERVES 4–6

I grew up with this dish. My old man is a County Kerry man who was born and raised in Killarney. He would always go on about how good this dish was, how the potatoes in Ireland were better than anywhere in the world and how important they were to the quality of this dish. In this recipe, I use two types of potatoes: a floury one that will break up and thicken the stew, and a waxy one, which holds its shape to add texture. There's no doubt that this is a nourishing and delicious meal. I wish I had appreciated it more as a kid.

1 kg (2 lb 3 oz) mutton or lamb neck or shoulder chops

1 tablespoon beef or duck fat (see page 229) or sunflower oil

salt and freshly ground black pepper

2 medium carrots, diced

8 shallots, peeled and cut in half through the root

2 thyme sprigs

4 medium waxy potatoes, peeled and sliced into large cubes

4 floury potatoes, sliced into quarters

1 tablespoon chopped flat-leaf (Italian) parsley

buttered crusty bread, to serve

Place the mutton or lamb in a large flameproof casserole dish or ovenproof pan and cover with water. Bring to the boil and blanch for 1–2 minutes, then drain and pat dry with paper towel.

Give the casserole dish a quick wipe and add the fat. Place over medium heat. Season the mutton with salt and pepper, then add it to the casserole and lightly brown all over. Remove the mutton and set aside. Add the carrots and shallots and sauté over medium heat for a few minutes, until soft and lightly coloured.

Preheat the oven to 160°C (320°F).

Return the mutton to the pan, along with 1 litre (34 fl oz/4 cups) water, and bring to a simmer. Stir in the thyme and both kinds of potatoes. Cover with the lid and cook in the oven for 1–1½ hours, until the mutton is tender.

Once cooked, drain the stock from the mutton into a cup or bowl. Tip a cup of ice into the stock so that the fat cools and rises to the top. Skim the fat off and return the stock to the mutton and vegetables. Bring everything to the boil on the stove top, add the chopped parsley, season again if needed, and serve with buttered crusty bread.

Shearer pie

SERVES 4–6

2 tablespoons sunflower oil
2 tablespoons roughly chopped rosemary
3 onions, finely chopped
3 garlic cloves, finely chopped
1 tablespoon Vegemite (yeast extract)
500 g (1 lb 2 oz) lamb leg or shoulder, cut into 2 cm (3¼ in) cubes
500 g (1 lb 2 oz) boneless lamb shank meat, cut into 2 cm (3¼ in) cubes (ask your butcher to cut the meat from about 3 shanks)
freshly ground black pepper
3 waxy potatoes, cut into 3 cm (1¼ in) pieces
75 g (2¾ oz/½ cup) cornflour (cornstarch)
120 g (4½ oz/1 cup) frozen peas
butter, for greasing
200 g (7 oz) or 2 sheets ready-rolled shortcrust pastry
200 g (7 oz) or 2 sheets ready-rolled puff pastry
2 egg yolks, lightly beaten

Using half lamb-shank meat in the filling gives this hearty pie a wonderfully rich flavour.

Heat the oil in a large heavy-based saucepan over medium heat. Add the rosemary and cook, stirring, for 30 seconds. Reduce the heat to low–medium, then add the chopped onions and cook, stirring occasionally, for 10–12 minutes, until soft and light golden. Add the garlic and Vegemite and stir for 1 minute to combine. The Vegemite will act as a stock base.

Season the lamb with pepper. Increase the heat to medium and fry the lamb, turning occasionally for 3–4 minutes, until the meat is sealed and pale in colour – avoid browning the lamb as this will give the filling a bitter taste. Add 2 litres (68 fl oz/8 cups) of water and bring to a simmer.

Turn the heat to low–medium, cover and cook for 1½ hours, or until the lamb is very tender. Add the potatoes and simmer for 15 minutes, or until tender.

In a small bowl, combine the cornflour with 60 ml (2 fl oz/¼ cup) water to make a wet paste, then rapidly stir the paste into the lamb filling and cook for 10–20 seconds, until the mixture has thickened. Stir in the frozen peas, then remove the pan from the heat and allow to cool.

Preheat the oven to 175°C (340°F). Grease a 14 cm × 26 cm × 5 cm (5½ in × 10¼ in × 2 in) rectangular ovenproof dish (or use a deep 24 cm/9½ in pie dish) with a little butter.

Lay the shortcrust pastry on a lightly floured surface, overlapping the 2 pieces slightly to form a long rectangle large enough to line the pie dish. Using a rolling pin, roll over the join to seal the 2 sheets together, then press gently into the bottom and corners of the dish. Spoon the filling into the pie dish. Next, place the puff pastry on a lightly floured surface, overlapping the 2 pieces slightly to form a long rectangle. As before, roll over the join to seal the 2 sheets together. Brush the rim of the shortcrust with a little beaten egg yolk.

Lay the puff pastry sheet over the filling and use a fork to crimp and press the edges of the shortcrust and puff pastries together, then trim away any excess pastry.

Finally, glaze the pie by brushing with the remaining egg yolk. Slash the top of the pie in 3 places, so that steam is able to escape and the pastry puffs. Place the pie dish on a baking sheet and bake for about 45 minutes, or until the pastry top is golden brown. Let the pie stand for 10–15 minutes before cutting and serving.

Lamb shanks with chickpeas and fried eggplant

SERVES 6

675 g (1½ lb) ripe tomatoes
600 ml (20½ fl oz) water
3 large garlic cloves, thinly sliced
4 tablespoons finely chopped flat-leaf (Italian) parsley
1 long red chilli, chopped
3 tablespoons extra-virgin olive oil
salt and freshly ground black pepper
6 lamb shanks
440 g (15½ oz) tinned chickpeas, drained
2 eggplants (aubergines), cut into large cubes
250 ml (8½ fl oz/1 cup) vegetable oil
1 tablespoon sherry or red-wine vinegar

Preheat the oven to 160°C (320°F).

First, peel the tomatoes. Score a cross in the base of each tomato. Place in a heatproof bowl and cover with boiling water. Leave for 30 seconds, then transfer to cold water and peel the skin away from the cross. Chop the tomatoes roughly and set aside.

In a large cast-iron casserole dish, add the tomatoes, water, garlic, 2 tablespoons of the parsley, the chilli, extra-virgin olive oil and salt. Submerge the lamb shanks in the liquid and add the chickpeas. Place over medium heat and bring the liquid to a steady simmer.

Put the lid on the casserole and transfer to the oven to cook for 3 hours. After this time, return the casserole to the stove top, remove the shanks to a plate and keep warm. Place the casserole over medium heat and bring to the boil. Turn the heat down to low–medium and simmer the sauce for 10 minutes, until reduced and thickened. Adjust the seasoning.

Meanwhile, heat the vegetable oil in a heavy-based saucepan or deep-fat fryer to around 175°C (345°F), or hot enough to make a small piece of bread sizzle in 15 seconds when dropped into the oil. Deep-fry the eggplant for 6–8 minutes, until golden and soft. Remove and drain well on a plate lined with paper towel. Season with salt and pepper and sprinkle over the vinegar.

Stir the fried eggplants into the chickpeas and tomato. To serve, divide the lamb shanks between plates, spoon over the chickpeas, tomato and eggplant, and sprinkle with the remaining chopped parsley.

Slow-cooked lamb belly

SERVES 4

1 × 600 g (1 lb 5 oz) lamb belly or boneless lamb breast
2 tablespoons chopped rosemary
2 tablespoons chopped garlic
1 tablespoon fennel seeds or dried oregano
1 tablespoon salt
½ tablespoon white peppercorns, crushed
2 tablespoons olive oil
250 ml (8½ fl oz/1 cup) water
salsa verde (page 192), to serve

This is my Aussie version of porchetta. It's the same principle: a herb-spiked roll of meat slowly cooked and then finished in a hot oven to achieve a lovely crackle. Belly of lamb can be quite rich so a salsa verde is a fantastic sauce to serve with it to cut through the fattiness. Alternatively, a simple crisp green salad would do the trick.

Preheat the oven to 150°C (300°F).

Lay the lamb belly flat on a work surface. Using a sharp knife, score the lamb skin in a lattice pattern to within 5 mm (¼ in) of the base.

Combine the rosemary, garlic, fennel seeds, salt, peppercorns and oil in a bowl.

Rub this mixture deep into scoring of the lamb, then roll the belly tightly and secure with kitchen string at intervals (at least 6) along its length. Season the rolled belly well with salt and pepper and place it in a roasting tin. Pour in the water and cook in the oven for 2½ hours, until very tender. Keep an eye on the lamb and add a little water if it looks a little dry.

Increase the temperature to 200°C (400°F) and continue to cook for a further 20 minutes, turning the lamb if necessary so that all sides crisp up.

Slice and serve with roasted root vegetables, such as heirloom carrots, parsnips and fennel, and Mexican salsa verde (page 221).

POULTRY

Casserole with lentils, green beans and salsa picante

SERVES 6

2 bulbs garlic
12 chicken thighs or drumsticks
½ bunch rosemary sprigs
½ bunch thyme
salt and freshly ground black pepper
drizzle of olive oil
500 ml (17 fl oz/2 cups) chicken stock (see page 216)
500 g (1 lb 2 oz) green beans, topped and tailed and evenly trimmed
400 g (14 oz) tinned brown lentils, rinsed and drained

SALSA PICANTE

1 red onion, very finely diced
2 long dried chillies, finely chopped
1 fresh red chilli, seeds removed, finely chopped
25 g (1 oz/½ cup) chopped basil
25 g (1 oz/½ cup) chopped flat-leaf (Italian) parsley
15 g (½ oz/¼ cup) chopped marjoram
1 tablespoon dried wild or regular oregano
2–3 tablespoons red-wine vinegar
2–3 tablespoons extra-virgin olive oil

Preheat the oven to 200°C (400°F).

Break the garlic bulbs up by hand and discard the skins. Slice off and discard the root end of the garlic cloves and gently squash each using the flat of a knife.

In a bowl, toss the chicken, garlic, rosemary, thyme and a good pinch of salt and pepper with a glug of olive oil. Tip into a roasting tin, making sure the chicken skin is facing up, and cook in the oven for 15 minutes. The chicken should have started to colour and become crisp. Remove from the oven and add the stock to half-cover the chicken. Turn the oven down to 180°C (350°F) and cook for a further 20 minutes. Add the green beans and the drained lentils and combine well. Cook for a further 15 minutes. Remove from the oven and allow to rest while you prepare the salsa picante.

Make the salsa by combining the onion, chillies and herbs in a bowl. Add the vinegar, season to taste and drizzle over the oil. Serve spooned over the chicken.

Chicken mole

SERVES 6

1 quantity Buttermilk brine (page 231)
2 small chickens (3.6 kg/7 lb 12 oz total), cut into 8 pieces each
50 g (1¾ oz) pork fat (see page 229) or olive oil
500 ml (17 fl oz/2 cups) chicken stock (see page 216)
40 g (1½ oz) dark chocolate, at least 70% cocoa solids
salt, to taste
1 quantity Guacamole (page 220), to serve
90 g (3 oz/⅓ cup) sour cream, to serve
12 corn tortillas, to serve
15 g (½ oz/½ cup) coriander (cilantro), leaves picked, to garnish

SPICE PASTE

4 pasilla chillies (see note)
6 ancho chillies (see note)
450 g (1 lb) tomatoes
2 onions, roughly chopped
4 garlic cloves
½ teaspoon fennel seeds
1 tablespoon sesame seeds, plus extra for sprinkling
2 tablespoons chopped coriander (cilantro)
1 toasted corn tortilla, broken
115 g (4 oz/½ cup) flaked almonds
60 g (2 oz/¼ cup) raisins
½ teaspoon ground cloves
½ teaspoon ground cinnamon
½ teaspoon ground coriander
½ teaspoon cracked black pepper

One day before cooking, prepare the brine according to the recipe on page 231 and add the chicken. Place in the refrigerator and brine overnight.

The next day, begin the spice paste by toasting the chillies in a dry pan. Pull off the stems and remove the seeds. Tear the chillies into pieces and soak in a bowl of hot water for 30 minutes.

Peel the tomatoes by scoring a cross in the base of each one. Place in a heatproof bowl and cover with boiling water. Leave for 30 seconds, then transfer to cold water and peel the skin away from the cross. To seed, cut the tomatoes in half and scoop out the seeds with a teaspoon. Set aside.

Heat half the fat in a large heavy-based frying pan over medium heat. Add the chicken pieces and brown all over for 10 minutes, until nicely golden and crispy. Remove and set aside while you finish the spice paste.

Drain the chillies and add these to a food processor, along with the tomatoes, onions, garlic, fennel seeds, 1 tablespoon of sesame seeds, fresh coriander, tortilla, almonds, raisins and ground spices, and process to a coarse paste.

In the same pan you browned the chicken in, heat the remaining fat and fry the spice paste over low–medium heat for 5 minutes. Stir in the stock and chocolate and season with salt. Simmer gently until the chocolate has melted. Return the chicken to the pan and cook for a further 15 minutes on low heat. Just before serving, sprinkle the mole with the remaining sesame seeds. Serve with guacamole, sour cream, coriander and tortillas.

NOTE

Pasilla chillies are the dried form of the long, brown, mild chilaca chilli. Ancho chillies are the dried form of the wide, green, mild–medium poblano chilli. They can be found in Mexican and South American grocers and some specialty food stores.

Malaysian chicken curry

SERVES 4

60 ml (2 fl oz/¼ cup) sunflower oil
1 star anise
2 cloves
1 cinnamon stick
35 g (1¼ oz/¼ cup) mild curry powder, mixed with enough water to form a paste
200 ml (7 fl oz) coconut cream
1.5 kg (3 lb 5 oz) bone-in chicken pieces
300 g (10½ oz) potatoes, cut into wedges
800 ml (27 fl oz/3¼ cups) water
1 tablespoon salt
½ teaspoon sugar
steamed rice, to serve
1 bunch coriander (cilantro), leaves picked, to serve
fresh red chillies, sliced, to serve
flatbread, poppadoms or crusty bread rolls, to serve

Heat the oil over low heat and sauté the star anise, cloves and cinnamon stick until coated with oil and aromatic.

Add the curry paste and stir-fry for 5 minutes, until well combined and fragrant.

Add 2–3 tablespoons of the coconut cream and continue to fry until the oil begins to separate.

Add the chicken pieces and stir-fry for 1 minute. Add the potatoes and water and bring to the boil. Lower the heat and simmer for 30 minutes, until the potatoes and chicken are tender and cooked. Add the remaining coconut cream and season with the salt and sugar to taste. Bring to the boil and continue to cook until the curry is slightly thickened.

Spoon the curry onto bowls of steamed rice and sprinkle with the coriander leaves and chilli. Serve with flatbread, poppadoms or crusty bread rolls to accompany.

Coconut and quinoa chicken fingers

SERVES 4

POULTRY

200 g (7 oz/2 cups) quinoa flakes (see note)
120 g (4½ oz/2 cups) shredded coconut
3 eggs
150 g (5½ oz/1 cup) plain (all-purpose) flour
1 teaspoon ground coriander
salt and freshly ground black pepper
500 g (1 lb 2 oz) chicken tenderloins, sliced into strips
250 ml (8½ fl oz/1 cup) coconut oil, for frying

In my house it's quite often a case of 'I don't like that', but never with this recipe. It's a quick and easy dish to whip up and the little terrors love it! Quinoa flakes add extra texture to the dish, and at the same time they are a good source of additional protein. Quinoa is a grain that has recently grown in popularity and is favoured for its gluten-free, high-protein properties. The flakes look similar to rolled oats, only smaller in size.

Combine the quinoa flakes and coconut in one bowl. In another bowl, whisk the eggs together. In a zip-lock bag, combine the flour with the coriander and season with salt and pepper.

Place the chicken in the bag with the flour and shake to coat. Dust off the excess flour and dip the chicken into the beaten eggs, followed by the quinoa mixture. Make sure to coat the chicken pieces well, pressing the crumbs down with your hands to ensure they stick.

Heat the oil in a large frying pan over a low–medium heat. Shallow-fry the chicken in batches for 5–7 minutes, or until golden and cooked. Remove to a baking tray lined with paper towel and transfer to a warm oven while you cook the remaining chicken.

Season with salt and pepper and serve with a salad of your choice.

NOTE

Quinoa flakes are available from health-food stores and some good supermarkets. If you want to go completely gluten-free for this recipe, replace the plain flour with coconut flour.

Gai yang

SERVES 4–6

1 × 1.2 kg (2 lb 10 oz) chicken
125 ml (4 fl oz/½ cup) coconut cream
1 tablespoon crisp-fried shallots (available from Asian supermarkets)
15 g (½ oz/¼ cup) coriander (cilantro) leaves, chopped
3 kaffir lime leaves, finely sliced
sweet chilli sauce, to serve
1 telegraph (long) cucumber, sliced, to serve

CURRY PASTE

10 white peppercorns
3 coriander (cilantro) roots, scraped and chopped
pinch of salt
4 garlic cloves
large pinch of palm sugar (jaggery) or soft brown sugar
3 tablespoons fish sauce

Gai yang, or Thai barbecued chicken, is one of those street foods you experience in Thailand and just hope you can replicate when you get home. Well, now you can. This dish really does benefit from being cooked over a charcoal flame. If this isn't possible, then don't let that dissuade you. Traditionally this recipe would include turmeric, but I like it without – sometimes the turmeric can be overpowering.

To butterfly the chicken, place breast side down on a chopping board. With a heavy knife or kitchen scissors, cut along both sides of the backbone and remove. Open up the bird and place on the board, skin side up. Press down on the breast to flatten out the chicken. (Alternatively, you can ask your butcher to do this for you.) Set aside in a tray that will comfortably fit the chicken.

Make the curry paste by pounding the peppercorns in a mortar and pestle until finely ground. Remove and set aside in a bowl. Next, pound the coriander roots until they start to break down, then add the salt and garlic and continue to pound until combined and paste-like. Remove and add to the peppercorns, along with the sugar and fish sauce. Stir until well combined.

Cover the chicken in the curry paste and allow to marinate for at least 4 hours or, ideally, overnight.

When ready to cook, heat your barbecue or chargrill pan on medium heat. Place the chicken, bone side down, onto the hot surface and cook for 5–8 minutes. Ensure that the chicken is nicely browned before turning and cooking for a further 5–8 minutes. Lift the chicken up onto the resting rack of the barbecue, if available, or remove from direct heat. If using a chargrill pan, lower the heat. Baste the chicken with most of the coconut cream and continue to cook (with the lid down if cooking on the barbecue) for a further 15 minutes, until the chicken is done.

Remove from the heat, place onto a board and chop into 8 pieces, splitting each leg and breast in half. Transfer to a bowl and drizzle with the remaining coconut cream and scatter with crisp-fried shallots, coriander and kaffir lime leaves.

Serve with chilli sauce and a few slices of cucumber.

Hainanese chicken

SERVES 4

This is one of the cleanest and healthiest meals you'll ever have. This simple meal of chicken steeped in broth is often considered Singapore's national dish. Every time I go there I will always eat this.

1 × 1.2 kg (2 lb 10 oz) chicken
150 ml (5 fl oz) rice vinegar or red-wine vinegar, plus extra to serve
1 lemongrass stem
1 red chilli, pricked with a fork
2 black peppercorns
2 kaffir lime leaves
1 star anise
1 tablespoon dark soy sauce
4 garlic cloves, smashed
2.5 cm (1 in) piece fresh ginger, peeled and thickly sliced
1 bunch spring onions (scallions), trimmed and sliced in half
¼ teaspoon salt
300 g (10½ oz) broccolini or broccoli broken into large florets
1–2 tablespoons oyster sauce
light soy sauce, to serve
sesame oil, to serve

DIPPING SAUCE

1 red chilli, chopped
3 tablespoons light soy sauce

Rinse the inside of the chicken with the vinegar and discard the liquid.

Smash the lemongrass with a rolling pin, cut in half and pop into the cavity of the chicken. Transfer the chicken to a stockpot and cover with water. Add the pricked chilli, peppercorns, lime leaves, star anise, dark soy sauce and half the amount of garlic, ginger and spring onions. Bring to the boil and add the salt. Reduce the heat and simmer for 5 minutes, then cover with the lid and turn off the heat. Allow to stand for 40 minutes.

Meanwhile, make the dipping sauce by combining the chilli with the soy sauce in a small bowl.

Remove the chicken from the stock and set it aside on a plate to drain. Place a colander in the stockpot for steaming and bring the stock back to the boil. Add the broccolini to the colander and steam for 5 minutes. Remove and plunge into ice-cold water. Transfer to a bowl and toss with the oyster sauce.

Carve the chicken and lay onto a serving platter. Slice the remaining garlic, ginger and spring onions into fine matchsticks and scatter over the chicken. Pour over a ladleful of stock and sprinkle with vinegar, soy sauce and sesame oil. Serve with the steamed broccolini and dipping sauce.

Lemon and olive tagine

SERVES 8

POULTRY

2 × 1.2 kg (2 lb 10 oz) chickens, quartered, with their livers if possible
6 garlic cloves
25 g (1 oz) salt, plus 1 teaspoon extra
1 teaspoon ground ginger
1 teaspoon sweet paprika
¼ teaspoon ground cumin
¼ teaspoon freshly ground black pepper
60 ml (2 fl oz/¼ cup) olive oil
2 large onions, grated and drained
¼ teaspoon ground saffron strands (mixed with a little turmeric if desired)
3 tablespoons chopped flat-leaf (Italian) parsley
3 tablespoons chopped coriander (cilantro)
450 ml (15 fl oz) water, plus extra if needed
225 g (8 oz) mixed green and black olives
2 preserved lemons
juice of 1–2 lemons

One day before cooking, marinate the chicken. Pound 2 garlic cloves with 25 g (1 oz) of the salt in a mortar and pestle until you have a smooth paste. Rub this over the chicken (and livers, if using). Transfer to a large bowl.

Rinse the remaining garlic under cold water until the water no longer smells like garlic. Thinly slice and combine with the ground ginger, sweet paprika, cumin, black pepper, 1 teaspoon of salt and the oil. Rub this mixture all over the chicken and the livers, then cover and refrigerate overnight.

Place the chicken and the marinade in a large flameproof casserole dish or slow cooker, along with 4 tablespoons of the grated onions, the saffron, fresh herbs and water. Bring to the boil, cover and cook gently for 20 minutes, turning the chicken in the sauce.

Meanwhile, rinse and pit the olives if needed. If using livers, remove them from the casserole and mash them finely using a mortar and pestle. Return to the casserole. Stir in the remaining grated onions and pour in a little more water if necessary. Continue to cook, partially covered, for 10–15 minutes, until the chicken is cooked.

Rinse the preserved lemons, discarding the pulp if necessary, and quarter. Once the chicken is cooked, add the olives and preserved lemons to the casserole. Continue cooking, uncovered, for a further 5–10 minutes.

Transfer the chicken to a serving dish and spoon over the olives and lemons. Cover and keep warm while you boil the remaining liquid to reduce it to roughly 400 ml (13½ fl oz/1⅔ cups). Stir in the lemon juice, check the seasoning and adjust to taste if necessary. Pour the sauce over the chicken and serve.

Lemongrass chicken

SERVES 6

POULTRY

- 60 ml (2 fl oz/¼ cup) fish sauce
- 1½ tablespoons sugar
- 2 lemongrass stems, white part only, tough outer skin removed, finely diced
- 4 garlic cloves, finely diced
- 2 long red chillies, finely diced
- 500 g (1 lb 2 oz) boneless, skinless chicken thighs, cut into bite-size pieces
- 60 ml (2 fl oz/¼ cup) vegetable oil
- 250 ml (8½ fl oz/1 cup) light coconut milk
- 1½ onions, sliced into wedges
- 15 g (½ oz/¼ cup) chopped coriander (cilantro), to serve
- steamed jasmine rice, to serve

This is a family favourite at our house as it's so quick and easy. We generally serve the chicken with steamed broccoli or similar brassicas when eating with the kids, but to jazz it up for adults I like to serve it with stir-fried shiitake mushrooms, spring onions and asparagus. If there's any left-over marinated chicken, just pan-fry and eat in rice paper rolls.

In a bowl, combine the fish sauce and sugar and mix until the sugar has dissolved. Add half the amount of lemongrass, garlic and chillies, then tip in all of the chicken. Use your hands to mix and coat the chicken, then cover and marinate in the refrigerator for 1 hour, or overnight for a better result.

Heat the oil in a large saucepan or wok and fry the remaining lemongrass, garlic and chilli over medium heat until fragrant and slightly brown. Turn the heat to high, add the chicken and brown for about 2 minutes on each side.

Add the coconut milk and the onions. Cover the pan with a lid and cook over medium heat for 5 minutes, or until the sauce has reduced by about half.

Transfer to a serving bowl, garnish with the coriander and serve with steamed jasmine rice.

Salt roast chicken

SERVES 6

POULTRY

1 whole garlic bulb, cloves separated
12 chicken thighs, skin on
1 bunch thyme
2 tablespoons black peppercorns
80 g (2¾ oz/¼ cup) coarse rock salt
olive oil, to drizzle
smoked or sweet paprika, to sprinkle

While working at the Atlantic Bar and Grill in London, we would make this dish to feed more than 30 staff members in one evening. The night before we would salt the chicken thighs on trays ready to go into the ovens the next day. The salt helps to intensify the flavour of the chicken and also allows the aromatic flavours of the thyme to really get into the chicken.

Smash the garlic cloves lightly and leave their papery skins on. Place the garlic, chicken, thyme and peppercorns in a bowl and turn the whole lot over a few times with your hands.

Arrange the chicken on a rack set over a roasting tin; this will allow any liquid to drain out. Scatter over the garlic, thyme and peppercorn mixture, poking it in amongst the chicken. Sprinkle over the salt, making sure that you cover all the pieces. Chill overnight or for at least 8 hours so the salt can draw out any excess moisture.

Preheat the oven to 160°C (320°F). Remove the rack of chicken from the roasting tin, brush off any excess salt and rinse out the tin. Return the chicken to the tin, drizzle with a little oil and dust with paprika. I prefer smoked paprika as it has a lovely warm flavour and a slightly sharp edge.

Roast in the oven for 45 minutes, until the skin is browned and crisp and the chicken is cooked through. Check for doneness by piercing the thickest part of the thigh with a knife: if the juices run clear it is done. Serve with the garlic cloves to squeeze out.

Buttermilk barbecued chicken with Cobb salad

SERVES 4

This is one of the most popular dishes on our lunch menu at Billykart Kitchen. Chicken is soaked in buttermilk brine overnight, then the next day it is barbecued and topped with lashings of home-made barbecue sauce. Paired with a simple Cobb salad, it's a real smasher! If you want to spice the chicken up, add a few teaspoons of Fermented chilli sauce (page 222) to the brine.

1 quantity Buttermilk brine (page 231)
8 chicken thighs, skin on
salt and freshly ground black pepper
100 g (3½ oz) Barbecue sauce (page 223)
100 ml (3½ fl oz) Blue cheese sauce (page 222), to serve
1 tablespoon chopped flat-leaf (Italian) parsley, to garnish

COBB SALAD

1 head cos (romaine) lettuce
4 slices streaky bacon
150 g (5½ oz) cherry tomatoes, cut in half
1 ripe avocado, stone removed and flesh sliced
4 hard-boiled eggs, peeled and cut in half

One day before cooking, prepare the brine according to the recipe on page 231 and add the chicken. Place in the refrigerator and brine overnight.

Heat up the barbecue or, alternatively, preheat your grill (broiler) to medium. Remove the chicken from the brine and use paper towel to pat dry. Season with salt and pepper and place, skin side down, on the barbecue. Cook over a medium flame for about 8 minutes, until you have nice grill marks and the skin becomes golden brown. Flip the chicken over and grill for a further 5 minutes. Transfer the chicken onto the resting rack of the barbecue, then use a pastry brush to coat the chicken with a generous amount of the barbecue sauce. Close the lid of the barbecue and allow the chicken to cook for a further 8–10 minutes. Check for doneness by piercing the thickest part of the thigh with a knife: if the juices run clear it is done. Remove from the heat and brush liberally with any remaining barbecue sauce.

Meanwhile, make the salad. Tear off and discard the large outer leaves of the lettuce. Separate the internal leaves and arrange on a serving plate. Heat a small frying pan over medium heat and fry the bacon until crisp. Drain on paper towel. Place the tomatoes on top of the lettuce and arrange the avocado slices and egg halves around the plate. Crumble the crisp bacon over the top.

Arrange the chicken in the centre of the salad, then drizzle with the blue cheese sauce and scatter with the chopped parsley.

Sopa de lima

SERVES 4–6

POULTRY

2 tomatoes
250 ml (8½ fl oz/1 cup) sunflower oil
4 × 15 cm (6 in) corn tortillas, sliced into fine strips
1 tablespoon Fire and smoke salt (page 226) or Togarashi salt (page 227)
1 medium onion, finely diced
1 celery stalk, finely diced
1 medium carrot, finely diced
1 habanero or jalapeño chilli, chopped
4 garlic cloves, chopped
1 bay leaf
good pinch of dried wild oregano or regular dried oregano
2 litres (68 fl oz/8 cups) chicken stock (see page 216)
500 g (1 lb 2 oz) boneless, skinless chicken breasts
2 spring onions (scallions), finely chopped
juice of 2–3 limes, to taste
¼ cup chopped coriander (cilantro), to garnish

While it sounds like this soup might come from the capital of Peru, Lima, it's actually a specialty of Mexico's Yucatán Peninsula. The 'lima' in this recipe's name comes from the Spanish word for 'lime', which is added to the soup just before serving to add a deliciously tangy flavour.

Score a cross in the base of each tomato. Place in a heatproof bowl and cover with boiling water. Leave for 30 seconds, then transfer to cold water and peel the skins away from the cross. Cut the tomatoes in half and scoop out the seeds with a teaspoon, then dice and set aside.

Heat the oil in a wok or large, deep frying pan and shallow-fry the tortilla strips for 1–2 minutes, or until crispy. Use a slotted spoon to remove the crispy tortillas and transfer to a plate lined with paper towel to drain. Season with a little fire and smoke salt.

In a large heavy-based pan, heat 2 tablespoons of the oil used to fry the tortilla strips. Add the onion, celery, carrot and chilli, then sauté over medium heat for 10 minutes, until the vegetables are soft and translucent. Stir in the garlic, bay leaf and oregano and cook for a further 2–3 minutes. Add the tomatoes and season with the remaining flavoured salt. Reduce the heat to low and cook gently for about 15 minutes, until the tomatoes have broken down and the mixture is almost dry.

Add the chicken stock, increase the heat to high and bring to the boil. Reduce the heat to a simmer and poach the chicken in the stock for about 10 minutes. Remove the chicken from the stock and allow to cool slightly. When cool enough to handle, use a knife to shred the chicken into pieces.

Return the shredded chicken to the stock, along with the chopped spring onions and lime juice. Simmer until the chicken is heated through. Taste and adjust the seasoning. Divide the soup between serving bowls and garnish with the fried tortillas and chopped coriander.

My Southern fried chicken

SERVES 4

¼ quantity Buttermilk brine (page 231)
1 kg (2 lb 3 oz) chicken thigh pieces
sunflower oil for deep-frying
1 quantity Blue cheese sauce (page 222)
flat-leaf (Italian) parsley leaves, chopped, to garnish

CRUMB

165 g (6 oz/1½ cups) besan (chickpea flour)
1 teaspoon onion powder
¼ teaspoon cayenne pepper
¼ teaspoon garlic powder
¼ teaspoon smoked paprika
1 heaped teaspoon Chicken salt (page 226)
1 teaspoon freshly ground black pepper
1½ teaspoons baking powder

Dude food like fried chicken is all the rage these days. This is my version of one of the Deep South's best comfort foods. I prefer to use chickpea flour in the crumb, as it has a really great flavour and provides an irresistible crunch.

One day before cooking, prepare the brine according to the recipe on page 231 and add the chicken. Place in the refrigerator and brine overnight.

When you are ready to cook, remove the chicken from the brine and reserve 3–4 tablespoons of the brine.

Make the crumb by combining all the ingredients in a large bowl. Add the reserved buttermilk brine and stir with a fork until even clumps form.

Coat the chicken, a few pieces at a time, in the crumb, pressing firmly so that it sticks to the chicken. Place the pieces onto a baking tray.

Line another tray with paper towel.

Fill a large heavy-based saucepan one-third with oil and heat to 175°C (345°F), or hot enough to make a small cube of bread sizzle in 15 seconds when dropped into the oil. Carefully lower a few pieces of chicken at a time into the oil so as not to overcrowd the pan. Fry for 5–7 minutes on one side, until golden, then turn and cook the other side for a further 5–7 minutes. Remove from the oil and drain on the lined tray; check one piece for doneness. Once drained, you can keep the chicken warm by placing it in a low oven. Fry the remaining chicken in batches, being careful not to overheat the oil.

Serve immediately with the blue cheese sauce and sprinkle over the parsley.

Brazilian cachaça chicken

SERVES 4

4 boneless, skinless chicken breasts, cut in half lengthways if very large

bamboo or metal skewers

coconut cream, to brush

1 handful chopped coriander (cilantro) leaves, to serve

lime wedges, to serve

MARINADE

60 ml (2 fl oz / ¼ cup) cachaça

grated zest and juice of 1 lime

1 handful coriander (cilantro) leaves, finely chopped

1 fresh green jalapeño chilli, seeds removed, finely chopped

2 tablespoons olive oil

1 tablespoon honey

1 garlic clove, crushed

1 teaspoon sea salt

This dish is ideal for barbecues or parties. The cachaça and lime gives the chicken a great flavour. If you like, serve it with aïoli for dipping; it will be like Carnival in your mouth.

Combine all of the ingredients for the marinade in a large non-reactive bowl. Add the chicken and toss to coat well. Refrigerate for at least 1–2 hours, or overnight.

If using bamboo skewers, soak them in water for 10 minutes before using.

Thread one piece of chicken onto each of the skewers. Heat a chargrill pan over medium heat (or crank up the barbecue) and brush the grill with coconut cream. Cook the chicken skewers for 6–8 minutes, turning occasionally and brushing with coconut cream frequently until the chicken is cooked through and lightly charred. Serve sprinkled with coriander and a squeeze of fresh lime.

NOTE

Cachaça is a Brazilian spirit made from sugarcane juice and is available from most bottle shops.

Roast chicken with yoghurt

SERVES 4

2 × 900 g (2 lb) chickens
grated zest and juice of 2 lemons
2 tablespoons dried wild Greek oregano
salt and freshly ground black pepper
100 ml (3½ fl oz) olive oil
150 g (5½ oz) unsalted butter, melted
175 ml (6 oz/⅔ cup) water
500 g (1 lb 2 oz/2 cups) plain Greek-style yoghurt
3 eggs
pinch of dried chilli flakes
steamed potatoes, to serve
chopped flat-leaf (Italian) parsley, to sprinkle

Rinse the inside and outside of the chicken with the lemon juice. Rub the cavity with the zest and oregano and refrigerate for at least 2 hours.

Preheat the oven to 200°C (400°F).

Remove the chicken from the refrigerator 20 minutes prior to cooking (this will help it come up to room temperature). Lay the chicken in a roasting tin and season well.

Combine the oil, melted butter and 100 ml (3½ fl oz) of the water in a bowl and pour over the chicken. Roast in the oven for 15 minutes, then turn the oven down to 180°C (350°F) and continue to roast for a further 30 minutes.

Whisk together the yoghurt, eggs, chilli and remaining water in a bowl. Pour this over the chicken and return to the oven for a further 15 minutes, until the sauce has thickened and the chickens are fully cooked.

Serve with steamed potatoes tossed in olive oil and a little flat-leaf (Italian) parsley to sprinkle.

Pan-roasted mascarpone-stuffed chicken

SERVES 4

2 × 900 g (2 lb) chickens, deboned (ask your butcher to do this)
8 slices prosciutto
250 ml (8½ fl oz/1 cup) chicken stock
knob of unsalted butter
250 g (9 oz) baby spinach

FILLING

110 g (4 oz/½ cup) mascarpone, plus 4 tablespoons for finishing and extra to serve
grated zest of 1 lemon
1 tablespoon finely chopped thyme
1 garlic clove, finely chopped
salt and freshly ground black pepper

In a bowl, make the filling by combining 110 g (4 oz/½ cup) of the mascarpone with the lemon zest, thyme, garlic and salt and pepper. Set aside.

Using a sharp knife, halve the deboned chickens so that each half has a thigh and a breast.

Lay one chicken half on your chopping board, skin side down. Use your fingers to gently separate the breast and thigh meat from the skin almost completely, keeping them attached at the outer edges. Fold back the breast and thigh to expose the skin beneath. Place one slice of prosciutto so the mid-point of its length sits where the breast and skin meet. Dollop a ½ tablespoon of the mascarpone filling on top of the prosciutto and fold the breast back over, pulling the tenderloin down to create a seal. Repeat the process with the thigh, so you have 2 pockets of prosciutto-wrapped filling between the skin and the meat. Repeat with the remaining chicken halves.

Preheat the oven to 180°C (350°F).

Heat the oil in a large heavy-based pan that will comfortably fit the chicken halves. Lay the stuffed birds in the pan, skin side down, and fry over medium heat for about 8 minutes, until the skin is golden. Transfer to the oven for 15 minutes, or until cooked – pierce the thickest part with a knife; if the juice runs clear, it is done. Remove from the oven, transfer to a tray and cover with a sheet of aluminium foil to keep warm.

Skim off any excess fat from the pan and set over medium heat. Add the stock and bring to the boil, then simmer for 5 minutes, until reduced by half. Add 4 tablespoons of the mascarpone and allow to melt slightly.

Melt the butter in a separate frying pan. Sauté the spinach for 6 minutes, or until wilted, then drain and season with salt and pepper. Divide the spinach between 4 plates and top with the stuffed chicken. Finish with a dollop of mascarpone and a glug of the gravy.

Duck confit

SERVES 6

Confit is a traditional method for preserving duck. The fat prevents air from contaminating the meat, allowing you to keep it for long periods of time if stored in the refrigerator. This is a great way to cook duck, and from this recipe you'll have many options for further dishes. You can either roast the duck and serve it as a stand-alone dish, perhaps with a little salad, or use it to make Duck nuggets (page 112) or Duck rillettes (page 197).

12 duck leg quarters, hip bone removed
50 g (1¾ oz/¼ cup) Chicken salt (page 226)
1 kg (2 lb 3 oz) duck fat (see page 229), melted

One day before cooking, prepare the duck. Trim any excess fat and skin from the edges of the duck. Lay the duck in a non-reactive tray and sprinkle over the chicken salt. Transfer to the refrigerator overnight.

The next day, preheat the oven to 150°C (300°F). Rinse the duck under cold running water to remove the salt and pat dry with paper towel. Place the duck legs into a casserole dish in a single layer. Pour over the melted fat and cover the dish with a sheet each of baking paper and foil.

Cook in the oven for 2 hours. After this time, check if the duck is cooked by using a knife to press down on the thigh – it should yield easily, and the meat should be very tender.

Remove the duck confit from the oven. Allow to cool completely, then transfer the duck and the fat to an airtight container and store in the refrigerator. You will find that once the duck has cooled, a jelly will form at the base of the container. Discard the jelly, but keep the fat, as it can be reused. If the duck is completely covered by fat, it will last for months.

To serve as a stand-alone dish, remove the duck legs from the fat, taking care not to pull the bone out of the meat. Heat a non-stick frying pan over medium–high heat and fry the duck for about 6 minutes, skin side down, until the skin is crisp and the meat is warmed through.

Duck nuggets

MAKES 20

500 g (1 lb 2 oz) shredded Duck confit (page 111 or store-bought)
1 tablespoon dijon mustard
1 tablespoon sherry vinegar
1 tablespoon olive oil
1 onion, finely diced
6 garlic cloves, finely chopped
½ teaspoon dried sage
½ teaspoon dried thyme
¼ teaspoon garlic powder
¼ teaspoon paprika
¼ teaspoon mustard powder
sunflower oil for deep-frying
sweet chilli sauce or Fermented chilli sauce (page 221), to serve

CRUMB

150 g (5½ oz/1 cup) plain (all-purpose) flour, seasoned with salt and freshly ground black pepper
4 eggs, lightly beaten
120 g (4½ oz/2 cups) Japanese panko breadcrumbs

At Billykart Kitchen, we serve this great party dish as finger food. The nuggets have a rich, deep flavour that goes well with our pear and mustard dipping sauce, but they taste just as good with trusty sweet chilli sauce.

Combine the confit duck, mustard and vinegar in a bowl.

Heat the olive oil in a frying pan and sauté the onion and garlic until translucent. Stir in the herbs and the remaining dry ingredients, and sauté for a further 2–3 minutes. Transfer the mixture to a bowl and allow to cool. Once cooled, combine the onion mixture and duck and mix well. Allow to rest in the refrigerator for 20 minutes to firm up.

Using a tablespoon as a guide, shape portions of the mixture into round nuggets with your hands, until all the duck has been used.

Prepare a crumbing station with the seasoned flour, beaten eggs and breadcrumbs in separate shallow bowls. Dip each nugget into the flour, followed by the egg and finally the breadcrumbs. You can choose to double the crumbing; simply omit the flour step the second time.

Heat the oil in a heavy-based saucepan or deep-fryer to 175°C (345°F), or hot enough to make a small piece of bread sizzle in 15 seconds when dropped into the oil. Working in batches to avoid overcrowding the pan, fry the nuggets for about 1½ minutes on each side, until golden brown. Drain on paper towel and serve with sweet chilli sauce.

Duck and tapioca pearl soup with crab

SERVES 6

- 3 tablespoons large tapioca pearls (see note)
- 1.25 litres (42 fl oz/5 cups) chicken stock (see page 216)
- pinch of salt
- 1 tablespoon oyster sauce
- 1–2 tablespoons light soy sauce
- large pinch of palm sugar (jaggery) or soft brown sugar
- 100 g (3½ oz) crabmeat
- 100 g (3½ oz) roasted duck, sliced
- 1 handful pea shoots
- 2 spring onions (scallions), sliced
- 1 tablespoon chopped coriander (cilantro) leaves
- 1 teaspoon crisp-fried garlic
- pinch of ground white pepper
- sesame oil, to drizzle

This is a beautiful, clean and simple soup that is a great way to start a meal. I like to make this when I have left-over roast duck. If you roasted your own duck, keep the bones and use it for the stock instead of chicken – this will make your money go that little bit further.

Clean the tapioca of any dust by tossing it in a sieve. Bring a large saucepan of water to the boil and whisk in the tapioca, stirring regularly to ensure that they don't stick to each other or the bottom of the pan. Simmer for 30 minutes, until the tapioca pearls are translucent. Remove, drain and refresh with cold water to stop them cooking further.

Bring the stock to the boil and season with the salt, oyster sauce, soy sauce and sugar. Skim off any froth that comes to the surface. Add the drained tapioca, crabmeat and duck, and heat through without letting it boil. The soup should be savoury and a little nutty. Serve topped with pea shoots, spring onions, coriander, crisp-fried garlic and pepper, and drizzle over the sesame oil to finish.

NOTE

Tapioca pearls are easy to find at Asian supermarkets. Choose the large variety for this soup.

Duck ragu with bucatini

SERVES 6

POULTRY

- 1 × 2.5 kg (5½ lb) duck
- 2 celery stalks
- 2 medium carrots
- 1 tomato, roughly chopped
- 1 red onion
- ½ bunch thyme
- ½ bunch sage
- 1 teaspoon black peppercorns
- 3 garlic cloves
- 3 tablespoons olive oil
- 800 g (1 lb 12 oz) tinned tomatoes, drained
- salt and freshly ground black pepper
- 500 g (1 lb 2 oz) bucatini or similar pasta
- 100 g (3½ oz) unsalted butter
- ½ nutmeg
- 100 g (3½ oz/1 cup) finely grated parmesan

I first came across a recipe like this in Verona, while travelling in Italy. I have replicated it several times, both at Monte's in London and also at Billykart Kitchen, for our Veneto monthly menu.

Using butcher's twine, wrap and tie the duck in muslin (cheesecloth) or a clean tea towel. Place it in a large saucepan, cover with water and set over medium heat. Roughly chop 1 celery stalk and 1 carrot and add them to the saucepan with the fresh tomato, ½ onion, herbs and peppercorns. Bring to a simmer and cook for 2 hours, keeping the duck submerged using a small plate or bowl, until the duck is very tender. Top up with water if it looks a little dry.

Once cooked, remove the bird from the stock and allow to cool sufficiently to handle.

Strain the stock, discarding the vegetables and herbs and reserving the liquid in the same pan.

Finely chop the garlic and the remaining celery, carrot and onion. Heat the oil in a medium-sized saucepan and sauté the vegetables over a low heat for about 10 minutes, until very soft. Stir in the drained tinned tomatoes and continue to cook gently, uncovered, until the tomatoes break down and thicken to a rich sauce.

Meanwhile, unwrap the duck and remove as much meat as you possibly can. Discard the skin and bones. Shred the meat and add it to the sauce, then continue to cook over low heat for 15 minutes to marry the flavours. Season with salt and freshly ground pepper.

Bring the stock to the boil and add the pasta. Cook for 8–10 minutes, or according to the packet instructions. As the pasta cooks, add the butter to the sauce and grate in the nutmeg. Using a pair of tongs, lift the cooked pasta from the stock and add it to the sauce. Combine well and check for seasoning. Divide the pasta between bowls and scatter with the parmesan.

Thai duck curry

SERVES 6

100 ml (3½ fl oz) coconut oil or duck fat (see page 229)

750 g (1 lb 11 oz/3 cups) coconut cream

2 teaspoons palm sugar (jaggery) or soft brown sugar

3 tablespoons fish sauce

1–2 confit duck legs (page 111, or shop-bought)

250 g (9 oz) waxy potatoes, cooked, peeled and sliced

230 g (8 oz) tinned lychees, drained

steamed jasmine rice, to serve

20 g (¾ oz/¼ cup) crisp-fried shallots (available from Asian supermarkets)

3 kaffir lime leaves, finely sliced

15 g (½ oz/½ cup) coriander (cilantro) leaves (optional)

CURRY PASTE

7 long dried red chillies

15 white peppercorns

1 tablespoon coriander seeds, roasted

2 teaspoons cumin seeds, roasted

1 teaspoon fennel seeds, roasted

1 whole nutmeg

1 teaspoon salt

2 red shallots

2 tablespoons chopped garlic

1 tablespoon chopped galangal

1 tablespoon chopped lemongrass stem

2 teaspoons scraped and chopped coriander (cilantro) root

Make the curry paste. Soak the chillies in a small bowl of water for 10 minutes. Meanwhile, pound the peppercorns, coriander seeds, cumin seeds, fennel seeds and nutmeg in a mortar and pestle until finely ground, or use a spice grinder. Remove and set aside.

Place the remaining ingredients for the curry paste in a food processor and blend to a paste-like consistency. Add the ground spices and combine well.

Heat the fat in a large saucepan or wok and fry the curry paste over a low heat for about 5 minutes, until fragrant. Pour in the coconut cream and bring to the boil, then reduce the heat. Adjust the seasoning with the sugar and fish sauce to achieve a balance of flavour.

Add the confit duck leg, along with the cooked potatoes and lychees. Stir well to coat with sauce and heat through for 15 minutes.

Serve alongside steamed jasmine rice and scatter with the crisp-fried shallots, kaffir lime leaves and coriander, if using.

Quail pastilla

SERVES 4

1 bunch coriander (cilantro) leaves and root
3 garlic cloves
salt and freshly ground black pepper
10 shallots, finely sliced
½ teaspoon ground ginger
1 teaspoon ground cumin
½ teaspoon turmeric
6 quails, butterflied (split in half down the backbone)
5 eggs, beaten
30 g (1 oz/1 cup) chopped flat-leaf (Italian) parsley
grated zest of 1 lemon
80 g (2¾ oz/½ cup) toasted almonds
80 g (2¾ oz/½ cup) toasted pine nuts
2 tablespoons ground cinnamon, plus extra to dust
2 tablespoons icing (confectioners') sugar, plus extra to dust
250 g (9 oz) clarified butter or salted butter, melted
8 sheets filo pastry

Pick the coriander leaves, chop and set aside. Rinse the stalks and root under cold water thoroughly, then roughly chop and place them in a food processor or mortar and pestle, along with the garlic and a pinch of salt. Blend or pound into a paste and add the shallots, ginger, cumin and turmeric.

In a roasting tin, combine the split quails with the shallot–spice mixture and enough water to just cover the quails. Place in the refrigerator to marinate for at least 2 hours.

Preheat the oven to 180°C (350°F).

Remove the quails from the refrigerator, cover with aluminium foil and roast in the oven for 20 minutes, or until they are just cooked but still a little pink. Remove and allow to cool. There should be about 250 ml (8½ fl oz/1 cup) liquid in the tin. If not, add enough water to top up. Once the quails have cooled, pick through and remove any bones. Roughly chop the meat and return it to the roasting tin.

Place the roasting tin on the stove top over low–medium heat and bring to a simmer. Stir in the beaten eggs and slowly heat until the sauce is thickened. Remove from the heat and allow to cool. Season with salt and pepper and stir in the chopped coriander leaves, parsley and lemon zest. The mixture should be quite thick and not at all watery.

Blend the toasted nuts together in a food processor, then combine with the cinnamon and icing sugar and set aside.

Brush a 25 cm (10 in) casserole dish or shallow cake tin with clarified butter. Lay 1 sheet of filo in the dish, making sure there is plenty of overhang, then brush with more butter and lay another sheet of filo on top. Continue with 2 more sheets of filo, ensuring that all of the dish is covered. Butter the fourth sheet of filo, then sprinkle with the nut mixture. Continue layering and buttering filo until the remaining 4 sheets have been used.

Tip the quail filling into the pan and fold back the overhanging pastry, pressing down to seal. Brush the top with more butter and bake in the oven for 20 minutes, until the pastry is golden. Remove from the oven and allow to stand for 5 minutes before turning out onto a serving plate and dusting with icing sugar and cinnamon. This is excellent served with a leaf salad dressed with pomegranate molasses.

Pot-roasted guinea fowl

SERVES 4

pinch of saffron threads
4 garlic cloves
1 × 1.1 kg (2 lb 7 oz) guinea fowl
8 thyme sprigs
2 tablespoons pomegranate molasses
salt and freshly ground black pepper
30 g (1 oz) salted butter
2 tablespoons olive oil
2 large red onions, chopped
½ teaspoon cardamom, crushed
½ teaspoon dried oregano
150 g (5½ oz) tinned chickpeas, rinsed and drained
10 g (¼ oz/⅓ cup) fresh oregano leaves
1 fresh bay leaf
300 ml (10 fl oz/1¼ cups) chicken stock
2 tablespoons currants
cooked couscous or steamed rice, to serve

Soak the saffron in 2 tablespoons of water for 10 minutes.

Using the flat part of a large knife, crush 2 of the garlic cloves and discard the papery skin. Peel and slice the remaining 2 cloves of garlic and set aside.

Preheat the oven to 160°C (320°F).

Stuff the guinea fowl with the sliced garlic and thyme, and rub the pomegranate molasses all over. Season well, inside and out, with salt and pepper. Melt the butter in a large flameproof casserole dish and brown the guinea fowl on all sides until golden. Remove to a tray and set aside.

Return the casserole to a low heat and add the olive oil. Sauté the onions and remaining garlic until the onions are soft and translucent. Stir in the crushed cardamom and dried oregano and cook until fragrant. Stir in the chickpeas and the fresh herbs.

Add the stock and saffron liquid and bring to the boil. Place the guinea fowl into the pan. Transfer to the oven and cook for 40 minutes, spooning the liquid, onion and chickpeas over the bird from time to time, until the chickpeas are very tender and the guinea fowl is cooked. To check for doneness, insert a sharp knife into the thickest part of the guinea fowl's thigh: if the juices run clear, it's ready. If the juices are bloody, continue to cook for another 7–10 minutes and test again. Towards the end of cooking, add the currants and season to your liking. Serve with couscous or rice.

Roast turkey with Grandma's stuffing

SERVES 8

You are going to need a fairly big pot or bucket and plenty of refrigerator space for this recipe, but it's worth it.

One day before cooking, make the cider brine according to the recipe on page 230. Place the turkey in a very large stockpot or bucket and pour over the prepared brine, turning to remove any air from the cavity. Refrigerate and brine for 1 hour per 500 g (1 lb) of turkey. If available, use a brining syringe to inject the breast and thighs with the brine occasionally.

Make the stuffing. First, soak the raisins in a bowl with the brandy. Melt the butter in a frying pan and sauté the onions, sage and garlic until soft. Remove from the heat and allow to cool.

In a bowl, soak the bread in the cream for 10 minutes. Use your hands to mash and soften the bread. Add the soaked raisins and onion mixture and season well with salt and pepper.

Preheat the oven to 200°C (400°F).

Remove the turkey from the brine and pat dry with paper towel. Stuff the turkey loosely, both in the rear cavity and the neck cavity. Rub 200 g (7 oz) of the butter all over the turkey. Place the thick onion slices in a large roasting tin and lay the turkey, breast side down, into the tin. Season well with salt and pepper.

Roast for 20 minutes on the bottom rack of the oven until well coloured. Turn the heat down to 165°C (325°F). Cook with its bum in the air for 1 hour. Using a large spoon, baste the turkey occasionally by spooning over the fat from the tray.

Remove from the oven and turn the turkey over, then return to the oven. Continue to cook, basting often, for a further 1½ hours, or until the internal temperature of both the turkey and the stuffing reaches 75°C (165°F). Remove from the oven, transfer the turkey to a platter and cover loosely with aluminium foil. Allow to rest for 20 minutes while you make the gravy.

Place the roasting tin on the stove top over medium heat. Pour in the stock and bring to the boil. Use a wooden spoon to scrape off any bits of onion or turkey stuck to the bottom of the tin. In a small bowl, mix 1 tablespoon of the butter with the flour and whisk this mixture into the stock, along with any juices from the resting bird. Bring to the boil, reduce the heat to low and simmer for about 10 minutes to cook the flour and thicken. Season with salt and pepper.

Carve the rested turkey and serve with the gravy.

1 quantity Cider brine (page 230)
1 × 4–5 kg (8 lb 13 oz–11 lb) turkey
200 g (7 oz) salted butter, softened, plus 1 tablespoon
2 large onions, thickly sliced
125 ml (4 fl oz/½ cup) chicken stock
1 tablespoon plain (all-purpose) flour

STUFFING

120 g (4½ oz/1 cup) raisins
80 ml (2½ fl oz/⅓ cup) brandy
50 g (1¾ oz) salted butter
2 brown onions, finely diced
1 bunch of sage, chopped
3 garlic cloves, finely chopped
6 slices sourdough bread, crusts removed
500 ml (17 fl oz/2 cups) cream
salt and freshly ground black pepper

Maple-glazed drumsticks

SERVES 6

½ quantity Maple brine (page 230)
6 turkey drumsticks or 12 chicken drumsticks
125 ml (4 fl oz/½ cup) maple syrup
50 g (1¾ oz) salted butter
1 clove, crushed
1 teaspoon cracked black pepper
1 teaspoon white sesame seeds, to serve (optional)
1 teaspoon black sesame seeds, to serve (optional)

One day before cooking, prepare the maple brine according to the recipe on page 230. Place the drumsticks in a large container and pour over the brine. Refrigerate overnight.

Preheat the oven to 180°C (350°F).

Remove the drumsticks from the brine and pat dry with paper towel. Set aside 250 ml (8½ fl oz/1 cup) of the brine in a cup with a pouring lip and discard the rest. Lay the drumsticks in a roasting tray lined with baking paper and cook in the oven for 15 minutes, until the skin starts to caramelise.

Meanwhile, make the glaze. Pour the reserved brine into a saucepan and bring to the boil. Turn the heat to low and simmer, uncovered, for about 5 minutes. Add the maple syrup, butter, crushed clove and cracked black pepper, and cook for a further 5 minutes. Pour the glaze over the drumsticks and return to the oven to cook, basting occasionally with the glaze, for about 10 minutes, until sticky. To finish, sprinkle with the sesame seeds, if desired.

Turkey parmigiana

SERVES 4

POULTRY

2 turkey breasts, sliced into 8 thick pieces
2 balls buffalo mozzarella, sliced
16 basil leaves
3 eggs, beaten
150 g (5½ oz/1 cup) plain (all-purpose) flour, seasoned with salt and pepper
180 g (6½ oz/3 cups) Japanese panko breadcrumbs
500 ml (17 fl oz/2 cups) tomato sugo (see note)
salt and freshly ground black pepper
100 ml (3½ fl oz) olive oil
50 g (1¾ oz) salted butter

Place the turkey slices in between 2 sheets of baking paper and use a rolling pin to beat the turkey until it is about 5 mm (¼ in) thick.

Top each slice of turkey with a single mozzarella slice and basil leaf, then sandwich with another piece of turkey and set aside for crumbing.

Set up a crumbing station with the beaten eggs, flour and breadcrumbs in separate bowls. Crumb the turkey by dipping into the flour, then the egg, followed by the breadcrumbs. Press well with your hands to ensure the crumb sticks to the turkey. Set aside.

Pour the tomato sugo into a saucepan and simmer, uncovered, to reduce by about a quarter – it should be quite thick. Season with salt and pepper.

Heat the oil and butter in a frying pan and shallow-fry the turkey in batches for 6–8 minutes, until golden on both sides. Remove and drain on a plate lined with paper towel. For each turkey parmigiana, spoon the tomato sauce on top, add a slice of mozzarella and grill (broil) for 2–3 minutes, or until the cheese is melted and oozing. Garnish each parmigiana with a single leaf of basil.

NOTE

Tomato sugo is an Italian tomato sauce, and can be bought in most supermarkets. You could also substitute tomato passata (puréed tomatoes).

Satay turkey skewers

SERVES 4–6

1 cm (½ in) piece fresh ginger, peeled
2 red shallots, peeled and sliced
2 lemongrass stalks, sliced
2 teaspoons salt
2 tablespoons sugar
2 teaspoons ground coriander
2 tablespoons sunflower oil
125 ml (4 fl oz/½ cup) coconut cream, plus extra for brushing
500 g turkey breast, cut into 2 cm (¾ in) cubes
metal or bamboo skewers
lime wedges, to serve

PEANUT DIPPING SAUCE

2 garlic cloves
2 red shallots, chopped
½ teaspoon salt
1 tablespoon sunflower oil
1 lemongrass stalk, bruised
1 tablespoon dried chilli flakes
250 ml (8½ fl oz/1 cup) coconut milk
2 tablespoons sugar
125 g (4½ oz/½ cup) crunchy peanut butter

Place the ginger, shallots, lemongrass, salt, sugar, coriander, oil and coconut cream into a food processor and blitz into a paste. Transfer to a bowl and coat the turkey pieces in the paste, then refrigerate for 2 hours or overnight if possible.

To make the dipping sauce, pound the garlic, shallots and salt in a mortar and pestle, or process in a food processor. Heat the oil in a small frying pan and fry the shallot mixture over medium heat until fragrant and beginning to brown. Add the lemongrass and chilli flakes and fry for a further minute. Stir in the coconut milk and sugar, bring to the boil, then reduce the heat and simmer for 5 minutes. Add the peanut butter, stirring well until the sauce is smooth and thick, then cook for another 5 minutes over low heat. If the sauce gets too thick, add a little hot water to thin out; the sauce should coat the back of a spoon without being runny. Remove the lemongrass stalk and set aside for serving.

If using bamboo skewers, soak them in water for 10 minutes before using. Thread the turkey onto the skewers.

Heat a chargrill pan over medium heat (or crank up the barbecue). Brush the pan with coconut cream and brown the turkey skewers for 5–6 minutes, basting them with coconut cream as they cook and turning them often to get a nice colour.

Serve with the peanut dipping sauce and a few lime wedges for squeezing.

PORK

Classic roast pork

SERVES 6

1 × 2.5 kg (5½ lb) pork belly
2 tablespoons sea salt or flavoured salt of your choice (see pages 225–227)

This method of cooking is a little different and is more Asian in concept, as the pork is poached before it is roasted. Once roasted, the pork can be accompanied by a variety of flavours. For a traditional meal, roast your choice of veg in the same tray as the pork and serve with a great apple sauce, or jazz it up with Asian accompaniments or Mexican sides.

Preheat the oven to 180°C (350°F).

Use a sharp knife to score the surface of the pork skin in a cross-hatch pattern. Rub 1 tablespoon of the salt all over the pork, especially the skin and scoring. Place in a roasting tin and pour over enough water to submerge the pork fully. Cover with a snug-fitting piece of baking paper and a large piece of aluminium foil.

Bake in the oven for 1½ hours, until tender and soft. Carefully drain the water from the tin and set the pork aside to dry out and cool. Once cooled, generously season the skin with the remaining salt, rubbing it into the scoring well. Crank the oven up to 240°C (480°F), as you need to blast the pork with heat to start off the crackling.

Roast in the oven for 30 minutes, until the skin starts to bubble, then reduce the heat to 180°C (350°F) and continue to roast for a further 30 minutes, or until the skin turns golden brown and crispy. Remove from the oven and allow to rest for 10 minutes before serving.

Cola baked ham

SERVES 8–10

1 × 4–5 kg (8 lb 13 oz–11 lb) bone-in ham
20 whole cloves
500 ml (17 fl oz/2 cups) cola
125 ml (4 fl oz/½ cup) apple-cider vinegar
95 g (3¼ oz/½ cup) soft brown sugar
1 teaspoon freshly ground black pepper
1 teaspoon English mustard powder

This is one bad-ass ham recipe! It's a ripper when cooked on the barbecue. Try throwing some soaked woodchips onto the burners to add a killer smoky flavour. I love eating this with a nice potato salad or slaw.

Preheat the oven to 150°C (300°F). If using a barbecue, set it up for indirect cooking with the outer burners on and the inner ones off.

Use a sharp knife to remove the skin from the ham, leaving as much of the fat as you like (I prefer as much as possible). Score the fat diagonally to form a cross-hatch pattern and pierce the centre of each 'diamond' with a whole clove. Place the ham, fat side up, on a rack over a roasting tin.

Combine the cola, vinegar, brown sugar, pepper and mustard powder in a bowl and pour this mixture over the ham. Bake for 30 minutes per kilogram (2 lb 3 oz), basting regularly with the liquid in the tin. Remove from the oven and allow to stand for at least 15 minutes before transferring to a serving platter.

While the ham is resting, drain the juices from the tin into a saucepan. Cook over medium heat for about 15 minutes, or until the juices have reduced to form a sticky glaze. Baste the ham with this glaze before serving.

This ham is excellent served simply with fresh bread rolls and good dijon mustard, warm or cold, so don't despair if there are leftovers.

Pork and cabbage potstickers

MAKES 30

¼ Chinese cabbage (about 150 g/5½ oz), finely shredded
1 teaspoon salt
500 g (1 lb 2 oz) minced (ground) pork
3 spring onions (scallions), finely chopped
1 tablespoon finely chopped garlic
1 tablespoon finely chopped fresh ginger
2 teaspoons light soy sauce
60 ml (2 fl oz/¼ cup) sesame oil
½ teaspoon freshly ground black pepper
2 teaspoons caster (superfine) sugar
2 tablespoons potato starch, plus extra to dust
30 round Shanghai (flour and water) dumpling wrappers (6–8 cm/2½–3¼ in diameter)
vegetable oil for frying

DIPPING SAUCE

60 ml (2 fl oz/¼ cup) light soy sauce
2 tablespoons rice vinegar
1 tablespoon chilli oil

Potstickers or gyozas are very easy to make. They are an excellent snack for when you're entertaining and freeze really well. Just place a sheet of baking paper between each layer of uncooked potstickers and freeze in an airtight container. Thaw them in the refrigerator prior to cooking and make sure they are hot all the way through before eating.

Mix the cabbage and salt in a bowl and let stand for 30 minutes for the flavours to develop. Squeeze out as much liquid as possible and add the cabbage to a bowl with the pork, spring onions, garlic, ginger, soy sauce, sesame oil, pepper, sugar and potato starch. Using your hands, mix the ingredients together until well combined. Set aside while you make the dipping sauce.

In a bowl, mix the soy sauce, vinegar and chilli oil. Set aside.

Dust a tray with a fine sprinkling of potato starch. Have ready a small bowl of cold water. Place a dumpling wrapper, floured side down (they are usually sold floured on one side), on a clean, floured surface, then dip your fingertips into the water and wet the edges of the wrapper.

Place a tablespoon of the filling in the centre of the wrapper. Using your index fingers and thumbs, fold the wrapper in half to form a semi-circle and seal by pinching the edges together; the aim is to keep the base as flat as you can, pinching to create pleats at the top. Repeat with the remaining wrappers, placing them upright on the floured tray as you go. Push down on the top of each potsticker to flatten its base.

Heat a dash of vegetable oil in a non-stick frying pan with a lid over high heat. (I find an electric frying pan works best.) Working in batches if necessary – don't pack the pan too tightly – fry the potstickers, flat side down, until the bases are golden, roughly 2–3 minutes. Pour in 250 ml (8½ fl oz/1 cup) water, taking care to avoid the spattering liquid. Bring to the boil, cover with the lid, turn the heat down to medium and cook for a further 6 minutes, until the water has evaporated and the potstickers are cooked all the way through. Repeat with the remaining uncooked potstickers.

Serve hot, accompanied with the dipping sauce.

Short soup

SERVES 4

1 litre (34 fl oz/4 cups) Hainanese chicken stock (see page 95) or Beef pho broth (see page 22)
20 Pork and cabbage potstickers (page 136) or store-bought dumplings (see note)
1–2 tablespoons light soy sauce, to taste
1 tablespoon oyster sauce
2 spring onions (scallions), chopped
1 tablespoon chopped coriander (cilantro) leaves
1 tablespoon crisp-fried shallots
1 teaspoon crisp-fried garlic
chilli oil, to serve

When I have left-over stock, I like to make this filling and super-easy soup. It's quick to make if you've got the Pork and cabbage potstickers (page 136) on hand, or if you simply use store-bought dumplings.

Place the chicken stock in a large saucepan. Arrange the dumplings in a large bamboo steamer and place the steamer on top of the saucepan, making sure it doesn't touch the liquid. Bring to a boil, reduce the heat to a simmer and steam, covered, for 15 minutes.

Remove the bamboo steamer and carefully take out the dumplings, then add them to the broth. Season the broth with the soy and oyster sauces, and stir gently to heat through. Divide the dumplings between serving bowls and ladle over the broth. Sprinkle with the spring onions, coriander, crisp-fried shallots and garlic, and a few drops of chilli oil.

NOTE

A wide range of pre-made dumplings can be found in Asian supermarkets.

Pot-roasted pork with porcini, tomato, garlic and sage

SERVES 6

1.5 kg (3 lb 5 oz) boneless rolled shoulder or loin roast
salt and freshly ground black pepper
50 g (1¾ oz) dried porcini mushrooms
100 g (3½ oz) unsalted butter
6 garlic cloves, sliced in half
1 bunch sage
pinch of dried chilli flakes
440 g (15½ oz) tinned chopped tomatoes

SOFT POLENTA

1.5 litres (51 fl oz/6 cups) water
300 g (10½ oz/2 cups) instant polenta
100 g (3½ oz) unsalted butter
100 g (3½ oz/1 cup) finely grated parmesan, plus extra to garnish

You can make this recipe in a slow cooker or an electric frying pan. I always use an electric frying pan as it's something I like to cook when I'm on holiday. Soft polenta is what I call 'Italian mash'. Served together with the pot-roasted pork, it has comfort written all over it.

Season the pork well with salt and pepper.

Soak the porcini mushrooms in a bowl of just-boiled water for 10–15 minutes, until soft. Remove the mushrooms (reserve the soaking liquid) and rinse in cold water, making sure that the mushrooms are grit-free. Strain the mushroom soaking liquid into a cup or bowl and set aside.

Melt half of the butter in a large, deep frying pan (or electric frying pan) over medium–high heat until it starts to foam. Add the pork and brown on all sides until nicely crusted. Remove the pork from the pan and set aside. Use a paper towel to wipe the pan clean. Heat the remaining butter in the pan until foaming, then add the garlic, sage and dried chilli flakes. Once the sage becomes crisp, add the soaked mushrooms and stir to combine. Return the pork to the pan and add the tomatoes. (If you want to use a slow cooker at this point, transfer everything to the slow cooker, add the reserved mushroom soaking liquid, cover and cook as per the manufacturer's instructions until the pork is cooked.)

Reduce the heat to low and cover with a wet sheet of baking paper. Cover and cook slowly, turning the pork from time to time and adding the mushroom soaking liquid to keep the sauce from getting too thick, for about 1 hour, or until well cooked. You may need to add a splash of water from time to time if you have used all of the mushroom liquid.

To make the polenta, bring the water to the boil in a large saucepan. Whisk in the polenta in a thin and constant stream. Continue to stir over medium heat until the polenta becomes the consistency of thick porridge. Reduce the heat to low and cook for 10 minutes. Stir in the butter and parmesan.

Divide the polenta between serving plates and slice the pork into nice thick slices. Place the pork slices on top of the polenta, along with the sauce. Garnish with a sprinkle of cheese and serve alongside some steamed spinach if you like.

Pork chops with grilled pears and gremolata

SERVES 4

4 × 300 g (10½ oz) thick skinless pork loin chops, bones removed
2 tablespoons finely chopped thyme
1 tablespoon finely chopped rosemary
pinch of dried chilli flakes (optional)
sea salt flakes and freshly ground black pepper
4 pears, cored and quartered
olive oil, to drizzle
2 handfuls rocket (arugula)
100 g (3½ oz/1 cup) shaved parmesan

SALAD DRESSING

60 g (2 oz/¼ cup) sour cream
60 ml (2 fl oz/¼ cup) buttermilk
60 g (2 oz/¼ cup) Japanese mayonnaise
1 tablespoon onion powder
1 garlic clove
1 teaspoon chopped fresh dill

GREMOLATA

30 g (1 oz/½ cup) chopped flat-leaf (Italian) parsley
1 tablespoon chopped garlic
shredded zest of 2 unwaxed lemons

Sandwich the pork between two sheets of baking paper and use a rolling pin to pound the meat until it is about 5 mm (¼ in) thick. A little thicker won't hurt – but the pork does need to cook quickly over high heat.

Sprinkle a baking tray with the herbs, chilli flakes (if using) and salt and pepper. Roll the pork chops in the seasoning, then toss the pears in any left-over seasoning and leave to rest while you prepare the remaining ingredients.

Make the salad dressing by combining all the ingredients in a small bowl. Season to taste with salt and pepper and set aside.

Next, make the gremolata. Combine the parsley, garlic and lemon zest well. Season with pepper and set aside.

Heat a chargrill pan over high heat (or crank up the barbecue) and grill the pear quarters for 5 minutes, or until nicely charred. Transfer to a bowl, drizzle with olive oil and set aside. Cook the pork on the chargrill pan for 3–5 minutes, then remove from the heat and drizzle with olive oil. Slice into wide strips and add to the bowl with the pears.

Arrange the pears and pork on serving plates and garnish with the rocket, shaved parmesan and lashings of dressing. Finally, sprinkle the gremolata liberally on top.

Crispy pork belly salad

SERVES 4–6

PORK

1 × 1 kg (2 lb 3 oz) boneless pork belly
2 tablespoons light soy sauce
3 large or 5 small coriander (cilantro) roots
large pinch of salt
4 garlic cloves
1 teaspoon white peppercorns
1 star anise, roasted and ground
100 g (3½ oz/½ cup) palm sugar (jaggery) or soft brown sugar
2–3 tablespoons water
3 tablespoons fish sauce
3 tablespoons oyster sauce
oil for deep-frying
1 tablespoon coconut oil
35 g (1¼ oz/¼ cup) crisp-fried shallots, to serve
sliced fresh red chillies, to serve

DRESSING

1 garlic clove
pinch of salt
2 bird's-eye chillies
1½ tablespoons lime juice
1 tablespoon fish sauce
pinch of sugar

CUCUMBER SALAD

2 Lebanese (short) cucumbers
1 small red onion, very finely sliced
½ bunch mint, leaves picked
1 bunch coriander (cilantro), leaves picked

One day before cooking, rub the pork with the soy sauce, cover and place in the refrigerator to marinate overnight.

Steam the pork belly for 1 hour in a bamboo steamer.

Meanwhile, combine the coriander roots, salt, garlic, peppercorns and star anise in a mortar and pestle or food processor and grind to a paste. Set aside.

Place the sugar and water in a saucepan and bring to the boil. Simmer for about 5 minutes to dissolve the sugar and make a caramel, then remove from the heat and add the fish and oyster sauces. Set aside.

Remove the pork from the steamer and set aside to cool slightly. Cut into 3 cm (1¼ in) cubes, then set aside.

Make the dressing by pounding the ingredients in a mortar and pestle (or use a food processor), then set aside while you make the salad. Halve the cucumbers lengthways, remove the seeds and slice thinly on an angle. Mix the cucumber, onion and herbs and pour over the dressing. Arrange half of the salad on a serving plate.

Fill a deep-fryer or large heavy-based saucepan one-third with oil and heat to 175°C (345°F), or hot enough to make a small cube of bread sizzle in 15 seconds when dropped into the oil. Gently lower the cubed pork into the hot oil (take care as it will spit and pop) and deep-fry for 5–8 minutes, or until crispy, then remove and drain well on paper towel. Cook the pork in batches so that the oil stays hot and the pork cooks evenly.

Heat the coconut oil in a non-stick frying pan and fry the spice paste until fragrant. Pour in the caramel and bring to the boil, then add the pork and stir until just coated; don't leave the pork in the caramel too long, otherwise it will lose its crispness.

Scatter the pork over the salad and top with the remaining salad. Sprinkle with fried shallots and sliced chilli and serve immediately.

Scotch eggs

MAKES 6

6 eggs
splash of white vinegar
8 fat pork sausages
100 g (3½ oz) pork fat, very finely diced
5 thyme sprigs, chopped
1 handful sage, leaves picked and chopped
45 g (1½ oz/½ cup) dried apple, finely diced
freshly grated nutmeg
salt and freshly ground black pepper
35 g (1¼ oz/¼ cup) plain (all-purpose) flour
2 eggs, lightly beaten
40 g (1½ oz/½ cup) Japanese panko breadcrumbs
oil for deep-frying
Togarashi or Thai salt (page 227) or sea salt flakes mixed with chopped flat-leaf (Italian) parsley, to serve (optional)

Bring a saucepan of water to the boil. Gently drop in the eggs, add the vinegar and simmer for 5 minutes, then drain and plunge immediately into ice-cold water. Allow to cool, then peel the eggs and set aside.

Squeeze the meat out of the sausage skins and mix in a bowl with the pork fat, chopped herbs and dried apple. Grate over some nutmeg and season with salt and pepper. Divide the mixture into 6 equal portions and flatten each into a 1 cm (½ in) thick disc.

Place an egg in the centre of a disc and mould the sausage mixture around the egg to enclose, ensuring there are no holes. Repeat with the remaining sausage mixture and eggs.

Set up a crumbing station with the flour, beaten egg and breadcrumbs in separate bowls. Take a scotch egg and dip it into the flour, followed by the beaten egg, then coat in the breadcrumbs. Repeat the crumbing process once more, omitting the flour step, then set aside on a plate while you do the same with the rest of the eggs.

Fill a deep-fryer or large heavy-based saucepan one-third with oil and heat to 175°C (345°F), or hot enough to make a small cube of bread sizzle in 15 seconds when dropped into the oil. Working in 2 batches, carefully lower the eggs into the hot oil and fry for 6–8 minutes, until crisp and golden, using a slotted spoon to turn them as they cook. Remove and drain on paper towel. Slice the eggs in half and serve with togarashi salt or sea salt flakes and chopped parsley, if you like.

Cajun-spiced pork fillet with beer sauce

SERVES 4

2 × 300 g (10½ oz) pork fillets, halved
150 g (5½ oz) salted butter, melted
sea salt flakes and freshly ground black pepper
2 tablespoons olive oil
steamed rice, to serve
1 teaspoon chopped coriander (cilantro) or celery leaves, to serve

CAJUN SPICE MIX

1 teaspoon each of the following:
cayenne pepper
smoked paprika
crisp-fried onions
crisp-fried garlic
celery salt
dried thyme
plain (all-purpose) flour

BEER SAUCE

2 tablespoons olive oil
2 garlic cloves, chopped
400g (14 oz) tinned chopped tomatoes
1 red capsicum (bell pepper)
1 green capsicum (bell pepper)
2 spring onions (scallions), finely sliced
250 ml (8½ fl oz/1 cup) pale ale
50 g (1¾ oz) salted butter
2 tablespoons sherry vinegar

Make the spice mix by blending all the ingredients for the spice mix together in a blender or food processor. Transfer to a shallow bowl or a plate and set aside.

Pour a third of the melted butter into a separate shallow bowl. Season the pork fillets with salt and pepper, dip into the melted butter and then roll them around in the spice mixture, making sure the pork is well coated. Transfer the pork to a plate and set aside any remaining spice mixture for the sauce.

Heat the oil and another third of the melted butter in a heavy-based frying pan over medium–high heat. Once the butter is foaming, add the pork and brown on all sides, turning occasionally, for about 5 minutes; the surface should blacken slightly because of the spice coating. Remove the pork from the pan and set aside to rest.

To make the sauce, heat the oil in a saucepan and fry the garlic until golden. Add the tomatoes and cook over low heat for 10–15 minutes, until thick and sweet.

Meanwhile, char the capsicums by placing them directly on the flame of a gas burner or under a hot grill (broiler), turning often to blacken and blister all over. Remove from the heat and allow to cool. Peel the skins off the capsicums, discard the cores and seeds and dice the flesh.

Wipe out the pan in which you fried the pork and add the remaining melted butter, followed by the spring onions and a good pinch of the reserved spice mix. Sauté until the spices are fragrant, then pour in the ale and simmer until reduced by about half. Add the charred capsicum and the tomato mixture, and reduce for a further 5 minutes. Finish by stirring through the 50 g (1¾ oz) of butter and the vinegar.

Return the pork to the pan and warm through. Serve with rice and sprinkle over the chopped coriander or celery leaves.

Lao minced pork salad

SERVES 6

This popular dish is known as *larb* in Laos and Thailand, and can be made with any kind of minced meat or fish. The combination of tangy lime, pungent fish sauce, chilli and a hint of sweetness will have you hooked in no time.

125 ml (4 fl oz/½ cup) chicken stock (see page 216)
1 kg (2 lb 3 oz) minced (ground) pork
1 tablespoon toasted ground glutinous rice (see note)
2 kaffir lime leaves, finely sliced
60 ml (2 fl oz/¼ cup) fish sauce
1 tablespoon sugar
juice of 2 limes
4 small dried red chillies, coarsely crushed
4 red shallots, thinly sliced

TO SERVE

1 Lebanese (short) cucumber, halved and finely sliced lengthways
6 snake (yard-long) beans, finely sliced diagonally
100 g (3½ oz) savoy cabbage, finely sliced
45 g (1½ oz/1 cup) mixed Thai basil, mint and coriander (cilantro) leaves
sliced green chillies
lime wedges, for squeezing

Heat the stock in a large saucepan over medium heat. Add the pork and the ground rice and cook, stirring continuously, for 3 minutes, or until the pork is just cooked. Throw in the lime leaves, add the fish sauce and sugar, and cook for 2 minutes. Check the seasoning and add more fish sauce or sugar to taste, if necessary. Remove from the heat and add the lime juice, crushed dried chillies and shallots. Serve with the vegetables, herbs, green chillies and lime wedges on the side.

NOTE

Toasted ground glutinous rice is used as a binding agent and adds an authentic texture to this dish that can't be beat. You should be able to find it in Asian supermarkets.

Okonomiyaki

SERVES 6

500 g (1 lb 2 oz) potatoes, peeled
100 g (3½ oz) plain (all-purpose) flour
75 g (2¾ oz) potato flour
½ teaspoon dashi granules (see note) or salt
2 eggs
375 ml (12½ fl oz/1½ cups) milk

FILLING

500 g (1 lb 2 oz) Chinese cabbage, finely shredded
25 g (1 oz/½ cup) tempura flakes (*tenkasu*)
1 tablespoon red pickled ginger (*beni shōga*)
60 g (2 oz/½ cup) spring onions (scallions), finely sliced
6 thin slices left-over Classic roast pork (page 132), or 6 slices smoked streaky bacon
250 g (9 oz/1 cup) okonomiyaki sauce or Barbecue sauce (page 223)
125 g (4½ oz/½ cup) Japanese mayonnaise
bonito flakes, to serve (optional)

These famous Japanese vegetable pancakes make a great savoury breakfast served with poached or fried eggs, and you can easily swap the roasted pork belly for bacon. The Japanese ingredients in this recipe can be found in either the international section of your local supermarket or at specialist Asian grocers.

First, make the okonomiyaki batter. In a large heavy-based pan, boil the potatoes for 10–15 minutes, until cooked; they should be tender when pricked with a knife. Drain and allow to steam dry. While still hot, add the potatoes to a blender with the flours, dashi, eggs and milk. Whizz into a thick batter, then leave to rest for 30 minutes.

Make the filling. Combine the cabbage, tempura flakes and pickled ginger in a large bowl with most of the spring onions. Pour the batter into the bowl and mix everything together well.

Lightly oil a hotplate or large frying pan and set over medium heat. Add a few spoonfuls of the mixture and spread them out into rough 15 cm (6 in) discs. Top with slices of pork, gently pressing them into the batter. Cook for 6–7 minutes, or until the bottoms of the pancakes are golden. Flip the pancakes over and poke a few holes in the top to allow steam to escape. Cook for a further 5 minutes, until the pancakes are firm and cooked through and the pork is browned and crispy. Alternatively, you could also make the okonomiyaki as one large pancake and cut it into portions. The thicker it is, the longer it will take to cook.

Transfer to plates with the pork side facing up and drizzle over the okonomiyaki or barbecue sauce and plenty of mayonnaise. Serve scattered with the remaining spring onions and the bonito flakes, if using.

NOTE

Dashi is a Japanese soup stock usually made from kelp and dried fish, and adds a great authentic flavour to this dish.

Pork cooked in milk

SERVES 6

1 × 1.5 kg (3 lb 5 oz) skinless and boneless pork shoulder
salt and freshly ground black pepper
100 g (3½ oz) butter
1 bunch sage, leaves picked
5 garlic cloves, halved
½ dried red chilli, crushed
zest of 2 unwaxed lemons, finely sliced into matchsticks
1.5 litres (52 fl oz/6 cups) full-cream (whole) milk

Preheat the oven to 150°C (300°F). Season the shoulder of pork with salt and pepper.

In a flameproof casserole dish, melt half the butter over medium heat until it foams. Add the pork, fat side down, and allow to brown, undisturbed, for 8–10 minutes, until the fat has rendered down. Turn and brown all over. Remove from the dish, drain the excess fat on paper towel and pat dry.

In the same pan, melt the remaining butter. Once foaming, add the sage, garlic and crushed chilli and cook gently for 1 minute. Add the lemon zest, cook gently for another minute, then add the pork. Pour in the milk and bring to the boil, then loosely cover with a round of damp baking paper (this will ensure moisture is maintained over the pork but will allow the liquid to evaporate). Transfer to the oven and cook for 3 hours, turning the pork halfway through the cooking time. When cooked, the meat will be meltingly tender and the milk reduced by about two-thirds.

This is excellent served with steamed spinach, cavolo nero or broccoli, and soft polenta (page 140) to soak up the juices.

Red-braised Japanese pork hock

SERVES 4

2 pork hocks (about 2 kg/4 lb 6 oz total)
1 tablespoon white rice
2 litres (68 fl oz/8 cups) water
100 g (3½ oz) fresh ginger, thickly sliced
1 star anise
1 tablespoon sea salt flakes
6 spring onions (scallions), finely sliced
steamed rice, to serve
pickled daikon (white radish) or kimchi, to serve

GLAZE

500 ml (17 fl oz/2 cups) dashi stock (see note)
100 ml (3½ fl oz) sake
100 ml (3½ fl oz) mirin
100 ml (3½ fl oz) dark soy sauce
100 g (3½ oz/⅓ cup) Japanese black rock sugar or soft brown sugar

We created this dish at Billykart Kitchen for our one-off Japanese menu. It's quite a classic. We used pork belly, but pork hocks work just as well and are a little less fatty.

One day before you want to eat this, prepare the pork. Preheat the oven to 150°C (300°F). In a large casserole dish or ovenproof saucepan, combine the pork with the rice, water, ginger, star anise, salt and most of the spring onions. Cover with a round of baking paper and a sheet of aluminium foil and cook for 3 hours, until the pork is tender; it should be easily pierced with a knife. Allow to cool completely in the stock. Chill overnight in the refrigerator.

The next day, preheat the oven to 150°C (300°F) and make the glaze. Mix the ingredients for the glaze in a saucepan and bring to the boil, then simmer for about 15 minutes, until reduced by half. Transfer the pork to a roasting tin that will hold the hocks snugly. Pour over the reduced glaze and bake in the oven for about 1 hour, basting regularly. The pork should take on a deep, rich red colour.

Serve the pork together with rice, pickled daikon and the remaining spring onions.

NOTE

Dashi is a Japanese soup stock usually made from kelp and dried fish, and adds a great authentic flavour to this dish. You can find it in Asian supermarkets.

Sausage rolls

MAKES 12–15

8 fat pork sausages
100 g (3½ oz) pork fat, very finely diced
5 thyme sprigs, chopped
1 handful sage, leaves picked and chopped
45 g (1½ oz/½ cup) dried apple, finely diced
pinch of freshly grated nutmeg
salt and freshly ground black pepper
1 tablespoon olive oil
1 brown onion, diced
2 teaspoons fennel seeds, lightly toasted and crushed
250 g (9 oz) ready-made puff pastry
100 g (3½ oz) salted butter, melted
2 eggs, lightly beaten

Squeeze the meat out of the sausage skins and mix in a bowl with the pork fat, chopped herbs and dried apple. Add the nutmeg, season with salt and pepper and set aside.

Heat the oil in a heavy-based frying pan over low–medium heat. Sauté the onion for 10–15 minutes, until soft and translucent. Add the fennel seeds and cook for a further 5 minutes. Remove from the heat and allow to cool before mixing through the pork mixture.

Preheat the oven to 165°C (320°F).

On a floured work surface, roll the pastry out into a large rectangle about 3 mm (⅛ in) thick. Cut the pastry lengthways, into 3 long, even rectangles. Spoon about a third of the sausage mix onto one piece of pastry, slightly off-centre, then brush the top edge of the pastry with melted butter. Roll the pastry over onto itself, encasing the filling to make a sausage shape, and press down to seal. Brush the top lightly with the beaten egg or the remaining butter. Repeat to make 3 rolls. Slice into 4 or 5 equal pieces and place them on a baking tray lined with baking paper. Bake for 20 minutes, or until golden brown, and serve immediately.

Tonkotsu miso ramen

SERVES 4

1 × 500 g (1 lb 2 oz) boneless pork loin, rind removed

salt and freshly ground black pepper

3 tablespoons white miso paste

4 teaspoons light soy sauce

2 teaspoons sake (optional)

1 teaspoon sugar

BROTH

2 litres (68 fl oz/8 cups) chicken stock (see page 216)

200 g (7 oz) minced (ground) pork

6 fresh shiitake mushrooms, brushed and sliced

3–4 cm (1¼–1½ in) piece ginger, peeled and sliced

3 garlic cloves, sliced

10 spring onions (scallions), white part sliced, green part finely sliced and reserved for garnish

piece of kombu seaweed (see note)

TO SERVE

2–3 baby bok choy (pak choy), sliced

100 g (3½ oz) dried wheat or soba noodles

2 soft-boiled eggs, peeled and halved

2 nori sheets, shredded

2 teaspoons sesame seeds

Ramen has really taken off over the past few years outside of its homeland. Recently, while on a ski trip in Japan, we spent a few days in Sapporo, where an entire street is dedicated to ramen. Dotted with tiny little ramen eateries, most of which we could hardly squeeze four adults and five children into, the street had the best ramen you could ever eat. This one comes a close second...

Season the pork with salt and pepper. Heat a small non-stick frying pan over medium–high heat and cook the pork for about 10 minutes, until well browned and cooked through. Set aside.

In a large stockpot over medium–high heat, bring all the ingredients for the broth, apart from the spring onion greens, to the boil. Reduce the heat and simmer for 20 minutes. Strain the broth into a bowl and return it to the stockpot. Stir the miso paste, soy sauce, sake and sugar into the broth and heat gently over low heat, taking care not to bring the stock up to the boil. Taste and adjust the seasoning if required.

Blanch the baby bok choy in a saucepan of boiling water for 1 minute. Drain and refresh under cold running water, then set aside. Cook the noodles according to their packet directions, then drain and divide between 4 large bowls, along with the bok choy. Slice the pork and add to the bowls. Place the eggs, nori, sesame seeds and reserved spring onion greens on top, then ladle over the miso tonkotsu broth to serve.

NOTE

Kombu is dried kelp seaweed and is available from most Asian supermarkets or Japanese food stores.

Meatball subs with gruyère and jalapeños

SERVES 6

70 g (2½ oz/1 cup) Japanese panko breadcrumbs
100 ml (3½ fl oz) milk
500 g (1 lb 2 oz) lean minced (ground) pork
1 onion, grated
salt and freshly ground black pepper
60 ml (2 fl oz/¼ cup) olive oil
2 garlic cloves, finely chopped
400 g (14 oz) tomato passata (puréed tomatoes)
2 jalapeño chillies, 1 whole and pricked, 1 thinly sliced (or use pickled jalapeños)
1 cinnamon stick
6 soft, long white bread rolls
100 g (3½ oz) gruyère cheese, thickly sliced
100 g (3½ oz) baby spinach leaves
1 ripe avocado, stone removed and flesh sliced
fries, to serve

I think the Americans own the sandwich world. This one, though, draws its inspiration from a couple of Greek girls who ran a café on Winn Lane in Brisvegas! Theirs was a wonderful interpretation of mum's meatballs stuffed in a bun with melting cheese. I've put a spicy spin on this and I'm sure you'll love it.

In a medium-sized bowl, soak the breadcrumbs in the milk for 5 minutes. Mix in the pork and onion, then season with salt and pepper. Wet your hands and roll the meatball mixture into 24 walnut-sized balls. Place them on a tray, cover and refrigerate for 10–15 minutes.

Preheat the oven to 180°C (350°F).

Heat 2 tablespoons of the oil in a large ovenproof frying pan over medium–high heat. Cook the meatballs for 6–8 minutes, turning often, until browned. Remove from the pan and set aside. Heat the remaining oil in the same frying pan and cook the garlic for 30 seconds, stirring, until fragrant. Add the tomato passata, whole pricked jalapeño, cinnamon and meatballs to the pan and stir to combine. Transfer to the oven and cook for 15 minutes, or until the meatballs are cooked through and the sauce is bubbling and thickened.

Preheat the grill (broiler) to medium–high. Slice the bread rolls lengthways but not all the way through, then toast until golden-brown. Arrange the cheese and jalapeño slices on top and grill for 1–2 minutes, or until the cheese is melted and oozing. Tuck some spinach leaves, avocado slices and 4 meatballs into each of the bread rolls. Spoon over some of the tomato sauce and serve immediately with fries.

Gammon steaks with pineapple and mustard crust

SERVES 4

4 × 180 g (6½ oz) slices leg gammon (smoked ham)
1 tablespoon olive oil
1 tablespoon hot English mustard
1 tablespoon white wine
4 tinned pineapple rings

CRUMB

½ onion, grated
170 g (6 oz) Japanese panko breadcrumbs or dried breadcrumbs
2 tablespoons chopped sage
1 tablespoon chopped flat-leaf (Italian) parsley
1 garlic clove, crushed
55 g (2 oz) salted butter, softened
salt and freshly ground black pepper

This recipe comes from English chef Brian Turner, with whom I have had the pleasure of working on British television and at various cooking events both in the UK and in South Africa. I've added my own little twist to this.

Preheat the oven to 180°C (350°F).

To make the crumb, mix the onion, breadcrumbs, sage, parsley, garlic and butter in a bowl. Season with salt and pepper and set aside.

Using a sharp knife or kitchen scissors, make a few snips at the edges of the steaks through the skin and into the fat layer. Heat the oil in a medium-sized frying pan and sear the gammon for about 3 minutes on each side, until golden brown. Remove from the heat.

Mix the mustard and wine in a small bowl to form a paste and brush this liberally over the gammon steaks. Place the pineapple rings on top, followed by the crumb mixture, then pat down to form a crust around the steaks. Transfer to a roasting tin and bake in the preheated oven for 15 minutes, until the crust is golden.

Steamed roast pork buns

MAKES 12

1½ tablespoons caster (superfine) sugar
250 ml (8 fl oz/1 cup) lukewarm water
1½ teaspoons dried yeast
1 tablespoon vegetable oil
1½ teaspoons baking powder
400 g (14 oz/2½ cups) plain (all-purpose) flour

FILLING

½ tablespoon peanut oil
1 teaspoon sesame oil
2 garlic cloves, finely chopped
1.5 cm (½ in) piece fresh ginger, finely chopped
4 fresh shiitake mushrooms, stems removed, diced
300 g (10½ oz) left-over Japanese red-braised pork hock (page 154) or store-bought Chinese barbecued pork (char siu), sliced
2 spring onions (scallions), finely sliced
1½ tablespoons black vinegar
3½ tablespoons hoisin sauce
1 tablespoon light soy sauce

In a bowl, mix the sugar with the lukewarm water until the sugar dissolves. Add the yeast, stir to dissolve and leave for 10 minutes, or until frothy. Add the oil and sift in the baking powder and flour. Knead the mixture with your hands until it comes together as a smooth and slightly wet dough. Cover the bowl with a damp cloth and allow the dough to rise for about 20 minutes, until doubled in size. Knock the dough back and scrape it out of the bowl. Use immediately or cover with plastic wrap, refrigerate and use within 12 hours.

To make the filling, heat the oils in a wok and stir-fry the garlic, ginger and mushrooms until fragrant. Add the pork, spring onions, vinegar, hoisin and soy sauces and cook for 1–2 minutes, or until the liquid has almost evaporated. Remove from the heat and set aside to cool.

Divide the dough into 12 balls. On a floured surface, roll each ball and press into a neat disc, about 8 cm (3 in) in diameter. Place a tablespoon of the pork mixture in the centre of each disc. Bring the edges of the dough up around the filling and pinch together at the top to seal.

Place the buns into a steamer lined with baking paper, allowing space between each bun for rising. Steam for 10–12 minutes, or until the tops have just slightly opened. Serve immediately.

Pea and ham soup

SERVES 4–6

40 g (1½ oz) salted butter
2 large onions, diced
2 carrots, diced
2 celery stalks, diced
4 garlic cloves, crushed
2 ham hocks
750 g (1 lb 11 oz) dried yellow split peas, rinsed and drained
300 g (10½ oz/2 cups) frozen baby peas
salt and freshly ground black pepper
extra-virgin olive oil, to serve

This is a great wholesome soup to warm you up on a cold winter's day. It also freezes very well, so you can have a healthy, comforting meal ready in minutes. I love this served with crusty buttered bread and hot English mustard.

Melt the butter in a large heavy-based saucepan and sauté the onions, carrots, celery and garlic for 10–15 minutes, until softened but not coloured. Add the ham hocks and split peas to the pan, along with enough water to cover. Bring to the boil and reduce the heat to low–medium and simmer for about 1½–2 hours, or until the ham hocks are very tender. You may need to top up with a little water during cooking if it looks a little dry. Remove the ham hocks from the pan and set aside to cool. When cooled, use a fork or your fingers to shred the meat from the ham hocks. Set aside. Discard the bones and skin.

Add the baby peas to the pan, bring to the boil and simmer for 4 minutes. Remove from the heat and allow to cool a little. Using a stick blender, blitz the soup until smooth. Taste and adjust the seasoning, then add the shredded ham and return to the heat until warmed through.

To serve, ladle the soup into serving bowls. Grind over some fresh black pepper and add a swirl of extra-virgin olive oil.

Bánh mì

SERVES 4

2 tablespoons vegetable oil
500 g (1 lb 2 oz) Classic roast pork (page 132), sliced
salt and freshly ground black pepper
4 Vietnamese baguettes (see note), halved horizontally
60 g (2 oz) chicken liver pâté
2 Lebanese (short) cucumbers, finely sliced lengthways into strips

PICKLED CARROT AND DAIKON

250 ml (8½ fl oz/1 cup) white-wine vinegar
115 g (4 oz/½ cup) caster (superfine) sugar
125 ml (4 fl oz/½ cup) warm water
1 carrot, sliced into fine matchsticks
½ medium daikon (white radish), sliced into fine matchsticks

TO SERVE

coriander (cilantro) leaves
1 fresh red chilli, finely sliced
light soy sauce

These legendary Vietnamese filled baguettes are delicious – the secret to the crispy crust of the roll being a little rice flour in the dough. While the pickled carrot and daikon can be made in 2 hours, you can prepare it up to a week in advance for a great flavour pay-off.

Start by making the pickled carrot and daikon. Combine the vinegar, sugar and warm water in a saucepan over medium heat and stir until the sugar dissolves. Transfer to an airtight container and set aside to cool. When cool, add the carrot and daikon, cover and refrigerate for at least 2 hours, or for up to a week.

When ready to eat, heat the oil in a frying pan and sauté the pork for 2–3 minutes, until hot, then season to taste with salt and pepper.

Spread the baguettes with pâté and top with the hot pork slices, cucumber, pickled carrot and daikon, coriander and chilli. Season to taste with light soy sauce and serve.

NOTE

Buy the long white rolls from a Vietnamese bakery if you can. If they're unavailable, use a white roll with a good crust.

GAME

BARBECUED KANGAROO TAIL WITH PIRI PIRI SAUCE

BLACK PEPPER KANGAROO

PIGEON, LENTIL AND PANCETTA SALAD

HARE PAPPARDELLE

JAMAICAN BARBECUED GOAT LEG

RABBIT WITH PRESERVED LEMON AND SOFT POLENTA

VENISON HUMBLE PIE

Barbecued kangaroo tail with piri piri sauce

SERVES 4

2 tablespoons sunflower oil
1 large kangaroo tail, cut into 4 pieces
1 brown onion, finely chopped
2 carrots, finely chopped
2 celery stalks, finely chopped
1 small bunch thyme sprigs
1 bay leaf
1 cinnamon stick
750 ml (25½ fl oz/3 cups) chicken stock
250 g (9 oz/1 cup) tomato passata (tomato purée)

PIRI PIRI SAUCE

4 red chillies, roughly chopped
8 small dried red chillies
4 garlic cloves, roughly chopped
1 tablespoon sea salt flakes
4 tablespoons whisky
1 tablespoon sherry vinegar or red-wine vinegar
1 tablespoon lemon juice
250 ml (8½ fl oz/1 cup) olive oil

I had this in Carnarvon while filming the second series of *Surfing the Menu*. We were having a barbecue with a bunch of people we had just met and I thought this dish was super-tasty. I didn't ask for the recipe but came up with this version after playing around with the flavours. If you can't get kangaroo tail, you could try using oxtail instead.

If you can, make the piri piri sauce a day or two in advance. Blend the chillies, garlic and salt in a food processor or blender until you have a smooth paste. Transfer the paste to a small saucepan and stir in the whisky, vinegar, lemon juice and 125 ml (4 fl oz/½ cup) of the oil. Bring to the boil, remove from the heat and whisk in the remaining oil. Set aside.

Preheat the oven to 160°C (320°F).

Heat the sunflower oil in a non-stick frying pan and brown the kangaroo over medium heat for 3–4 minutes. Add the onion, carrots, celery, thyme sprigs, bay leaf and cinnamon stick. Sauté for about 5 minutes, or until the vegetables are well coloured. Pour in the stock, add the tomato passata, bring to the boil and place a tight-fitting lid on the pan. Cook in the oven for 2 hours, or until the meat is very tender.

Remove from the oven and transfer the kangaroo to a plate. Reduce the sauce over medium–high heat for 5–10 minutes. Add 3 tablespoons of piri piri to the sauce (or more to taste) and stir to combine. Any leftover piri piri can be stored in an airtight jar and refrigerated for up to 1 month. Use it to jazz up a mayonnaise or as a condiment in a burger.

Heat the barbecue to medium or set a large chargrill pan over medium heat.

Cut 4 large sheets each of aluminium foil and baking paper. Place the paper on top of the foil. Brush the cooked kangaroo in the piri piri–spiked sauce, lay one piece on top of each paper and foil stack and wrap into a parcel. Cook the kangaroo parcels on the hot barbecue or chargrill pan for about 20 minutes, turning a few times to ensure they cook evenly. Open the parcels up carefully and allow to cool slightly before serving.

Black pepper kangaroo

SERVES 4

500 g (1 lb 2 oz) kangaroo sirloin, cut into thin strips
2 tablespoons cornflour (cornstarch)
salt and freshly ground black pepper
2 tablespoons sunflower oil
6 spring onions (scallions), finely chopped
4 salad onions, cut into 3 cm (1¼ in) lengths
1 tablespoon chicken stock
2 bunches broccolini, tough stems removed and florets sliced in half
2 green capsicums (bell peppers), cut into strips
steamed rice, to serve
1 tablespoon chopped coriander (cilantro), to serve

BLACK PEPPER SAUCE

2 tablespoons kecap manis
2 tablespoons oyster sauce
2 tablespoons light soy sauce
250 ml (8½ fl oz/1 cup) chicken stock
20 g (¾ oz) ginger
20 g (¾ oz) garlic
10 g (¼ oz) red chilli
10 g (¼ oz) dried shrimp, soaked in hot water to soften, then drained
10 g (¼ oz) black peppercorns, cracked
1 tablespoon sunflower oil
20 curry leaves
3 spring onions (scallions), white parts only, finely sliced
2 tablespoons cornflour (cornstarch)
50 g (1¾ oz) salted butter

First, make the black pepper sauce. Combine the kecap manis, oyster and soy sauces and 250 ml (8½ fl oz/1 cup) of stock in a small bowl and set aside. In a mortar and pestle or food processor, pound or process the ginger, garlic, chilli and soaked shrimp to a paste. Stir in the cracked pepper.

Heat the tablespoon of the oil in a wok or large frying pan over medium–high heat. Add the curry leaves and fry for a few seconds, then add the spring onion whites and ginger-garlic paste and stir-fry for 3–4 minutes, until fragrant. Stir in the sauce mixture and bring to the boil. In a small bowl, combine the 2 tablespoons of cornflour with an equal amount of water and whisk this mixture into the sauce, along with the butter. Whisk until well combined and simmer for a few minutes to thicken – the sauce should coat the back of a wooden spoon. Set aside in a bowl or cup.

Prepare the kangaroo for frying by seasoning the remaining 2 tablespoons of cornflour with salt and pepper and transfer to a plate. Lightly dredge the kangaroo strips with the seasoned cornflour.

Heat 1 tablespoon of oil in a wok or large frying pan over high heat. Add the kangaroo, in 2 batches, and sear for 2–3 minutes, until browned but still rare in the middle. Remove and set the kangaroo aside.

Use paper towels to wipe the wok clean and add the remaining oil. Reheat the wok over high heat and sauté the spring and salad onions with the stock to get them cooking. Add the broccolini and stir-fry for 2 minutes, then add the capsicum and continue to cook for a further 2 minutes, until the vegetables are beginning to soften. Add the kangaroo and stir in 3 tablespoons of the black pepper sauce. Continue to stir-fry over high heat for about 2 minutes, until the vegetables are well coated in the sauce. Remove and serve immediately with steamed rice and freshly chopped coriander.

NOTE

Kecap manis is an Indonesian soy sauce that can be found in Asian supermarkets or the international aisle of large supermarkets. If you don't have any, use soy sauce mixed with a little soft brown sugar.

Pigeon, lentil and pancetta salad

SERVES 6–8

4 pigeons
7 garlic cloves, 2 finely chopped and 5 lightly crushed with the flat of a knife
½ red onion, finely chopped
½ bunch thyme, leaves picked
120 ml (4 fl oz/½ cup) sweet red wine
salt and freshly ground black pepper
12 slices pancetta or bacon
3 large red chillies
100 g (3½ oz/½ cup) dried green or puy lentils
1 celery stalk with leaves, roughly chopped
½ bunch sage leaves
500 ml (17 fl oz/2 cups) cold water
⅔ tablespoon red-wine vinegar
2 tablespoons extra-virgin olive oil
1 head radicchio, leaves separated
2 large handfuls baby rocket (arugula)
2 baby cos (romaine) lettuce heads, cut in half

I love the richness of pigeon. If you're lucky enough to live on a farm, try shooting a wood pigeon for this one. You can also use squab – young pigeons – which are very tasty indeed.

First, butterfly the pigeons. Using a large, sharp knife, cut down both sides of the backbone of each pigeon. Remove the backbone and all the small rib bones. Use the heel of your palm to flatten the pigeons down and pat them dry with paper towel. In a small bowl, combine the finely chopped garlic and onion with the thyme and wine. Rub this mixture all over the pigeons and allow to marinate for 2 hours.

Heat the barbecue to medium (or use a chargrill pan over medium–high heat). Remove the pigeons from the marinade, lightly pat dry with paper towel and season with salt and pepper. Grill the pigeons, skin side first, for 8 minutes to create some grill marks, then flip over and continue to cook the other side for another 5 minutes, until medium rare. As the pigeons cook, add the slices of pancetta to the barbecue or pan and crisp up well on both sides. Add the chillies and allow them to brown and blister. Remove the chillies, allow them to cool briefly, then peel off the charred skins and tear the flesh into strips.

In a medium-sized saucepan, add the lentils, celery stalk and leaves, sage and the remaining garlic, then pour in the cold water. Bring to the boil over high heat, then reduce the heat to a rolling simmer. Cook for a further 15–20 minutes, until the lentils are tender. Drain and add the vinegar and oil, then season with salt and pepper. Arrange on a large platter and set aside while you prepare the salad leaves.

Rinse the leaves well and spin-dry them in a salad spinner, then scatter over the dressed lentils, along with the chillies and crisp pancetta. Slice each of the barbecued pigeons into 4 pieces and arrange them on the platter over the lentils and salad leaves.

Hare pappardelle

SERVES 6

150 g (5½ oz/1 cup) plain (all-purpose) flour, to dust
salt and freshly ground black pepper
1 hare, jointed into legs and saddle (divided into 4 pieces)
120 ml (4 fl oz/½ cup) olive oil
1 medium red onion, finely diced
2 small carrots, finely diced
2 celery stalks, finely diced
3 garlic cloves, sliced
400 g (14 oz) tinned chopped tomatoes
375 ml (12½ fl oz/½ cup) cabernet sauvignon
3 cloves
½ cinnamon stick
125 ml (4 fl oz/½ cup) cream
250 g (9 oz) dried egg pappardelle
45 g (1½ oz) parmesan, shaved

This is one of the first game dishes I cooked while I was working at the River Café in London. It was my introduction to proper furred game and handling the whole untouched beast – fairly intimidating – but the results were so delicious it was worth it. The hare is cooked slowly, which is one of the best ways to enjoy this particular meat. Hare is more similar to venison than rabbit when it comes to cooking; you can substitute either if you're having trouble finding hare.

Place the flour, salt and pepper in a zip-lock plastic bag. Add the hare pieces and shake well to coat.

Preheat the oven to 150°C (300°F).

Heat half the oil in a large ovenproof saucepan or flameproof casserole dish over medium–high heat. Working in batches, brown the hare pieces evenly all over. Remove and set aside.

Using paper towel, wipe the pan clean and heat the remaining olive oil over low–medium heat. Add the onion, carrots and celery, scraping any browned meat and flour off the bottom of the pan with a wooden spoon. Sauté the vegetables for 15 minutes, until they begin to soften and lightly brown. Stir in the garlic and tomatoes and simmer for 15 minutes. Pour in the wine and simmer for a further 10 minutes. Season with salt and pepper to taste. Add the cloves, cinnamon and the hare, then cover loosely with a sheet of dampened baking paper and the lid, and bake in the oven for 1 hour. Remove the saddle of the hare to a bowl and continue to cook the legs for a further 30 minutes, until very tender. If the sauce seems too dry, add about 125 ml (4 fl oz/½ cup) water as needed.

Remove the legs from the sauce. Use a fork to remove the meat from the bones, discarding the bones as you go, and keeping the leg meat separate from the saddle meat. Pick through the meat, carefully shredding it as you do so. Discard the cinnamon and cloves from the sauce.

Transfer the sauce and shredded leg meat to a food processor and blitz until the meat is finely chopped. Pour this into a saucepan and add the cream and the shredded saddle meat. Gently heat through and taste to check the seasoning.

Bring a large saucepan of salted water to the boil and cook the pappardelle as per the packet instructions. Drain thoroughly and combine well with the sauce. Garnish with the shaved parmesan.

Jamaican barbecued goat leg

SERVES 6–8

2 tablespoons allspice berries
2 tablespoons black peppercorns
1 teaspoon ground cinnamon
1 teaspoon ground nutmeg
4 garlic cloves, crushed
8 cm (3¼ in) piece ginger, peeled and chopped
2 tablespoons chopped thyme leaves
90 g (3¼ oz/¾ cup) finely chopped spring onions (scallions)
60 ml (2 fl oz/¼ cup) honey
2 teaspoons salt
drizzle of olive oil
zest of 1 lime
1 × 2 kg (4 lb 6 oz) boneless young goat leg

Blitz all the ingredients except the goat in a food processor to make the marinade.

Place the goat leg into a large bowl, pour over the marinade and toss to coat completely. Cover the bowl with plastic wrap and refrigerate for 2 hours or preferably overnight. Remove from the refrigerator 1 hour before cooking.

Crank up the barbecue (or heat a chargrill pan). Remove the goat from the bowl, reserving the marinade, and cook for about 15 minutes over medium–high heat, until nicely browned. Move the goat onto the resting rack of the barbecue, close the lid and cook for 35–40 minutes, basting occasionally with the reserved marinade. This will give you medium-rare meat – ideal for goat. Alternatively, if using a chargrill pan, transfer the browned goat to an oven preheated to 180°C (350°F) and bake for 30–40 minutes, or until cooked to your liking.

Transfer the goat to a platter and rest, covered with foil, for 10 minutes before serving.

KIWI-BRAND

Rabbit with preserved lemon and soft polenta

SERVES 6–8

100 g (3½ oz/⅔ cup) plain (all-purpose) flour
salt and freshly ground black pepper
1 × 1.5 kg (3 lb 7 oz) rabbit, jointed into legs and shoulders, saddle cut in two
80 ml (2½ fl oz/⅓ cup) olive oil
1 garlic clove, peeled
1 tablespoon finely chopped rosemary leaves
300 ml (10 fl oz/1¼ cups) dry white wine
470 ml (16 fl oz) chicken stock
200 g (7 oz) tinned chickpeas, rinsed and drained

PRESERVED LEMON

zest of 2 lemons, cut into thin matchsticks
110 g (4 oz/½ cup) sugar
125 ml (4 fl oz/½ cup) water

SOFT POLENTA

1 litre (34 fl oz/4 cups) water
300 g (10½ oz/2 cups) instant polenta
100 g (3½ oz) salted butter
100 g (3½ oz/1 cup) parmesan cheese, finely grated, plus extra to serve

Season the flour with salt and pepper. Lightly dredge the rabbit in the seasoned flour, shaking off the excess. Heat 3 tablespoons of the oil in a large heavy-based saucepan or flameproof casserole dish and fry the rabbit, in batches, until golden brown. Remove from the pan and drain on a plate lined with paper towel.

Preheat the oven to 180°C (350°F). Use paper towels to wipe out the pan, then add the remaining oil and return the pan to the heat. Place the rabbit in the pan, along with the garlic and rosemary, and fry for 1–2 minutes. Stir in the wine, stock and chickpeas, and bring to the simmer. Cover with baking paper, then the lid. Transfer to the oven and bake for 1 hour, until cooked. To check for doneness, press the rabbit meat with your fingers; it should give way under pressure. Use tongs to remove the rabbit, leaving the sauce in the pan, and shred the meat off the bones with a fork.

Make the preserved lemon by heating the lemon zest, sugar and water in a small saucepan. Bring to the boil and simmer for 15 minutes, until thickened and the consistency of syrup, taking care not to allow the mixture to caramelise.

Place the pan with the sauce over medium–high heat and reduce the sauce for 5–10 minutes, until it coats the back of a wooden spoon. Season to taste with salt and pepper. Add the shredded rabbit meat and the preserved lemon to the sauce and heat through. Keep warm while you make the polenta.

In a large saucepan, bring the water to the boil and whisk in the polenta. Stir over medium–high heat until thickened and simmer, partially covered, for 10 minutes. Dot in the butter and scatter over the grated parmesan. Divide between serving plates, top with the rabbit and sauce, and garnish with extra parmesan.

Venison humble pie

SERVES 4–6

300 g (10½ oz) ready-made shortcrust pastry (ideally, ready-rolled)

1 egg, beaten

150 g (5½ oz) Stilton or other strong, semi-soft blue cheese

VENISON FILLING

500 ml (17 fl oz/2 cups) Beer brine (page 231)

1 kg (2 lb 3 oz) venison leg, cut into chunks

75 g (2¾ oz/½ cup) plain (all-purpose) flour, plus extra to dust

2 tablespoons salted butter

olive oil for frying

12 shallots, peeled and left whole

2 onions, diced

3 carrots, diced

3 celery stalks, diced

2 celeriac (optional), diced

about 1 litre (34 fl oz/4 cups) beef stock (see page 216)

1 bay leaf

½ bunch thyme sprigs

10 black peppercorns

One day before cooking, make the beer brine according to the recipe on page 231. Place the venison in a large bowl and cover with the brine. Transfer to the refrigerator to marinate for 24 hours.

The next day, strain the brine into a bowl and reserve for later.

Preheat the oven to 160°C (320°F).

Lightly dredge the venison in the flour. Heat the butter and a splash of oil in a large flameproof casserole dish. Working in batches, brown the venison all over for 10 minutes over medium heat. Add another dash of oil, along with the whole shallots and diced vegetables, and fry for another 5 minutes, until the vegetables are beginning to colour. Pour in the reserved beer brine and top up with stock to ensure that all of the meat is submerged in liquid. Add the bay leaf, thyme sprigs and peppercorns, then cover with the lid and braise in the oven for 2–3 hours. The venison should be very soft and the liquid should be similar in consistency to thick gravy. Remove from the oven and set aside to cool while you prepare the pie.

Increase the oven temperature to 200°C (400°F).

Dust a clean work surface with flour and, if necessary, roll out a sheet of pastry so that it is a little larger than your pie dish. Trim roughly to the size and shape of the pie dish, leaving a 1 cm (½ in) overhang, and gently press into the dish. Chill the pastry in the refrigerator for 20 minutes.

Remove the pastry from the refrigerator, line with baking paper and fill with pastry weights, uncooked rice or dried beans. Blind bake in the oven for 12–15 minutes, or until lightly golden. Remove from the oven and set aside to cool for 10 minutes. Meanwhile, if necessary, roll out the remaining pastry dough and trim it to the size of the pie dish (this will be the pie lid).

Spoon the venison mixture into the pie casing. Brush the edge of the pastry lid with egg, then lay it, egg side down, over the pie filling, pinching the edges together to seal. Use a sharp knife to score a couple of lines in the lid to allow steam to escape while the pie is baking. Brush the top liberally with the remaining egg wash and bake in the oven for 20–25 minutes, or until light golden brown. Remove from the oven and crumble the Stilton over the top of the pie. Place the pie on a baking tray to catch any drips and return to the oven for a further 7–10 minutes, until the cheese is melted and golden.

COLD CUTS & CHARCUTERIE

MEXICAN BREAKFAST

BOUDIN BLANC, GOAT'S CURD AND OLIVE TAPENADE

COTECHINO AND LENTILS WITH SALSA VERDE

SPICY CHORIZO SOUP

BEEF CARPACCIO

DUCK RILLETTES

AMAZING HOT DOG

BOSTON BAKED BEANS

CURRIED SAUSAGES

DUCK LIVER PÂTÉ

BRESAOLA AND RADICCHIO

SMOKED VENISON SAUSAGE WITH BEETROOT RELISH

HAM HOCK TERRINE

TOAD IN THE HOLE

MAIALE TONNATO

Mexican breakfast

SERVES 4

4 chorizo sausages, sliced in half lengthways

⅓ quantity Boston baked beans (page 200) or 500 g (1 lb 2 oz) tinned baked beans

3 litres (101 fl oz/12 cups) water

60 ml (2 fl oz/¼ cup) white vinegar

8 eggs

4 tablespoons Chipotle salsa (page 220)

2 tablespoons finely chopped coriander (cilantro)

2 ripe avocados, stone removed, flesh sliced

8 corn tortillas

A Billykart Kitchen favourite.

Place a frying pan over medium heat and pan-fry the chorizo sausages for 10 minutes. As the sausages cook, they will release their oils – these will add a lot of flavour to the finished dish.

Meanwhile, in a small saucepan, heat the baked beans over low heat to warm through. Keep them on low heat while you poach the eggs.

Fill a very wide saucepan with the water. Add the vinegar and bring to a gentle boil over medium heat. Crack one of the eggs into a cup and gently drop it into the boiling water in one fluid movement. Repeat with 1 or 2 more eggs, taking care not to crowd the pan. (Depending on how large the pan is, you could poach 4 eggs at a time.) Cook over a gentle simmer for 3–4 minutes, until cooked to your liking. Use a slotted spoon to remove the eggs to a plate lined with paper towels. Repeat with the remaining eggs.

Divide the baked beans between plates. Place two sausage halves on top of each serving of beans, followed by a couple of poached eggs and a tablespoon of chipotle salsa. Drizzle over the reserved chorizo cooking oils, sprinkle with the chopped coriander and serve with the avocado slices and warmed tortillas on the side.

Boudin blanc, goat's curd and olive tapenade

SERVES 8

500 g (1 lb 2 oz) skinless chicken breasts, roughly diced
2–3 egg whites
crushed ice
500 ml (17 fl oz/2 cups) pouring cream
½ cup goat's curd (I like Milawa's)
sea salt flakes and ground white pepper
olive oil, for greasing
8 teaspoons Olive tapenade (page 219)
micro leaves, to serve

Place the chicken in a food processor, along with the egg whites. Process for about 5 minutes, until you have a fine paste. Remove and, if possible, push the chicken paste through a fine sieve into a large bowl. Cover and refrigerate for 2 hours.

Fill a large bowl halfway with crushed ice. Place the bowl containing the chicken directly into the bowl containing the crushed ice. Using a rubber spatula or wooden spoon, slowly beat in the cream, a little at a time, followed by the goat's curd; the mixture should be smooth. Season well with salt and white pepper and transfer to a piping (icing) bag.

Lightly grease 8 dariole moulds with olive oil and place a teaspoonful of olive tapenade into the bottom of each mould. Pipe an equal amount of the chicken mousse into each mould, ensuring there are no air pockets.

Place the moulds in a steamer and steam gently for about 20 minutes, until the chicken is fully cooked. Carefully remove and allow to rest for 5 minutes before serving with a few micro leaves.

Cotechino and lentils with salsa verde

SERVES 4

2 × 300 g (10½ oz) cotechino sausages
1 carrot, finely chopped
2 celery stalks, 1 finely chopped and the other halved
1 onion, finely chopped
2 bay leaves
370 g (13 oz/2 cups) puy lentils or dried green lentils
¼ bunch sage
½ garlic bulb (cut horizontally through the centre)
2–3 tablespoons red-wine vinegar
60 ml (2 fl oz/¼ cup) extra-virgin olive oil

SALSA VERDE

30 g (1 oz/1 cup) flat-leaf (Italian) or curly parsley
60 g (2 oz/1 cup) basil leaves
50 g (1¾ oz/1 cup) mint leaves
2 tablespoons capers, rinsed and drained
4 anchovy fillets
1 garlic clove, peeled
1 tablespoon red-wine vinegar
2 teaspoons dijon mustard
185 ml (6 fl oz/¾ cup) extra-virgin olive oil
salt and freshly ground black pepper

I think I fell in love with cotechino in the early nineties, when I was working at a restaurant called Goodfellas in Newtown. These rich and coarse-textured pork sausages, not dissimilar to salami, require long, slow cooking and are perfect on a cold winter's night. The salsa verde is the perfect condiment, as its freshness cuts through the richness of the sausage.

First, make the salsa verde. Place the herbs in a food processor with the capers, anchovies and garlic, and process until finely chopped. If necessary, gradually add the vinegar to loosen the mixture (you may not need all of it). Stir in the mustard and oil and blitz again to combine well. Season with salt and pepper.

Allow the salsa to stand for 30 minutes before using. You will have made more than you need for this recipe; store the rest in an airtight container in the refrigerator for up to 1 week.

Next, cook the cotechino sausages. Place the sausages, carrot, chopped celery, onion and bay leaves in a large pan and cover with cold water. Slowly bring to the boil, turn down to a very gentle simmer, cover with a lid slightly ajar, and cook for 2 hours. Once cooked, turn off the heat and allow to stand for about 15 minutes.

About 30 minutes before the sausages are done, cook the lentils. Use kitchen string to tie the sage between the halved celery stalks. Place the lentils, celery, sage and garlic in a saucepan and cover with cold water. Bring to the boil, reduce the heat and simmer gently for about 15 minutes, until the lentils are tender. The exact timing will vary depending on how fresh the lentils are, so keep an eye on them. Drain off almost all of the liquid, reserving about 125 ml (4 fl oz/½ cup) to keep the lentils nice and moist. Remove and discard the celery, sage and garlic. Season with the vinegar, oil and salt and pepper, and keep warm.

To serve, divide the lentils between plates. Drain the sausages and slice them, removing the thick outer skin. Arrange the sliced sausages on top of the lentils, and finish with a dollop of salsa verde.

Spicy chorizo soup

SERVES 4–6

220 g (8 oz/1 cup) dried white beans, rinsed, drained and picked over
2 litres (68 fl oz/8 cups) chicken stock
1 bay leaf
pinch saffron threads
2 tablespoons extra-virgin olive oil
3 Spanish chorizo sausages, sliced
1 large onion, finely chopped
4 garlic cloves, finely chopped
1 large red capsicum (bell pepper), finely diced
1 tablespoon sweet smoked paprika
1 small bunch kale, tough stems removed, washed well and coarsely chopped
salt and freshly ground black pepper
sherry vinegar, to taste

Bring the beans and stock to the boil in a large saucepan over high heat. Reduce the heat to medium and add the bay leaf. Partially cover the pan with a lid and cook for about 2 hours, stirring often and adjusting the heat to keep it at a slow, steady simmer, until the beans are tender. Remove and discard the bay leaf.

In a small bowl, soak the saffron in 125 ml (4 fl oz/1/2 cup) of the hot stock.

Heat the oil in a large frying pan over medium–high heat. Stir in the chorizo and cook for about 5 minutes, until lightly browned. Use a slotted spoon to transfer the chorizo to a plate and set aside. Add the onion, reduce the heat to medium and cook, stirring often for about 5 minutes, until softened. Add the garlic and cook for a further 1 minute. Stir in the capsicum and the paprika. Cook for a further 10 minutes, then transfer to the pan of beans. Stir in the saffron with its soaking liquid, the chorizo and the kale. Bring back to a simmer and cook for 10 minutes, until the kale is wilted and tender. Season with salt and pepper, stir in the vinegar and serve hot in warmed soup bowls.

Beef carpaccio

SERVES 4

20 black peppercorns
small bunch thyme, leaves picked and chopped
2 teaspoons sea salt flakes
500 g (1 lb 2 oz) beef fillet, thick end trimmed
200 g (7 oz) parmesan
juice of 1 lemon
good-quality extra-virgin olive oil

I love carpaccio, and the simplest ones are the best. Choose really good-quality beef and pair with a simply dressed rocket salad.

Crush the peppercorns in a mortar and pestle until cracked but not ground. Stir in the thyme and sea salt. Scatter the seasoning onto a chopping board or plate and roll the beef in the seasonings to coat completely. Wrap the beef tightly in a few layers of plastic wrap, which will help press the pepper into the beef. Refrigerate for 1 hour.

Lightly oil a large frying pan and set over high heat. Sear the beef on all sides until golden brown, then remove from the heat, cool, and chill for a further hour.

Slice the beef thinly; each slice should be about 2 mm (1/12 in). Lay the beef slices on a chopping board and use the back of a chef's knife to gently flatten. Some pieces will be wafer thin and flatter than others, which is just fine.

Transfer the beef to a large serving platter and refrigerate while you prepare the other ingredients.

Use a fine grater to grate the parmesan into a small bowl. Pour in the lemon juice and use a spoon to work it into the parmesan to form a paste. Stir in the oil gradually to make a thick cheesy dressing.

When ready to serve, spoon the dressing over the beef and serve immediately.

Duck rillettes

SERVES 4

Carefully shred the duck confit and remove any bones and gristle. Season with salt and pepper, and mix in the parsley, cornichons and capers. Using a spatula, mix in three-quarters of the fat. Check the seasoning and add more fat if required. Divide the mixture between four 125 ml (4 fl oz/½ cup) ramekins and smooth the tops with a spoon, pressing the mixture down firmly.

Melt the remaining fat in a small saucepan over low heat. Pour the melted fat over each of the ramekins and refrigerate for 30 minutes, until set; the rillettes will keep for a week like this. Remove the rillettes from the refrigerator about 10 minutes before serving to soften up slightly.

Serve with toasted sourdough and quince jam, or a relish of your choice.

NOTE

If you have any left-over Classic roast pork (page 132), use it in place of the confit duck.

500 g (1 lb 2 oz) Duck confit (page 111)
salt and freshly ground black pepper
1 tablespoon chopped flat-leaf (Italian) parsley
1 tablespoon finely chopped cornichons
½ tablespoon finely chopped capers
250 ml (8½ fl oz/1 cup) duck or pork fat (see page 229)

Amazing hot dog

SERVES 4

4 cheesy kransky sausages
300 g (10½ oz/2 cups) sauerkraut
4 soft, long white bread rolls
60 g (2 fl oz/¼ cup) Japanese mayonnaise
2 tablespoons dijon mustard
60 ml (2 fl oz/¼ cup) German currywurst sauce, or tomato sauce mixed with 1 teaspoon mild curry powder
125 g (4½ oz/1 cup) cheddar cheese, grated

Heat a chargrill pan (or your barbecue) over low–medium heat. Cook the sausages for about 15 minutes, being careful not to split them.

Add the sauerkraut to the same pan and heat through for 5 minutes.

Slice the buns open and toast them.

Divide half the sauerkraut between the buns. Place the sausages on top and layer on the remaining sauerkraut. In a bowl, combine the mayonnaise with the mustard. Squeeze the currywurst sauce and mustard mayonnaise over each roll, then sprinkle with the cheese. Place under a hot grill (broiler) for 5 minutes, or until the cheese melts. Tuck in and wash it down with a nice German beer.

Boston baked beans

SERVES 8

400 g (14 oz/2 cups) dried borlotti (cranberry) beans, soaked overnight in water

125 ml (4 fl oz/½ cup) olive oil

1 bay leaf

500 g (1 lb 2 oz) smoked pancetta, diced

1 onion, finely chopped

150 ml (5 fl oz/½ cup) molasses

1½ tablespoons freshly ground black pepper

1½ tablespoons English mustard powder

500 ml (17 fl oz/2 cups) tomato sauce (ketchup)

75 ml (2½ fl oz/⅓ cup) worcestershire sauce

100 g (3½ oz/½ cup) soft brown sugar

salt, to taste

These beans are awesome! Try them as part of a Mexican breakfast (page 188) with grilled chorizo sausages, poached eggs, chipotle salsa and a wedge of avocado – it's the perfect way to start your weekend.

Drain the beans, place them in a large saucepan and cover with water. Add the olive oil and bay leaf, and bring to the boil. Simmer over low–medium heat for about 45 minutes, or until the beans are tender. The beans should be completely submerged; if they start to get too dry, add more just-boiled water from a kettle (never add cold water).

Preheat the oven to 165°C (325°F).

Once the beans are tender, drain off enough water so the beans are only just covered. Stir in the pancetta and onion.

In a large flameproof casserole dish, combine the molasses, pepper, mustard powder, tomato and worcestershire sauces and brown sugar. Bring the mixture to a boil over high heat, then add the beans and mix well. Season to taste with salt, if necessary, and cover the casserole with a round of baking paper and a sheet of aluminium foil.

Bake for 2 hours in the preheated oven, until the beans are very tender. Uncover halfway through cooking, adding more water if necessary to prevent the beans from drying out. Remove from the oven, check the seasoning and serve hot.

Curried sausages

SERVES 4

2 tablespoons olive oil
8 beef sausages
1 large brown onion, chopped
2 teaspoons curry powder
2 large potatoes, roughly diced
2 carrots, diced
125 ml (4 fl oz/½ cup) chicken stock
40 g (1½ oz/¾ cup) peas, fresh or frozen
1 tablespoon cornflour (cornstarch)
2 tablespoons mango chutney
1 tablespoon apple sauce (optional)
salt and freshly ground black pepper

This is an Aussie classic in my book. My wife, Dee, reminisces endlessly about growing up eating curried sausages. This one is for you, Dee!

In a deep heavy-based frying pan, heat the oil over medium heat. Add the sausages and cook for 1–2 minutes, stirring occasionally until lightly browned. Stir in the onion and curry powder, and fry for 10 minutes, until the onions are softened. Add the potatoes and carrots, pour in the chicken stock and 250 ml (8½ fl oz/1 cup) of water, then bring to the boil. Reduce the heat to a very low simmer and cook for about 10–15 minutes, until the vegetables soften. Add the peas and simmer for a further 4 minutes.

In the meantime, combine the cornflour and 2 tablespoons of water in a small cup. Stir this mixture into the pan, bring to the boil and cook for a further 5 minutes, until the sauce has thickened. Stir in the mango chutney and the apple sauce, if using. Check the seasoning and add salt and pepper to taste.

Duck liver pâté

SERVES 4

200 g (7 oz) unsalted butter, at room temperature, plus 2 tablespoons for frying
2 shallots, finely chopped
500 g (1 lb 2 oz) duck livers
1 large garlic clove, finely chopped
1 tablespoon marjoram leaves
2 thyme stalks
salt and freshly ground black pepper
2 tablespoons brandy
2 tablespoons port
2 tablespoons Madeira wine
1 tablespoon balsamic vinegar
125 ml (4 fl oz/½ cup) chilled pouring cream
8 sage leaves

This is one of my indulgences. If I could, I would eat duck liver pâté every day on nice crusty bread with some pickles. It really is worth making your own.

In a large frying pan, melt the 2 tablespoons of butter over high heat until the foam subsides, then add the shallots. Sauté for 30 seconds, or until the shallots just start to soften. Add the livers, garlic, marjoram and thyme, and season with salt and pepper. Continue to sauté for a further 1½ minutes, until the livers colour on the outside and are just pink in the middle. Add all the alcohol to the pan and toss the livers a few more times. Remove to a bowl, allow to cool slightly, and refrigerate to cool completely.

Once the livers are completely cool, discard the thyme stalks and stir in the vinegar. Transfer to a food processor and process to a purée. Slowly pour in the cream and stir until the mixture is smooth. Adjust the seasoning. Transfer to four 125 ml (4 fl oz/½ cup) ramekins.

In a small saucepan, melt the remaining butter. Remove from the heat, allow to cool, then pour the melted butter over each pâté and top with a couple of sage leaves. Refrigerate for at least 2 hours, or until the butter has set.

Bresaola and radicchio

SERVES 4

240–250 g (8½–9 oz) bresaola, very thinly sliced
2 tablespoons extra-virgin olive oil, plus extra for drizzling
½ head radicchio
1 tablespoon lemon juice
1 tablespoon aged balsamic vinegar
1 teaspoon finely chopped rosemary
sea salt flakes and freshly ground black pepper
80 g (2¾ oz) parmesan, finely shaved

Bresaola is air-dried cured beef that is lean and good for you. If you get the chance to visit the Collingwood Farmers' Market in Melbourne, look out for Warialda Belted Galloways' bresaola – hands down one of the best I've ever tasted. A little goes a long way and you only need about 60–70 g (2–2½ oz) of thinly sliced bresaola per person to make a delicious salad.

Arrange the sliced bresaola on a board, laying it out so that it is not completely flat, but has some depth and texture. Drizzle with a little oil.

Using a Japanese mandoline slicer or a peeler, very finely shave the radicchio into a bowl and season with the lemon juice, balsamic, 2 tablespoons of oil, rosemary and salt and freshly ground black pepper. Toss together and scatter over the bresaola.

Scatter the parmesan over the top of the salad. The nutty saltiness of the cheese will balance the bitterness of the radicchio and the sharpness of the dressing.

Smoked venison sausage with beetroot relish

SERVES 8

I cooked this rich and smoky dish on *The Best in Australia* and it won! I recommend using beef casings for the sausages, but you could also use caul fat – this just makes them extra-rich.

You will need a barbecue with a lid in order to smoke the sausages. If you prefer, you could serve this with the Horseradish crème fraîche (page 219) instead of the beetroot relish.

500 g (1 lb 2 oz) lean venison, cut into chunks
450 g (1 lb) pig's livers
750 g (1 lb 11 oz) boneless pork belly, cut into chunks
60 g (2 oz) salt
2 garlic cloves, crushed
1 tablespoon chopped rosemary leaves
2 mace blades, ground
1 teaspoon freshly ground black pepper
1 teaspoon juniper berries, ground
1 tablespoon soft brown sugar
1 wine glass of red wine
1 kg (2 lb 3 oz) beef casings or caul fat, rinsed and soaked overnight in water

BEETROOT RELISH

500 g (1 lb 2 oz) grated cooked beetroot
190 g (6½ oz/1 cup) soft brown sugar
125 ml (4 fl oz/½ cup) balsamic vinegar
1 star anise

TO SMOKE

lump charcoal
about 2 cups hickory barbecue woodchips, soaked in water for 1 hour and drained

Make the sausage filling by combining the venison, livers, pork, salt, garlic, rosemary, mace, pepper, juniper berries and sugar in a large bowl. Pass the mixture twice through a meat grinder set to medium. Mix in the red wine and allow to stand.

If using beef casings, take out your sausage maker (or secure your sausage-making attachment to your mixer). Push the beef casing onto the sausage nozzle and tie a knot in the loose end of the casing. Place the sausage mixture into the hopper of the sausage machine and turn it on to its slowest speed. Push the meat down into the machine until the meat starts to slowly fill the beef casing. Once the entire casing is full, use your hands to twist into small sausages, tying the last one with kitchen string to secure.

If using caul fat, drain the caul fat and take a piece large enough to make a sausage 20 cm (8 in) long and 7.5 cm (3 in) thick; you will need enough fat to wrap at least 3 layers around the meat. Shape the meat inside the fat into a firm sausage and tie each end with kitchen string. Repeat this process using the remaining filling to get 3 thick sausages.

To make the relish, combine the grated beetroot, sugar, vinegar and star anise in a small saucepan. Set over medium heat and simmer for 15–20 minutes, or until the beetroot reaches a chutney-like consistency. Remove from the heat and set aside to cool.

Prepare the barbecue for smoking (I use a big, green, egg-shaped barbecue). Light about 12 large pieces of lump charcoal, allowing the coal to burn evenly with the lid up. Once alight, close the lid and set the airflow and temperature to low to slow down the burning. The temperature should be around 100°C (210°F). Add the pre-soaked hickory chips. Allow the smoke to start; it should be a thin stream through the top of the lid.

Add your sausages to the barbecue, close the lid and smoke them for 45 minutes. Don't allow the temperature to exceed 100°C (210°F).

After 45 minutes, open the airflow to full and let the temperature rise to 200°C (400°F) – this will happen quickly. Cook for a further 5–10 minutes to allow the sausages to colour and cook. Carefully remove from the barbecue and slice the sausages into small sections. Serve with the beetroot relish.

Ham hock terrine

SERVES 8

10 leaves titanium-strength gelatine
1 garlic clove, finely chopped
2 tablespoons finely chopped shallots
30 g (1 oz/⅔ cup) finely chopped flat-leaf (Italian) parsley
1 tablespoon finely chopped tarragon
2 tablespoons white-wine vinegar
salt and freshly ground black pepper

STOCK

2 pickled ham hocks, about 2.5–3 kg (5½ lb–6 lb 10 oz) total
2 large onions, finely diced
2 carrots, finely diced
2 celery stalks, finely diced
4 garlic cloves, crushed
1 bay leaf
2 parsley stalks
2 thyme sprigs
1 teaspoon black peppercorns

Here the stock needs to be as clear as possible to make a nice clean jelly. The left-over stock can be used in the Pea and ham soup on page 166.

Begin by making the stock. Place the ham hocks in a large heavy-based pan and cover with water. Bring to the boil over high heat. Drain and rinse well under cold water.

Return the hocks to the pan and add enough cold water to cover, along with the remaining stock ingredients. Bring to the boil, reduce the heat to low–medium, and gently simmer for 3 hours, until the meat is falling off the bone.

Use tongs to carefully remove the ham hocks to a tray and set aside to cool.

Strain the stock into a bowl, measure out 1 litre (34 fl oz/4 cups) of stock and return this to the pan. Bring to the boil, reduce the heat to low–medium and simmer for 30 minutes to reduce the liquid by half.

Meanwhile, soak the gelatine in a small bowl of cold water for 5 minutes until soft. Drain and squeeze well. Add the gelatine to the reduced stock in the pan and stir gently over low heat to dissolve. Remove the pan from the heat and allow to cool to about 40°C (104°F).

Once the ham hocks have cooled enough to handle, remove the skin and bone and cut the meat into chunks about 3–4 cm (1¼ in) in size. Transfer to a large bowl and set aside.

Add the garlic, shallots, parsley, tarragon and vinegar to the stock and season to taste with salt and pepper. Be a little more generous with the seasoning, bearing in mind that when it's cold it will taste less seasoned. Pour the stock over the ham in the bowl and combine well.

Line a 20 cm (8 in) loaf tin or terrine dish well with plastic wrap, then use a tea towel to smooth out any wrinkles in the base of the tin (what will become the top of the terrine). Add the ham, along with the stock, pressing the mixture down into the tin. Cover with a final layer of plastic wrap and weigh it down with something heavy on top to press the terrine (I like to use a couple of tins of tomatoes). Refrigerate overnight.

To serve, turn the terrine out onto a board or plate, remove the plastic wrap and slice. This ham hock terrine goes very well served with toast and Olive tapenade (page 219) or salsa verde (page 192).

Toad in the hole

SERVES 6

250 ml (8½ fl oz/1 cup) pork or duck fat (see page 229), melted

400 g (1 lb 2 oz) good-quality black pudding, sliced

1 apple, peeled, cored and diced

6 rosemary sprigs

salt and freshly ground black pepper

6 eggs

1 tablespoon very finely chopped flat-leaf (Italian) parsley, to garnish (optional)

YORKSHIRE PUDDING BATTER

225 g (8 oz/1¾ cups) plain (all-purpose) flour

3 whole eggs

200 ml (7 fl oz) milk

pinch of salt

200 ml (7 fl oz) water

A British classic with a twist. Here I've used black pudding instead of the traditional pork sausages. Black pudding is a favourite sausage of mine; I love the spicy crumbling texture of Clonakilty Irish black pudding, but any good-quality one will do.

To make the batter, whisk the flour, eggs, milk, salt and water in a small bowl until smooth. Cover and chill in the refrigerator for 1 hour.

Preheat the oven to 220°C (430°F).

In a 6-hole muffin tin, pour a little of the fat into each hole. Turn the oven down to 180°C (350°F) and place the tin in the oven for 15 minutes. At this point, the fat will be furiously hot and smoking.

Carefully remove the tin from the oven and divide the slices of black pudding into each muffin tin hole (be careful, as the hot fat will spit). Top with the diced apple and the rosemary, then sprinkle with salt and pepper. Pour in the batter so that it comes up to about two-thirds the height of the sausages – you don't have to use all the batter. Transfer to the hot oven and cook for about 20 minutes, until the Yorkshires are golden and puffed up.

Meanwhile, fill a very wide saucepan with water and bring to a gentle boil over medium heat. Crack one of the eggs into a cup and gently drop it into the boiling water in one fluid movement. Repeat with 1 or 2 more eggs, taking care not to crowd the pan. (Depending on how large the pan is, you could poach 4 eggs at a time.) Cook over a gentle simmer for 3–4 minutes. Use a slotted spoon to remove the eggs to a plate lined with paper towels. Repeat with the remaining eggs.

Carefully remove the tin from the oven. Let it cool briefly before removing each pudding to a serving plate and topping with a poached egg. Garnish with chopped parsley, if desired.

Maiale tonnato

SERVES 4

1 kg (2 lb 3 oz) kipfler (fingerling) or similar potatoes, scrubbed
sea salt flakes and freshly ground black pepper
500 g (1 lb 2 oz) green beans, trimmed and cut into 5 cm (2 in) lengths
1 lemon
2 tablespoons extra-virgin olive oil
100 g (3½ oz) baby spinach
500 g (1 lb 2 oz) left-over Classic roast pork (page 132), thinly sliced
4 tablespoons good-quality store-bought aïoli
8 anchovy fillets, cut into thin strips

Maiale tonnato, an Italian cold roast pork salad, makes for a great summer lunch and is an excellent way to use left-over roast pork. Traditionally, the Italians use veal, but pork works equally well.

Place the potatoes in a large saucepan and cover with water. Bring to the boil and cook the potatoes over medium heat for 20–30 minutes, until tender. Drain off the water and allow the potatoes to cool in their skins. When cool enough to handle, peel the skins and cut the potatoes in half. Sprinkle them with salt, transfer to a mixing bowl and leave to cool.

Bring a large saucepan of water to the boil. Add the green beans and cook over a rapid boil for 1–2 minutes, then drain and refresh under cold running water.

Toss the potatoes and green beans together and season with a squeeze of lemon juice and the olive oil. Gently mix in the spinach.

To serve, divide the pork between serving plates alongside the potatoes and green beans. Add a dollop of the aïoli to each plate, scatter with the anchovies and season with a final fresh grinding of black pepper before serving.

STOCKS, SAUCES & SEASONINGS

BEEF OR VEAL STOCK

CHICKEN STOCK

RED WINE JUS

PEPPER SAUCE

ESTRAGON SAUCE

HORSERADISH CRÈME FRAÎCHE

OLIVE TAPENADE

GUACAMOLE

CHIPOTLE SALSA

MEXICAN SALSA VERDE

FERMENTED CHILLI SAUCE

BLUE CHEESE SAUCE

VANILLA BOURBON SYRUP

BARBECUE SAUCE

PICCALILLI

MEAT SALT

CHICKEN SALT

FIRE AND SMOKE SALT

THAI SALT

TOGARASHI SALT

MEAT RUBS

RENDERING FAT

CIDER BRINE

MAPLE BRINE

BEER BRINE

BUTTERMILK BRINE

Beef or veal stock

1.5 kg (4½ lb) beef or veal bones (with a little meat still on, if possible)
4 litres (135 fl oz/16 cups) water
1 pig trotter
400 g (1 lb 2 oz) chicken bones (optional), rinsed under cold water
2 ripe tomatoes
1 celery stalk
1 carrot
1 onion
1 bouquet garni
4 garlic cloves
8 black peppercorns

Preheat the oven to 180°C (350°F).

Arrange the beef bones in a roasting tin and bake in the oven for 20 minutes, until lightly coloured. Remove from the oven and transfer the bones to a large stockpot. Place the roasting tin directly on the stove top over medium heat and add 250 ml (8½ fl oz/1 cup) of the water to deglaze, scraping any browned meat from the bottom of the tin with a wooden spoon. Pour the liquid into the stockpot with the beef bones.

Add the pig trotter, chicken bones (if using), vegetables, bouquet garni, garlic and pepper. Cover with the remaining cold water. Slowly bring the stock to the boil, removing any scum that rises to the surface. Once boiling, reduce the heat to low and simmer for at least 3–4 hours and up to 8 hours, skimming the away the froth occasionally. Keep an eye on the water level and top up with water if necessary. Strain the stock into an airtight container where it will keep, refrigerated, for up to 4 days, or decant into several smaller containers and freeze.

MAKES ABOUT 3 LITRES (101 FL OZ/12 CUPS)

Chicken stock

800 g (1 lb 12 oz) left-over chicken carcass and trimmings
1 carrot, chopped
1 onion, chopped
1 celery stalk, chopped
5 black peppercorns
1 tomato
4 thyme sprigs
1 parsley stalk
3 litres (101 fl oz/12 cups) water

Rinse the chicken carcass in cold water and place it in a stockpot. Add the remaining ingredients and bring to the boil over medium heat, removing any scum that rises to the surface. Once boiling, reduce the heat to low and simmer for 2–3 hours, skimming away the froth and fat occasionally. Keep an eye on the water level and top up with water if necessary. Strain the liquid into an airtight container where it will keep, refrigerated, for up to 4 days, or decant into several smaller containers and freeze.

MAKES ABOUT 2 LITRES (68 FL OZ/8 CUPS)

Red wine jus

This basic red wine jus forms the basis of a few sauces in this section. I like to make extra and refrigerate it to have it on hand.

1 quantity Beef or veal stock (page 216)
1 wine glass of red wine
1 red onion, finely sliced
1 garlic clove, crushed
1 tablespoon finely chopped thyme leaves
1 teaspoon black peppercorns

Bring the stock to the boil in a saucepan. Lower the heat to a gentle simmer, skimming off the foam and scum that rises to the surface. The stock will thicken and develop a rich, dark colour as it reduces.

When the stock has reduced by about two-thirds, combine the remaining ingredients in a separate saucepan and bring to the boil over high heat. Reduce the heat to low and simmer, uncovered, until the wine has almost evaporated. Pour in the reduced stock and simmer for 2–3 minutes, then pass the jus through a fine sieve into a bowl. Keep the jus warm until required, or decant into a container and refrigerate until needed.

MAKES 500 ML (17 FL OZ/2 CUPS)

Pepper sauce

50 g (1¾ oz) salted butter
1 onion, finely diced
100 ml (3½ fl oz) brandy
1 quantity Red wine jus (page 217)
1 tablespoon cracked white or green peppercorns

This pepper sauce goes really well with red meat. It's a delicious alternative to the béarnaise sauce in the Steak, smashed potatoes and béarnaise recipe on page 42.

Melt the butter in a saucepan until foaming. Add the diced onions and sauté for 10 minutes, until soft and translucent. Pour in the brandy, bring to the boil, then simmer until almost all of the liquid has evaporated. Stir in the red wine jus and simmer for 2–3 minutes. Finally, add the peppercorns and keep warm until required.

MAKES ABOUT 500 ML (14 FL OZ/2 CUPS)

Estragon sauce

2 tomatoes
250 ml (8½ fl oz/1 cup) Red wine jus (page 217)
1 tablespoon chopped tarragon

This is a variation on your basic red wine jus and is gorgeous served with the Roast lamb saddle on page 70.

Score a cross in the base of the tomatoes. Place them in a heatproof bowl and cover with boiling water. Leave for 30 seconds, then transfer to cold water and peel the skin away from the cross. Cut the tomatoes in half, discard the seeds and dice the flesh.

Bring the jus to the boil in a saucepan and simmer for 5 minutes. Stir in the chopped tomatoes and tarragon. Reduce the heat to low and simmer for 1–2 minutes, then serve.

MAKES ABOUT 200 ML (7 FL OZ)

Horseradish crème fraîche

Horseradish is a traditional accompaniment for beef. If you're not a fan of beetroot, it's also a real winner with the Smoked venison sausages on page 207.

20 g (¾ oz) fresh or prepared horseradish

200 g (7 oz/1 cup) crème fraîche

salt and freshly ground black pepper, to taste

If using fresh horseradish, finely grate it.

In a small bowl, combine the crème fraîche and horseradish. Season to taste with salt and pepper.

MAKES ABOUT 200 G (7 OZ/1 CUP)

Olive tapenade

Tapenade is a classic preparation eaten with grilled red meat and poultry. It's also great rubbed under the skin of chicken or all over lamb before roasting.

125 g (4½ oz/1 cup) pitted black Spanish olives

10 g (¼ oz/½ cup) flat-leaf (Italian) parsley

6 anchovy fillets

1 tablespoon baby capers, rinsed and drained

125 ml (4½ fl oz/½ cup) extra-virgin olive oil

juice of ½ lemon

freshly ground black pepper, to taste

Combine all of the ingredients except the pepper in a food processor and process until smooth. Season with pepper to taste.

MAKES ABOUT 250 G (9 OZ/1 CUP)

Guacamole

3 ripe avocados
2 tablespoons finely chopped onion
1 jalapeño chilli, finely chopped
sea salt, to taste
1 ripe peach, peeled and diced
90 g (3 oz/½ cup) seedless grapes
juice of 1 lime or to taste
seeds of 1 pomegranate

This guacamole is out of this world. It's a real change from your average run-of-the-mill tomato-coriander-lime combo.

Remove the stones from the avocados, scoop the flesh into a bowl and mash roughly with the back of a fork.

In a serving bowl, mix the chopped onion, chilli and salt together to a rough paste. Stir in the mashed avocado, peach, grapes, lime juice and half the pomegranate seeds. Mix well and serve sprinkled with the remaining pomegranate seeds.

SERVES 4 AS A SIDE OR STARTER

Chipotle salsa

450 g (1 lb) tomatoes
30 ml (1 fl oz) olive oil
1 onion, finely chopped
1 garlic clove
½ teaspoon dried oregano
6 canned chipotle chillies in adobo
2 tablespoons white vinegar

To peel the tomatoes, score a cross in the base of each tomato. Place in a heatproof bowl and cover with boiling water. Leave for 30 seconds, then transfer to cold water and peel the skin away from the cross. Cut the tomatoes in half and remove the seeds by scooping them out with a teaspoon. Set aside.

Heat the oil in a saucepan and fry the onion and garlic until soft. Transfer to a food processor, add the tomatoes and the remaining ingredients, then purée. Return the purée to the saucepan and reduce until it is thick and the flavours are balanced.

MAKES ABOUT 500 G (1 LB 2 OZ/2 CUPS)

Mexican salsa verde

500 g (1 lb 2 oz) tomatillos
1 teaspoon apple-cider vinegar
1 small onion
1 garlic clove
2 jalapeño chillies, seeds removed, chopped
2 tablespoons chopped coriander (cilantro) leaves
1 teaspoon ground cumin
1 tablespoon olive oil
salt, to taste

In a food processor, combine all of the ingredients except for the oil and the salt. Purée, check the seasoning and add salt to taste, if necessary. Heat the oil in a large frying pan over medium heat. Add the purée and simmer over low heat for about 10–15 minutes, until thickened slightly. Allow to cool completely before serving.

MAKES ABOUT 500 G (1 LB 2 OZ/2 CUPS)

Fermented chilli sauce

This is a store-cupboard chilli sauce. You'll use it in everything from burgers to Beef pho (page 22).

800 ml (27 fl oz/3¼ cups) water
200 ml (7 fl oz) white-wine vinegar
50 g (1¾ oz) salt
5 garlic cloves
5 coriander (cilantro) roots
10 allspice berries
1 teaspoon cumin seeds
500 g (1 lb 2 oz) fresh chillies (an assortment of chillies is good)
12 dried red chillies
1 teaspoon xanthan gum (see note)

Heat the water and vinegar in a large saucepan over medium heat. Add the salt, garlic, coriander roots and spices, stirring to dissolve the salt completely. Place the chillies in an airtight container and pour over the vinegar mixture. Cover with the lid and allow to ferment for 2 weeks in a cool place (I use the laundry).

After fermentation, transfer the chillies and the liquid to a large saucepan. Bring to the boil over medium heat and skim away any scum that rises to the surface. Pour into a food processor and blitz until you have a smooth liquid, then add the xanthan gum to thicken the sauce. Decant into sterilised jars and store in the refrigerator for up to 1 month.

NOTE
Xanthan gum is a common thickening and stabilising agent. It can be found in large supermarkets and specialist food stores.

MAKES ABOUT 1 LITRE (34 FL OZ/4 CUPS)

Blue cheese sauce

½–1 onion, finely diced
2 tablespoons apple-cider vinegar
120 g (4½ oz) blue cheese
125 g (4½ oz/½ cup) sour cream
125 ml (4 fl oz/½ cup) buttermilk
125 g (4½ oz/½ cup) Japanese mayonnaise
1 tablespoon chopped tarragon
salt and freshly ground black pepper

This sauce is superb served with barbecued meats. Try it instead of the salsa in the recipe for Cordon bleu veal snizza (page 24), or served alongside the Pulled beef burger (page 38) or My Southern-fried chicken (page 104).

In a small bowl, steep the onion in the vinegar for 20 minutes. Drain the onions and place them in a food processor with the remaining ingredients. Blitz and season to taste. If possible, prepare this a day in advance, as the flavours really develop overnight.

MAKES ABOUT 500 G (1 LB 2 OZ/2 CUPS)

Vanilla bourbon syrup

375 ml (12½ fl oz/1½ cups) bourbon
1 vanilla bean, split
½ cup caster (superfine) sugar
good splash maple syrup

In a small saucepan, combine the ingredients and set over medium heat, gently stirring until the sugar has completely dissolved.

Bring the mixture to the boil, then lower the heat and allow to simmer until reduced by a third, roughly 5 minutes. Transfer to a sterilised jar and store in the refrigerator for up to 2 weeks.

MAKES ABOUT 250 ML (8½ FL OZ/1 CUP)

Barbecue sauce

We generally make five times the amount of this recipe at Billykart Kitchen and bottle it up. It's a store-cupboard basic and is delicious eaten with grilled sausages – or in fact any grilled or roasted meat. This sauce also rocks in a bacon sarnie!

230 g (8 oz/1 cup) dark brown sugar
250 ml (8½ fl oz/1 cup) sherry vinegar or red-wine vinegar
1 onion
1 teaspoon ground cumin
½ teaspoon ground cinnamon
1 star anise
1 chipotle chilli
2 teaspoons smoked paprika
60 ml (2 fl oz/¼ cup) tomato sauce (ketchup)
200 g (7 oz) tinned chopped tomatoes
1 tablespoon salt

Combine all the ingredients in a heavy-based saucepan. Bring to the boil, then reduce to a low simmer and cook for 30–40 minutes, until the sauce coats the back of a wooden spoon. Allow the sauce to cool briefly, then use a stick blender to purée until completely smooth. If the sauce is still a little too thin, you can continue to simmer and reduce it. Remove from the heat and allow the sauce to cool to room temperature. Store in an airtight container in the refrigerator for up to 3 months.

MAKES 500 ML (17 FL OZ/2 CUPS)

Piccalilli

1 head cauliflower, cut into small florets
1 bunch radishes, each radish quartered
500 g (1 lb 2 oz) green beans, sliced on an angle into 3 cm (1½ in) pieces
1 telegraph (long) cucumber, seeds removed, sliced on an angle
1 bunch baby carrots, peeled and sliced very thinly
1 red onion, finely diced
75 g (2¾ oz/½ cup) sea salt flakes

SPICE PASTE

1 tablespoon yellow mustard seeds
2 tablespoons cumin seeds
2 tablespoons coriander seeds
20 g (¾ oz) ground turmeric
20 g (¾ oz) English mustard powder
20 g (¾ oz) ground ginger
1 litre (34 fl oz/4 cups) apple-cider vinegar
300 g (10½ oz) sugar
100 g (3½ oz) honey
60 g (2 oz) cornflour (cornstarch)

Prepare the vegetables one day in advance. Place all of the vegetables in a large colander and use your hands to mix through the salt. Place the colander over a bowl and cover with plastic wrap. Refrigerate for 24 hours.

The next day, rinse the vegetables very well with ice-cold water and drain them thoroughly.

To make the spice paste, use a mortar and pestle to grind the mustard, cumin and coriander seeds as fine as you can get them. Transfer to a small bowl and stir in the turmeric, mustard powder and ginger. Add 1 tablespoon of the vinegar – just enough to form a paste.

Heat the remaining vinegar, the sugar and the honey in a preserving pan over medium heat and bring slowly to the boil. Once the vinegar is boiling, add the spice paste and stir well for 2–3 minutes to allow the spices to release their flavour. Whisk in the cornflour and cook for 2–3 minutes until the mixture thickens slightly. Turn off the heat and gently stir in the drained vegetables. Decant into sterilised jars and store for up to 1 year.

MAKES ABOUT 2 KG (4 LB 6 OZ)

Meat salt

130 g (4½ oz/1 cup) sea salt flakes
1 tablespoon celery salt
1 teaspoon freshly ground black pepper
1 teaspoon finely chopped rosemary
1 teaspoon finely chopped thyme
1 teaspoon finely chopped sage
1 teaspoon onion powder
1 teaspoon garlic powder
1 teaspoon smoked paprika
½ teaspoon ground cumin

Salt is the most basic form of seasoning. Just about every cook will sprinkle some on their meat before it is cooked. Salt is one of those marvels of human discovery, its properties elevating cooking beyond its simple function.

Acclaimed chef Ferran Adrià, of El Bulli fame, once declared salt 'the only product that changes cuisine'. It has the ability to change flavour profiles for the better and has also been used for centuries as a means to preserve food. In the days before refrigeration, combinations of salt, herbs and spices were rubbed over meat and left to 'cure' and draw out moisture. Without moisture, bacteria cannot grow, allowing the meat to be kept for longer periods – the intensified flavour of the protein an added benefit.

For this recipe, and the ones on the following pages, I would recommend using good-quality salt, because quality ingredients are key to a delicious end result. Start experimenting with flavour combinations and discover how these basic seasonings can transform a humble piece of meat into something sublime.

Preheat the oven to 60°C (140°F).

Combine the salts, pepper and herbs in a mortar and pestle and grind until you have a fine powder. Add the onion and garlic powders, paprika and cumin, and grind some more until completely combined.

Tip the mixture out onto a baking tray lined with baking paper and dry out in the oven for about 6 hours, or until the salt is completely dry. Remove from the oven and allow to cool on the tray. Transfer to an airtight container where it will keep for up to a month, or store in a refillable salt grinder.

MAKES ABOUT 200 G (7 OZ)

Chicken salt

130 g (4½ oz/1 cup) sea salt flakes
1 tablespoon white peppercorns, crushed
dried grated zest of 1 lemon
1 tablespoon finely chopped lemon thyme
1 tablespoon finely chopped sage
1 tablespoon finely chopped flat-leaf (Italian) parsley
1 teaspoon sumac

Preheat the oven to 60°C (140°F).

Rub all the ingredients together in a large bowl. Tip the mixture out onto a baking tray lined with baking paper and leave to dry out in the oven for 6 hours.

Remove from the oven and allow to cool on the tray. Transfer to an airtight container, where it will keep for up to a month, or store in a refillable salt grinder.

MAKES ABOUT 200 G (7 OZ)

Fire and smoke salt

130 g (4½ oz/1 cup) smoked salt flakes (available from good supermarkets)
1 teaspoon smoked sweet paprika
1 dried chipotle, toasted and finely chopped
1 teaspoon dried chilli flakes (I like using Aleppo chilli flakes)
1 tablespoon garlic flakes
½ teaspoon ground cumin
1 tablespoon onion flakes
1 teaspoon ground coriander
1 tablespoon dried wild oregano or regular oregano

Combine all the ingredients in a bowl and rub together well with your hands. Transfer to a refillable salt grinder, where it will keep for up to 1 month.

MAKES ABOUT 200 G (7 OZ)

Thai salt

130 g (4½ oz/1 cup) sea salt flakes
5 dried bird's eye chillies, finely chopped (seeds removed if you prefer)
2 stalks lemongrass, finely grated
zest of 1 lime
2 dried kaffir lime leaves
1 teaspoon chopped garlic
1 teaspoon chopped ginger
1 tablespoon cracked white peppercorns
1 tablespoon coriander seeds, crushed
½ teaspoon ground cumin
1 tablespoon shredded coconut, toasted

Preheat the oven to 60°C (140°F).

In a bowl, combine the salt with the chillies, lemongrass, lime zest, lime leaves, chopped garlic and ginger. Stir in the cracked pepper, coriander seeds and cumin and use your hands to rub the ingredients together. Tip the mixture out onto a baking tray lined with baking paper and dry out in the oven for 6 hours.

Remove from the oven, scatter over the shredded coconut and allow to cool on the tray. Transfer to an airtight container, where it will keep for up to 1 month, or store in a refillable salt grinder.

MAKES ABOUT 200 G (7 OZ)

Togarashi salt

130 g (4½ oz/1 cup) sea salt flakes
1 tablespoon white sesame seeds
1 tablespoon Sichuan peppercorns
1 sheet nori seaweed, toasted
1 large piece of dried tangerine peel (see note)
1 tablespoon chilli powder
1 teaspoon black sesame seeds
1 teaspoon ground ginger

Combine all of the ingredients in a food processor and blend well, then transfer to a refillable salt grinder, where it will keep for up to 1 month.

NOTE

Dried tangerine peel adds a unique fruity and floral note to this salt. It is available from Asian supermarkets or specialist stores.

MAKES ABOUT 200 G (7 OZ)

Meat rubs

1 tablespoon Fire and smoke salt (page 226) or other flavoured salt of your choice per kilogram of meat

1 tablespoon sugar of choice per kilogram of meat

Rubs combine the techniques of curing and seasoning, and usually consist of sugar, salt and flavourings. The mixture is rubbed over meat and left for a short period of time to impart its flavours and draw out moisture, which in turn intensifies the flavour of the meat.

You can transform any flavoured salt into a rub simply by adding sugar. The choice of sugar will determine the ultimate flavour of your dish. If you want the salt's flavour to be the most pronounced, then use caster (superfine) sugar. Use less processed sugars, such as brown, golden caster, raw (demerara) or muscovado, to increase the richness and depth of flavour. You could also experiment with sweet syrups (like golden or agave) or honey: the darker the syrup, the stronger the flavour. I like to use dark syrups such as molasses or malt in rubs for strongly flavoured meat like beef short ribs, brisket and pork ribs.

Any of the salts on the previous pages can be turned into rubs with this simple method.

Use your hands to combine the salt and sugar in a bowl. Mix well.

Take the rub and massage it all over the cut of meat. Refrigerate for at least 2 hours, or up to 24 hours. Proceed to cook as directed by the recipe.

MAKES 2+ TABLESPOONS

Rendering fat

3 kg (6 lb 10 oz) minced (ground) pork back fat or duck fat

4–5 litres (139–169 fl oz/16–20 cups) cold water

Fats are finally back in fashion! Once much maligned, good old animal fats are now considered better than all the processed rubbish that is out there. The beauty of rendering your own fat is that it promotes the use of the whole animal, or 'nose-to-tail eating', a notion that all chefs like to talk about.

Rendering fat entails heating the animal fat slowly enough that it melts and separates from anything else within the fat. You can also buy pre-rendered animal fats: I love Luv-a-Duck duck fat and the wagyu fats available at the markets in Canberra, Australia, and goose fat is quite easy to come by at good supermarkets or specialist food stores. The basic difference between the fats lies in the subtle flavours of each, although they all pretty much perform the same. The only fat that is particularly strong in flavour is lamb fat.

The process of rendering fat is pretty easy to do, and once you have done it, the possibilities are endless. You can use rendered fat in place of oil or butter in many recipes, and it will increase the depth of flavour. To render fat yourself, ask your butcher for your fat of choice (duck, beef, pork, etc.) and have them mince it. Your yield will be about 40 per cent of the weight of the solid fat.

Blitz the fat in a food processor in small batches to break it down. Place the fat in a large saucepan and cover with the cold water. Bring to the boil and simmer over medium heat for about 1 hour, or until the water has evaporated and the fat separates out. At this point you need to be careful and lower the heat slightly to avoid burning the fat.

Line a sieve with muslin (cheese cloth) and strain the fat into a bowl. Allow to cool before transferring to a jar or airtight container. Store in the refrigerator or in a cool, dark place, where it will keep for up to 3 months.

Once you've used the fat, you can strain it again for re-use. Simply pass through a muslin-lined sieve again and let it cool in a bowl (any liquid left in the fat will sink to the bottom as it will be denser than the fat). Once cold, you can scoop the fat off to use again, bearing in mind that it may take on the flavour of anything it cooks.

There are many uses for rendered fat: duck fat potatoes (page 42) are out of this world, as are Duck confit (page 111) and Duck rillettes (page 197). Fat can be used in pastry, for basting, in terrines, or – if you're feeling really naughty – to fry up some thick toast.

MAKES ABOUT 1.2 KG (2 LB 10 OZ)

Cider brine

500 ml (17 fl oz/2 cups) apple cider
230 g (8 oz/1 cup) soft brown sugar
3 oranges, cut into quarters
230 g (8 oz) table salt or kosher salt
2 tablespoons chopped rosemary
5 garlic cloves, finely chopped
3 tablespoons black peppercorns
5 bay leaves
2 litres (68 fl oz/8 cups) cold water

Heat the cider in a very large stockpot over medium heat and bring to a simmer. Stir in the sugar and allow it to dissolve in the cider. Add the remaining ingredients except for the water and stir to combine. Remove from the heat, cover and set aside for 20 minutes.

Pour the water into the container you will be using to brine your meat. Add the apple cider mixture and stir well to combine. Allow the brine to cool completely before using.

MAKES ABOUT 2.5 LITRES (85 FL OZ/10 CUPS)

Maple brine

1 litre (34 fl oz/4 cups) water
450 g (1 lb/2 cups) dark brown sugar
250 ml (8½ fl oz/1 cup) maple syrup
100 g (3½ oz/¾ cup) sea salt flakes
6 garlic cloves, peeled
4 bay leaves
3 large thyme sprigs
2 teaspoons whole black peppercorns
2 cloves

Place all of the ingredients in a stockpot and bring to the boil over medium heat. Stir to dissolve the sugar and maple syrup. Remove from the heat and allow the brine to cool completely before using.

MAKES ABOUT 1.2 LITRES (41 FL OZ/5 CUPS)

Beer brine

This recipe works well for stronger meats, such as beef short ribs and brisket, pork belly, pork chops and cuts of meat that suit slow cooking. The brining not only adds saltiness, it also intensifies the flavour and helps to tenderise the meat.

500 ml (17 fl oz/2 cups) water
500 ml (17 fl oz/2 cups) dark ale beer
100 g (3½ oz) coarse salt
3 tablespoons firmly packed dark brown sugar
3 tablespoons light molasses
1 teaspoon black peppercorns
2 bay leaves
6 garlic cloves
4 thyme sprigs

Combine the water and beer in a stockpot and bring to a gentle boil over medium heat. Add the remaining ingredients and stir until the salt and sugar have dissolved. Allow to cool completely, then chill in the refrigerator before use.

MAKES ABOUT 1 LITRE (34 FL OZ/4 CUPS)

Buttermilk brine

This brine is perfect for poultry. We use it a lot at Billykart Kitchen to flavour our birds, and are lucky enough to have a vacuum-pack machine that seals the poultry and brine in an airtight bag, providing maximum penetrating power. At home, I suggest using a large airtight container that will allow the meat to be covered completely in the brine. You can also buy a large brining needle, which allows you to inject the meat with the brine, from specialist kitchen stores.

500 ml (17 fl oz/2 cups) buttermilk
1 onion, finely diced
2 garlic cloves
1 tablespoon salt
1 teaspoon cracked black pepper

Combine the buttermilk, onion and garlic in a bowl and mix thoroughly. Add the salt and cracked black pepper and stir until the salt has dissolved.

MAKES 500 ML (17 FL OZ/2 CUPS) OR ENOUGH TO BRINE 1 LARGE CHICKEN

INDEX

T

V

W

Y

Acknowledgements

There are so many people to thank:

Dee, my steadfast, beautiful and organised wife, for helping me realise my dreams and for joining me in opening a restaurant that we can call our own!

My beautiful children, Ruby, Herb and Cash.

My kitchen, for running things while I have been focussing on other projects, including this book; Murray Coulter, for the support from front of house that means we can still have a family life; and all our staff, past and present.

Julie Pinkham, Paul McNally, Jane Willson, Rihana Ries and Kate Wanwimolruk, for your support and patience with me, and Mark Campbell, Benito Martin, Vanessa Austin, Arum Shim and Sekju Maing, for the amazing shoot. I really appreciate everything you guys have done to help me write and pull this book together!

Big shout out to Melita Hodge and the guys at One Management.

To the awesome Kimmy – your assistance has been invaluable! I knew you'd be indispensable ever since I watched you roast a chicken back in the Wilson Street days.

To Curtis, thank you for the kind words! 'You're the bench mark' and wing man!

To 'Goat', thanks for the tips and the flat-bottomed wok.

To Tara – sorry, no recipe this time ... we only cook fish with you guys!

Big love to all.

Bender

About the author

Ben O'Donoghue is one of Australia's most popular culinary personalities, having enjoyed more than two decades of success as a chef, television presenter, author and columnist.

After kicking off his food career in the 1990s at some of Australia's top restaurants, Ben honed his talents in London, where he made a name for himself working at the world-famous River Café for four years before joining his mate Jamie Oliver at the exclusive Monte's Club, where he was executive chef. He went on to become head chef at the famous Atlantic Bar & Grill and helped Oliver Peyton open the National Dining Room at the National Gallery, renowned for its creative seasonal menus.

After cutting his teeth on *Surfing the Menu* with fellow chef Curtis Stone, Ben has since gone on to host *The Best in Australia* and *Drive Thru Australia*, released four cookbooks and written for *Delicious* magazine. 2014 saw the opening and success of Ben's Brisbane restaurant Billykart Kitchen, with a second Billykart Kitchen scheduled to open soon.

For Ben, cooking is a passion and a reflex. He believes food should be simple, distinctive and authentic. His larrikin sense of humour, his high-end culinary expertise and his passion for sharing what he knows about food, cooking and having a great time has ensured he continues to be one of Australia's most-loved celebrity chefs.

When he's not cooking, Ben loves surfing, fly fishing, music and playing with his three kids.

Published in 2015 by Hardie Grant Books

Hardie Grant Books (Australia)
Ground Floor, Building 1
658 Church Street
Richmond, Victoria 3121
www.hardiegrant.com.au

Hardie Grant Books (UK)
5th & 6th Floors
52–54 Southwark Street
London SE1 1UN
www.hardiegrant.co.uk

A Cataloguing-in-Publication entry is available from the catalogue of the National Library of Australia at www.nla.gov.au

Ben's Meat Bible
ISBN 978 1 74270 999 4

Publishing Directors: Paul McNally and Jane Willson
Project Editor: Rihana Ries
Editor: Kate Wanwimolruk
Indexer: Max McMaster
Design Manager: Mark Campbell
Typesetter: Cannon Typesetting
Photographer: Benito Martin
Stylist: Vanessa Austin
Home Economist: Arum Shim
Production Manager: Todd Rechner

Colour reproduction by Splitting Image Colour Studio
Printed and bound in China by 1010 Printing International Limited

GCSE Higher Maths Solving Strategies

for Grade 9-7 topics.

First published 2020
United Kingdom

Written, designed and edited by Dr Darko

ISBN 978-1-8380444-0-4

Preface:

This book contains innovation of carefully selected questions on Higher GCSE Maths topics that are uttermost importance to students. I have taught students at various levels of their education and have found these topics as the areas where improvements are needed.

It is one of the books dearest to my heart as I have to take the time to invest and bring out the strategies in solving most of the higher GCSE maths questions. It is one of the first books that interact and teaches the student, thus minimising the over-reliance of a maths tutor. It is the focus to give students self-learning practices and build their confidence. I will recommend this book to any student who will like to achieve the best grades in their GCSE Maths exams.

The book tackles problems in Geometry, Algebra and Numbers with much emphasizes on how to resolve complex shapes using basic mathematical approaches. It improves the students' strength of thinking outside the box when facing questions. The questions have been created to strategically challenge the students' ability and provide a way to guide their problem-solving skills.

The author has several years of teaching experience at the secondary school level with many industrial experiences and currently lecture at the university level.

Dedication:

I dedicate this book to Ivy, Mario, Mackenzie, Maximilian and Malcolm for their support, assistance, motivation and encouragement.

Table of contents

Contents *Page*

1. Pythagoras, Trigonometry and Geometry

Strategy: All

<table>
<tr><th colspan="2">Right-Angle Triangle</th><th>Scalene Triangle</th></tr>
<tr>
<td>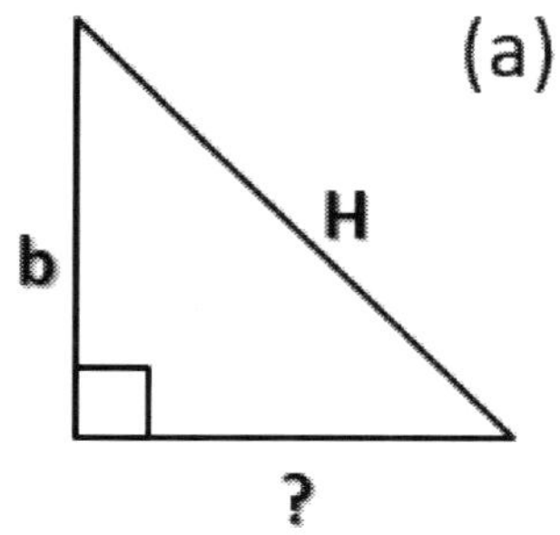

Note:
▪ Two sides given,
▪ One unknown side.
▪ No ANGLE
→ Use
PYTHAGORAS</td>
<td>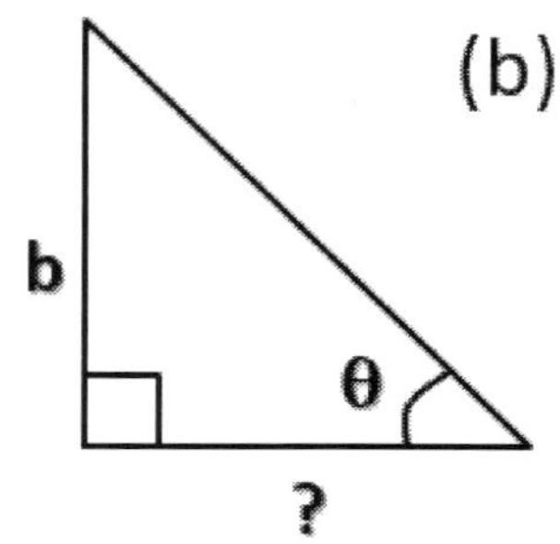

Note:
▪ When an ANGLE is involved.
→ Use
TRIGONOMETRY (SOH, CAH & TOA)</td>
<td>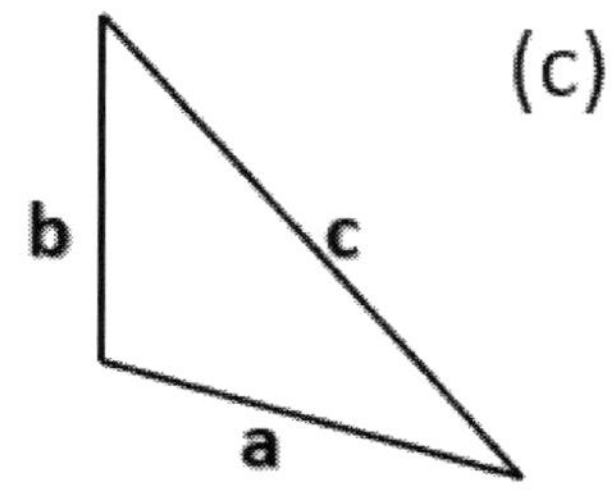

Note:
▪ All angles and sides not equal,
→ Use
TRIGONOMETRY (SINE & COSINE RULE)</td>
</tr>
</table>

A. Pythagoras

I. First, identify the missing sides of the question.

II. Use one of the two methods below.

1. Finding the **Longest** Side	2. Finding the **Shortest** Side
➢ SQUARE	➢ SQUARE
➢ SQUARE	➢ SQUARE
➢ **ADD**	➢ **SUBTRACT**
➢ SQUARE ROOT	➢ SQUARE ROOT

Questions

Q1. Calculate the length of the missing sides for the triangles below and give your answers to one decimal place.

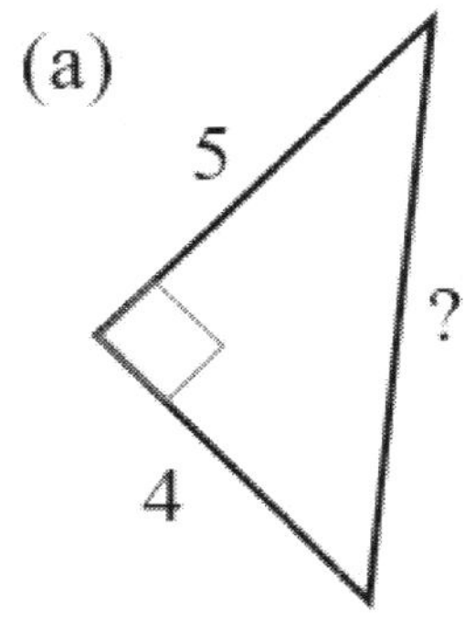

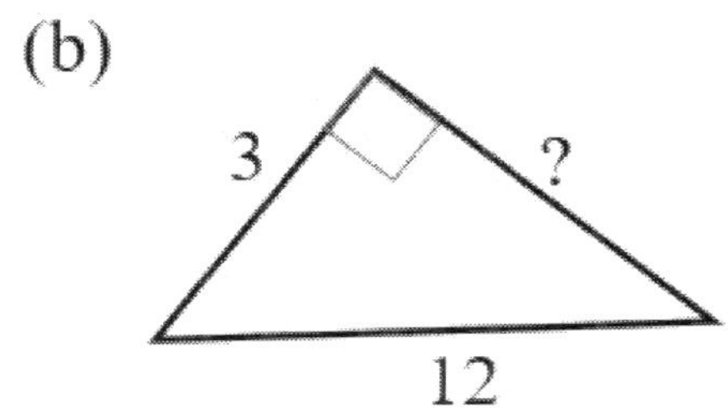

<u>Solution:</u>

(a)

$\rightarrow SQUARE = 5^2 = 25$

$\rightarrow SQUARE = 4^2 = 16$

$\rightarrow \boldsymbol{ADD} = 25 + 16 = 41$

$\rightarrow \boldsymbol{SQUARE\ ROOT} = \sqrt{41} = 6.4$

(b)

$\rightarrow SQUARE = 12^2 = 144$

$\rightarrow SQUARE = 3^2 = 9$

$\rightarrow \boldsymbol{SUBTRACT} = 144 - 9 = 135$

$\rightarrow \boldsymbol{SQUARE\ ROOT} = \sqrt{135} = 11.6$

Q2. Calculate the length of the missing sides for the triangles below and give your answers to one decimal place.

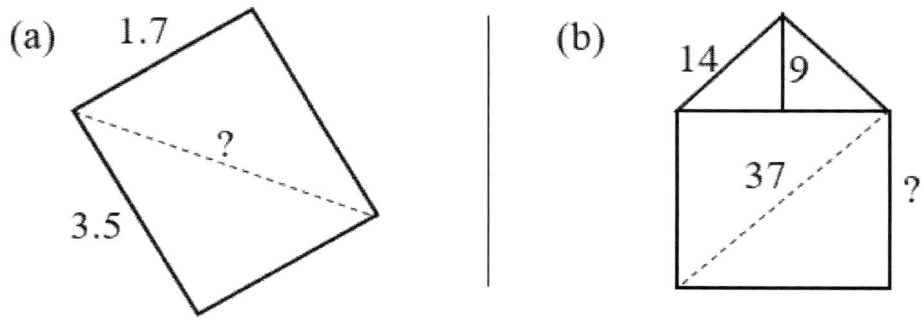

<u>***Solution:***</u>

(a) Separate the shape into two right-angled triangles.

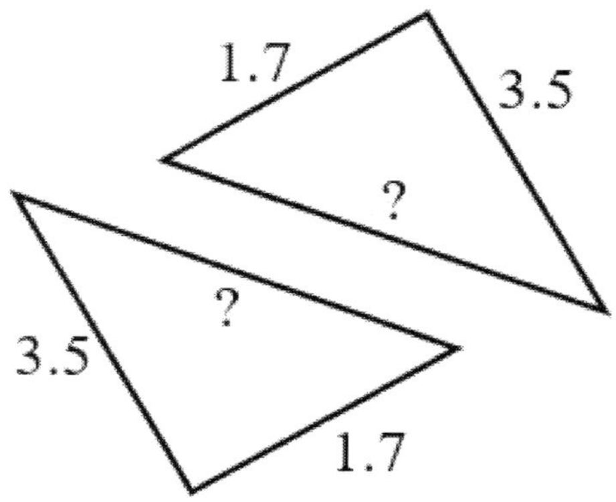

One of them gives a right-angle triangle with the longest side missing.

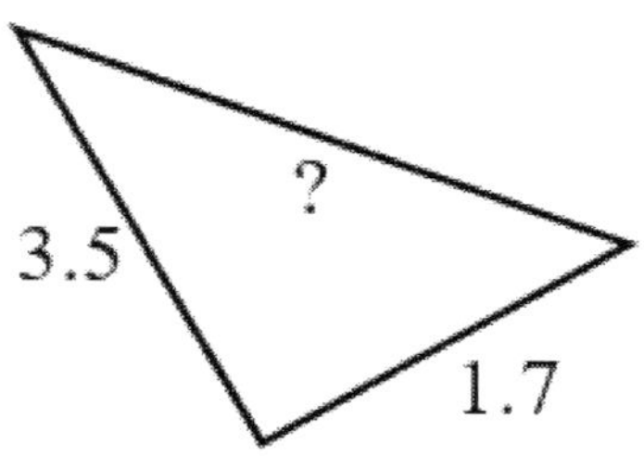

$\rightarrow SQUARE = 3.5^2 = 12.25$

$\rightarrow SQUARE = 1.7^2 = 2.89$

$\rightarrow \boldsymbol{ADD} = 12.25 + 2.89 = 15.14$

$\rightarrow \boldsymbol{SQUARE\ ROOT} = \sqrt{15.14} = 3.9$

It means that the diagonal length is <u>**3.9**</u>.

(b) Separate the shape into four right-angle triangles.

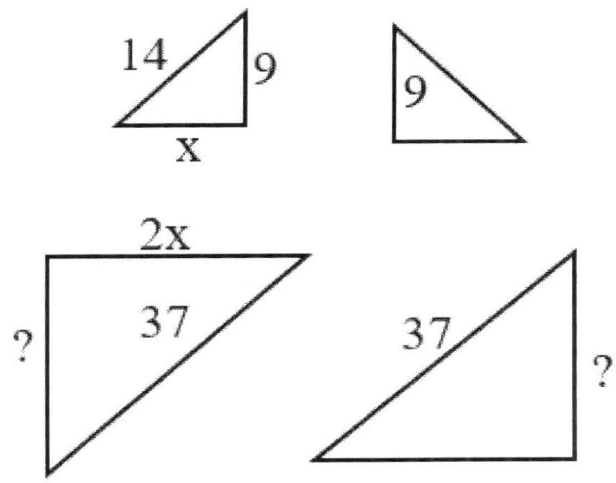

There will be two right-angle triangles with missing ***shortest*** sides to solve.

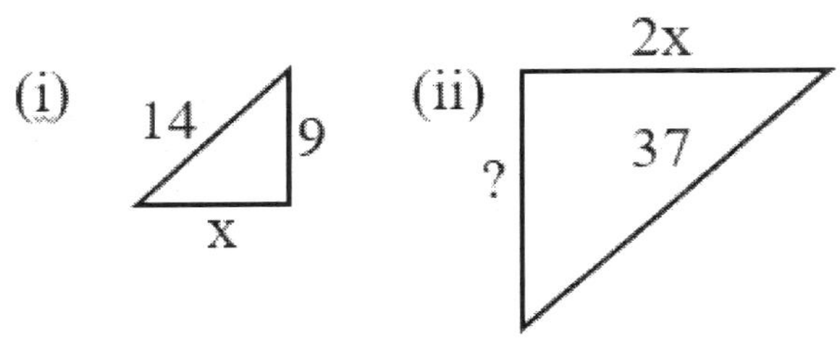

(i)

$\rightarrow SQUARE = 14^2 = 196$

$\rightarrow SQUARE = 9^2 = 81$

$\rightarrow \boldsymbol{SUBTRACT} = 196 - 81 = 115$

$\rightarrow \boldsymbol{SQUARE\ ROOT} = \sqrt{115} = 10.7$

Hence, $x = 10.7$.

(ii) It implies that; $2x = 21.4$.

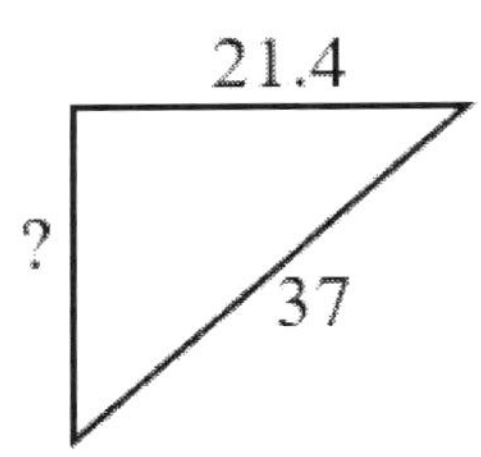

$\rightarrow SQUARE = 37^2 = 1369$

$$\rightarrow SQUARE = 21.4^2 = 457.96$$

$$\rightarrow \boldsymbol{SUBTRACT} = 1369 - 457.96 = 911.04$$

$$\rightarrow \boldsymbol{SQUARE\ ROOT} = \sqrt{911.04} = 30.2$$

Hence, the length of the missing side = 30.2.

Q3. A young boy can fit two of his dolls in a toy house as indicated below. If the height of the two sides is 26 cm, each side of the roof is 33 cm and the dolls are placed at a distance of 29 cm apart, calculate the height of the big doll.
Note: *diagram not drawn to scale.*

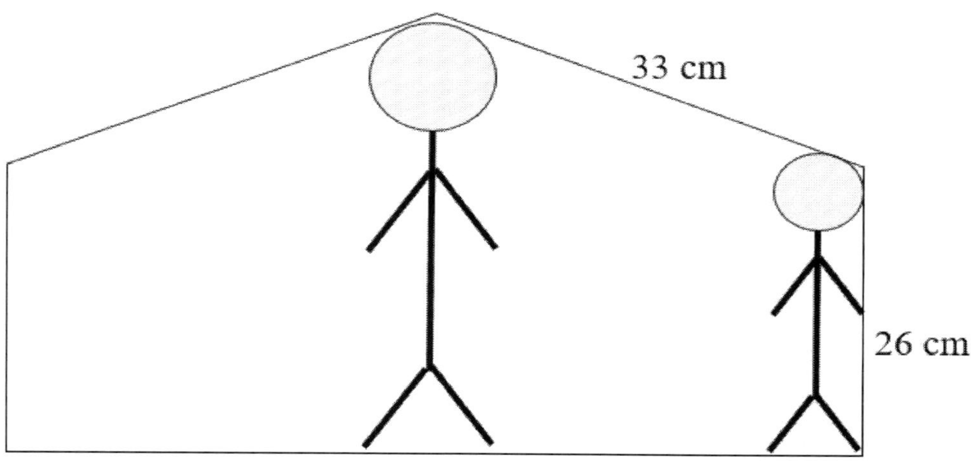

Solution:
The height of the small doll is known (i.e. 26 cm). Hence the difference between the height of the big and small doll can be calculated using a right-angled triangle model.
Once the difference (Dh) is obtained, the height of the big doll will be;

$$\boldsymbol{Big\ doll\ height = small\ doll\ height + Dh}$$

See illustrated below. ***Note***: you must not stick to the illustrated sketch always. Any reasonable sketch is accepted.

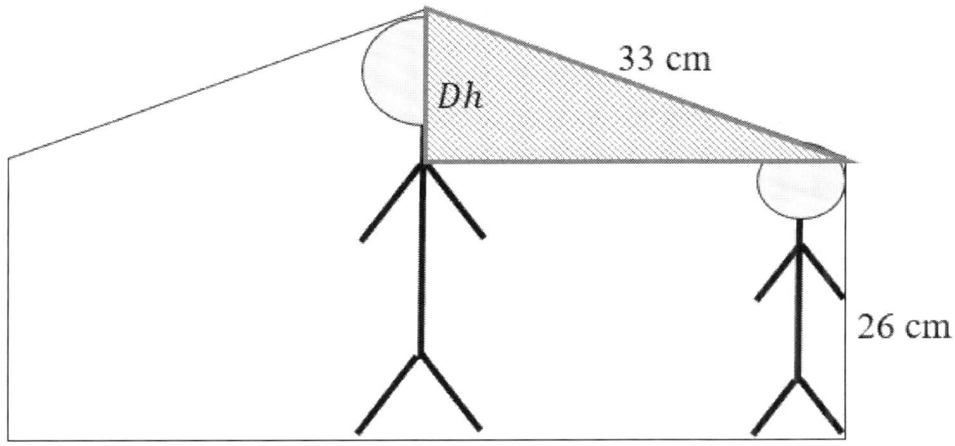

This means, the triangle can be taken out and the shortest side calculated using Pythagoras as follows; ***Remember***: that the base length is 29 cm.

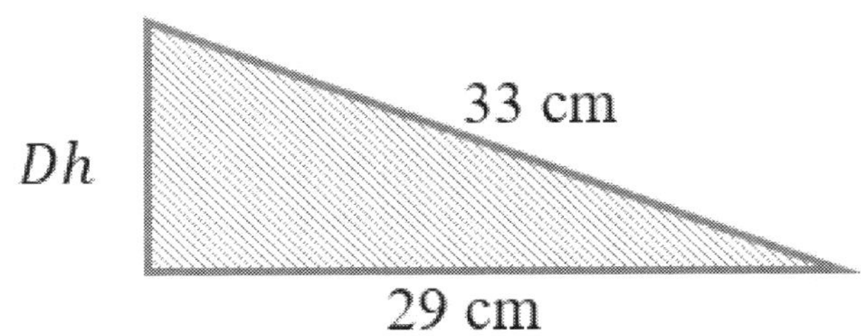

- SQUARE = $33^2 = 1089$
- SQUARE = $29^2 = 841$
- **SUBTRACT** = $1089 - 841 = 248$
- SQUARE ROOT = $\sqrt{248} = 15.8$

$\rightarrow$ It means $Dh = 15.8$

And since the small doll's height is 26 cm,

$$\boldsymbol{Big\ doll\ height = 26 + 15.8} = \mathbf{41.8\ cm \approx 42\ cm}$$

Q4. A ladder of unknown height is leaned against a wall and its base is supported by a horizontal platform. The platform is also supported by rigid circled metal rods, each having an area of 96,212 cm^2. Calculate the length of the ladder if it is leaned at a height of 10 m from the ground.

Note: *diagram not drawn to scale.*

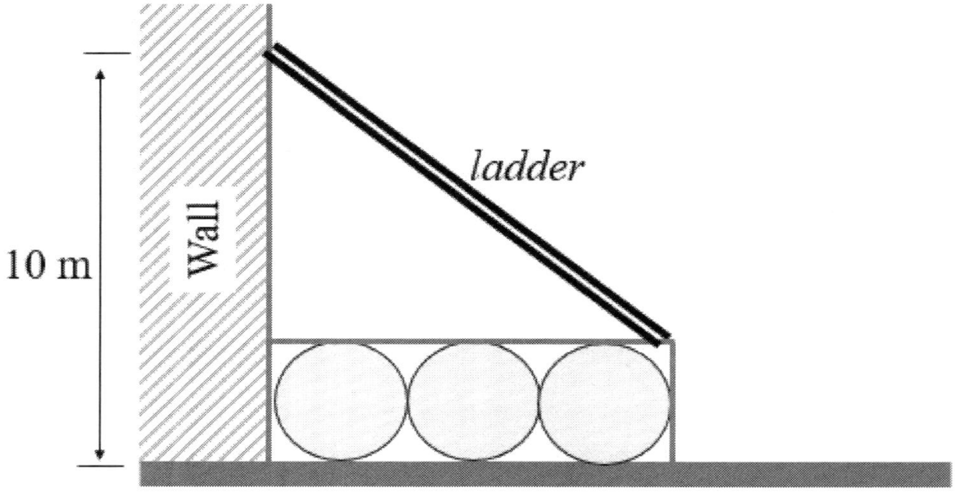

Solution:
Remember: ***No Angles*** involved, hence use ***Pythagoras***.
We must find an appropriate model to use.
The ladder, the base and the height of the wall are making right-angled - triangles.

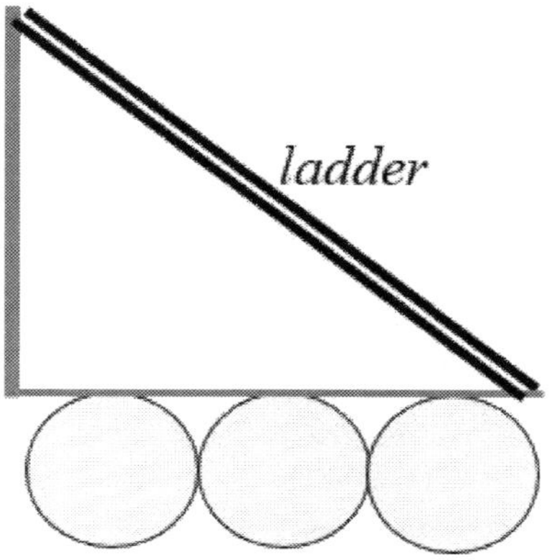

To find the base and the height (***h***), the ***radius*** of the circles needs to be calculated.

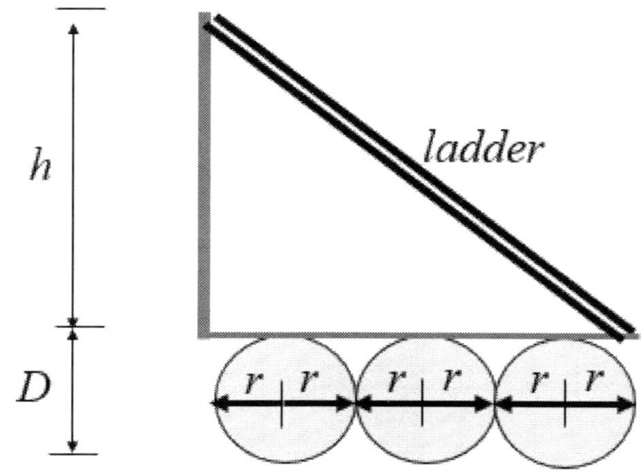

$$\boldsymbol{Base\ length = 6 \times r}$$

$$\boldsymbol{Height\ (h) = 10\ m - D}$$

Since the Diameter (***D***) of the circle $= 2 \times r$

Calculating the radius of the circle;

$$\boldsymbol{Area\ of\ circle\ (A) = \pi r^2}$$

$$r = \sqrt{\frac{A}{\pi}} = \sqrt{\frac{96{,}212}{\pi}} = \boldsymbol{175.3\ cm}$$

Hence,

$$\boldsymbol{Base\ length = 6 \times 175.3 = 1051.8\ cm}$$
$$\boldsymbol{Base\ length \approx 10.52\ m}$$

And,

$$\boldsymbol{D = 2 \times 175.3 = 350.6\ cm}$$
$$\boldsymbol{D = 3.506\ m \approx 3.51\ m}$$

Therefore,

$$\boldsymbol{Height\ (h) = 10\ cm - 3.51 = 6.49\ m}$$

The length of the ladder can now be calculated by Pythagoras using the dimensions of the right-angled triangle as illustrated below;

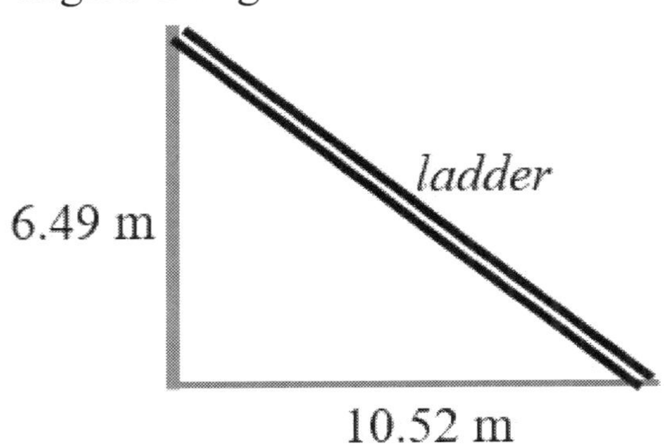

- SQUARE $= 6.49^2 = 42.12$
- SQUARE $= 10.52^2 = 110.67$
- **ADD** $= 42.12 + 110.67 = 152.79$
- SQUARE ROOT $= \sqrt{152.79} = 12.36$

→ It means *the ladder's length* = **12.4 m**

Q5. In the diagram below, a triangle has been inserted into a large rectangle (width, w = 6 m). The triangle is then separated into big and small triangles, having areas of $A_1 = 16$ m^2 and $A_2 = 8$ m^2, respectively. Calculate the length, L, of the large triangle attached to the rectangle.

Note: *diagram not drawn to scale.*

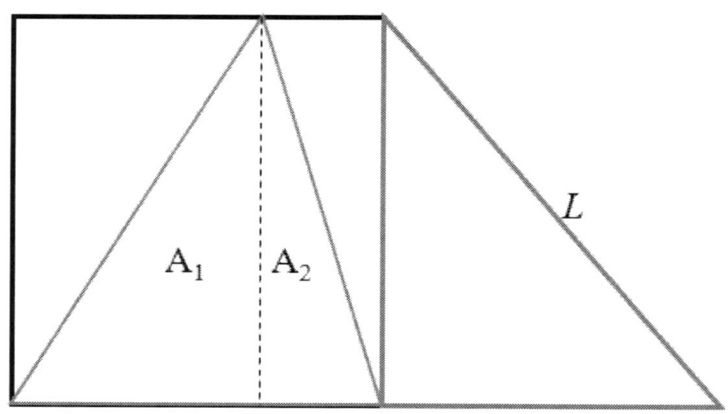

Solution:

Remember: ***No Angles*** involved and they have right-angled triangles hence use ***Pythagoras***.

First of all, find the two bases of the big (b_1) and small (b_2) triangles within the rectangle.

Area of a triangle is based on the ***base*** and the ***height***.

Since the two inserted triangles have the same HEIGHT (H), b_1 and b_2 can be obtained using the ratio of their areas;

$$\underline{A_1} : \underline{A_2}$$
$$16 : 8$$
$$\mathbf{2 : 1}$$

It implies that,

$$\underline{\boldsymbol{b_1}} : \underline{\boldsymbol{b_2}}$$
$$\mathbf{2 : 1}$$

$$Fraction\ of\ \boldsymbol{b_1} = \frac{2}{3}$$

$$Fraction\ of\ \boldsymbol{b_2} = \frac{1}{3}$$

Hence, the total width of a rectangle of ***6* m** can be divided into

$$\boldsymbol{b_1} = \frac{2}{3} \times 6 = \mathbf{4}$$

$$\boldsymbol{b_2} = \frac{1}{3} \times 6 = \mathbf{2}$$

The final diagram will be;

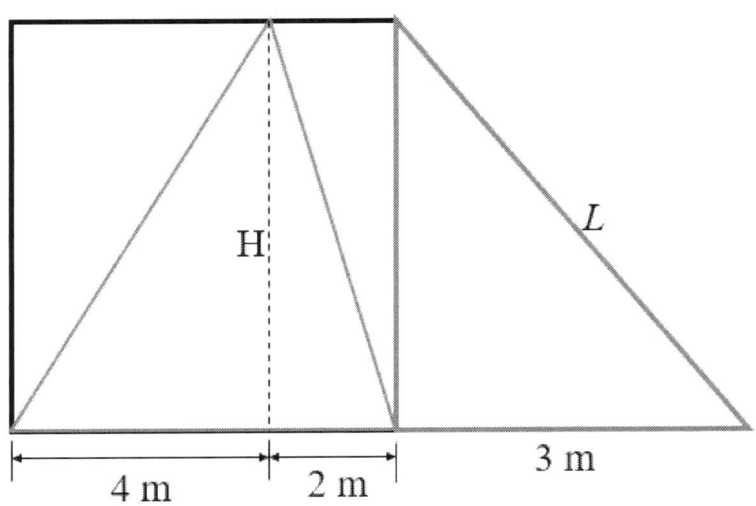

Since the area of a triangle is $\boldsymbol{A} = \frac{1}{2}\boldsymbol{bh}$

The Height (H) of the inserted triangle can be calculated by using the areas of one of the separated triangles and its base.

$$A_1 = \frac{1}{2} b_1 H$$

$$16 = \frac{1}{2} \times 4 \times H$$

$$H = 8\ m$$

Therefore to find L, the large triangle will have a height of 8 m and can be calculated as follows.

- SQUARE $= 8^2 = 64$
- SQUARE $= 3^2 = 9$
- **ADD** $= 64 + 9 = 73$
- SQUARE ROOT $= \sqrt{73} = 8.5$

→ It means L = **8.5 m**

Q6. Calculate the length, Q, when a rectangular beam is placed within a cube. The beam has a perimeter of 124 cm and makes an inclination to the inner wall of the cube as shown below.

Note: *diagram not drawn to scale.*

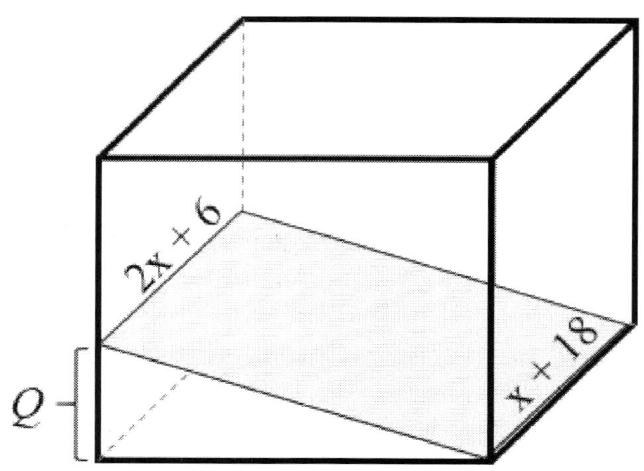

Solution:

The height, $\boldsymbol{Q}$, makes a right-angled triangle with the base of the cube and the length of the rectangular beam.

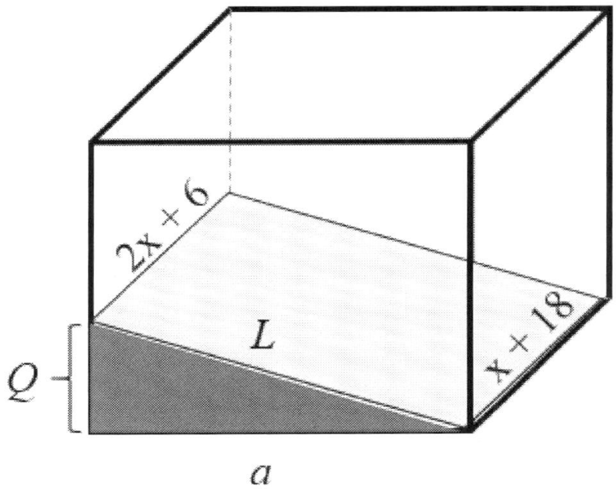

Using the laws of a rectangle,

$$2x + 6 = x + 18$$
$$2x - x = 18 - 6$$
$$x = 12$$

Meaning,

$$2x + 6 = 2 \times 12 + 6 = 30\ cm$$

or

$$x + 18 = 12 + 18 = 30\ cm$$

The perimeter of the rectangular beam is 124 cm.
Hence,

$$2L + 2 \times 30 = 124\ cm$$
$$2L = 124 - 60 = 64$$
$$L = 32\ cm$$

But since the width ($\boldsymbol{w}$) of the beam has the same length as one of the sides of the cube, the base length, $\boldsymbol{a}$, as shown in the sketch above, is also **30 cm** (i.e. $\boldsymbol{a = 30\ cm}$).

It implies that,

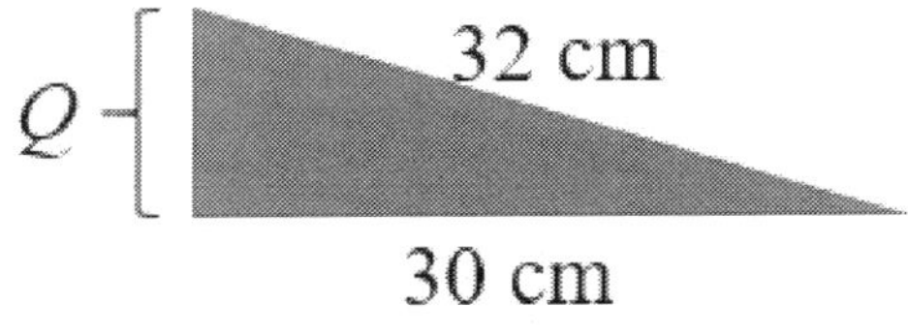

- SQUARE = $32^2 = 1024$
- SQUARE = $30^2 = 900$
- **SUBTRACT** = $1024 - 900 = 124$
- SQUARE ROOT = $\sqrt{124} = 11.134$

$\rightarrow$ It means the length, $Q = 11.1$ cm

Q7. Calculate the diagonal length, *B*, of the right-angled triangle within the cube below.

Note: *diagram not drawn to scale.*

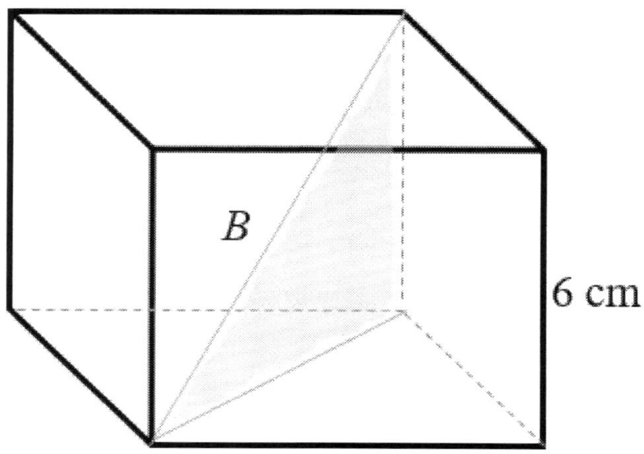

Solution:
Since all the sides of the cube are equal, each side of the cube is 6 cm.

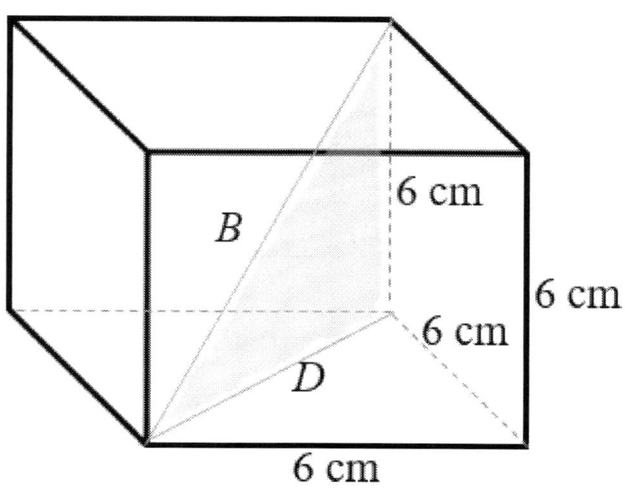

From the above sketch, there will be two triangles that can be deducted.

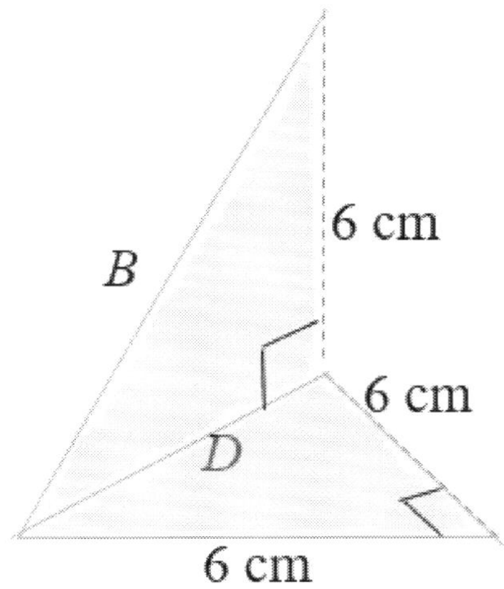

To find the length (***B***), the diagonal length (***D***) must be obtained first from the base triangle.
To find ***D***;

- SQUARE = $6^2 = 36$
- SQUARE = $6^2 = 36$
- **ADD** = $36 + 36 = 72$
- SQUARE ROOT = $\sqrt{72} = 8.5$

$\rightarrow D$ = **<u>8.5 m</u>**

Hence, the length B can be calculated by;

- SQUARE = $6^2 = 36$
- SQUARE = $8.5^2 = 72.25$
- **ADD** = $36 + 72.25 = 108.25$
- SQUARE ROOT = $\sqrt{108.25} = 10.4$

Hence, *length B* = **<u>10.4 m</u>**

B. Trigonometry

The focus will be on the following topics;

I. SOH CAH TOA
II. Sine Rule
III. Cosine Rule
IV. Area of Non-Right Angle Triangle
V. Finding trigonometry exact angles

I. SOH CAH TOA

<table>
<tr><th colspan="2">Right-Angle Triangle</th><th>Scalene Triangle</th></tr>
<tr><td></td><td>(b)
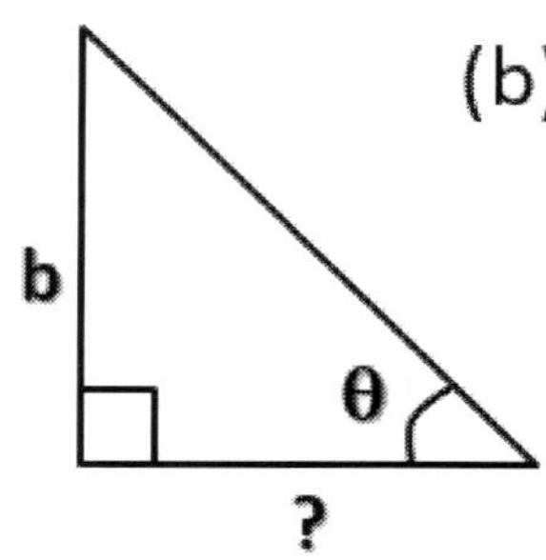

Note:
▪ When an ANGLE is involved.
→ Use TRIGONOMETRY (SOH, CAH & TOA)</td><td></td></tr>
</table>

Strategy for SOH CAH TOA

(a) Triangle must be labelled

- **Opposite**: Opposite to the ***ANGLE*** in question → **O**
- **Adjacent**: Adjacent (or ***near***) to the ***ANGLE*** in question → **A**

- **Hypotenuse**: ***Longest side*** or ***opposite*** to the ***Right-Angle*** → **H**

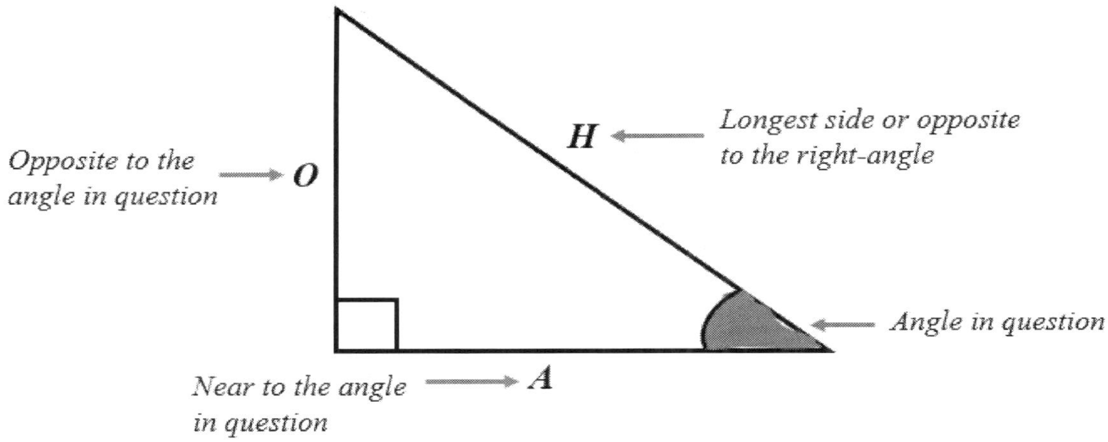

OR

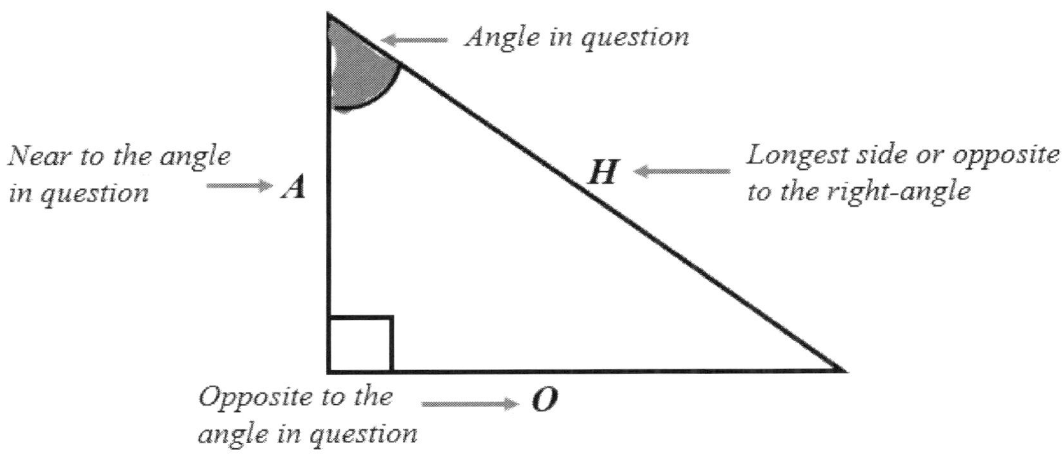

(b) *Select the right SOH CAH TOA formula*

- Put the **SOH**, **CAH**, **TOA** in a triangle.
- Always put the **CENTRE letter** at the **middle-top** and the **SIDE letters** on the **same sides**.

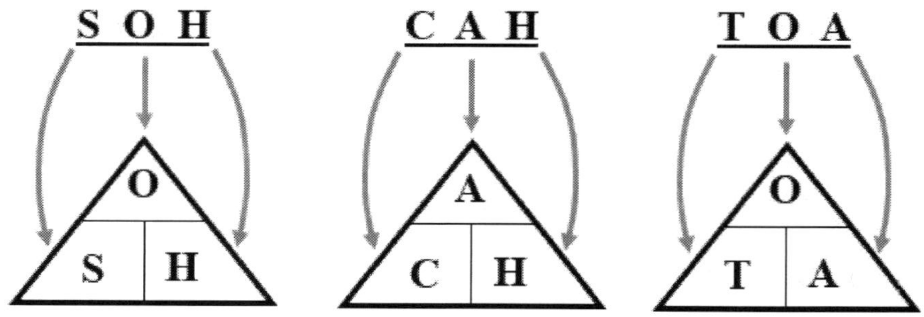

- Use the triangle to ***create*** the required formula.
  Example:

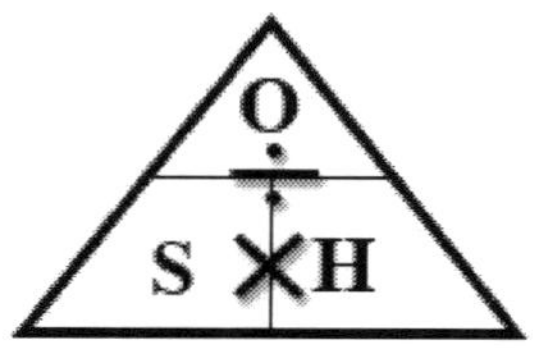

Meaning $\rightarrow \boldsymbol{O = S \times H}$

$$\boldsymbol{S = O \div H}$$

$$\boldsymbol{H = O \div S}$$

- **Note** the full meaning of ***S***, ***C*** and ***T*** that start the ***S***OH, ***C***AH and ***T***OA, respectively.
  That is:

$$\boldsymbol{S \rightarrow Sin\ of\ the\ angle.;\ e.g.\ sin(x)}$$
$$\boldsymbol{C \rightarrow Cos\ of\ the\ angle.;\ e.g.\ Cos(x)}$$
$$\boldsymbol{T \rightarrow Tan\ of\ the\ angle.;\ e.g.\ Tan(x)}$$

(c) When finding the angles, always use the <u>inverse</u> Sin, Cos or Tan.
That is:

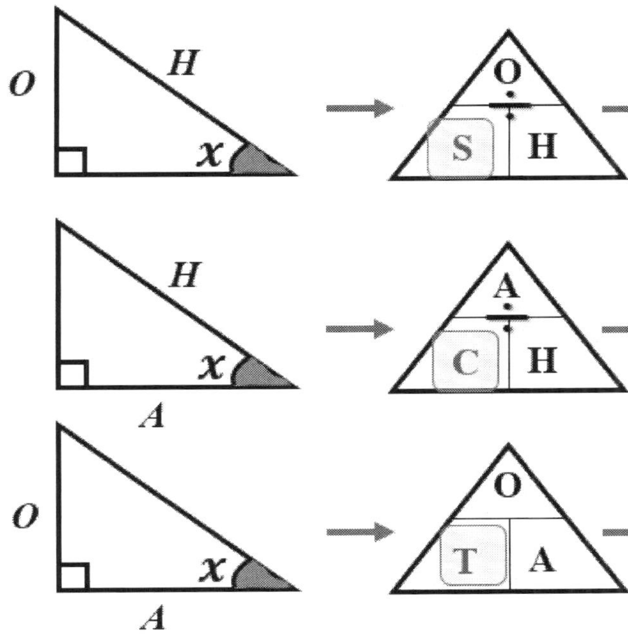

$$x = \sin^{-1}\left(\frac{O}{H}\right)$$

$$x = \cos^{-1}\left(\frac{A}{H}\right)$$

$$x = \tan^{-1}\left(\frac{O}{A}\right)$$

Remember: The appropriate formula depends on what has been given.

Questions

Q1. Find the length of the missing side.
Note: *diagram not drawn to scale.*

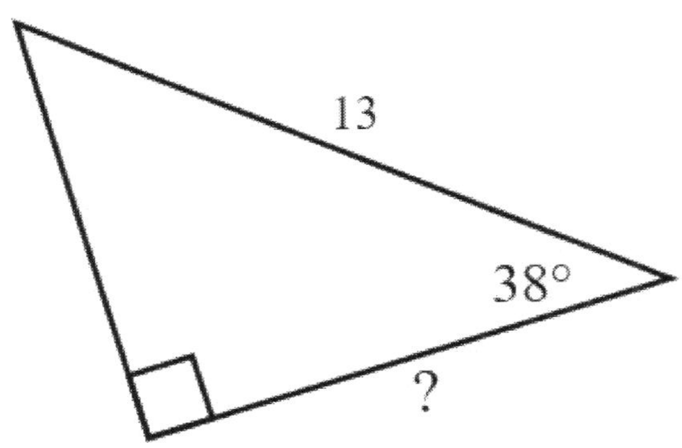

Solution:

Note that this involves an **angle**, hence trigonometry approach needed.

a. Try and label the ***SIDES*** that has been given and what is needed only!!!

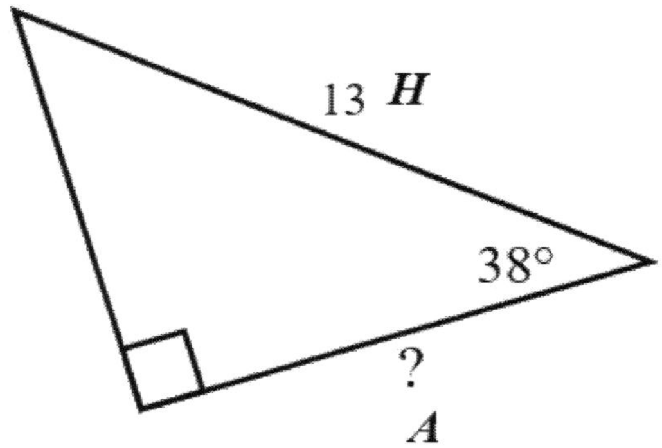

a. Select appropriate ***TRIANGLE*** that has <u>***A***</u> and <u>***H***</u>. Use the formula to solve the question.

<u>***A***</u> is needed and when <u>***A***</u> is covered,

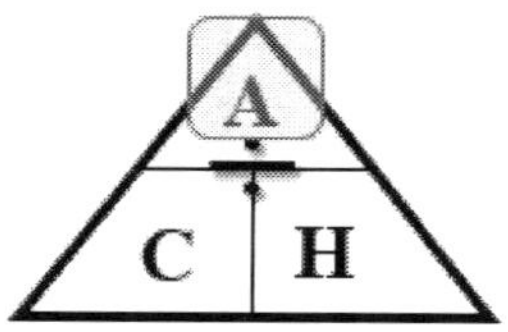

$$A = C \times H$$
$$\rightarrow A = Cos(38) \times 13$$
$$A = 10.2$$

Q2. Find the missing angle from the diagram below.

Note: *diagram not drawn to scale.*

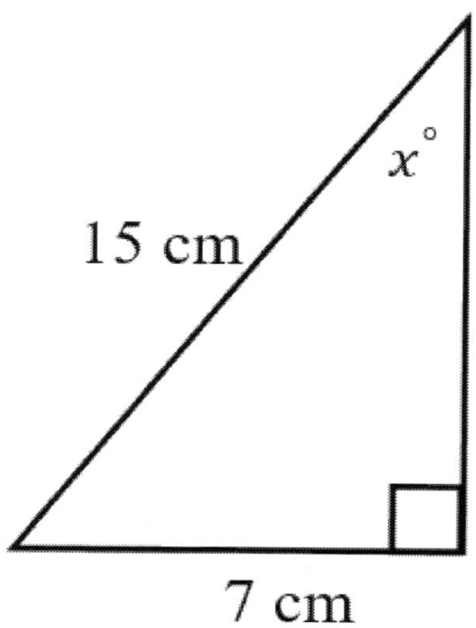

<u>Solution:</u>

a. Try and label the <u>***SIDES***</u> that has been given only!! The angle is needed but do not label it.

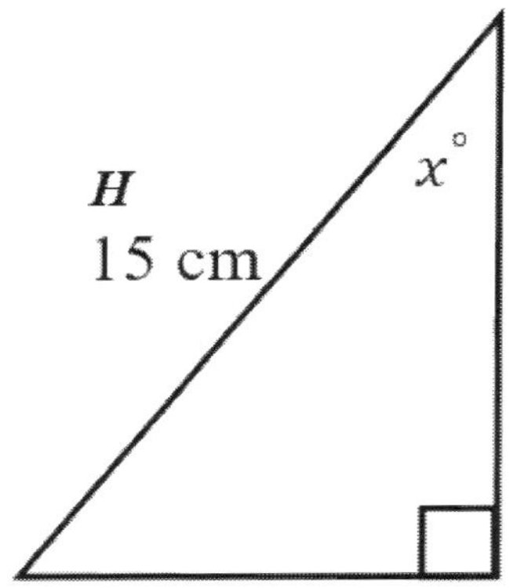

b. Select appropriate ***TRIANGLE*** that has ***O*** and ***H***. Use the formula to solve the question.

The angle x° is needed but we need a triangle that has ***O*** and ***H***

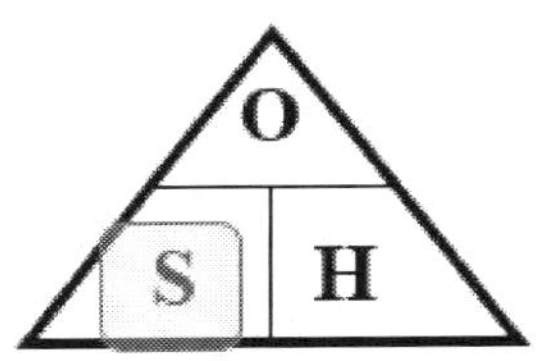

Cover the ***S*** (Sin of x°) to find x°.

$$\boldsymbol{S = O \div H}$$

$$\rightarrow \quad \boldsymbol{\sin(x) = \frac{O}{H}}$$

$$\boldsymbol{x = \sin^{-1}\left(\frac{O}{H}\right) = \sin^{-1}\left(\frac{7}{15}\right)}$$

$$\boldsymbol{x = 27.8^{\circ}}$$

Q3. A car knocks down a tall tree to fall on 10 m pole. If the tree was about 3.5 m from the pole, calculate the angle of the tree from its initial position.

Note: *diagram not drawn to scale.*

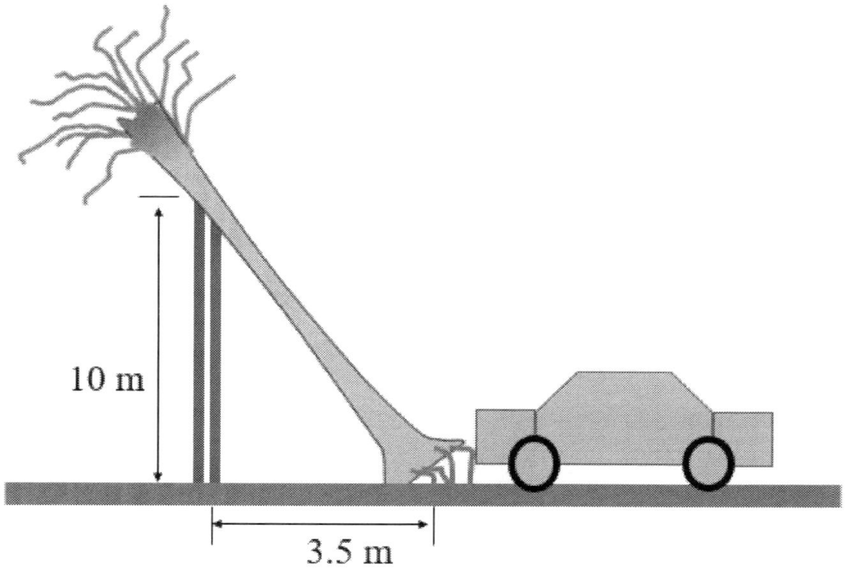

Solution:

a. Try and get the right-angle triangle from the diagram.

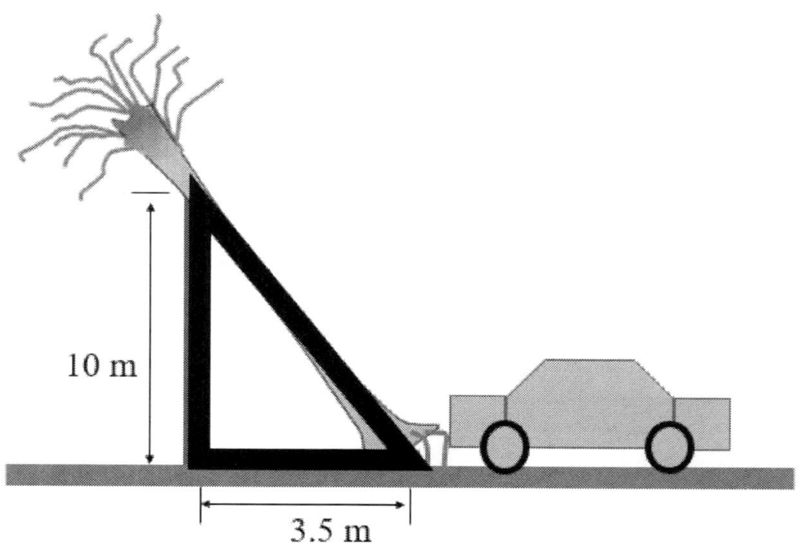

This gives,

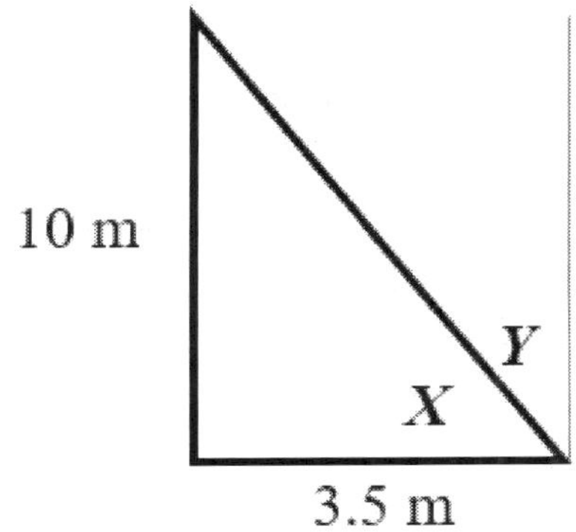

To find angle A, label the triangle;

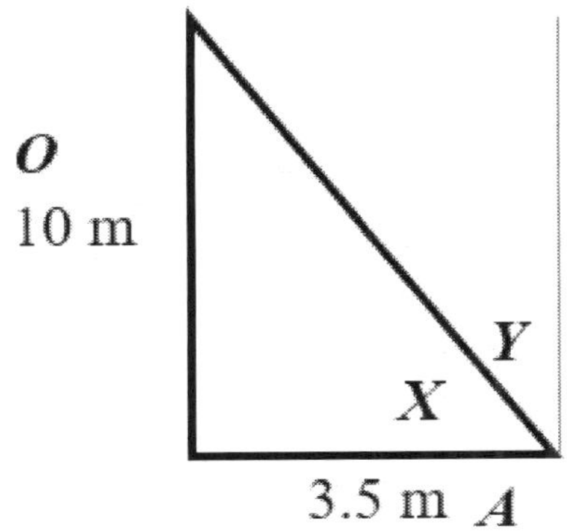

b. Select appropriate ***TRIANGLE*** that has ***O*** and ***A***. Use the formula to solve the question.

The angle X is needed but we need a triangle that has ***O*** and ***A***

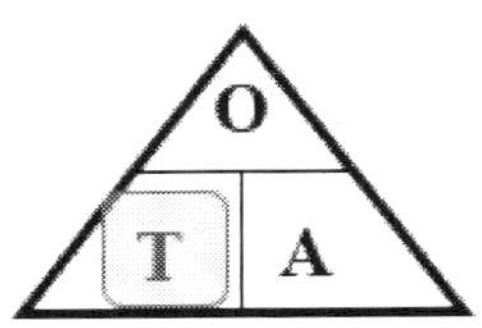

Cover the ***T*** (tan of X) to find X.

$$T = O \div A$$

$$\rightarrow \quad \mathbf{Tan}(X) = \frac{O}{A}$$

$$X = \tan^{-1}\left(\frac{O}{A}\right) = \tan^{-1}\left(\frac{10}{3.5}\right)$$

$$X = 70.7^\circ$$

Hence, the angle of the tree from its initial position = **90 – 70.7 = <u>19.3°.</u>**

Q4. In the diagram below, a triangle has been inserted into a big circle. The longest side of the triangle represents the diameter of the circle.
Calculate,

i. The radius of the circle.
ii. The area of the shaded region. (***Note**: diagram not drawn to scale).*

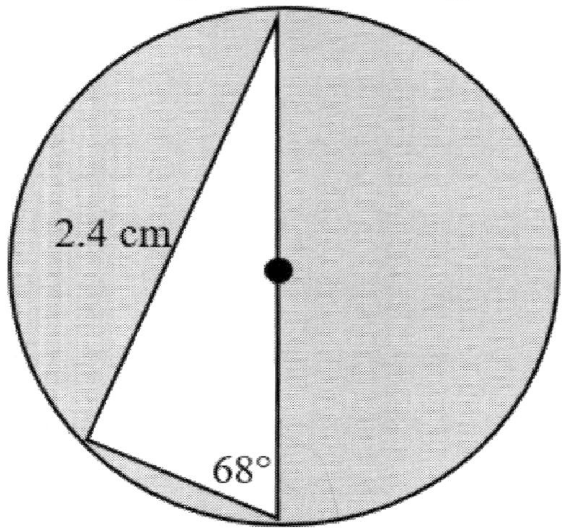

Solution:

i. To find the radius of the circle, the longest distance of the triangle must be calculated. **The radius = Diameter ÷ 2.**

Using SOH, CAH, TOA, the triangle must be labelled.

This gives,

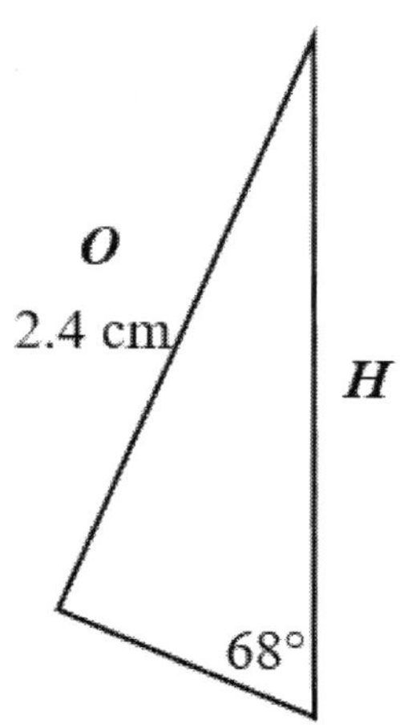

We need the formula with ***O*** and ***H***.
Cover ***H*** and use the formula.

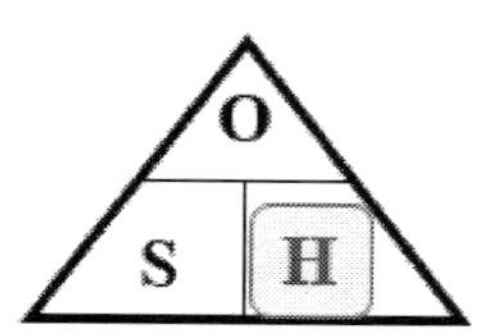

$$H = O \div S$$

$$\rightarrow \quad H = \frac{2.4}{\sin(68)}$$

$$H = 2.6\ cm$$

Hence, **the radius** = **2.6 ÷ 2 = 1.3 cm.**

ii. To find the area of the shaded region, the area of the circle and the triangle need to be calculated.

The area of the shaded region = **Area of the circle** – **Area of the triangle**.

$$\boldsymbol{Area\ of\ circle} = \pi r^2 = \pi \times 1.3^2 = 5.3\ cm^2$$

To find the area of the triangle, the base of the triangle needs to be calculated.

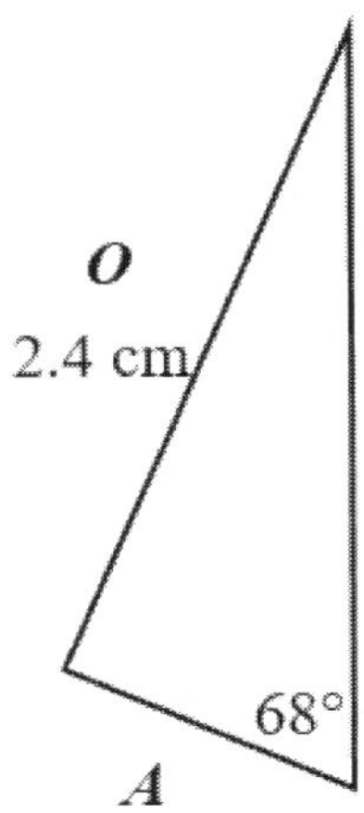

We need the formula with ***O*** and ***A***.
Cover ***A*** and use the formula.

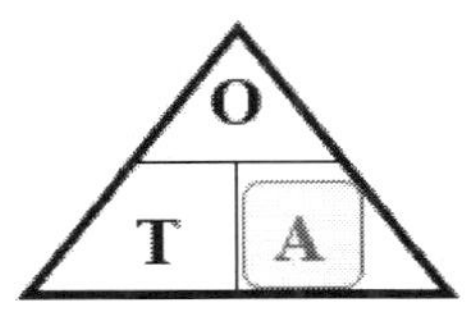

$$A = O \div T$$

$$\rightarrow \quad A = \frac{2.4}{\text{Tan}(68)}$$

$$A = 0.97cm$$

Therefore,

$$\boldsymbol{Area\ of\ the\ triangle} = \frac{1}{2}bh = \frac{1}{2} \times 0.97 \times 2.4 = 1.2\ cm^2$$

The area of the shaded region = **5.3 – 1.2 = <u>4.1 cm²</u>**.

Q5. The diagram below shows a cuboid, ABCDEFGH, and right-angled triangle, AGF, drawn inside. Using the information given, calculate the volume of the cuboid.

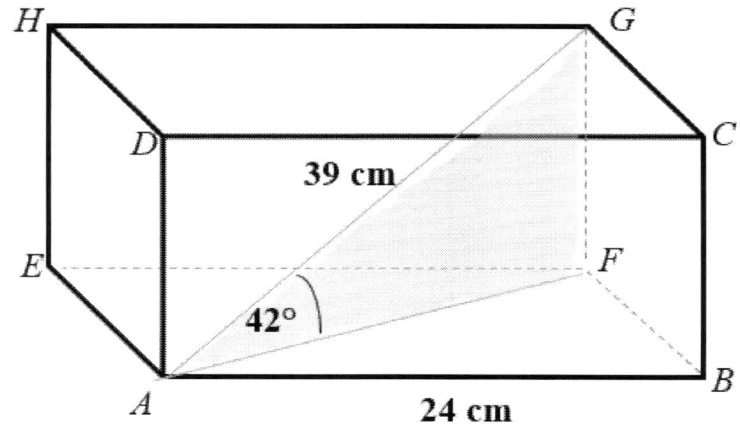

Solution:

Volume of a cuboid = ***L*** x ***W*** x ***H***.
The missing length are;

- Width (***W***) = length FB
- Height (***H***) = length FG

Finding the Width, W (FB);
First find length **AF** and secondly, **FB**.

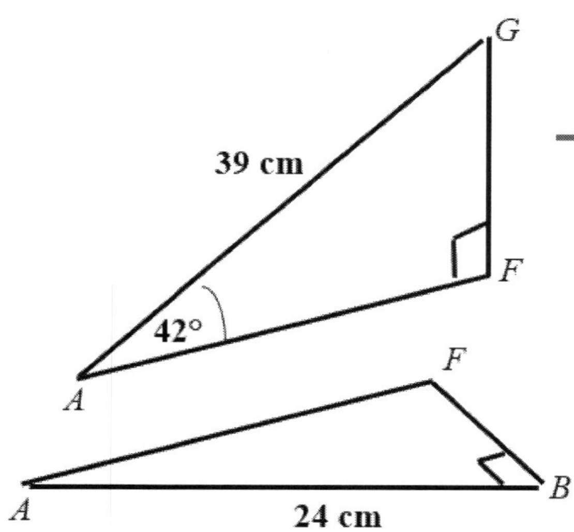

First triangle involves ***an angle***;

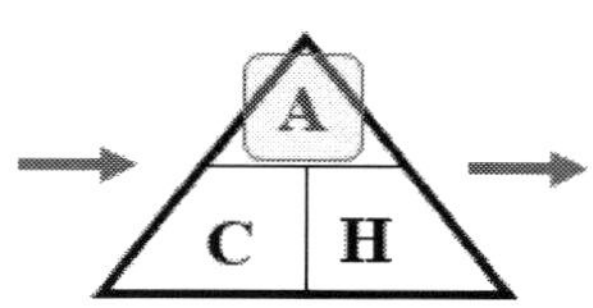

$$AF = C \times H$$

$$AF = \cos(42) \times 39$$

$$AF = 28.89\ cm$$

Second triangle has ***no angle***;

- SQUARE = $24^2 = 576$
- SQUARE = $28.89^2 = 834.63$
- **SUBTRACT** = 834.63 - 576 = 258.63
- SQUARE ROOT = $\sqrt{258.63}$ = 16.1 cm

It means the Width, ***W*** = **16.1 cm**

Finding the Height, *H* (FG);
From the first diagram,

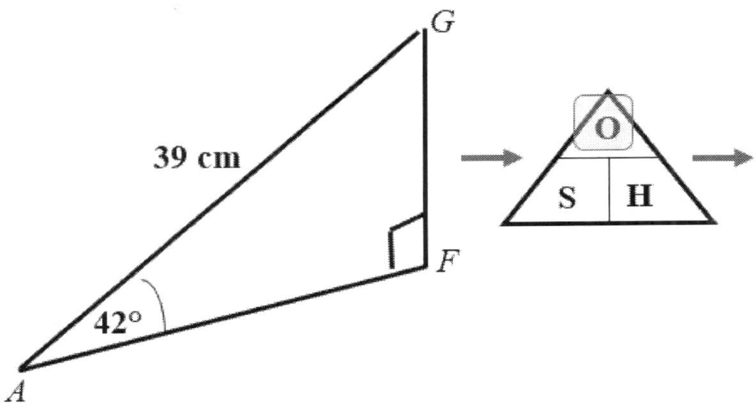

$$FG = S \times H$$

$$FG = \sin(42) \times 39$$

$$FG = 26.1\ cm$$

Hence, the height is 26.1 cm.

Volume of a cuboid = ***L*** x ***W*** x ***H***. = 24 cm x 16.1 cm x 26.1 cm
= **10085.04 cm^3**.

II. SINE RULE

<table>
<tr><th colspan="2">Right-Angle Triangle</th><th>Scalene Triangle</th></tr>
<tr><td></td><td></td><td>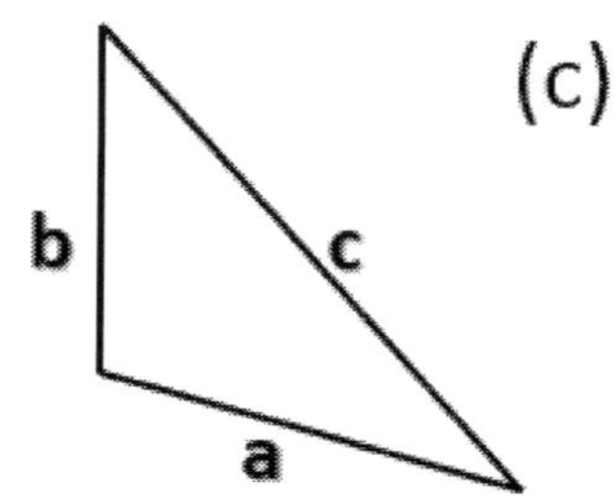

<u>Note:</u>
▪ All angles and sides not equal,
→ Use
TRIGONOMETRY (SINE & COSINE RULE)</td></tr>
</table>

Strategy for Sine Rule

(1) Triangle must be labelled even if they have letters.

- **ANGLES**: The ***ANGLEs*** are placed at the **vertices** of the triangle as ***A***, ***B*** and ***C*** in CAPITAL letters.

- **Lengths**: The lengths are placed ***OPPOSITES*** to the **Angles**.
  - Length ***a*** → opposite to Angle ***A***
  - Length ***b*** → opposite to Angle ***B***
  - Length ***c*** → opposite to Angle ***C***

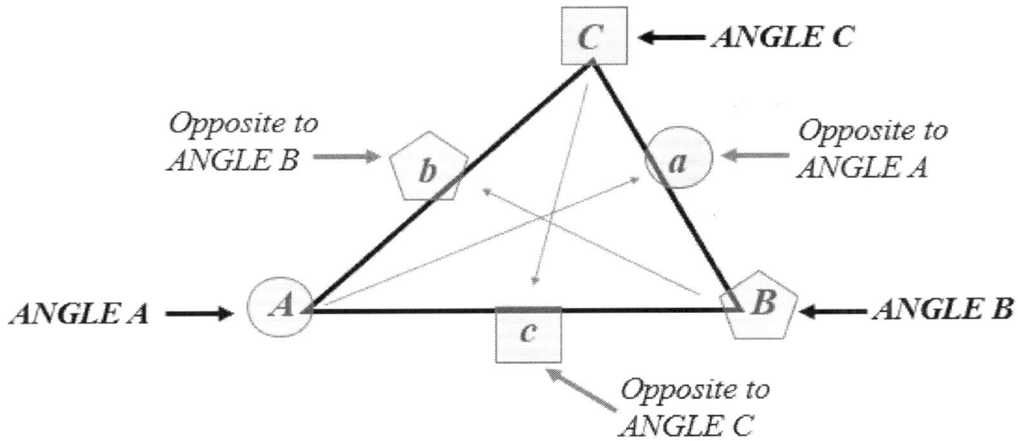

(2) Then use the following RATIOS to solve the question.

To find ***Lengths***; $\dfrac{a}{\sin A} = \dfrac{b}{\sin B} = \dfrac{c}{\sin C}$

Or

To find ***Angles***; $\dfrac{\sin A}{a} = \dfrac{\sin B}{b} = \dfrac{\sin C}{c}$

Note that you need ONLY TWO Ratios to solve the problem.

To find ***Lengths***; $\dfrac{a}{\sin A} = \dfrac{b}{\sin B}$ **or** ; $\dfrac{a}{\sin A} = \dfrac{c}{\sin C}$

Or

To find ***Angles***; $\dfrac{\sin A}{a} = \dfrac{\sin B}{b}$ **or** ; $\dfrac{\sin A}{a} = \dfrac{\sin C}{c}$

Questions

Q1. Find the length *AC* from the diagram below.
Note: *diagram not drawn to scale.*

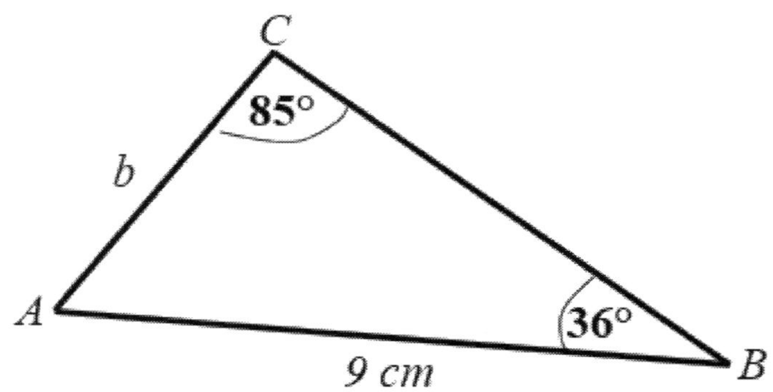

Solution:

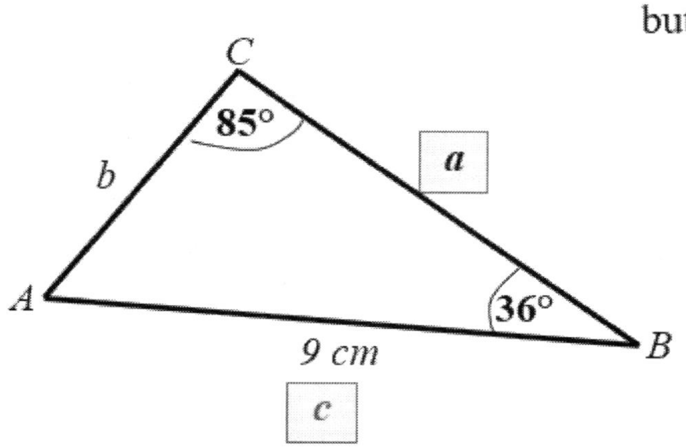

The triangle needs to be labelled but ***b*** and ***B*** are given.

$$\frac{b}{\sin B} = \frac{c}{\sin C}$$

$$b = \frac{c}{\sin C} \times \sin B$$

$$b = \frac{9}{\sin 85} \times \sin 36$$

$$b = 5.3\ cm$$

Q2. Find the missing angle displayed in the diagram below from the diagram below.

Note: *diagram not drawn to scale.*

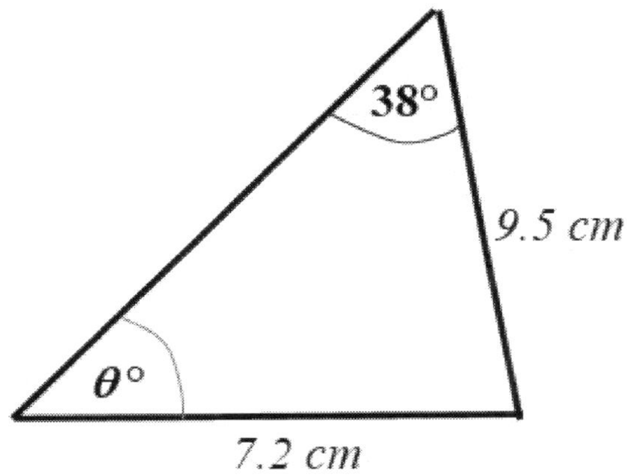

Solution:

The triangle needs to be labelled in ***A***, ***B*** and ***C*** format.

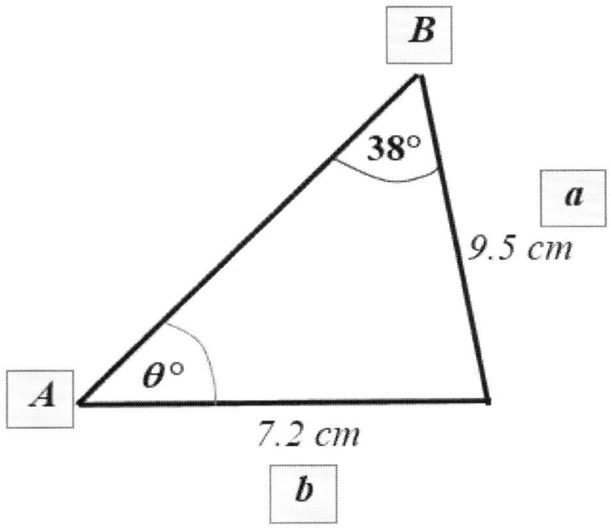

$$\frac{\sin A}{a} = \frac{\sin B}{b}$$

$$\sin A = \frac{\sin B}{b} \times a$$

$$A = \sin^{-1}\left[\frac{\sin B}{b} \times a\right]$$

$$A = \sin^{-1}\left[\frac{\sin 38}{7.2} \times 9.5\right]$$

$$A = 54.3\,°$$

Q3. In the triangle *X*, *Y*, *Z*, angle *ZXY* is 95° and the length *ZY* is 10.5 m. If the length *XZ* is 5 m, calculate the angle *XYZ*.
Note: *diagram not drawn to scale.*

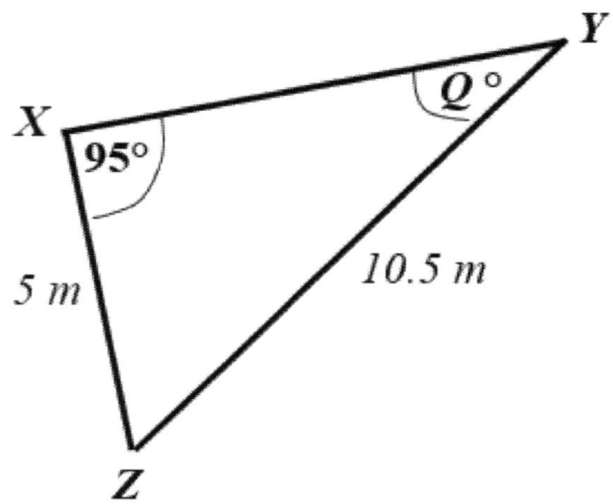

Solution:
The triangle needs to be labelled in ***A***, ***B*** and ***C*** format even though it has letters assigned to the vertices.

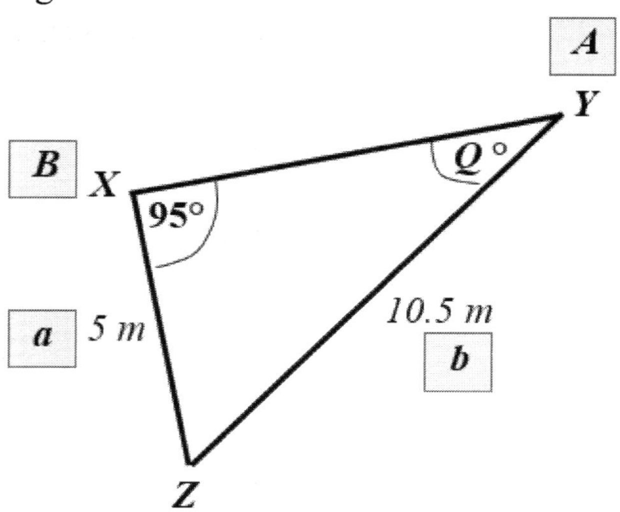

$$\frac{\sin A}{a} = \frac{\sin B}{b}$$

$$\sin A = \frac{\sin B}{b} \times a$$

$$A = \sin^{-1}\left[\frac{\sin B}{b} \times a\right]$$

$$A = \sin^{-1}\left[\frac{\sin 95}{10.5} \times 5\right]$$

$$A = 28.3°$$

Hence, the angle *XYZ* is **28.3°**.

Q4. A car and a bus set out from a station at the same time. The car moves down south and the bus moves to the south-east at a bearing of 096°. If the car then turns after 16 km and moves north-east at a bearing of 046°, calculate the distance travelled by the car when it meets the bus.

Solution:
The information can be sketched into a triangle and the appropriate model applied.

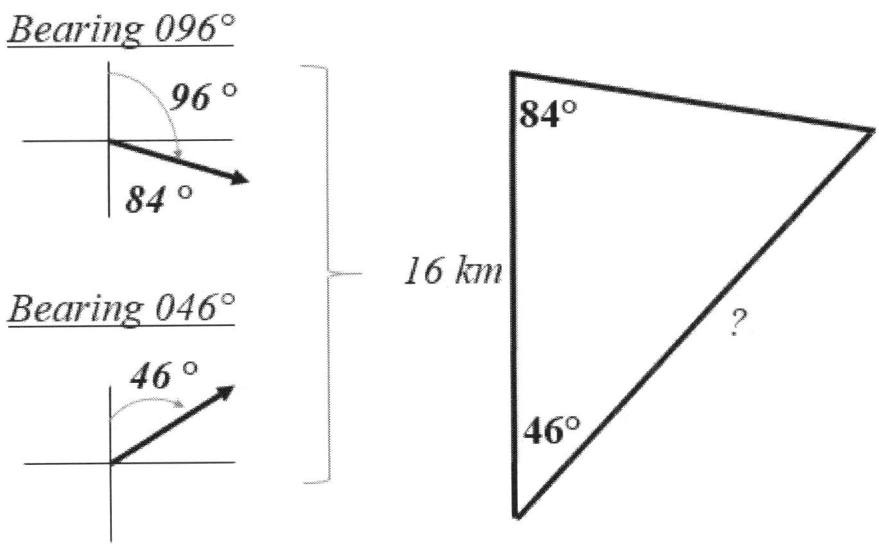

The triangle needs to be labelled in ***A***, ***B*** and ***C*** format and should be assigned in such a way that it will be easy to use the Sine Rule.

Important point: For the ***sign rule***, opposite angles and lengths needed.

Hence, using the *sum of angles in a triangle*, the **third angle** can be calculated.

$$\textit{The third angle} = 180 - [46 + 84] = 50^\circ$$

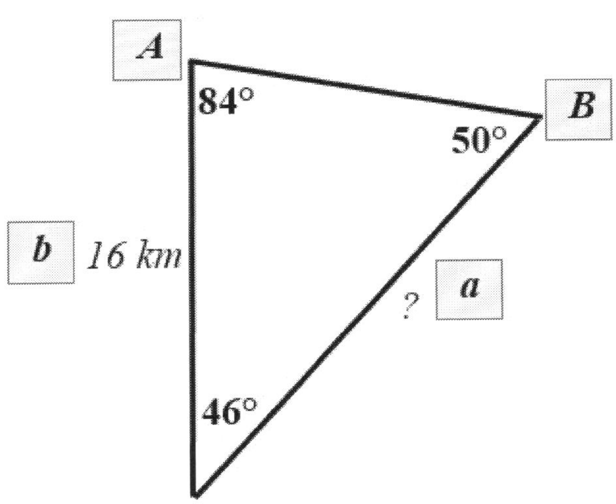

$$\frac{a}{\sin A} = \frac{b}{\sin B}$$

$$a = \frac{b}{\sin B} \times \sin A$$

$$a = \frac{16}{\sin 50} \times \sin 84$$

$$a = 20.8\ km$$

Therefore, the distance the car travelled before meeting the bus is **20.8 km**.

Q5. A ship starts from position X and moves south-west at a bearing of 215° for a distance of 19 km to position Y. From position Y, the ship then moves north-west at a bearing of 315° to position Z which is located at a distance of 25 km from Y. Calculate the bearing of position Z from X if the Z is located at a distance of 28 km from X.

Solution:

The information can be sketched into a triangle and the appropriate model applied.

__Note__: that the angle at ***Y*** needs to be resolved. There is an alternative angle of **35°** and the angle going north-west of about **45°** that needs to be added.

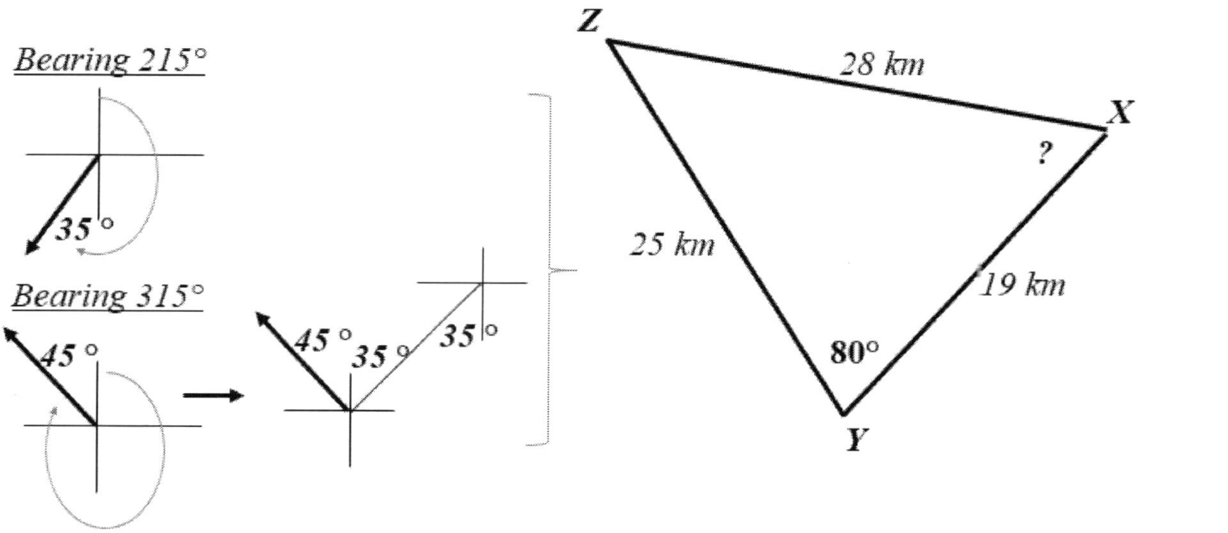

The angle at ***X*** is needed in order to calculate the bearing of ***Z*** from ***X***.

The triangle needs to be labelled in ***A***, ***B*** and ***C*** format and should be assigned in such a way that it will be easy to use the Sine Rule.

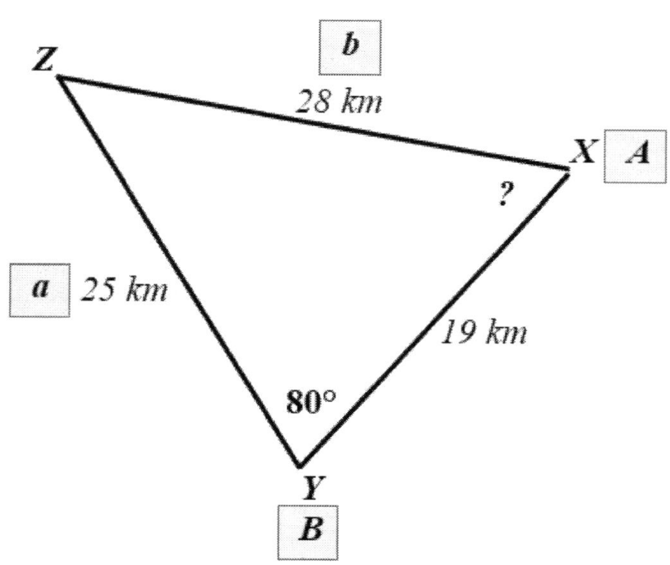

$$\frac{\sin A}{a} = \frac{\sin B}{b}$$

$$\sin A = \frac{\sin B}{b} \times a$$

$$A = \sin^{-1}\left[\frac{\sin B}{b} \times a\right]$$

$$A = \sin^{-1}\left[\frac{\sin 80}{28} \times 25\right]$$

$$A = 61.6^{\circ}$$

Hence, the bearing of ***Z*** can be obtained by comparing its angle at ***X*** and the north in an anticlockwise direction as shown below.

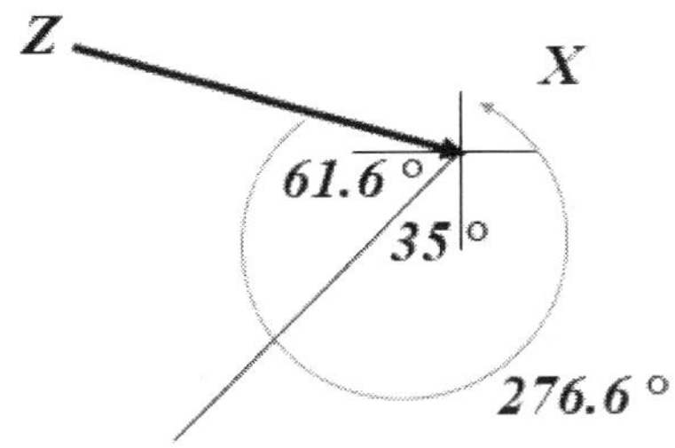

Therefore, the bearing of position ***Z*** from ***X*** is **<u>276.6°</u>**.

III. <u>COSINE RULE</u>

Remember, the conditions for using *COSINE* and *SINE RULEs* are **ALMOST** the same.

<u>Strategy for Cosine Rule</u>

(1) Triangle must be labelled even if they have letters.

- **ANGLES**: The ***ANGLEs*** are placed at the **vertices** of the triangle as ***A***, ***B*** and ***C*** in CAPITAL letters.

- **Lengths**: The lengths are placed ***OPPOSITES*** to the **Angles**.
  - Length ***a*** → opposite to Angle ***A***
  - Length ***b*** → opposite to Angle ***B***
  - Length ***c*** → opposite to Angle ***C***

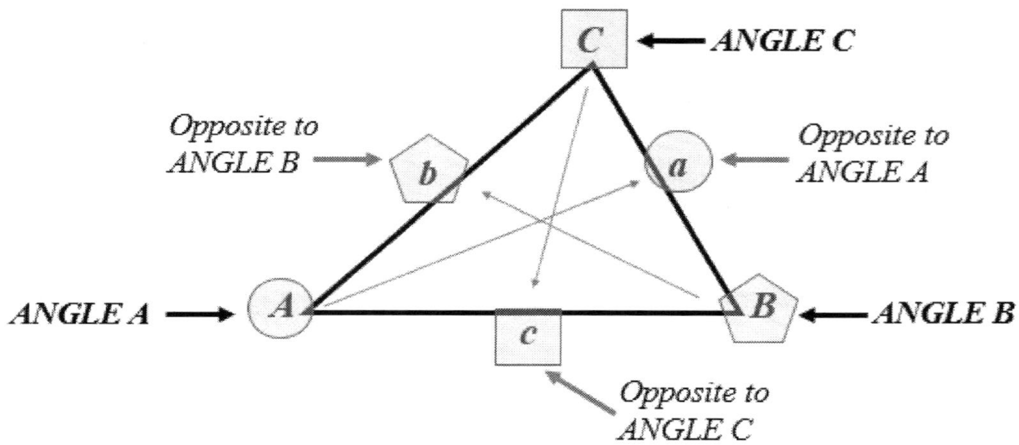

(2) ***REMEMBER***: For all values given and to use the ***Cosine rule***, an **ANGLE** needs to be **SANDWICHED** between TWO of the Side lengths.

That is;

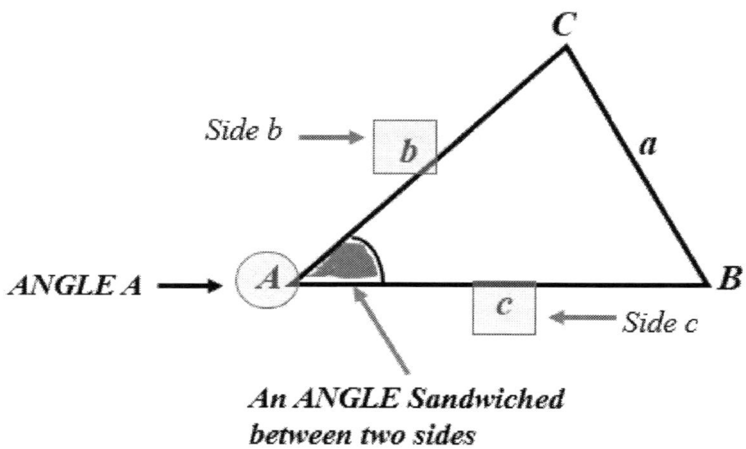

(3) ***The formula for Cosine Rule***:

$$\textit{For side length} \rightarrow a^2 = b^2 + c^2 - 2bc\cos A$$

$$\textit{For Angle} \rightarrow A = \cos^{-1}\left[\frac{b^2+c^2-a^2}{2bc}\right]$$

Questions

Q1. Find the length QR from the diagram below.
Note: *diagram not drawn to scale.*

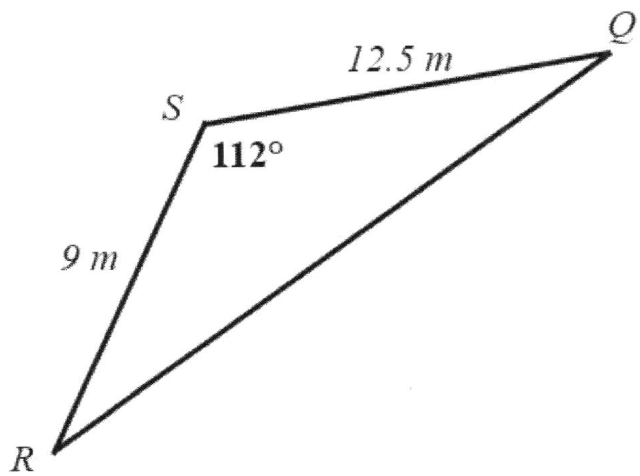

Solution:

The triangle needs to be labelled in ***A***, ***B*** and ***C*** format and use the Cosine rule to solve the question.

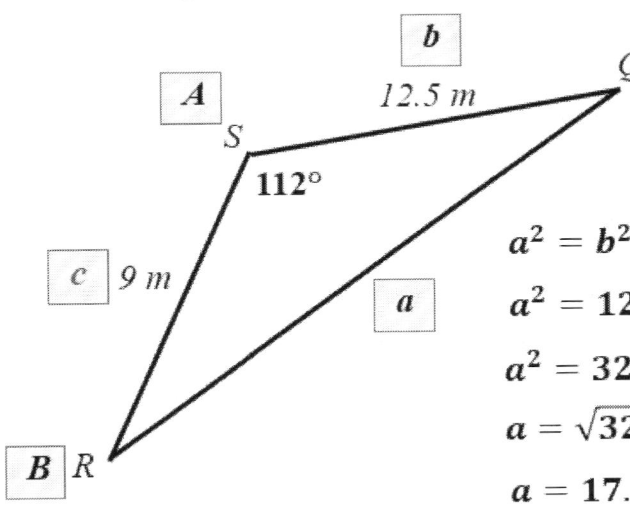

$$a^2 = b^2 + c^2 - 2bc\cos A$$

$$a^2 = 12.5^2 + 9^2 - 2 \times 12.5 \times 9 \times \cos 112$$

$$a^2 = 321.5$$

$$a = \sqrt{321.5}$$

$$a = 17.9\ m$$

Q2. The diagram below shows a triangle JKL representing a piece of plot to be used for farming. Calculate the angle JLK.

Note: *diagram not drawn to scale.*

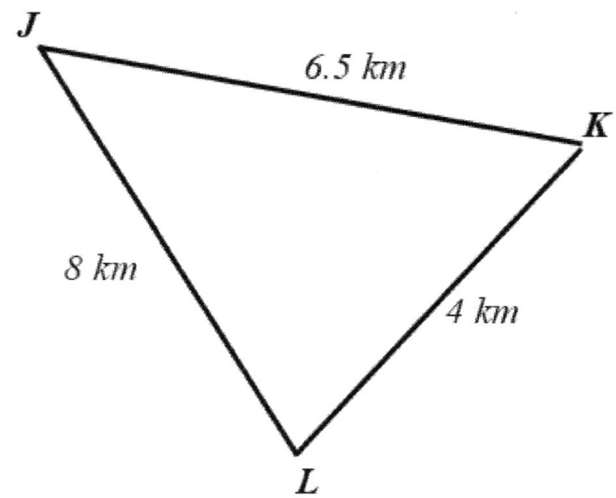

Solution:

The triangle needs to be labelled in ***A***, ***B*** and ***C*** format and use the Cosine rule to solve the question.

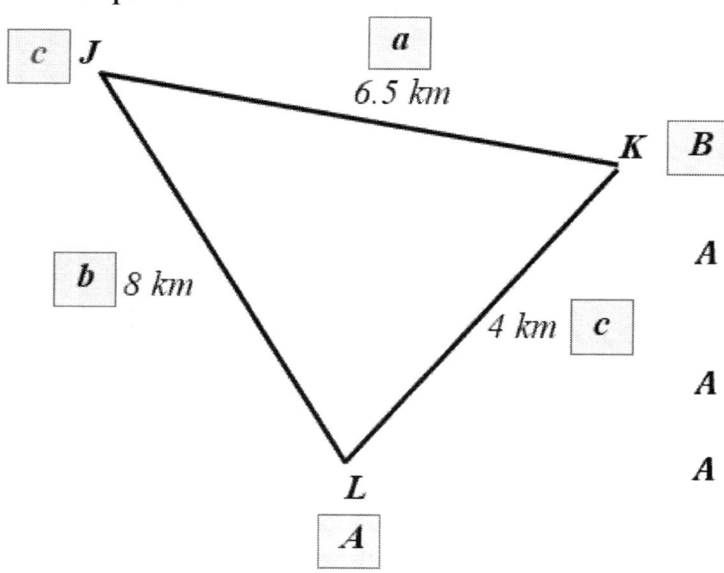

$$A = \cos^{-1}\left[\frac{b^2 + c^2 - a^2}{2bc}\right]$$

$$A = \cos^{-1}\left[\frac{8^2 + 4^2 - 6.5^2}{2 \times 8 \times 4}\right]$$

$$A = 53.9^\circ$$

Therefore, angle JLK is **53.9°.**

Q3. An ice company is trying to design the latest structure of their new ice cream product but realized that the side lengths are different. Nevertheless, they want to find out the area of the shaded region. Calculate the area of the shaded region and give your answer to one decimal place.

Note: *diagram not drawn to scale.*

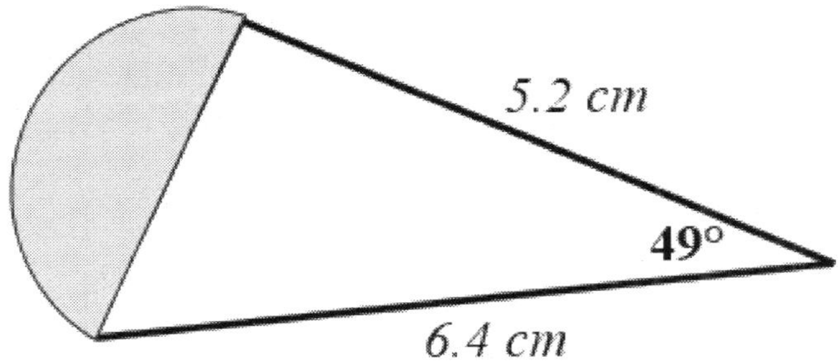

Solution:

The structure needs to be separated and then relabeled.
The triangle needs to be labelled in ***A***, ***B*** and ***C*** format and use the Cosine rule to solve the question.

The length BC will then be the diameter of the semi-circles which is twice the radius.

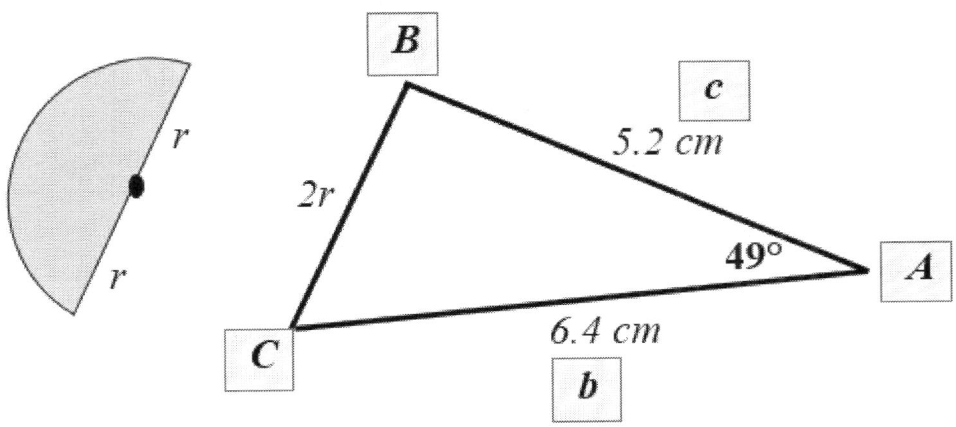

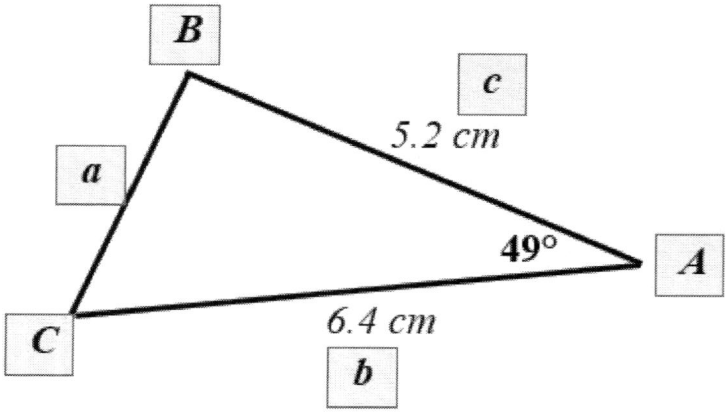

$$a^2 = b^2 + c^2 - 2bc \cos A$$

$$a^2 = 6.4^2 + 5.2^2 - 2 \times 6.4 \times 5.2 \times \cos 49$$

$$a^2 = 24.3$$

$$a = \sqrt{24.3}$$

$$a = 4.9\ cm$$

Hence, the diameter of the semi-circle is 4.9 cm. **Radius = 2.45 cm.**

$$Area\ of\ semi-circle = \frac{1}{2}\pi r^2 = \frac{1}{2} \times \pi \times 2.45^2 = 9.4\ cm^2$$

Therefore the shaded area is **$\underline{9.4\ cm^2}$**.

Q4. Calculate the length QR from the compound shape below.
Note: *diagram not drawn to scale.*

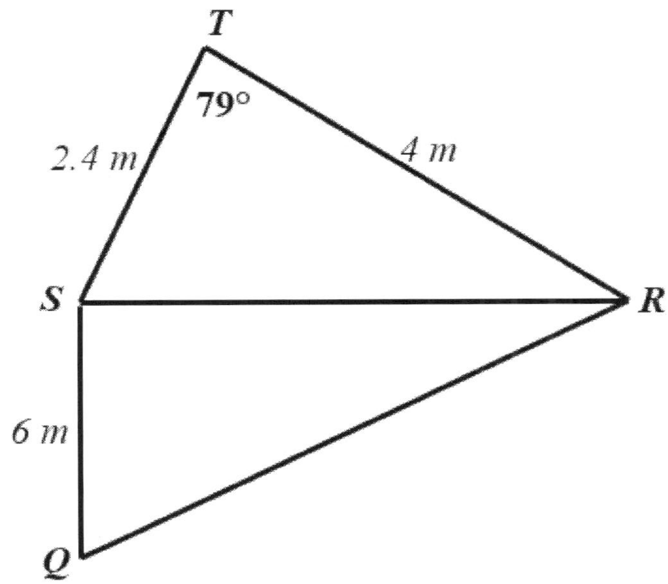

Solution:

The shape needs to be separated into two triangles and then relabeled.
The triangle needs to be labelled in ***A***, ***B*** and ***C*** format and use the Cosine rule to solve the length SR.
When SR is known, the length QR can be calculated using Pythagoras.

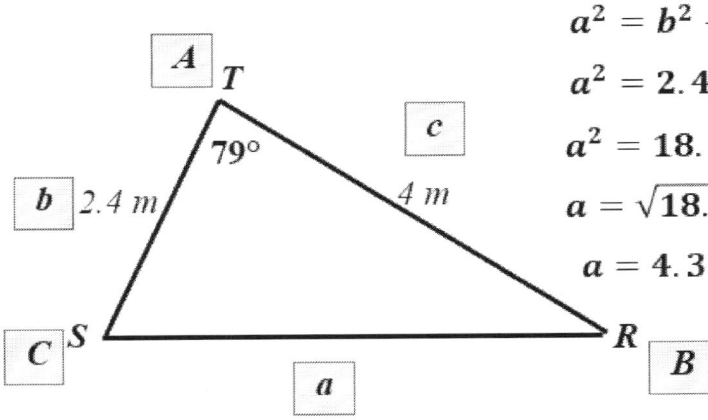

$$a^2 = b^2 + c^2 - 2bc\cos A$$

$$a^2 = 2.4^2 + 4^2 - 2 \times 2.4 \times 4 \times \cos 79$$

$$a^2 = 18.1$$

$$a = \sqrt{18.1}$$

$$a = 4.3\ m$$

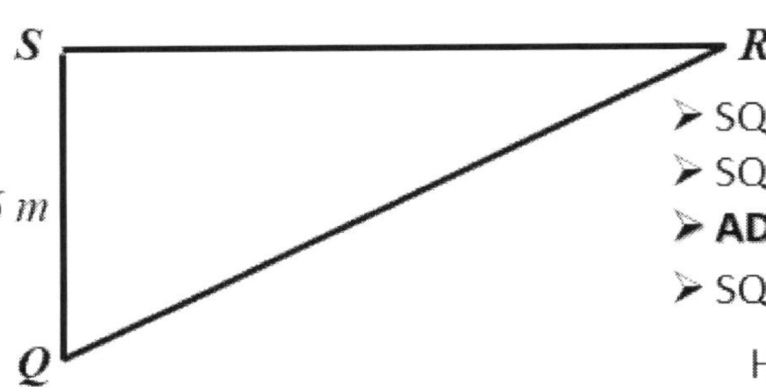

- SQUARE = $4.3^2 = 18.49$
- SQUARE = $6^2 = 36$
- **ADD** = $36 + 18.49 = 54.49$
- SQUARE ROOT = $\sqrt{54.49} = 7.4$

Hence, *length QR* = **<u>7.4 m</u>**

Q5. A delivery van set out from position K and moves north-west at a bearing of 300°. It reaches position L at a distance of 33 km and after delivery, it moves to position M at a bearing of 207°. If the van reaches position M at a distance of 42 km from L,

i. Calculate the distance between position M and K.
ii. From (i), what will happen if the van moves at a bearing of 200° from L to M. comment whether the distance between M and K will decrease or increase in that situation. You must show all your working.

Solution:

The information needs to be sketched into a suitable diagram that will enable the use of a mathematical model.

Note that the bearings at each location must be resolved and plotted into the diagram. That is;

Bearing 300° *Bearing 207°*

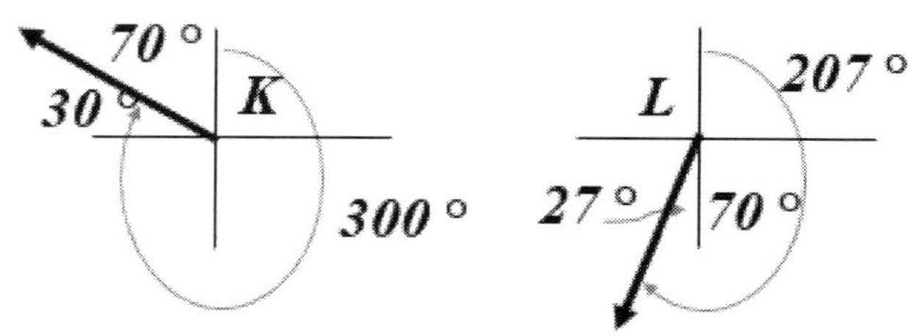

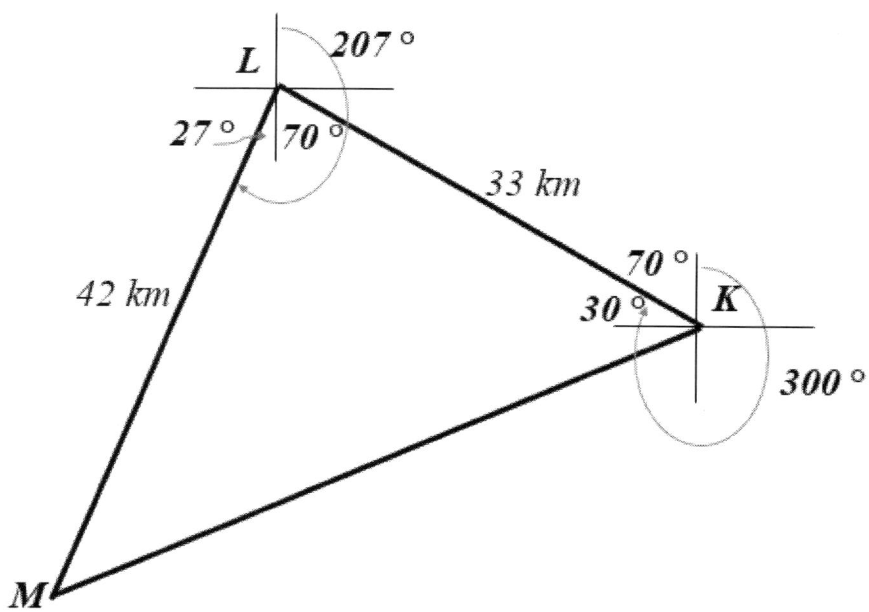

(i) This means that *Cosine* rule can be used to find the length *MK* as follows;

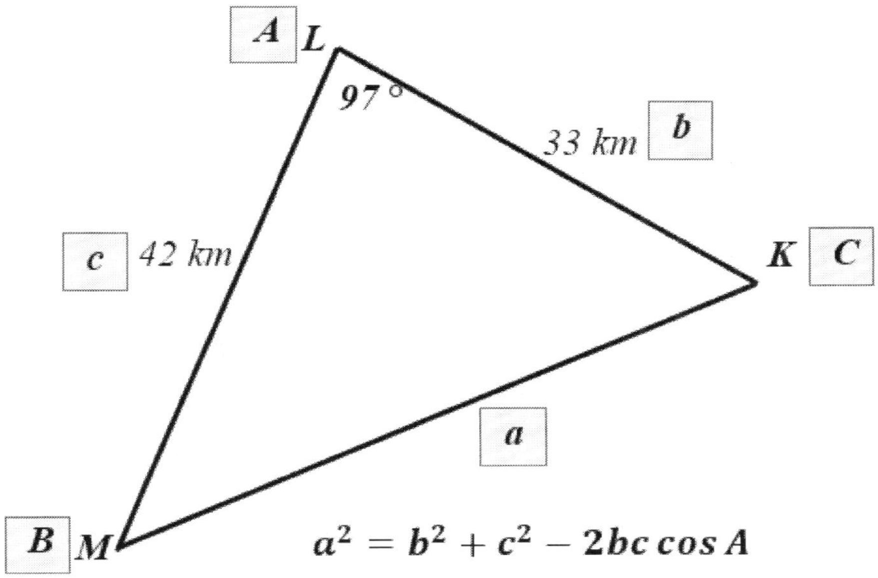

$$a^2 = b^2 + c^2 - 2bc\cos A$$

$$a^2 = 33^2 + 42^2 - 2 \times 33 \times 42 \times \cos 97$$

$$a^2 = 3190.82$$

$$a = \sqrt{3190.82}$$

$$a = 56.5\ km$$

(ii) If the van moves at a bearing of 200° from *L* to *M*, the angle at *L* will be reduced by 7°. Hence, the angle will be 90° and we can use Pythagoras theorem to solve the longest distance as follows;

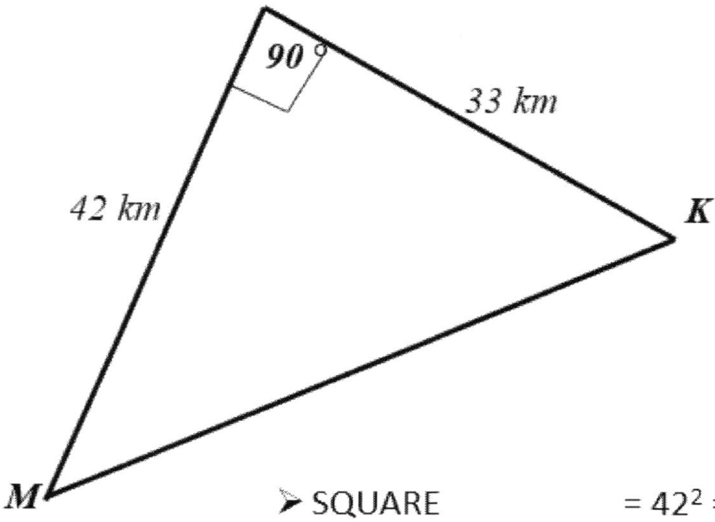

- SQUARE = $42^2 = 1764$
- SQUARE = $33^2 = 1089$
- **ADD** = $1764 + 1089 = 2853$
- SQUARE ROOT = $\sqrt{2853} = 53.4$

Hence, *length MK* = **53.4 km**

Comment: If the bearing is from *L* is reduced to 200°, the distance between *M* and *K* will decrease.

IV. AREA OF NON-RIGHT-ANGLED TRIANGLE

Remember, the **conditions** for finding the ***Area of Non-Right-Angled Triangle*** is similar to the *COSINE RULE* condition.

Strategy for Finding the Area of Non-Right-Angled Triangle

(1) Triangle must be labelled even if they have letters.

- **ANGLES**: The ***ANGLEs*** are placed at the **vertices** of the triangle as ***A***, ***B*** and ***C*** in CAPITAL letters.

- **Lengths**: The lengths are placed ***OPPOSITES*** to the **Angles**.
  - Length ***a*** → opposite to Angle ***A***

- Length $b \rightarrow$ opposite to Angle B
- Length $c \rightarrow$ opposite to Angle C

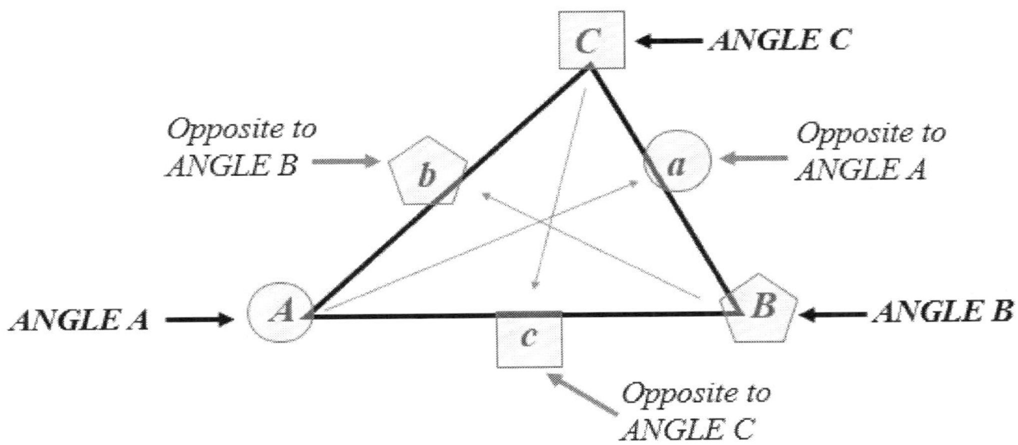

(2) ***REMEMBER***: For all values given and to find the ***AREA OF NON-RIGHT-ANGLED TRIANGLE***, an **ANGLE** needs to be **SANDWICHED** between TWO of the Side lengths.

That is;

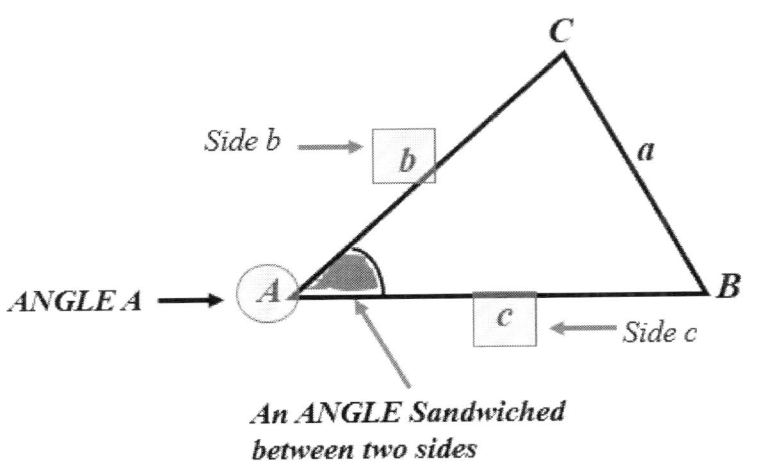

(3) ***The formula for finding the AREA OF NON-RIGHT-ANGLED triangle***:

$$\textit{Area of a triangle} \rightarrow \boldsymbol{Area} = \frac{1}{2} \times \boldsymbol{b} \times \boldsymbol{c} \times \sin \boldsymbol{A}$$

Note: the letters must not be the same. It must simply be half the product of the two side lengths times the Sine of the Sandwiched angle.

Questions

Q1. Find the area of the triangle below.

Note: *diagram not drawn to scale.*

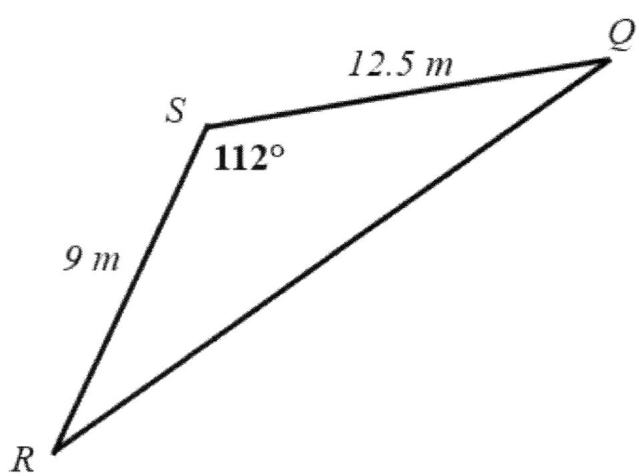

Solution:

The triangle needs to be labelled in the following format. A sandwiched angle ***A***, and two sides (i.e. ***b*** and ***c***) and simply use the formula to solve the question.

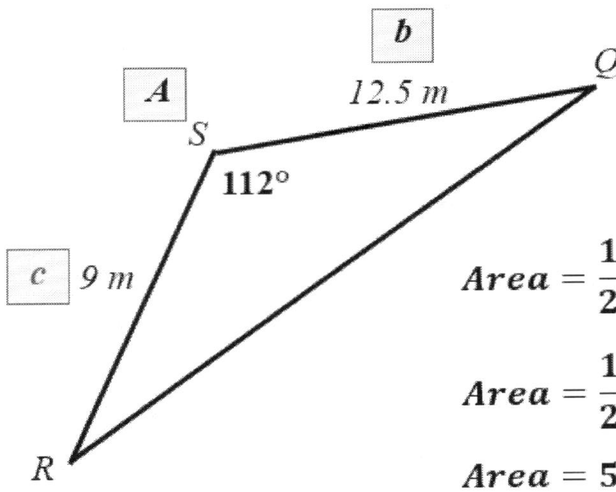

$$Area = \frac{1}{2} \times b \times c \times \sin A$$

$$Area = \frac{1}{2} \times 12.5 \times 9 \times \sin 112$$

$$Area = 52.2\ m^2$$

Q2. The triangle *XYZ* represent an area of 325000 cm^2 of a plot to be used as a playground. Find the length of the side *XZ* in meters.

Note: *diagram not drawn to scale.*

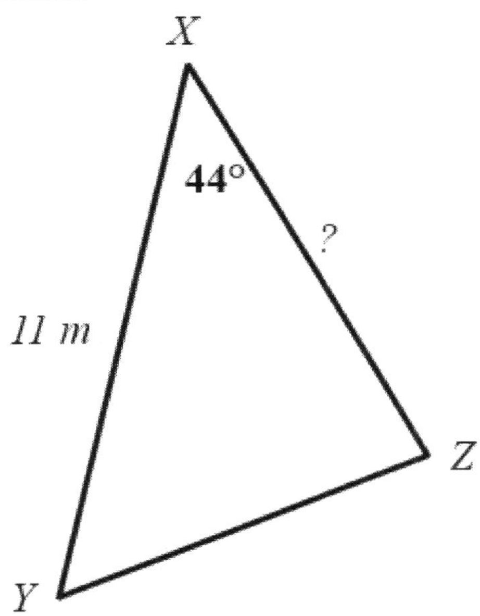

Solution:

The triangle needs to be labelled in the following format. A sandwiched angle ***A***, and two sides (i.e. ***b*** and ***c***) and simply use the formula to solve the question.

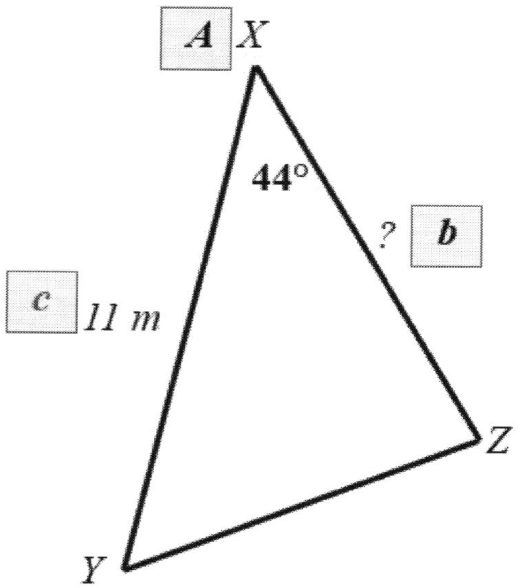

Meaning, b is needed.

From.

$$Ar = \frac{1}{2} \times b \times c \times \sin A$$

$$b = \frac{2 \times Ar}{c \times \sin A}$$

But.

$$325000\ cm^2 = 32.5\ m^2$$

$$b = \frac{2 \times 32.5}{11 \times \sin 44}$$

$$b = 8.5\ m$$

Q3. The diagram below shows a sector of a circle. Calculate the area of the shaded region.

Note: *diagram not drawn to scale.*

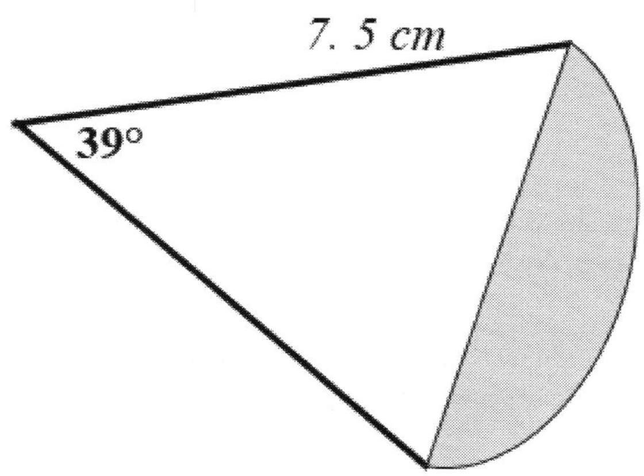

Solution:

First of all, the area of the whole sector needs to be calculated.
Secondly, the area of the non-right angled triangle needs to be calculated.
The **shaded area** is = **Area of the sector – Area of the triangle**.

Area of the sector

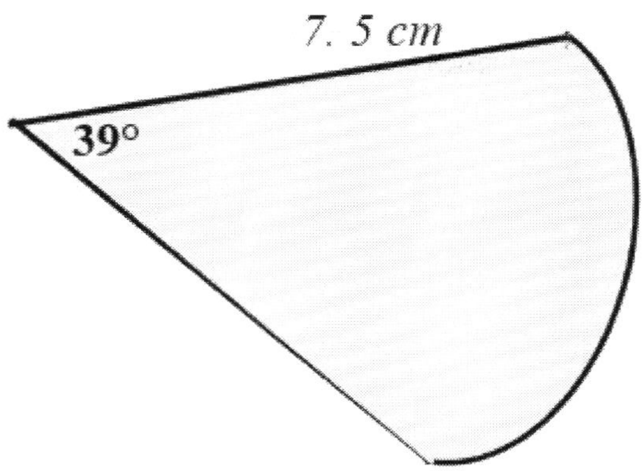

Area of sector is given by

$$Ar = \frac{Angle}{360} \times \pi \times r^2$$

R = 7.5 cm and angle = 39°

$$Ar = \frac{39}{360} \times \pi \times 7.5^2$$

$$Ar = 19.1\ cm^2$$

Area of the triangle

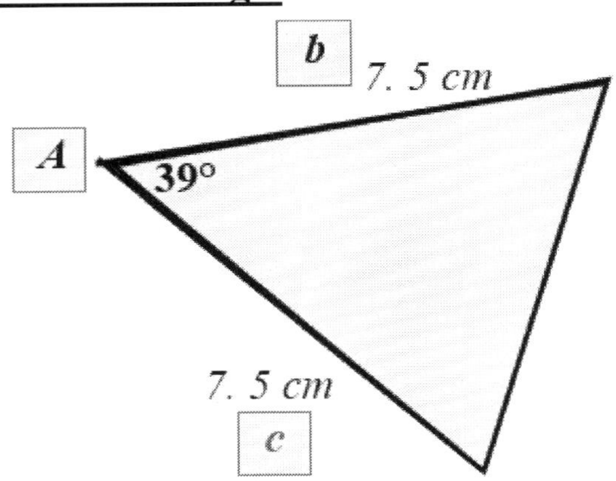

Area of the triangle is given by

$$Area = \frac{1}{2} \times b \times c \times \sin A$$

b is radius and ***c*** is radius of the sector

$$Area = \frac{1}{2} \times 7.5 \times 7.5 \times \sin 39$$

$$Area = 17.7\ cm^2$$

Therefore, the **shaded area** is = **19.1 – 17.7 =** **1.4 cm²**.

Q4. Calculate the area of the shaded region in the diagram below if the circumference of the circle is 8.8 cm.

Note: *diagram not drawn to scale.*

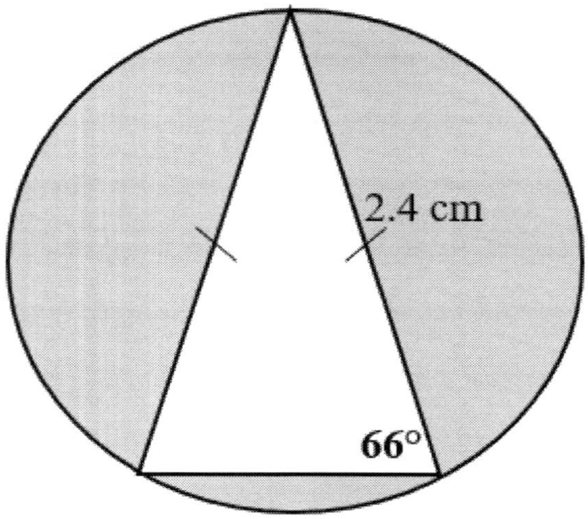

Solution:
First of all, the area of the circle needs to be calculated.
Secondly, the area of the triangle needs to be calculated.
The **shaded area** is = **Area of the circle – Area of the triangle**.

Area of the circle

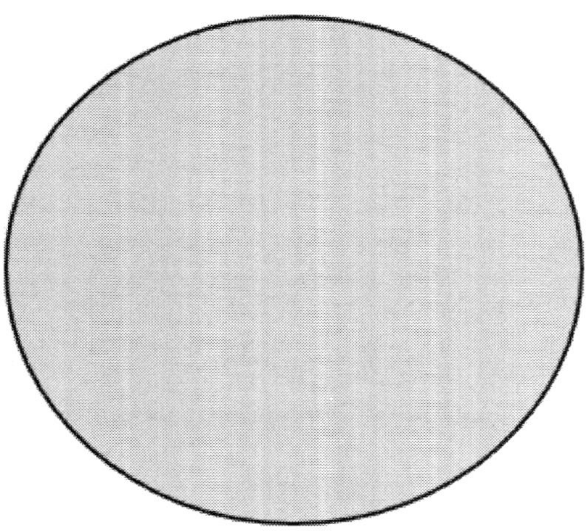

Area of circle is given by

$$A = \pi \times r^2$$

But, circumference (C) is given by

$$C = 2 \times \pi \times r$$

Meaning, the radius, r is given by

$$r = \frac{C}{2 \times \pi} = \frac{8.8}{2 \times \pi} = 1.4\ cm$$

Therefore,

$$A = \pi \times 1.4^2$$

$$A = 6.2\ cm^2$$

Area of the triangle
For the isosceles triangle, the two lengths are the same (i.e. 2.4 cm). It means the angles at each base is the same (i.e. 66° each).

The angle at the top of the triangle = $\mathbf{180 - [66 + 66] = 48°}$.
Resolving these values on the triangle gives;

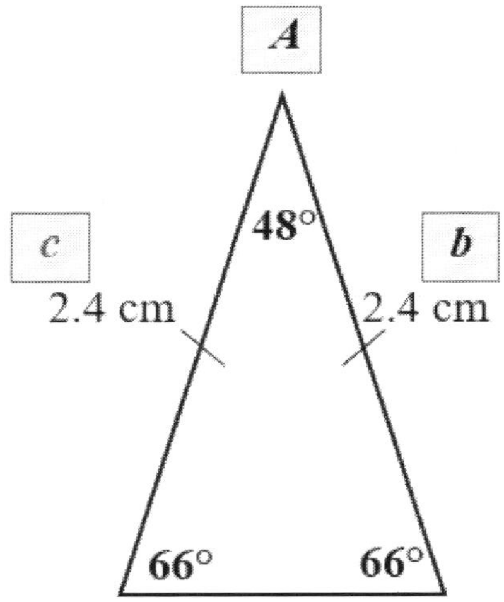

Area of the triangle is given by

$$Area = \frac{1}{2} \times b \times c \times \sin A$$

$$Area = \frac{1}{2} \times 2.4 \times 2.4 \times \sin 48$$

$$Area = 2.1\ cm^2$$

The **shaded area** is = **6.2 – 2.1 = 4.1 cm²**.

Q5. The shape *EFGH* is a trapezium that is made of two triangles. The line *HG* is parallel to line *EF*. Calculate the area of the triangle *EGH*.

Note: *diagram not drawn to scale.*

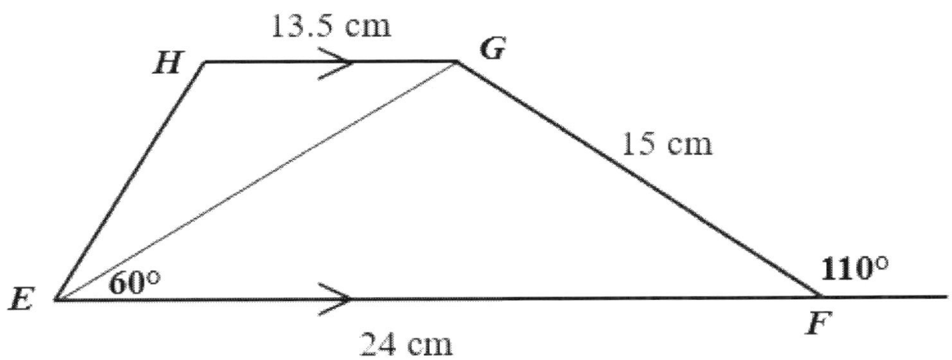

Solution:

To calculate the area of the triangle *EGH*, the length *EG* and the angle *EGH* are needed.

Finding the length EG

The angle on a straight line adds up to 180°. Hence, Angle EFG = **180° - 110° = 70°**.

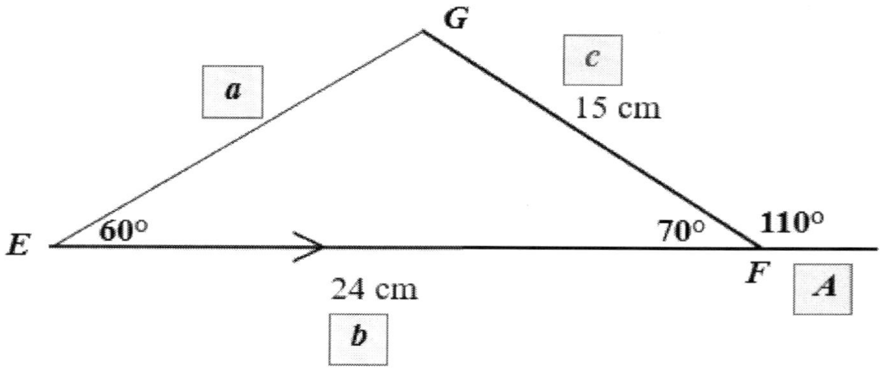

$$a^2 = b^2 + c^2 - 2bc\cos A$$

$$a^2 = 24^2 + 15^2 - 2 \times 24 \times 15 \times \cos 70$$

$$a^2 = 554.8$$

$$a = \sqrt{554.8}$$

$$a = 23.6\ cm$$

<u>Finding the area of the triangle EGH</u>

Angles *EGH* and *FEG* are ***ALTERNATE*** angles. Hence, ∠ ***EGG* = *FEG* = 60°**.

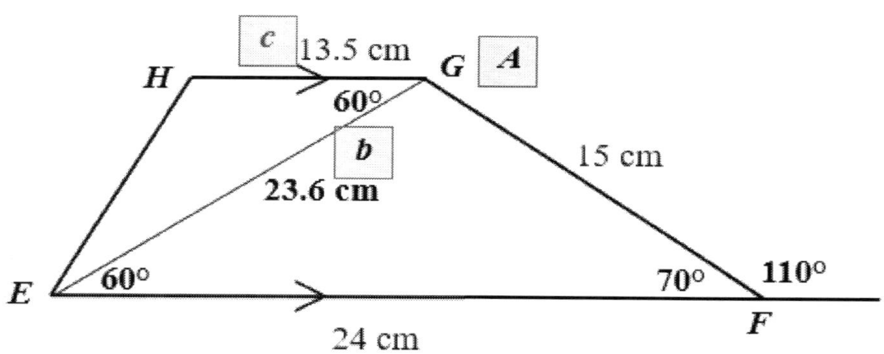

Area of the triangle EGH is given by

$$Area = \frac{1}{2} \times b \times c \times \sin A$$

$$Area = \frac{1}{2} \times 23.6 \times 13.5 \times \sin 60 = \mathbf{138\ cm^2}$$

V. TRIGONOMETRY EXACT ANGLES

Strategies

(1) Finding Exact values of **Sine 0°, 90°, 180°, 270° and 360° ($y = \sin x$)**.

- Create a graph plot of ***x***- and ***y***-axis having ***angles*** on the *x*-axis and amplitudes on the **y**-axis.

- Space your angles on the ***x***-axis evenly at 0, 90, 180, 270 and 360°. On the *y*-axis, keep the maximum height or amplitude at **+1** and the minimum to -**1**.

- Draw a sinusoidal curve starting from **ZERO on the *x*-axis and ZERO on the *y*-axis**.

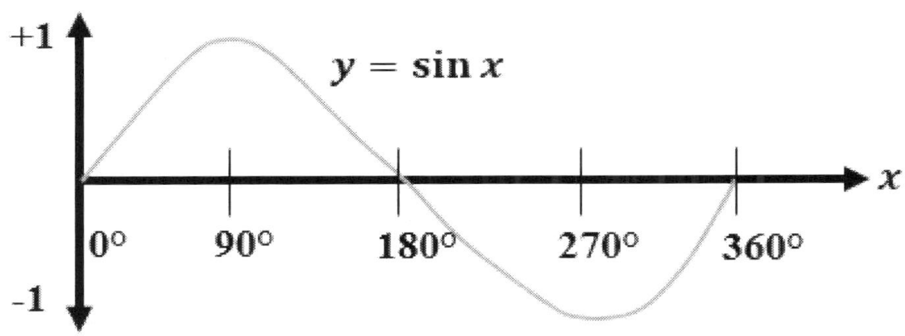

- From the graph, exact values of 0, 90, 180, 270 and 360° can be obtained without a calculator. Pick a value on the ***x-axis***, move up until it touches the curve and read off the corresponding value on the ***y-axis***.
  Example;
    - Sin **0°** → **0**.
    - Sin **90°** → **1**.
    - Sin **180°** → **0**.
    - Sin **270°** → **0**.
    - Sin **360°** → **0**.

(2) <u>Finding Exact values of **Cosine 0°, 90°, 180°, 270° and 360°** ($y = \cos x$)</u>.

- Create a graph plot of ***x***- and ***y***-axis having ***angles*** on the *x*-axis and amplitudes on the **y**-axis.

- Space your angles on the ***x***-axis evenly at 0, 90, 180, 270 and 360°. On the *y*-axis, keep the maximum height or amplitude at **+1** and the minimum to -**1**.

- Draw a sinusoidal curve starting from **ZERO on the *x*-axis but at the MAXIMUM amplitude of +1 on the *y*-axis** as shown below. It means the sinusoidal curve from the sine graph must be shifted by 90° to the left to create the cosine graph.

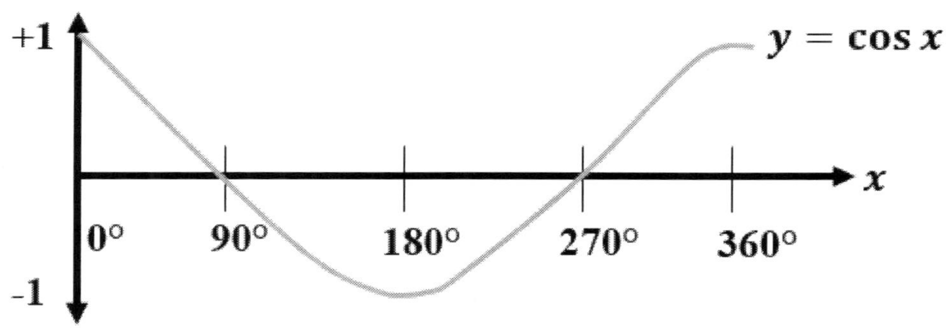

- From the graph, exact values of 0, 90, 180, 270 and 360° can be obtained without a calculator. Pick a value on the ***x-axis***, move up until it touches the curve and read off the corresponding value on the ***y-axis***.
Example;
  - Cos **0°** → **1**.
  - Cos 90° → **0**.
  - Cos **180°** → **-1**.
  - Cos **270°** → **0**.
  - Cos **360°** → **1**.

(3) <u>Finding Exact values of **Tangent 0°, 90°, 180°, 270° and 360°** ($y = \cos x$)</u>.

- Create a graph plot of ***x***- and *y*-axis having ***angles*** on the *x*-axis and amplitudes on the **y**-axis.

- Space your angles on the ***x***-axis evenly at 0, 90, 180, 270 and 360°. On the *y*-axis, keep the maximum height or amplitude at **+3** and the minimum to -**3**.

- Draw a straight perpendicular line at 90 and 270° that must extend to the level of the *y*-axis.

- Draw a curve starting from **ZERO on the *x*-axis and ZERO on the *y*-axis** as shown below. The curve must not touch the perpendicular line at the 90°.

- Draw another curve from the lower part of the perpendicular line at 90° which must not touch it. Extend this curve such that it passes through 180° horizontally and raises again towards 270°. Again, it must not touch the line at 270°. Lastly, draw the final curve from the lower part of the perpendicular line at 270° that must not touch it. Extend this curve such that it passes through 360° horizontally as shown below.

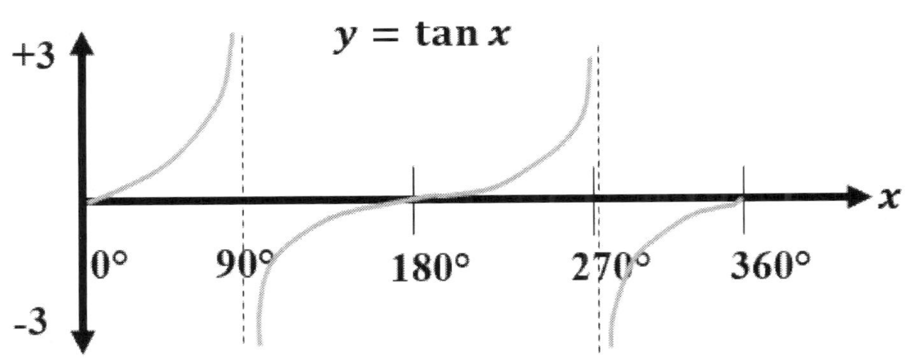

- **Note**: Tan **90°** and Tan **270°** cannot be obtained as shown on the graph.

- Apart from the above, all other values can be obtained without a calculator. Pick a value on the ***x-axis***, move up until it touches the curve and read off the corresponding value on the ***y-axis***.
  Example;
  - Tan **0°** → **0**.
  - Cos **180°** → **0**.

- Cos **360° → 0.**

(4) <u>Finding Exact values of **Sine, Cosine and Tan of 30°** and **60°**,</u>

- Start by drawing an equilateral triangle with side lengths of **2 units**. Each interior angle is 60°.

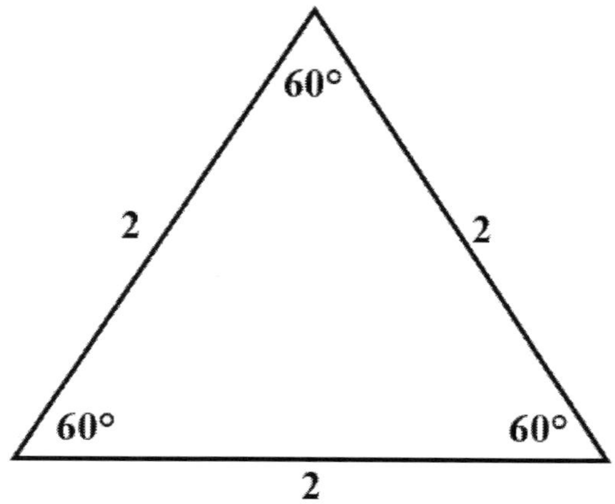

- Divide the triangle into ***two*** right-angled triangles. The top angle divides into **30°** each and the base length divided into **1 unit each**.

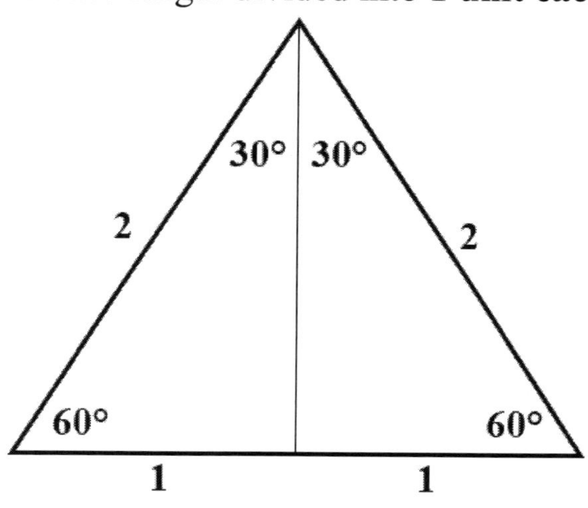

- Separate the triangles and use Pythagoras to solve the missing height as follows;

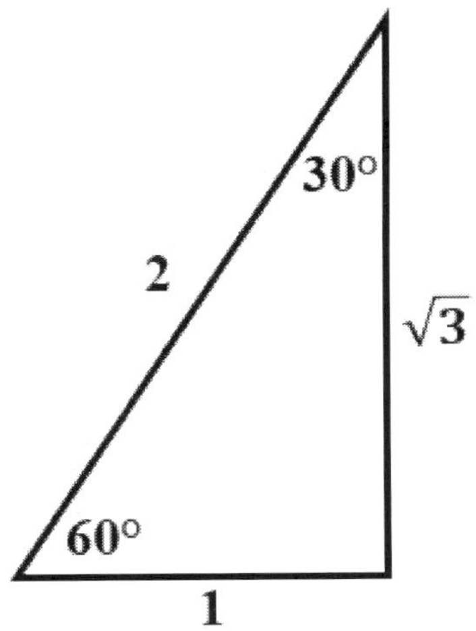

The height of the triangle is given by

- ➢ SQUARE = $2^2 = 4$
- ➢ SQUARE = $1^2 = 1$
- ➢ **SUBTRACT** = $4 - 1 = 3$
- ➢ SQUARE ROOT = $\sqrt{3}$

- Based on the angle in question the EXACT Values can be obtained;

<u>For example 60°</u>

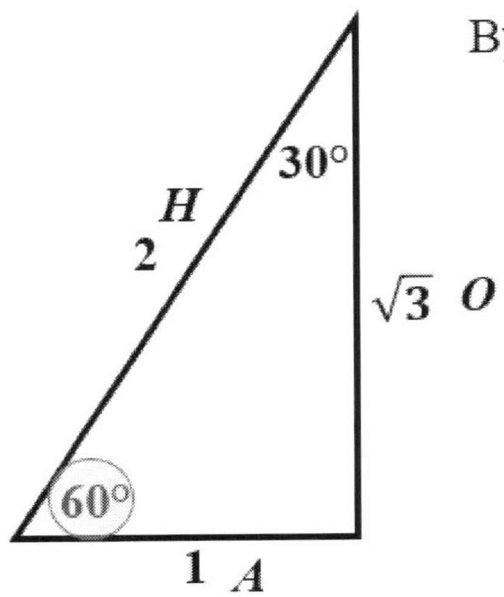

By using SOH CAH TOA

$$\cos \mathbf{60°} = \frac{A}{H} = \frac{1}{2} = 0.5$$

$$\sin \mathbf{60°} = \frac{O}{H} = \frac{\sqrt{3}}{2} = 0.866$$

$$\tan \mathbf{60°} = \frac{O}{A} = \frac{\sqrt{3}}{1} = \sqrt{3}$$

<u>For example 30°</u>

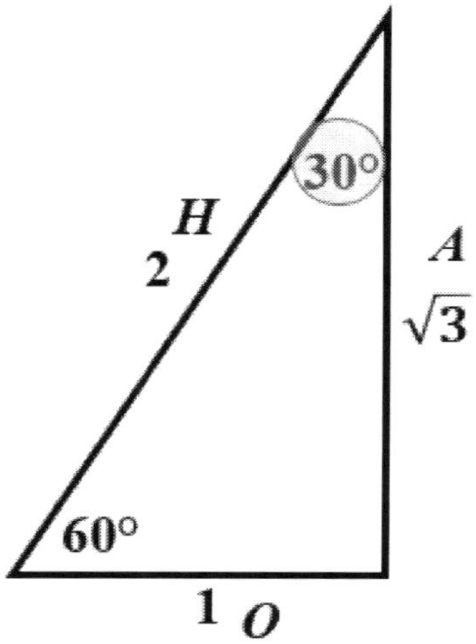

By using SOH CAH TOA

$$\cos 30° = \frac{A}{H} = \frac{\sqrt{3}}{2} = 0.866$$

$$\sin 30° = \frac{O}{H} = \frac{1}{2} = 0.5$$

$$\tan 30° = \frac{O}{A} = \frac{1}{\sqrt{3}} = \frac{\sqrt{3}}{3}$$

(5) <u>Finding Exact values of **Sine, Cosine and Tan of 45°**</u>

- Start by drawing a right-angled ***isosceles*** triangle having equal sides of1 units. That means, the interior angles at the opposite lengths will have 45° each as shown.

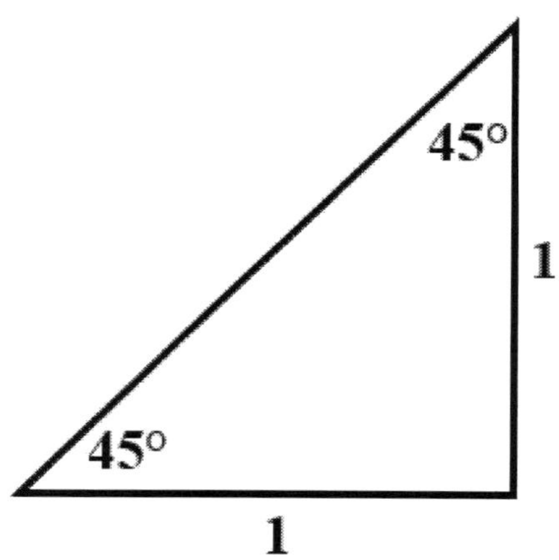

- Using Pythagoras, the longest length can be calculated as follows;
- Separate the triangles and use Pythagoras to solve the missing height as follows;

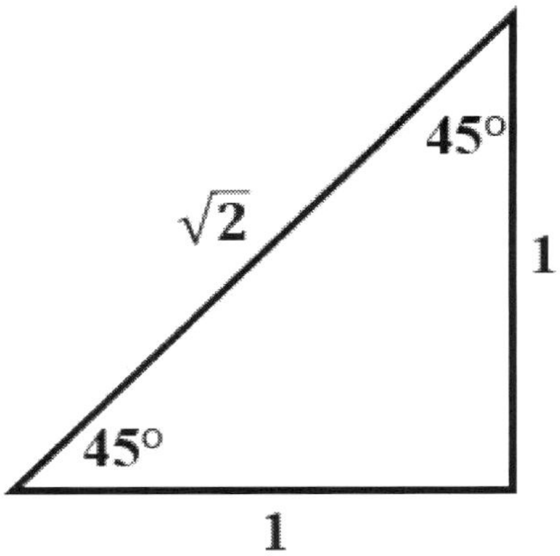

The longest side is given by

- ➢ SQUARE $= 1^2 = 1$
- ➢ SQUARE $= 1^2 = 1$
- ➢ **ADD** $= 1 + 1 = 2$
- ➢ SQUARE ROOT $= \sqrt{2}$

- EXACT Values of 45° can be obtained since each side is 45°;

For example 45°

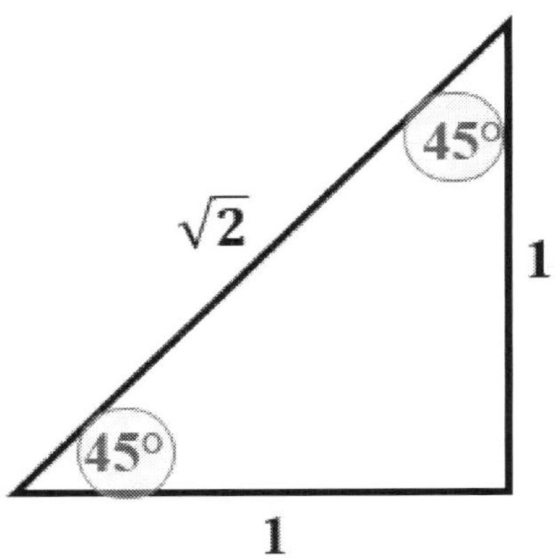

By using SOH CAH TOA

$$\cos \mathbf{45°} = \frac{A}{H} = \frac{1}{\sqrt{2}} = \frac{\sqrt{2}}{2}$$

$$\sin \mathbf{45°} = \frac{O}{H} = \frac{1}{\sqrt{2}} = \frac{\sqrt{2}}{2}$$

$$\tan \mathbf{45°} = \frac{O}{A} = \frac{1}{1} = 1$$

Questions

Q1. Find the solutions for the following equations of x from 0° and 360°;

i. $\sin x = 0.4.$

ii. $\sin x = 0.5.$

iii. $\sin x = 0.9.$

Solution:
To be able to solve the above equations, the sine graph above needs to be drawn.

i. $\sin x = 0.4$.

For this, go to the y-axis where $y = \mathbf{0.4}$ and draw a ***horizontal line*** across the curve as shown.

It can be seen that when you solve x,

$$x = \sin^{-1}(0.4) = \mathbf{24°}$$

This will be the first point on the graph.

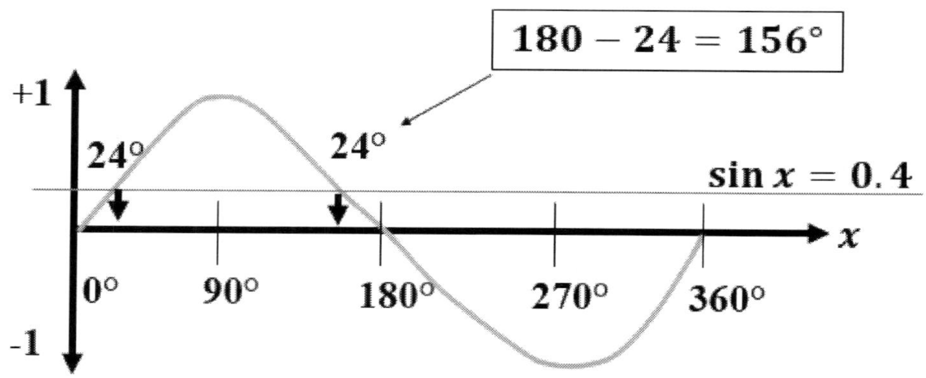

The other value is **156°**. That is subtracting 24° from the minimum value of 180° on the other side.
The two values must be symmetric on both sides of the curve.

ii. $\sin x = 0.5$.

Repeat the procedure in (i) and draw a horizontal line.
It can be seen that when you solve x,

$$x = \sin^{-1}(0.5) = \mathbf{30°}$$

This will be the first point on the graph.

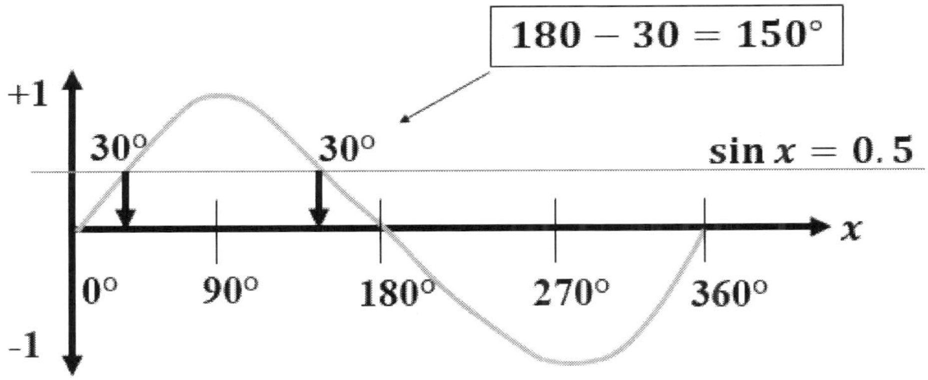

The other value is **150°**. That is subtracting 30° from the minimum value of 180° on the other side.

The two values must be symmetric on both sides of the curve.

iii. $\sin x = 0.9.$

Repeat the procedure in (*i*), (*ii*) and draw a horizontal line.
It can be seen that when you solve *x*,

$$x = \sin^{-1}(0.9) = 64.2°$$

This will be the first point on the graph.

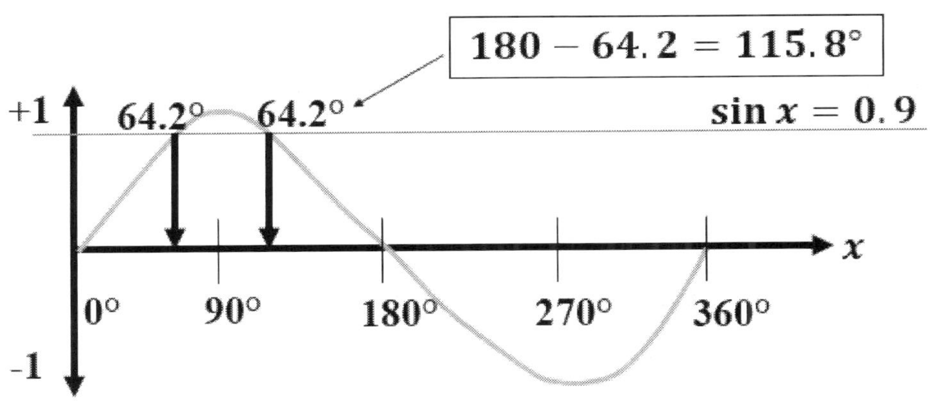

The other value is **115.8°**. That is subtracting 64.2° from the minimum value of 180° on the other side.

The two values must be symmetric on both sides of the curve.

Q2. Find the solutions for the following equations of x from 0° and 360°;

i. $\cos x = 0.4.$

ii. $\cos x = 0.5.$

iii. $\cos x = 0.9.$

<u>Solution:</u>

To be able to solve the above equations, the cos graph above needs to be drawn.

i. $\mathbf{\cos x = 0.4.}$

For this, go to the y-axis where y = **0.4** and draw a ***horizontal line*** across the curve as shown.

It can be seen that when you solve x,

$$x = \cos^{-1}(0.4) = \mathbf{66.4°}$$

This will be the first point on the graph.

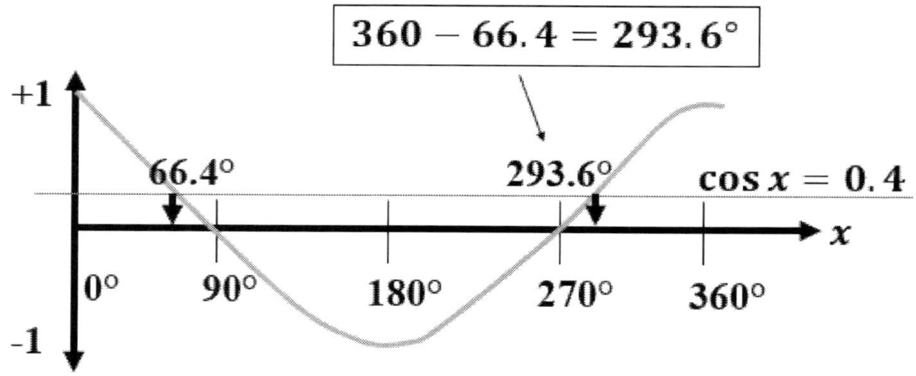

The other value is **293.6°**. That is subtracting 66.4° from the maximum value of 360°.

This is because the first angle of 66.4° is from the maximum point at 0°. It means that it is always 66.4° from the maximum point.

ii. $\mathbf{\cos x = 0.5.}$

Repeat the procedure in (*i*) and draw a horizontal line.

It can be seen that when you solve x,

$$x = \cos^{-1}(0.5) = \mathbf{60°}$$

This will be the first point on the graph.

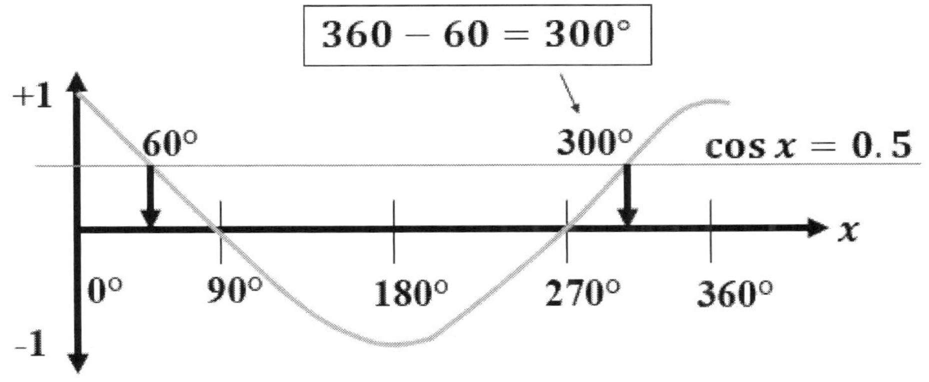

The other value is **300°**. That is subtracting 60° from the maximum value of 360°.

This is because the first angle of 60° is from the maximum point at 0°. It means that it is always 60° from the maximum point.

iii. $\cos x = 0.9$.
Repeat the procedure in (*i*), (*ii*) and draw a horizontal line.
It can be seen that when you solve x,

$$x = \cos^{-1}(0.9) = \mathbf{26°}$$

This will be the first point on the graph.

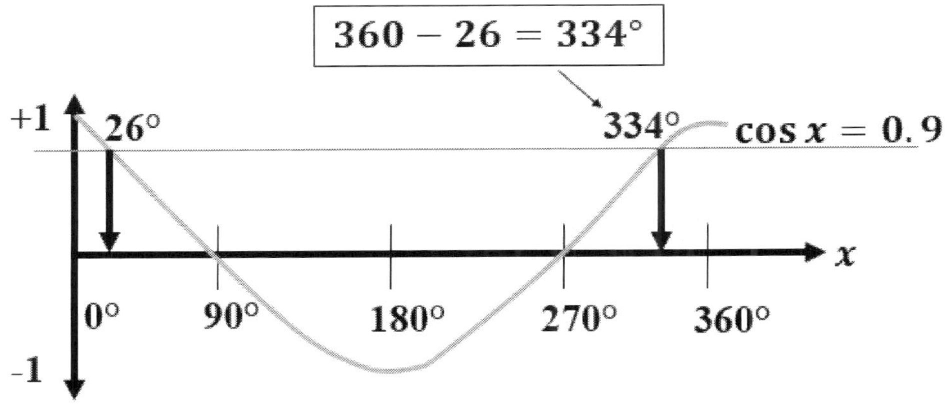

The other value is **334°**. That is subtracting 26° from the maximum value of 360°.

This is because the first angle of 26° is from the maximum point at 0°. It means that it is always 26° from the maximum point.

Q3. Find the exact values of the following equations of *x* from 0° and 360°;

i. $2\sin x = \sqrt{3}$

ii. $\frac{2}{\sqrt{3}}\cos x = 1$

iii. $\frac{3}{\sqrt{3}}\tan x = 1$

Solution:

To be able to solve the above equations, they must first be rearranged and then the triangle generated above to find the angles.

i. $\mathbf{2\sin x = \sqrt{3}}$

$\mathbf{\sin x} = \frac{\sqrt{3}}{2}$, From the triangle below;

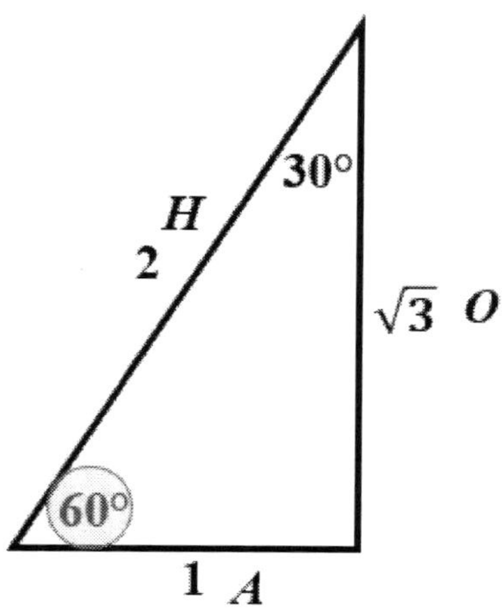

$$\sin 60° = \frac{O}{H} = \frac{\sqrt{3}}{2} = 0.866$$

$\underline{x = 60°}$

ii. $\frac{2}{\sqrt{3}}\cos x = 1$

$\cos x = \frac{\sqrt{3}}{2}$, From the triangle below;

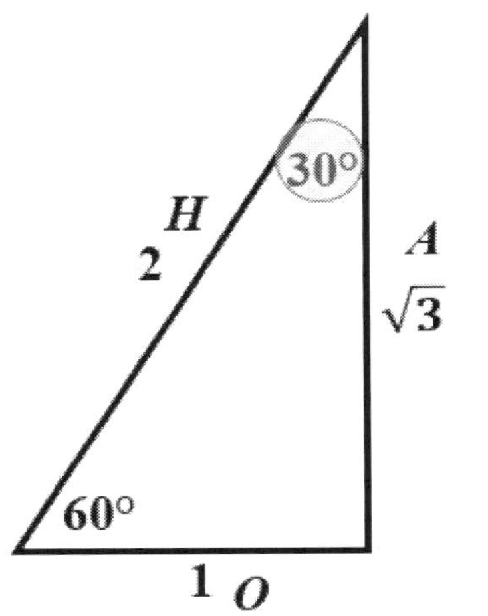

$$\cos 30° = \frac{A}{H} = \frac{\sqrt{3}}{2} = 0.866$$

$\underline{x = 30°}$

iv. $\frac{3}{\sqrt{3}}\tan x = 1$

$\tan x = \frac{\sqrt{3}}{3}$, From the triangle below;

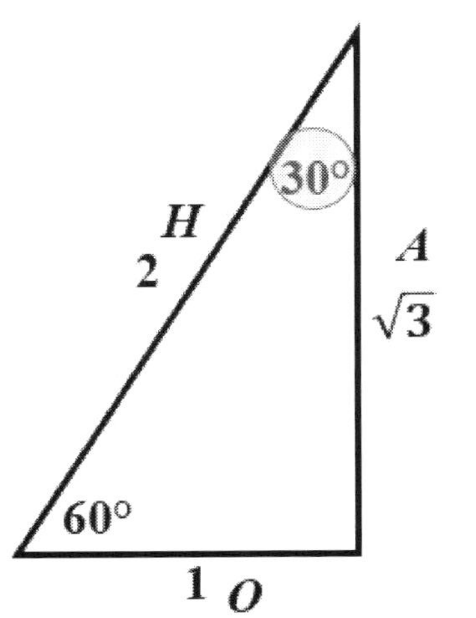

$$\tan 30° = \frac{O}{A} = \frac{1}{\sqrt{3}} = \frac{\sqrt{3}}{3}$$

$\underline{x = 30°}$

Q4. Find the exact values of x.

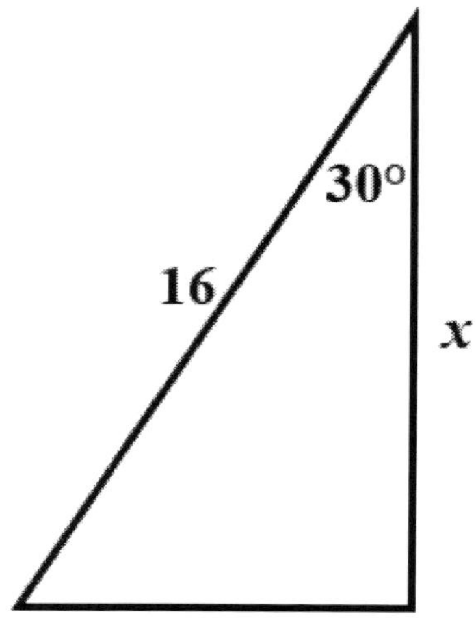

Solution:

Using SOH, CAH, TOA and comparing the triangle to the general triangle for trigonometry exact values the question can be solved by;

General Exact value triangle

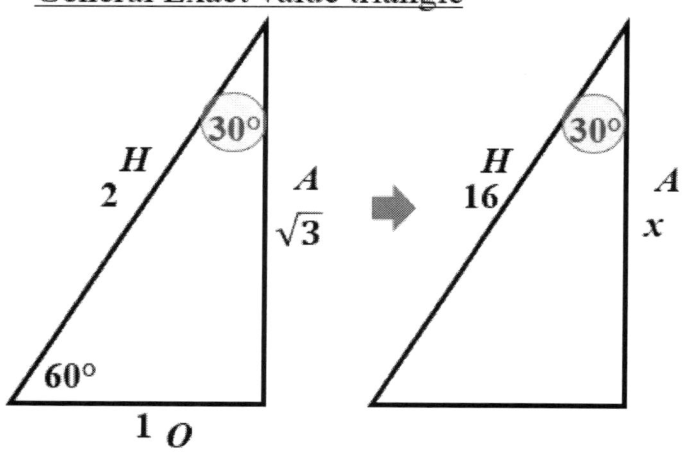

$$\cos 30° = \frac{A}{H} = \frac{\sqrt{3}}{2}$$

$$\frac{x}{16} = \frac{\sqrt{3}}{2}$$

$$x = \frac{16\sqrt{3}}{2}$$

$$x = 8\sqrt{3}$$

$\underline{x = 8\sqrt{3}}$

Q5. Find the exact values of x.

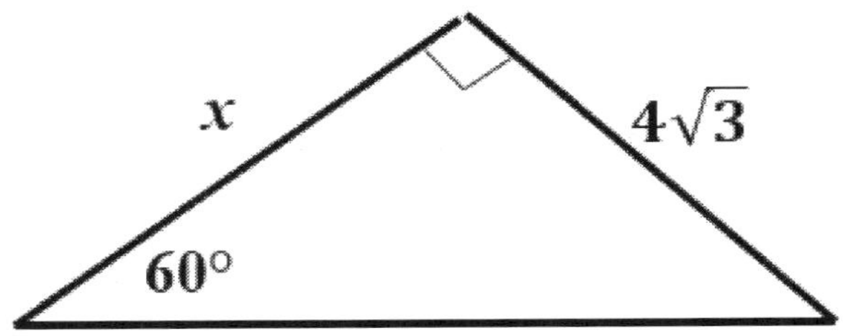

Solution:
Using SOH, CAH, TOA and comparing the triangle to the general triangle for trigonometry exact values the question can be solved by;

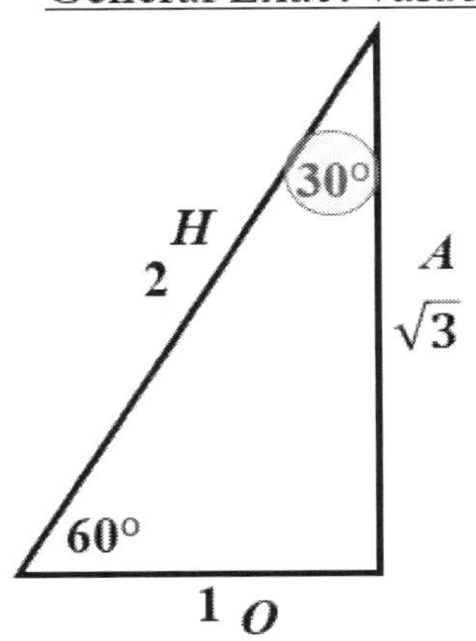

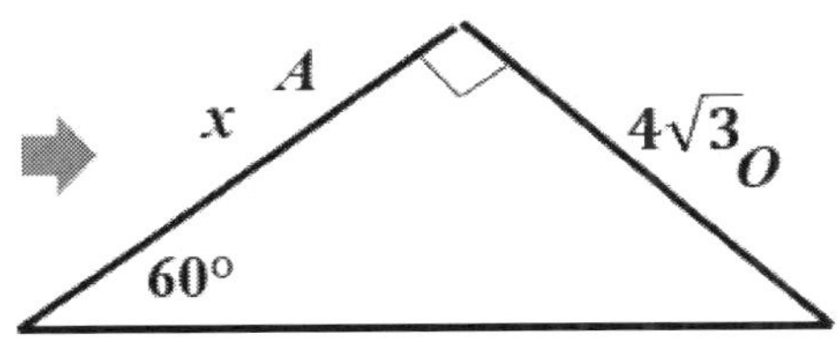

$$\tan 60° = \frac{O}{A} = \frac{\sqrt{3}}{1}$$

$$\frac{4\sqrt{3}}{x} = \frac{\sqrt{3}}{2}$$

$$x = \frac{2 \times 4\sqrt{3}}{\sqrt{3}}$$

$$x = 8$$

$\underline{x = 8}$

C. Geometry

The focus will be on the following topics;

I. Triangles
II. Rectangles, Rhombus and Parallelogram
III. Trapeziums
IV. Kites

I. Triangles

All the methods associated with Pythagoras, Trigonometry and most importantly Shapes must be applied in resolving any geometry questions.

Questions

Q1. Find the values of ***a*** and ***b***.
Note: *diagram not drawn to scale.*

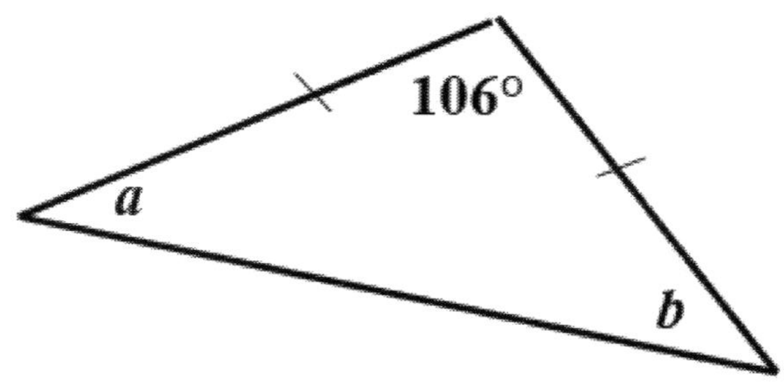

Solution:
The triangle is isosceles. Angle ***a*** and ***b*** must be equal because the side lengths are ***equal***;

$$a + b = 180 - 106 = 74$$

Since, a = b,

$$2a = 74$$
$$a = 37$$

Hence, ***a*** and ***b*** are all 37 each.

Q2. Calculate the angle ***a*** in the diagram shown below.
Note: *diagram not drawn to scale.*

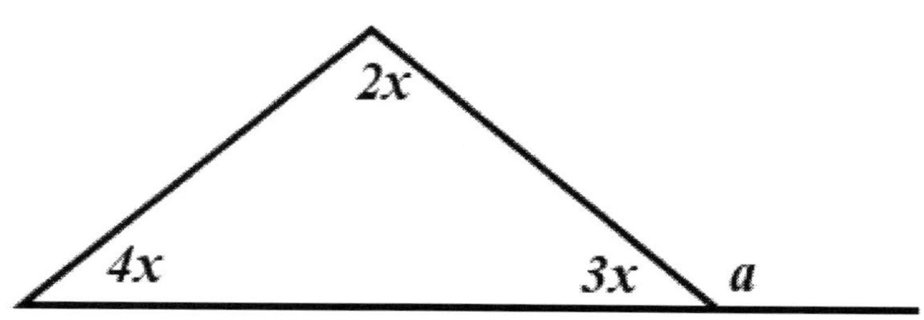

Solution:
The sum of angles in a triangle adds up to 180°. It means that;

$$4x + 2x + 3x = 180°$$
$$9x = 180°$$

$$x = 20°$$

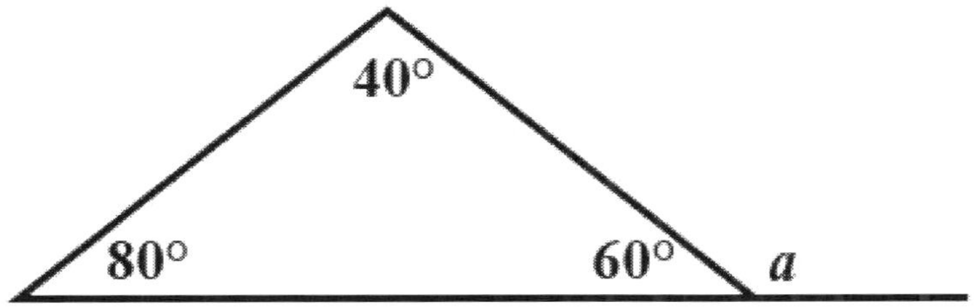

Hence, considering angles on a straight line,

$$a = 180° - 60° = 120°$$

Q3. Find the largest angle in the diagram below;
Note: *diagram not drawn to scale.*

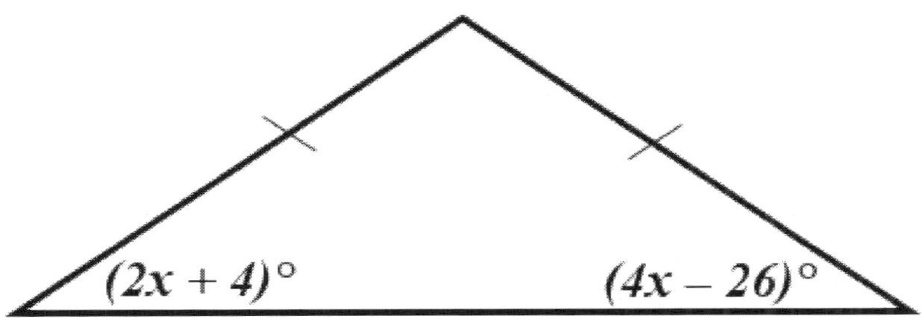

Solution:
The triangle is isosceles. Angle ***a*** and ***b*** must be equal because the side lengths are ***equal***;

$$2x + 4 = 4x - 26$$
$$26 + 4 = 4x - 2x$$
$$30 = 2x$$
$$x = 15°$$

The value of ***x*** can be inserted into the expressions at the isosceles angles and the other angle can be resolved by considering that angle within a triangle adds up to 180°,

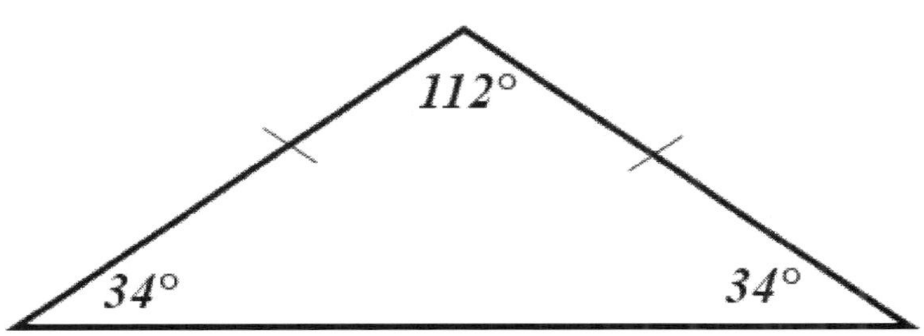

Hence, the largest angle is **112°**.

Q4. Calculate one side length of the triangle in the diagram below if the perimeter of the triangle is 87 cm.
Note: *diagram not drawn to scale.*

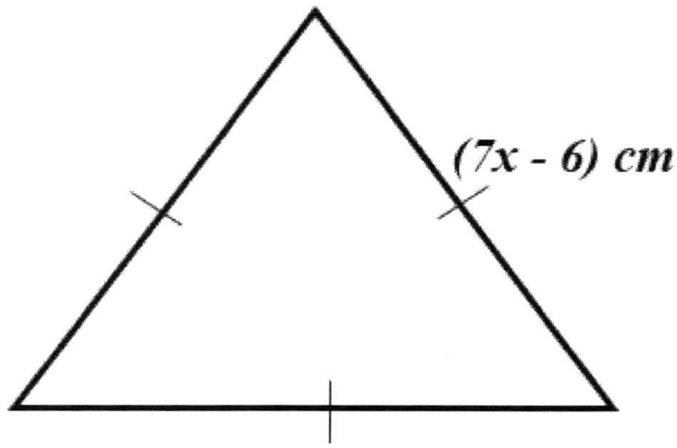

Solution:
The triangle is equilateral. All side lengths are ***equal***;

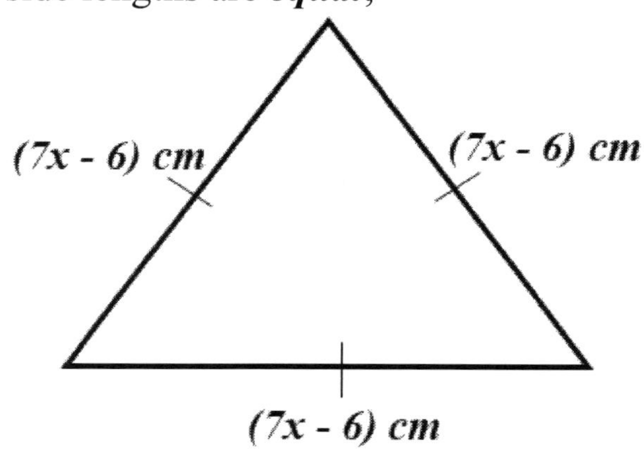

Hence, the perimeter is given by;

$$3(7x - 6) = 87$$
$$21x - 18 = 87$$
$$21x = 105$$
$$x = 5$$

Hence, each side has a length $= 7 \times 5 - 6 = 29$ cm.

Q5. Calculate the base length, x, of the triangle below if the area of the shaded region is 105000 cm^2.

Note: *diagram not drawn to scale.*

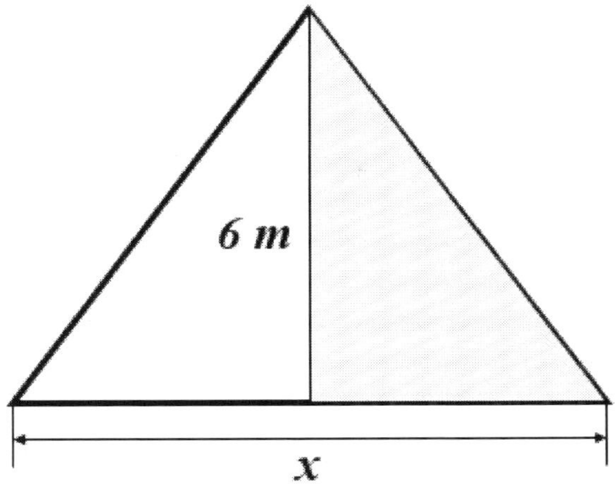

Solution:

The base length of the shaded triangle can be obtained and doubled to find x.

Area of shaded region;

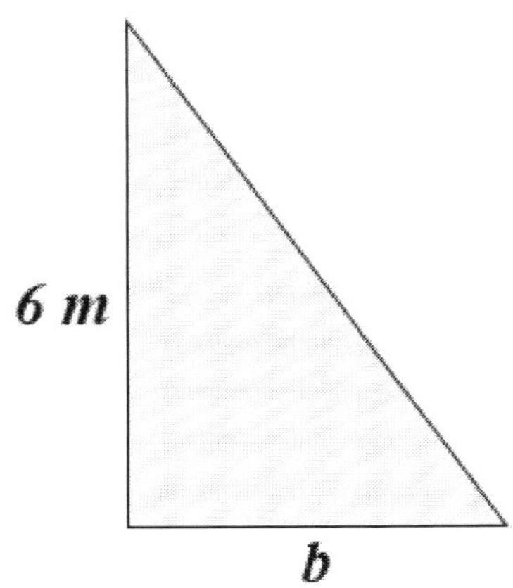

The area ($105000\ cm^2 = 10.5\ m^2$) is given by;

$$\frac{1}{2} \times b \times h = 10.5$$

$$b = \frac{2 \times 10.5}{h} = \frac{2 \times 10.5}{6} = 3.5\ m$$

Hence, base length, x, = $\mathbf{2 \times 3.5 = 7}$ **m**.

II. Rectangles, Rhombus and Parallelogram

All the basic rules associated with rectangles, rhombus and parallelograms must be applied in resolving any of their geometry questions. It is essential to learn them before going through the questions.

Q1. Calculate the value of x in the diagram below.
Note: *diagram not drawn to scale.*

Solution:

For rectangles, the widths are the same on both sides.
Hence,

$$4x - 8 = 2x + 28$$
$$4x - 2x = 28 + 8$$
$$2x = 36$$
$$x = 18$$

Q2. Calculate the area of the shaded region if the perimeter of the rectangle is 320 cm.
Note: *diagram not drawn to scale.*

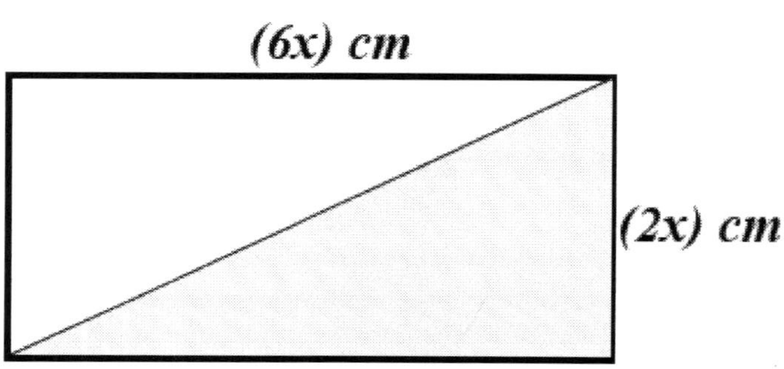

Solution:

Considering the perimeter of the rectangles, all the sides must be added and equated to the perimeter.
That is;

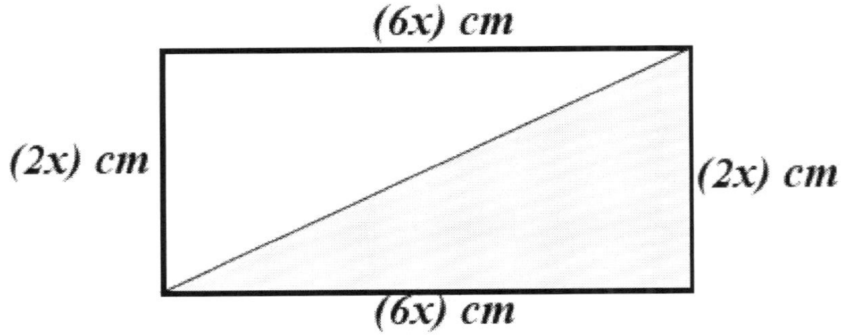

$$2(6x) + 2(2x) = 320$$
$$16x = 320$$
$$x = 20$$

It means,

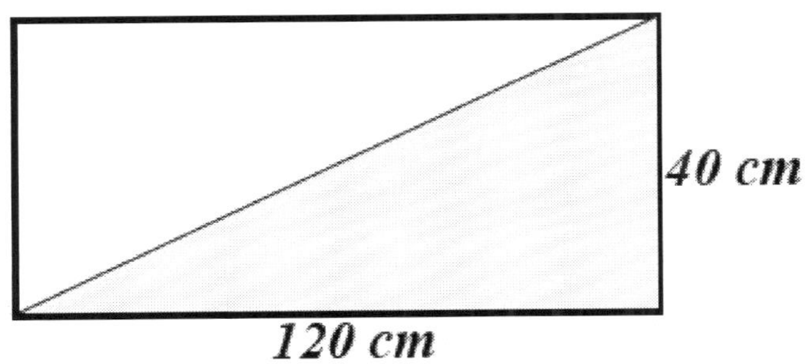

Therefore, the $\boldsymbol{Area\ of\ the\ triangle} = \frac{1}{2}bh = \frac{1}{2} \times 40 \times 120 = 2400\ cm^2$

The area of the shaded region = **2400 cm^2**.

Q3. Calculate the largest angle in the diagram below.
Note: *diagram not drawn to scale.*

Solution:
Note that the angles at the opposite side of the quadrilateral above are ***equal***.

$$2x + 30 = 4x$$
$$30 = 4x - 2x$$
$$30 = 2x$$
$$x = 15$$

It means the largest angles are $\mathbf{8 \times 15 = 120^\circ}$ each.

Q4. Find the value of x in the diagram below.

Note: *diagram not drawn to scale.*

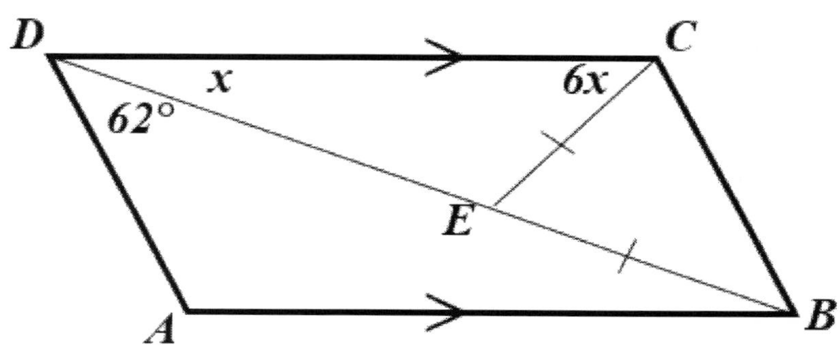

Solution:
The question can be solved in the following order;

(a) Angle $ADB = EBC$, because the two angles are ***ALTERNATE*** in a **parallel line**.

Hence, **∠ABC = 62°.**

(b) Since, $EC = EB$, **∠EBC = ∠ECB = 62°.**

It means, ∠**CEB = 180 – (62°+ 62°) = 56°.**

(c) Therefore, ∠**DEC = 180 – 56 = 124°**

The diagram now becomes;

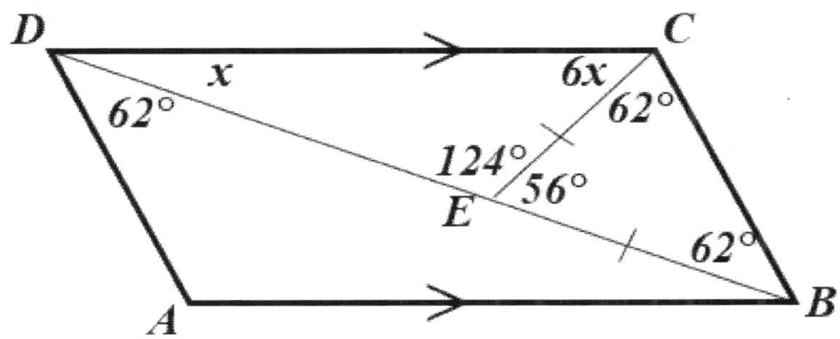

(d) All interior angles from triangle ***DEC*** must add up to 180°.

$$x + 6x + 124° = 180°$$
$$7x = 180 - 124$$
$$7x = 56$$
$$x = 8$$

Q5. Calculate the area of the shaded region if the perimeter of the rectangle is 36 cm.
Note: *diagram not drawn to scale.*

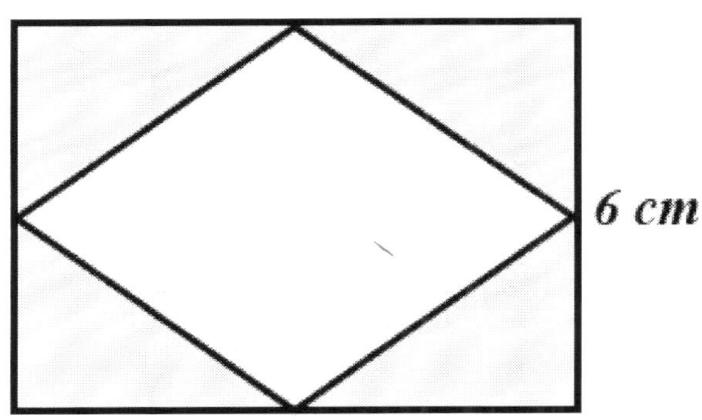

Solution:
First of all, the area of the rectangle needs to be calculated.
Then subtract the area of the rhombus from the area of the rectangle.
That is,
the **shaded area** is = **Area of the rectangle – Area of the rhombus**.

Finding the Area of rectangle

(a) If the length of the rectangle is x, then the perimeter will be given by;

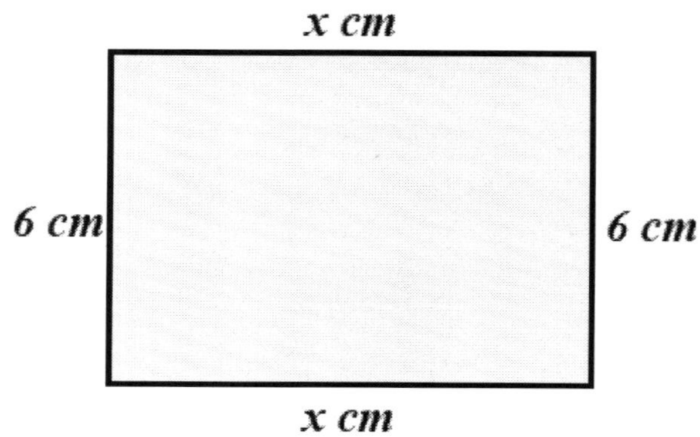

$$2x + 12 = 36$$
$$2x = 24$$
$$x = 12$$

Therefore, the $\boldsymbol{Area\ of\ the\ rectangle} = \mathbf{L \times W = 12 \times 6 = 72\ cm^2}$

Finding the Area of the rhombus

(a) Consider the complete rhombus as two triangles.

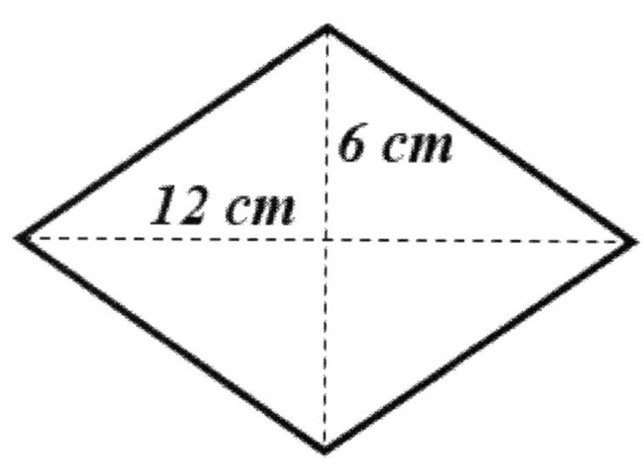

The two areas of the triangles can be added into one big area for the rhombus as follows;

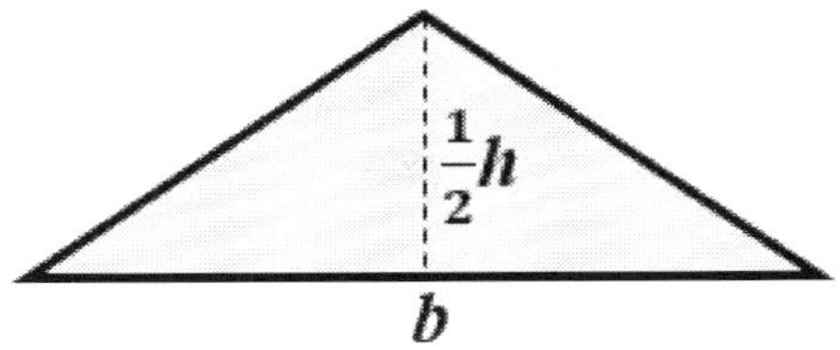

$$A_1 = \frac{1}{2} \times b \times \frac{1}{2}h$$

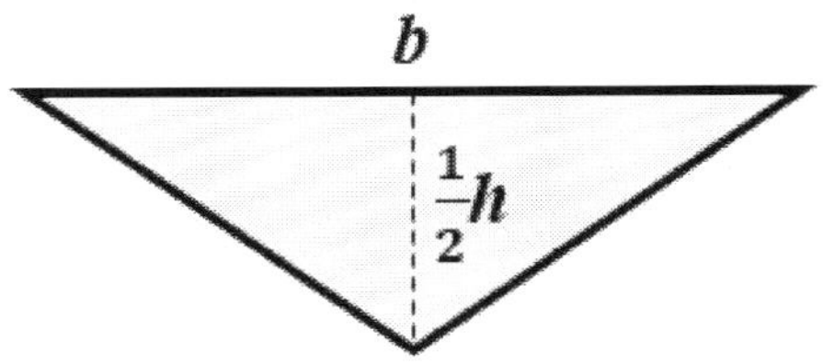

$$A_2 = \frac{1}{2} \times b \times \frac{1}{2}h$$

$$\textbf{\textit{Area of the rhombus}} = A_1 + A_{12} = \frac{1}{2} \times b \times \frac{1}{2}h + \frac{1}{2} \times b \times \frac{1}{2}h$$

$$= \frac{1}{4}bh + \frac{1}{4}bh$$

$$= \frac{1}{2}bh$$

Therefore, the $\textbf{\textit{Area of the rhombus}} = \frac{1}{2}bh = \frac{1}{2} \times 12 \times 6 = 36\ cm^2$

Hence, the **shaded area** is = **72 – 36 = 36 <u>cm</u>^{2}**.

III. <u>Trapeziums</u>

All the basic rules associated with trapeziums must be applied in resolving any of its geometry questions. It is essential to learn them before going through the questions.

Q1. Calculate the area of the diagram below.
Note: *diagram not drawn to scale.*

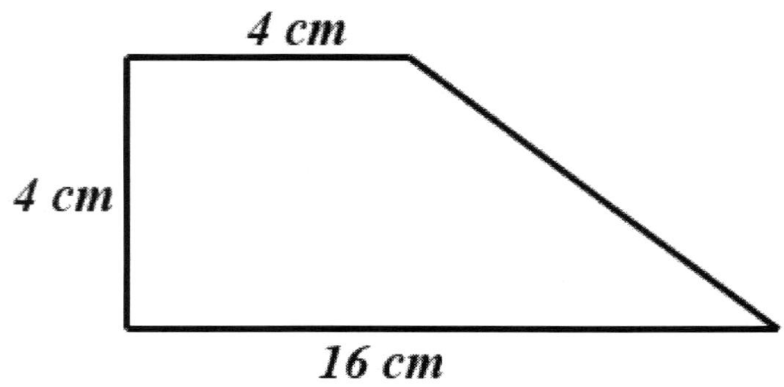

Solution:

The area of a trapezium is given by.

$$A = \frac{1}{2}(a + b)h$$

a = 4 cm, b = 16 and h = 4 cm.

$$A = \frac{1}{2}(4 + 16)4$$

$$A = 40\ cm^2$$

Q2. Find x if the area of the diagram below is 50 cm^2.
Note: *diagram not drawn to scale.*

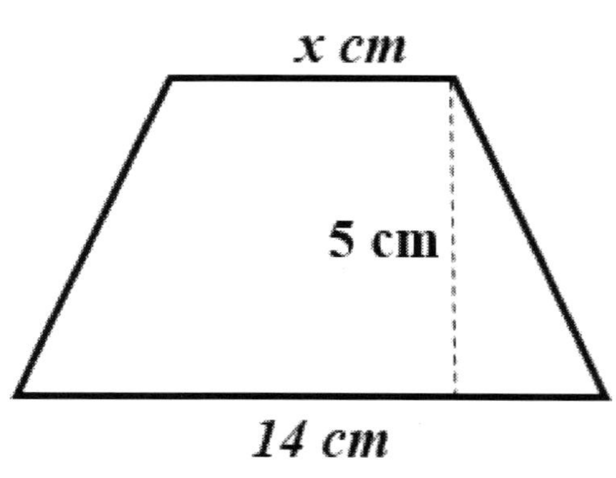

Solution:

The area of a trapezium is given by.

$$A = \frac{1}{2}(a + b)h$$

$a = x$ cm, b = 14 a, h = 5 cm and A = 50 cm^2.

$$a = \frac{2A}{h} - b$$

$$a = \frac{2 \times 50}{5} - 14$$

$$a = 6\ cm$$

Q3. Calculate the value of x if the areas of the trapezium and circle are 50 cm^2 and 12.6 cm^2, respectively.
Note: *diagram not drawn to scale.*

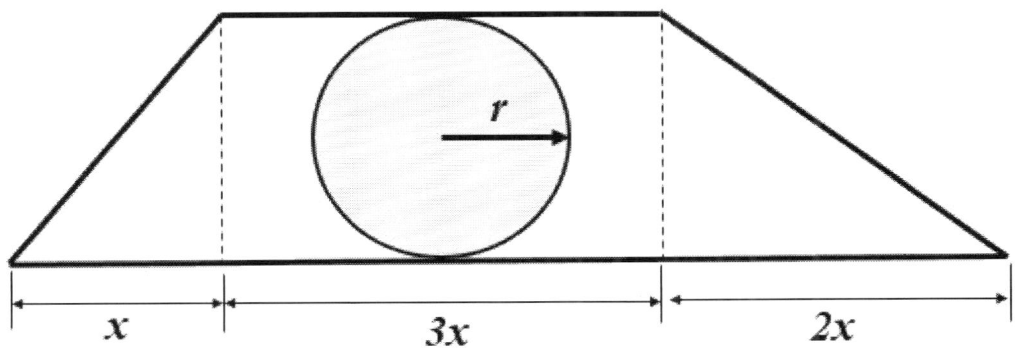

Solution:
First and foremost, the height of the trapezium needs to be calculated. This can be obtained from the radius of the circle. $\boldsymbol{Height} = 2 \times r = D$
The area of the circle is given by.

$$A = \pi r^2$$

$$r = \sqrt{\frac{A}{\pi}} = \sqrt{\frac{12.6}{\pi}} = 2$$

$$Height = 2 \times 2 = 4$$

The area of a trapezium is given by.

$$A = \frac{1}{2}(a + b)h$$

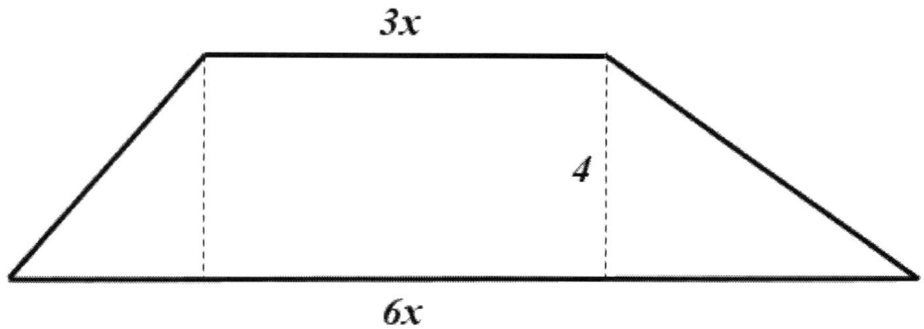

It means that;

$$54 = \frac{1}{2}(3x + 6x)4$$

$$9x = \frac{2 \times 54}{4}$$

$$x = 3$$

Q4. The perimeter of the rectangle shown below is 34 cm and the area of the quarter circle is 3.15 cm^2. If the ratio of $x : y$ is $2 : 1$, calculate the area of the shaded region.

Note: *diagram not drawn to scale.*

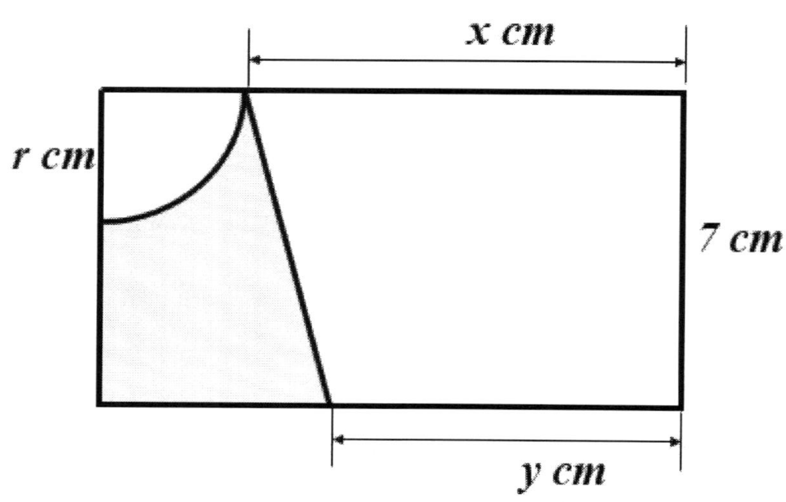

Solution:

The shaded area is given by

= **Area of the rectangle – (area of quarter circle + area of the trapezium).**

The question can be solved in the following order;

(a) Find the radius of the quarter circle; This is given by

$$A = \frac{1}{4}\pi r^2$$

$$r = \sqrt{\frac{4 \times A}{\pi}} = \sqrt{\frac{4 \times 3.15}{\pi}} = 2\ cm$$

(b) Find the dimensions of the rectangle;

The width = 7 cm

The length = (2 + *x*) cm

Hence, the perimeter is given by;

$$2(7) + 2(2 + x) = 34$$
$$14 + 4 + 2x = 34$$
$$2x = 16$$
$$x = 8$$

(c) Find the dimensions of the trapezium; The ratio $x : y$ is such that

$$x : y = 2 : 1$$
$$x : y = 8 : 4$$

Hence, $y = 4$

This means;

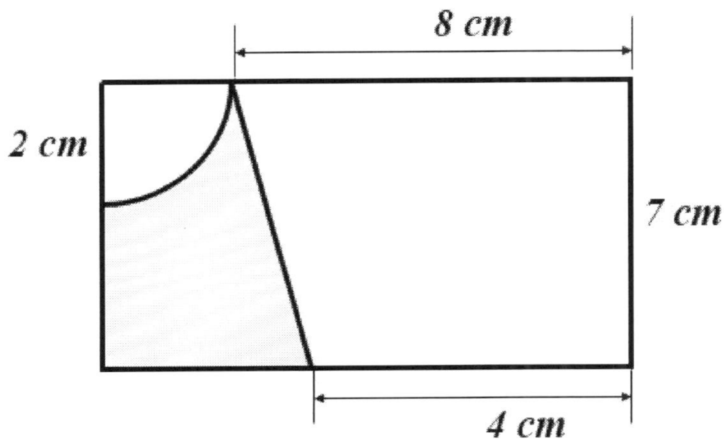

The shaded area =

= Area of the rectangle – (area of quarter circle + area of the trapezium).

$$= 7 \times 10 - \left(3.15 + \frac{1}{2} \times [8 + 4] \times 7\right)$$

$$= 70 - 45.15$$

$$= 24.5\ cm^2$$

Q5. The polygon below is a regular hexagon with a side length of 6 units. Calculate the area of the shaded region.
Note: *diagram not drawn to scale.*

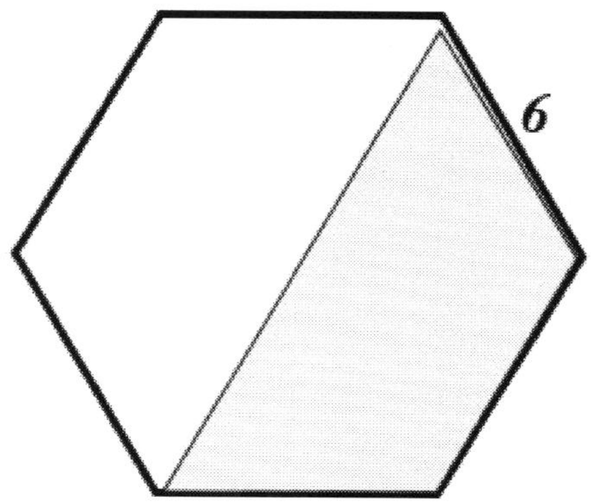

Solution:
The question can be solved in the following order;

(a) Finding the dimensions of the trapezium;
The sum of interior angles in a polygon is given by;

$$= (n - 2)180°$$

where n = number of sides. For a hexagon, $n = 6$.
Hence; Sum of interior angles = $(6 - 2)180°$ = **720°.**

Therefore, one interior angle is $= \frac{720}{6} = 120°$

It means that; the top end of the diagram can be illustrated as;

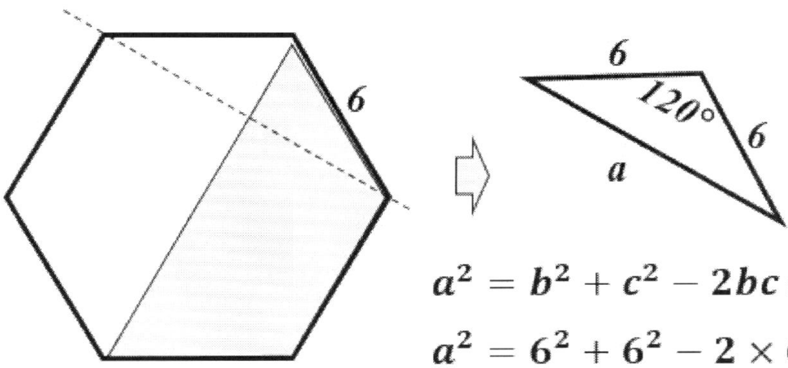

$$a^2 = b^2 + c^2 - 2bc\cos A$$

$$a^2 = 6^2 + 6^2 - 2 \times 6 \times 6 \times \cos 120$$

$$a^2 = 108$$

$$a = \sqrt{108}$$

$$a = 10.4$$

Separating the big triangle into two small triangles gives;

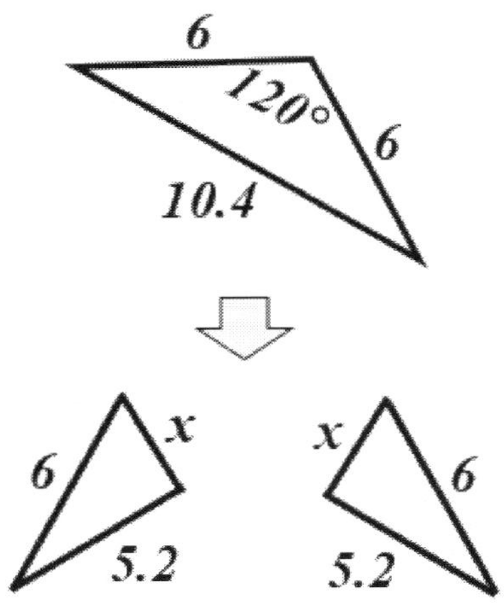

The value x can be obtained by;

- ➢ SQUARE $= 6^2 = 36$
- ➢ SQUARE $= 5.2^2 = 27.04$
- ➢ **SUBTRACT** $= 36 - 27.04 = 8.96$
- ➢ SQUARE ROOT $= \sqrt{8.96}$

  $\boldsymbol{x = 3}$

(b) Calculating the area of the trapezium;
Resolving all the dimensions of the trapezium gives;

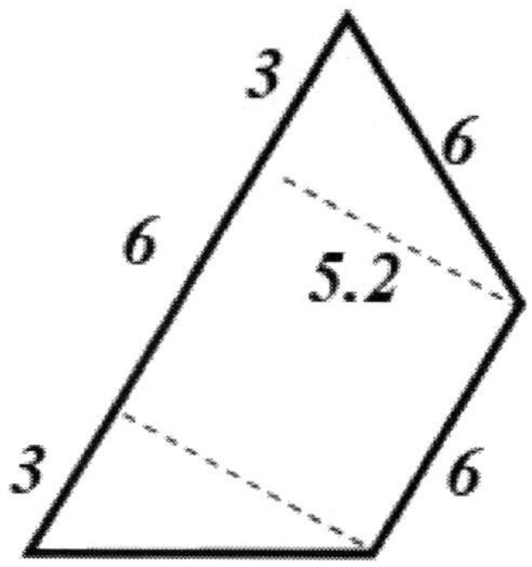

The area of a trapezium is given by.

$$A = \frac{1}{2}(a + b)h$$

$a = 6$, $b = 12$ and $h = 5.2$ cm.

$$A = \frac{1}{2}(6 + 12) \times 5.2$$

$$A = 46.8\ units^2$$

2. Quadratic Equations

A quadratic equation written in the form:

$$ax^2 + bx + c$$

Where ***a***, ***b*** and ***c*** are constants; $a \neq 0$.
These equations represent quadratic graphs where there are ***two solutions*** where the graph crosses the x-axis.

Two things to note on the coefficient of $\underline{x^2}$

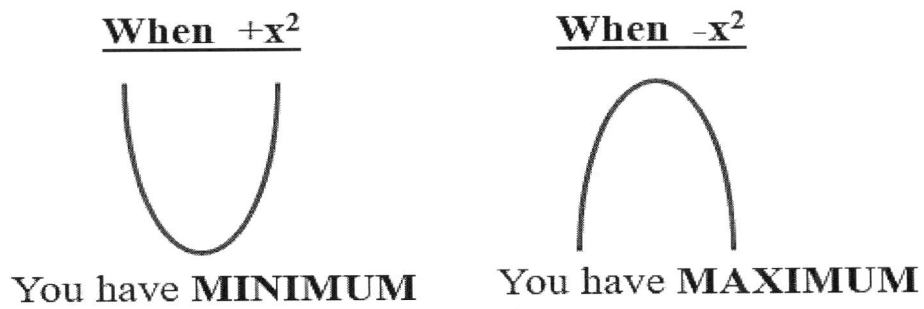

Information from a quadratic equation:

$$y = ax^2 + bx + c$$

Where $a \neq 0$.

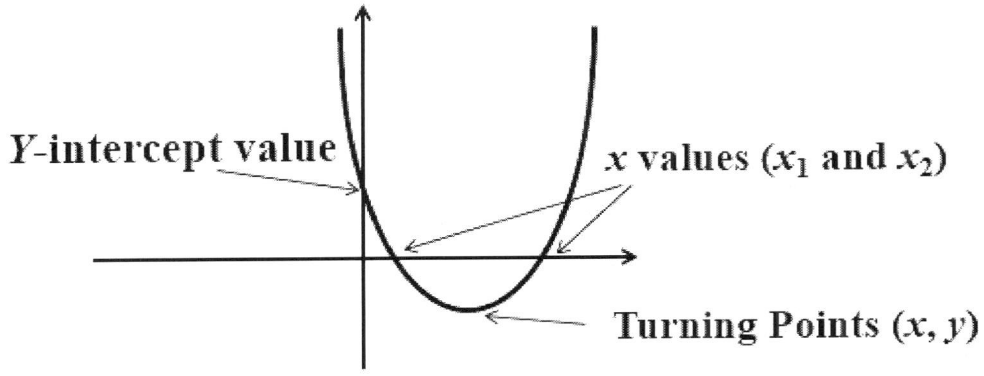

[1]. ***Y*-Intercept**: This is where the graph crosses the y-axis and can be obtained by putting $x = 0$ in the equation, $y = ax^2 + bx + c$.

[2]. ***x*-values**: This is where the graph crosses the x-axis and can be obtained by putting $y = 0$ in the equation $y = ax^2 + bx + c$ and solving the equation using the THREE methods discussed below.

[3]. ***<u>Turning point (x, y)</u>***: This is where the turning point of the graph and can be calculated from the equation $\boldsymbol{y = ax^2 + bx + c}$ by ***COMPLETING*** the *SQUARES.*

<u>Strategy for solving *x*-values:</u>

Apart from the graphical methods, there are **<u>THREE main</u>** methods of solving Quadratic Equations: These are;

A. <u>By Factorization</u>

There are again TWO forms of Factorizing quadratics.

I. When the coefficient of $x^2 = 1$.

$\boldsymbol{x^2 + 11x + 30 = 0}$
$\boldsymbol{a} = 1$, $\boldsymbol{b} = 11$ and $\boldsymbol{c} = 30$.

This is solved by finding the ***<u>factor pairs</u>*** *(F. P) of the constant,* **<u>c</u> (i.e. 30)**, *such that when added can be equal to* ***<u>b</u>*** **(i.e. 11)**,

F. P of 30	
3 X 10	
2 X 15	
5 X 6	= 5 + 6 = **<u>11</u>**

Hence, the solution is by +5 and +6;

$$\boldsymbol{(x + 5)(x + 6) = 0}$$

This means that either;

$$\boldsymbol{(x + 5) = 0} \textit{ and } \boldsymbol{x = -5}.$$

(That is the value of *x* that can make the equation ZERO)

Or;

$$\boldsymbol{(x + 6) = 0} \textit{ and } \boldsymbol{x = -6}.$$

(That is the value of *x* that can make the equation ZERO).

*Therefore the **Two** solutions for the equations are; x = -5 and x= -6.*

II. When the coefficient of x^2 >1.

$$2x^2 - 3x - 9 = 0$$

a = 2 (***Note***: a >1), ***b*** = -3 and ***c*** = -9.

Remember: *This is slightly different from **x<1**.*

*It is solved by finding the **factor pairs** (**F. P**) of the* **constants**, ***a × c***

(i.e. 2 × -9 = -18), *such that when added can be equal to **b*** **(i.e. -3),**

F. P of -18			
1	X	-18	
-6	X	3	= -6 + 3 = **-3**
2	X	-9	

Note: At this point, the selected factors are placed within the equation before factorization. They are placed in the place of ***b***.

It means, replacing ***-3x*** *by -6x+3x. (i.e.* ***-3x*** *= -6x+3x).*

It means, the equation now becomes;

$$2x^2 - 6x + 3x - 9 = 0$$

Factorization *is done by factorizing the first two terms and the last two terms.*

$$\boxed{2x^2 - 6x} + \boxed{3x - 9} = 0$$

This becomes;

$$2x(x - 3) + 3(x - 3) = 0$$

It means, we have 2x lots of (x-3) and 3 lots of (x-3).
In all, we have (2x+3) lots of (x-3).

Hence, the factorization becomes;

$$(2x + 3)(x - 3) = 0$$

This means that either;

$$(2x + 3) = 0 \text{ and } x = -\frac{3}{2} = -1.5.$$

(That is the value of *x* that can make the equation ZERO)

Or;

$$(x - 3) = 0 \text{ and } x = 3.$$

(That is the value of *x* that can make the equation ZERO).

*Therefore the **Two** solutions for the equations are; x = -1.5 and x= 3.*

B. By Completing the squares

A quadratic equation written in the form:

$$ax^2 + bx + c$$

(where ***a***, ***b*** and ***c*** are constants; ***a*** = 1).

Can be solved by ***completing the squares*** using the formula;

$$\left(x + \frac{b}{2}\right)^2 - \left(\frac{b}{2}\right)^2 + c$$

Please ensure that the constant ***a*** = 1 and is ***NOT USED*** in the formula.

The above formula will generate ***two solutions*** of $\boldsymbol{x}$ as obtained above.

<u>Examples;</u>

I. When the coefficient of $x^2 = 1$.

$$x^2 + 11x + 30 = 0$$

$\boldsymbol{a} = 1$, $\boldsymbol{b} = 11$ and $\boldsymbol{c} = 30$.

Using the formula,

$$\left(x + \frac{11}{2}\right)^2 - \left(\frac{11}{2}\right)^2 + 30 = 0$$

Resolving it becomes;

$$\left(x + \frac{11}{2}\right)^2 - \frac{121}{4} + 30 = 0$$

That gives;

$$\left(x + \frac{11}{2}\right)^2 - \frac{1}{4} = 0$$

Rearranging gives;

$$\left(x + \frac{11}{2}\right)^2 = \frac{1}{4}$$

Which gives;

$$x + \frac{11}{2} = \pm\sqrt{\frac{1}{4}}$$

Note: Every Square root can have ± **answers**.
(i.e. **+5** × **+5** = **25** and **-5** × **-5** = **25**).

Therefore x values can be obtained by;

$$x = -\frac{11}{2} \pm \sqrt{\frac{1}{4}}$$

This means that x can be either;

$$x = -\frac{11}{2} + \sqrt{\frac{1}{4}} = -5$$

or

$$x = -\frac{11}{2} - \sqrt{\frac{1}{4}} = -6$$

Therefore the ***Two*** *solutions for the equations are;* $x = -5$ *and* $x = -6$.
These are the same answers obtained from the **Factorization Method**.

II. When the coefficient of $x^2 > 1$.

$$2x^2 - 3x - 9 = 0$$

$\boldsymbol{a} = 2$ (***Note***: $a > 1$), $\boldsymbol{b} = -3$ and $\boldsymbol{c} = -9$.

Note: *To use the formula, the value of* ***a*** *must be changed to 1 by diving through by* ***a****.*

Since ***a*** *=* ***2****, the equation can be divided by* ***2*** *as follows;*

$$x^2 - 1.5x - 4.5 = 0$$

Using the formula,

$$\left(x - \frac{1.5}{2}\right)^2 - \left(\frac{1.5}{2}\right)^2 + -4.5 = 0$$

Note that b is NEGATIVE, hence$(x - \frac{b}{2})$ is used.

Resolving it becomes;

$$\left(x - \frac{1.5}{2}\right)^2 - \frac{2.25}{4} - 4.5 = 0$$

That gives;

$$\left(x - \frac{1.5}{2}\right)^2 - 5.0625 = 0$$

Rearranging gives;

$$\left(x - \frac{1.5}{2}\right)^2 = 5.0625$$

Which gives;

$$x - \frac{1.5}{2} = \pm\sqrt{5.0625}$$

Note: Every Square root can have ± **answers**.

Therefore x values can be obtained by;

$$x = \frac{1.5}{2} \pm \sqrt{5.0625}$$

This means that x can be either;

$$x = \frac{1.5}{2} + \sqrt{5.0625} = 3$$

or

$$x = \frac{1.5}{2} - \sqrt{5.0625} = -1.5$$

*Therefore the **Two** solutions for the equations are; x = 3 and x= -1.5.*
These are the same answers obtained from the **Factorization Method**.

C. By using the Quadratic Formula

A quadratic equation written in the form:

$$ax^2 + bx + c$$

(where ***a***, ***b*** and ***c*** are constants;).

Can be solved by ***the Quadratic formula***;

$$x = \frac{-b \pm \sqrt{b^2 - 4ac}}{2a}$$

Note: ***a*** can be any number. It is normally used when ***Factorization*** and ***Completing of squares*** become **COMPLEX**.

The above formula will generate ***two solutions*** of ***x*** as obtained above.

Examples;

I. When the coefficient of $x^2 = 1$.

$$x^2 + 11x + 30 = 0$$

a = 1, ***b*** = 11 and ***c*** = 30.

Using the formula,

$$x = \frac{-11 \pm \sqrt{11^2 - 4 \times 1 \times 30}}{2 \times 1}$$

Resolving it becomes;

$$x = \frac{-11 \pm \sqrt{1}}{2}$$

Therefore x values can be obtained by;

$$x = \frac{-11 \pm 1}{2}$$

This means that x can be either;

$$x = \frac{-11 + 1}{2} = -5$$

or

$$x = \frac{-11 - 1}{2} = -6$$

Therefore the **Two** *solutions for the equations are; x = -5 and x= -6.* These are the same answers obtained from the **Factorization and the Completing of Squares methods**.

II. When the coefficient of $x^2 > 1$.

$$2x^2 - 3x - 9 = 0$$

a = 2 , ***b*** = -3 and ***c*** = -9.

Note: *It does not matter what the value of* ***a*** *is.*

Using the formula,

$$x = \frac{- -3 \pm \sqrt{(-3)^2 - 4 \times 2 \times -9}}{2 \times 2}$$

Resolving it becomes;

$$x = \frac{3 \pm \sqrt{81}}{4}$$

Therefore x values can be obtained by;

$$x = \frac{3 \pm 9}{4}$$

This means that x can be either;

$$x = \frac{3+9}{4} = 3$$

or

$$x = \frac{3-9}{4} = -1.5$$

Therefore the ***Two*** *solutions for the equations are; x = 3 and x= -1.5.* These are the same answers obtained from the **Factorization and the Completing of Squares methods**.

D. Strategy for finding *Turning point* and *Y*-intercept:

I. Finding the Turning Point.

To find the turning point, you must COMPLETE the SQUARES using of a quadratic equation $y = \boldsymbol{ax^2 + bx + c}$ *by*

$$\left(x+\frac{b}{2}\right)^2 - \left(\frac{b}{2}\right)^2 + c$$

(where ***a***, ***b*** and ***c*** are constants).

After resolving the above equation, it can be left in the form;

$$(x+q)^2 + p$$

From the above expression; the turning point is (-***q***, ***p***).

NOTE*:*

1. If ***q*** is POSITIVE, the **x-value** of the turning point is **NEGATIVE**. If ***q*** is NEGATIVE, the **x-value** of the turning point is **POSITIVE**.

2. The ***p***-value remains **THE SAME**.

Example 1: To find the turning point of the following equation;

$$y = x^2 + 11x + 30$$

a = 1, ***b*** = 11 and ***c*** = 30.

Use the formula,

$$\left(x + \frac{11}{2}\right)^2 - \left(\frac{11}{2}\right)^2 + 30$$

Resolving it becomes;

$$\left(x + \frac{11}{2}\right)^2 - \frac{121}{4} + 30$$

That gives;

$$(x + 5.5)^2 - 0.25$$

The **turning point** *which is the* ***MINIMUM point*** *(i.e.* The quadratic graph has a minimum point since the coefficient of x^2 is POSITIVE*)*
= **(-5.5, -0.25).**

Example 2: To find the turning point of the following equation;

$$y = 2x^2 - 3x - 9$$

a = 2, ***b*** = -3 and ***c*** = -9.

Note: *This is slightly different than the methods for finding the x-values. To use the formula, the value of* ***a*** *must be* ***FACTORIZED OUT****.*

Since ***a*** *= 2,* ***2*** *must be factorized out of the equation as follows;*

$$y = 2[x^2 - 1.5x - 4.5]$$

Then using the completing of squares formula above;

$$y = 2\left[\left(x - \frac{1.5}{2}\right)^2 - \left(\frac{1.5}{2}\right)^2 + -4.5\right]$$

Resolving it becomes;

$$y = 2\left[\left(x - \frac{1.5}{2}\right)^2 - \frac{2.25}{4} - 4.5\right]$$

That gives;

$$y = 2[(x - 0.75)^2 - 5.0625]$$

Finally, the equation can be expressed as;

$$y = 2[(x - 0.75)^2] - 10.125$$

The **turning point** *(or **MINIMUM point**)* = **(0.75, -10.125).**

II. Finding the *Y*-Intercept.

To find the y-intercept, simply put x =0 in the equation and find the value of y. This is because at the y-axis x = 0.

Example 1: To find the ***y***-intercept of the following equation;

$$y = x^2 + 11x + 30$$

Put x =0,

$$y = (0)^2 + 11(0) + 30$$

Resolving it becomes;

$$y = 30$$

The graph intercepts the y-axis at ***y =30****.*

Since we have the solutions of x-values from above, the graph can be sketched as;

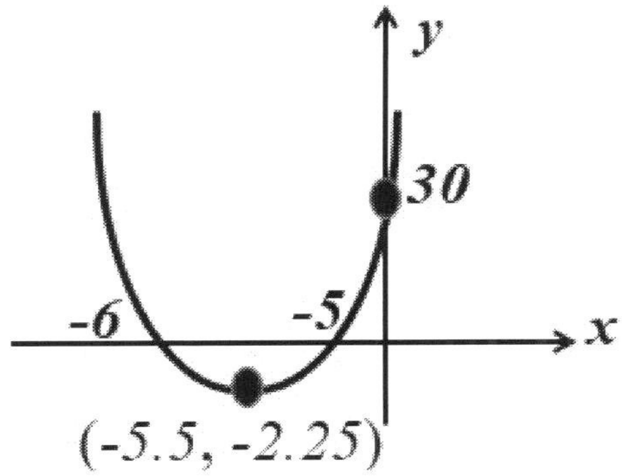

Example 2: To find the ***y***-intercept of the following equation;

$$y = 2x^2 - 3x - 9$$

Put x =0,

$$y = 2(0)^2 - 3(0) - 9$$

Resolving it becomes;

$$y = -9$$

*The graph intercepts the y-axis at **y = -9**.*

Since we have the solutions of x-values from above, the graph can also be sketched as;

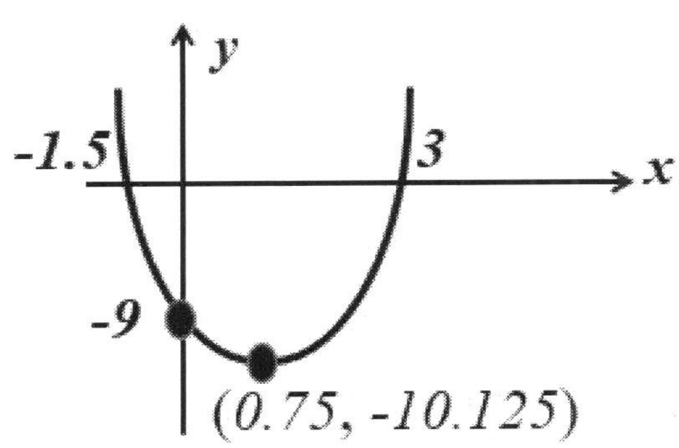

Questions

Q1. Solve the following quadratic equations by factorization.

i. $x^2 - 3x - 10 = 0$

ii. $2x^2 - 4x - 126 = 0$

Solution:

i. From the equation:

$$x^2 - 3x - 10 = 0$$

a = 1, ***b*** = -3 and ***c*** = -10.

Using the solution described above; find the ***factor pairs*** (***F. P***) of **c** (i.e. -**10**) such that when added it will be ***b*** (i.e. **-3**).

F. P of -10	
1 X -10	
-2 X 5	
2 X -5	= 2 + -5 = **-3**

Hence, the solution is by +2 and -5;

$$(x + 2)(x - 5) = 0$$

This means that either;

$$(x - 2) = 0 \; and \; x = -2.$$

(That is the value of *x* that can make the equation ZERO)

Or;

$$(x - 5) = 0 \; and \; x = 5.$$

(That is the value of *x* that can make the equation ZERO).

*Therefore the **Two** solutions for the equations are; x = -2 and x= 5.*

ii. From the equation:

$$2x^2 - 4x - 126 = 0$$

a = 2, ***b*** = -4 and ***c*** = -126.

It is solved by finding the ***factor pairs*** *(F. P) of the* **constants**, ***a × c***

(i.e. 2 × -126 = -252), *such that when added can be equal to* ***b*** **(i.e. -4),**

Determination of factor pairs: For big numbers, please use a factor tree to generate all the factors required.

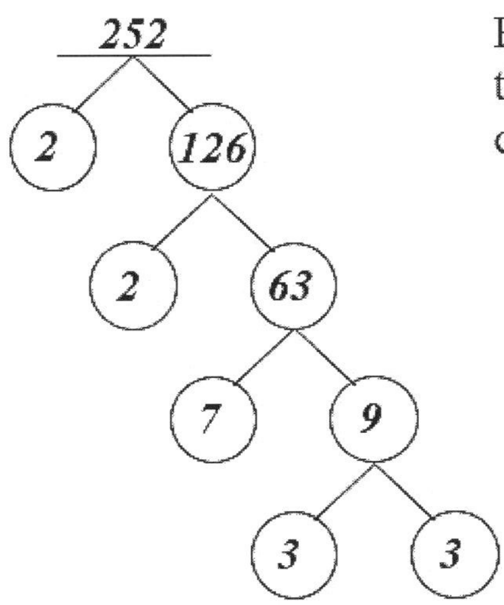

From the all the **PRIME FACTORS**, the possible combinations of *-252* that can get me close to **-4** are;

F. P of -252

- **-28 X 9**
  (i.e. 28 = 2x2x7) and (i.e. 9 = 3x3)
- **-42 X 6**
  (i.e. 42 = 2x7x3) and (i.e. 6 = 2x3)
- **14 X -18** = 14 + -18 = **-4**
  (i.e. 14 = 2x7) and (i.e. 18 = 2x3x3)

Note: At this point, the selected factors are placed within the equation before factorization. They are placed in the place of ***b***.

It means, replacing ***-4x*** *by -18x+14x. (i.e.* ***-4x*** *= -18x+14x).*

It means, the equation now becomes;

$$2x^2 - 4x - 126 = 0$$

Factorization *is done by factorizing the first two terms and the last two terms.*

$$\boxed{2x^2 - 18x} + \boxed{14x - 126} = 0$$

This becomes;

$$2x(x - 9) + 14(x - 9) = 0$$

It means, we have 2x lots of (x-9) and 14 lots of (x-9).
In all, we have (2x+14) lots of (x-9).

Hence, the factorization becomes;

$$(2x + 14)(x - 9) = 0$$

This means that either;

$$(2x + 14) = 0 \text{ and } x = -\frac{14}{2} = -7.$$

(That is the value of *x* that can make the equation ZERO)

Or;

$$(x - 9) = 0 \text{ and } x = 9.$$

(That is the value of *x* that can make the equation ZERO).

Therefore the ***Two*** *solutions for the equations are; x = -7 and x = 9.*

Q2. Solve the following quadratic equations by completing squares.

i. $x^2 - 3x - 10 = 0$

ii. $2x^2 - 4x - 126 = 0$

Solution:

i. The formula for ***completing the squares*** is given by;

$$\left(x + \frac{b}{2}\right)^2 - \left(\frac{b}{2}\right)^2 + c$$

From the equation:

$$x^2 - 3x - 10 = 0$$

a = 1, ***b*** = -3 and ***c*** = -10.

Using the formula,

$$\left(x-\frac{3}{2}\right)^2-\left(\frac{-3}{2}\right)^2-10=0$$

Resolving it becomes;

$$\left(x-\frac{3}{2}\right)^2-\frac{9}{4}-10=0$$

That gives;

$$\left(x-\frac{3}{2}\right)^2-\frac{49}{4}=0$$

Rearranging gives;

$$\left(x-\frac{3}{2}\right)^2=\frac{49}{4}$$

Which gives;

$$x-\frac{3}{2}=\pm\sqrt{\frac{49}{4}}$$

Note: Every Square root can have ± **answers**.
(i.e. **+5** × **+5** = **25** and **-5** × **-5** = **25**).

Therefore x values can be obtained by;

$$x=\frac{3}{2}\pm\frac{7}{2}$$

This means that x can be either;

$$x=\frac{3}{2}+\frac{7}{2}=5$$

or

$$x = \frac{3}{2} - \frac{7}{2} = -2$$

Therefore the ***Two*** *solutions for the equations are; x = -2 and x= 5.*

ii. From the equation:

$$2x^2 - 4x - 126 = 0$$

a = 2, ***b*** = -4 and ***c*** = -126.

Note: *To use the formula, the value of* ***a*** *must be changed to 1 by diving through by* ***a****.*

Since ***a*** *=* ***2****, the equation can be divided by* ***2*** *as follows;*

$$x^2 - 2x - 63 = 0$$

Using the formula,

$$\left(x - \frac{2}{2}\right)^2 - \left(\frac{2}{2}\right)^2 - 63 = 0$$

Resolving it becomes;

$$(x - 1)^2 - 1 - 63 = 0$$

That gives;

$$(x - 1)^2 - 64 = 0$$

Rearranging gives;

$$(x - 1)^2 = 64$$

Which gives;

$$x - 1 = \pm\sqrt{64}$$

Note: Every Square root can have ± **answers**.

Therefore x values can be obtained by;

$$x = 1 \pm 8$$

This means that x can be either;

$$x = 1 + 8 = 9$$

or

$$x = 1 - 8 = -7$$

Therefore the ***Two*** *solutions for the equations are; x = 9 and x= -7.*

Q3. Solve the following quadratic equations by using the quadratic formula.

i. $x^2 - 3x - 10 = 0$

ii. $2x^2 - 4x - 126 = 0$

Solution:

i. The ***quadratic formula*** is given by;

$$x = \frac{-b \pm \sqrt{b^2 - 4ac}}{2a}$$

From the equation;

$$x^2 - 3x - 10 = 0$$

a = 1, ***b*** = -3 and ***c*** = -10.

Using the formula,

$$x = \frac{- -3 \pm \sqrt{(-3)^2 - 4 \times 1 \times -10}}{2 \times 1}$$

Resolving it becomes;

$$x = \frac{3 \pm \sqrt{49}}{2}$$

Therefore x values can be obtained by;

$$x = \frac{3 \pm 7}{2}$$

This means that x can be either;

$$x = \frac{3 + 7}{2} = 5$$

or

$$x = \frac{3 - 7}{2} = -2$$

Therefore the ***Two*** *solutions for the equations are; x = 5 and x= -2.*

ii. From the equation:

$$2x^2 - 4x - 126 = 0$$

a = 2, ***b*** = -4 and ***c*** = -126.
Using the formula,

$$x = \frac{- -4 \pm \sqrt{(-4)^2 - 4 \times 2 \times -126}}{2 \times 2}$$

Resolving it becomes;

$$x = \frac{4 \pm \sqrt{1024}}{4}$$

Therefore x values can be obtained by;

$$x = \frac{4 \pm 32}{4}$$

This means that x can be either;

$$x = \frac{4 + 32}{4} = 9$$

or

$$x = \frac{4 - 32}{4} = -7$$

*Therefore the **Two** solutions for the equations are; x = 9 and x= -7.*

Q4.

(a) Write the equation $\boldsymbol{x^2 + 14x + 46}$ in the form $\boldsymbol{(x + q)^2 + p}$, where $\boldsymbol{q}$ and $\boldsymbol{p}$ are constants. Find the values of $\boldsymbol{q}$ and $\boldsymbol{p}$.

(b) Find the coordinates at the minimum point of $\boldsymbol{x^2 + 14x + 46}$.

Solution:

(a) The equation can be transformed by ***completing the squares***.

The formula for completing the squares is;

$$\left(x + \frac{b}{2}\right)^2 - \left(\frac{b}{2}\right)^2 + c$$

From the equation:

$\boldsymbol{a} = 1$, $\boldsymbol{b} = 14$ and $\boldsymbol{c} = 46$.

Using the formula,

$$\left(x + \frac{14}{2}\right)^2 - \left(\frac{14}{2}\right)^2 + 46$$

Resolving it becomes;

$$(x + 7)^2 - (7)^2 + 46$$

That gives;

$$(x + 7)^2 - 49 + 46$$

Finally, it can be expressed as;

$$(x + 7)^2 - 3$$

Hence, $q = 7$ and $p = -3$.

(b) Using the transformed equation obtained by ***completing the squares***.

$$(x + 7)^2 - 3$$

The minimum points can be obtained as **(-7, -3)**.

Q5. Solve the following simultaneous equation.

$$x^2 + y^2 = 5$$

$$y = 3x - 1$$

<u>**Solution:**</u>

From the two equations,

$$x^2 + y^2 = 5 \quad (1)$$

$$y = 3x - 1 \ (2)$$

Put $y = 3x - 1$ *into equation (1). And that gives;*

$$x^2 + (3x - 1)^2 = 5$$

This can be solved as follows;

$$x^2 + 9x^2 - 6x + 1 = 5$$

$$10x^2 - 6x - 4 = 0$$

This can easily be solved by factorization.

Factor Pairs for ***a*** x ***c*** (*10* x *-4*) = **-40**.

Factor pairs of ***-40*** that can be added to give ***-6*** (i.e. ***b***) are **-10** and **4**.

Hence, the above equation can be extended as;

$$10x^2 - 10x + 4x - 4 = 0$$

The equation can be factorized as discussed above as;

$$10x(x-1) + 4(x-1) = 0$$

This gives;

$$(10x + 4)(x-1) = 0$$

This means that either;

$$(10x+4) = 0 \text{ and } x = -\frac{4}{10} = -0.4.$$

Or;

$$(x-1) = 0 \text{ and } x = 1.$$

This means that;

For x = -0.4,

$$y = 3(-0.4) - 1 = -2.2$$

For x = 1,

$y = 3(1) - 1 = 2$

The solutions are **(-0.4, -2.2)** and **(1, 2)**.

Q6. Find the equation of a quadratic graph whose turning point is at (-5, 6).

Solution:

The turning point can be expressed in a transformed quadratic equation obtained from the complete of squares as;

$$(x+q)^2+p$$

Where the turning point is (-q, p).

Hence, if the turning point is (-5, 6), the transformed equation can be given by;

$$(x+5)^2+6$$

Expanding the brackets;

$$x^2+10x+25+6$$

Therefore the quadratic equation is given by;

$$x^2+10x+31$$

Summary on solving quadratic equations

A quadratic equation written in the form;

ax^2+bx+c

*where **a**, **b** and **c** are constants; $a \neq 0$.*

Can be solved by any of the methods shown above unless specified.
You must not limit yourself to any of the methods.

They can be used in the areas of;

1. Quadratic simultaneous equations as shown in question 5 on this chapter.

2. Circles and Geometry etc.

3. Cones and Frustums

The formula surrounding cones frustums are;

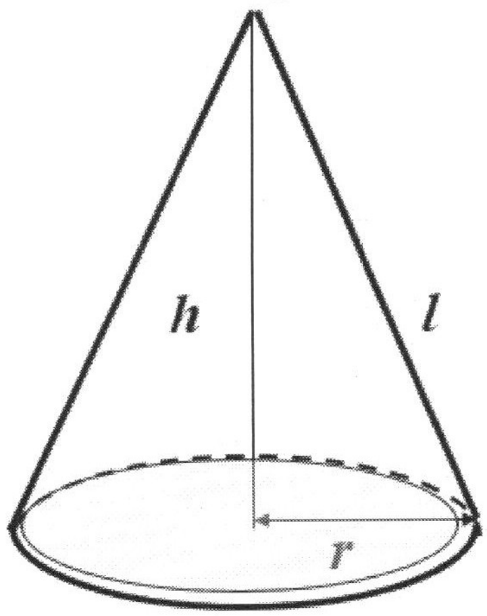

For Cone Volume;

$$V = \frac{1}{3}\pi r^2 h$$

For Cone Curve Surface Area;

$$CSA = \pi r l$$

For Cone **Total** Surface Area;

$$CSA = \pi r l + \pi r^2$$

The terminologies surrounding cones and frustums are;

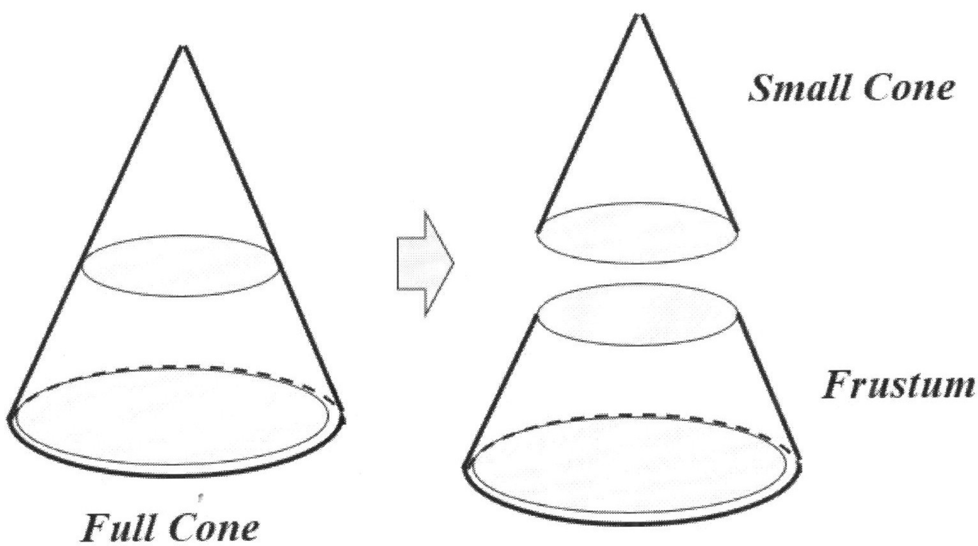

A. **Frustums:**

Note that the Frustums will have a volume by subtracting the small cone from the big cone but the total surface area will be the curve surface area plus the two areas of the circles at its ends.

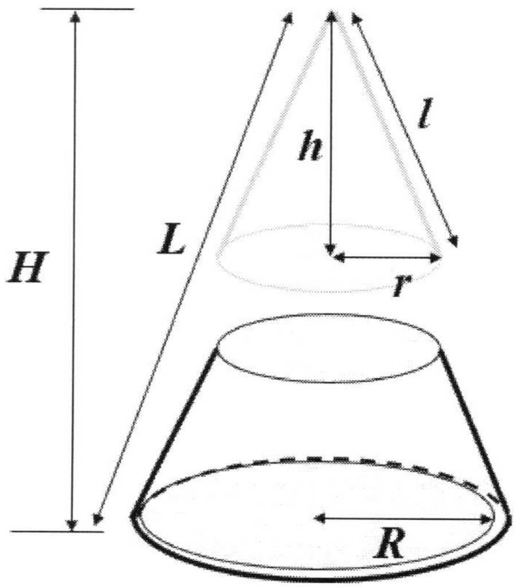

For Frustum Volume;

$$V = \frac{1}{3}\pi R^2 H - \frac{1}{3}\pi r^2 h$$

R and ***H*** are radius and height of Big Cone.
r and ***h*** are radius and height of Small Cone.

For Frustum Curve Surface Area;

$$CSA = \pi RL - \pi rl$$

For Frustum **Total** Surface Area;

$$CSA = \pi RL - \pi rl + \pi R^2 + \pi r^2$$

L and ***l*** are slant height of Big and Small Cone.

Strategies:

(A) Using Scale factors	*(B) Using Linear, Area & Volume Ratios*
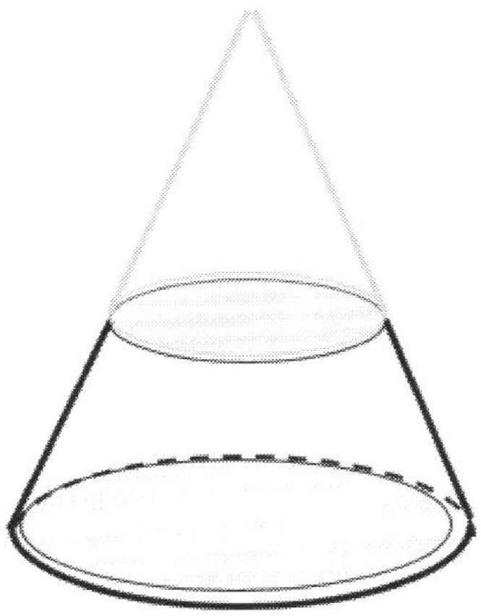	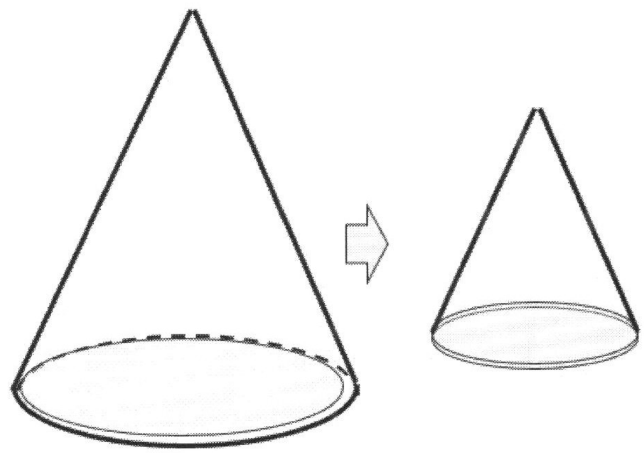
For: ▪ *Same Cone* ▪ *Frustum & imaginary small cone*	▪ *Similar cones* ▪ *And comparing linear, area and volume ratios*

B. Using Scale-Factor from SAME Cone

I. The main point is to compare **Heights (*H, h*)**, **Radii (*R, r*)** and **Slant height (*L, l*)**.

Note: Do not combine them!!!

$$\textbf{Scale fatcor} = \frac{\textit{Radius of Big Cone } (R)}{\textit{Radius ofSmall Cone } (r)}$$

$$= \frac{\textit{Height of Big Cone } (H)}{\textit{Height ofSmall Cone } (h)}$$

$$= \frac{\textit{Slant length of Big Cone } (L)}{\textit{Radius ofSmall Cone } (l)}$$

Questions

Q1. The diagram below shows a cone which has been cut into a small Cone and Frustum. Calculate the volume and total surface area of the Frustum.

Note: *diagram not drawn to scale.*

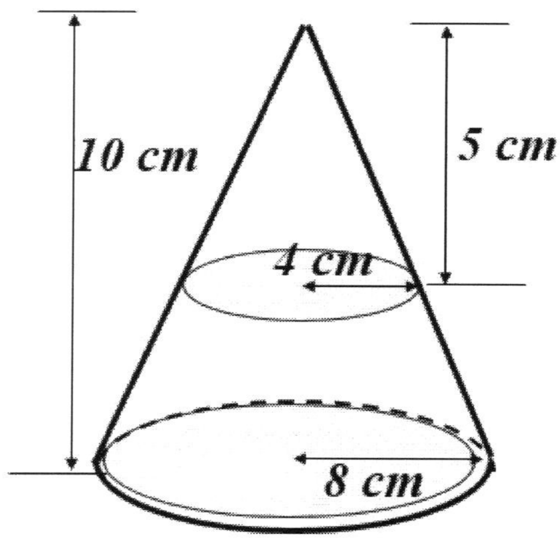

Solution:

(i) The volume of the Frustum;

The volume of the Frustum = **Volume of Big Cone – Volume of Small Cone.**

$$\textit{Volume of Big Cone} = \frac{1}{3}\pi R^2 H$$

$$\textit{Volume of Big Cone} = \frac{1}{3} \times \pi \times 8^2 \times 10 = 670.2\ cm^3$$

$$\textit{Volume of Small Cone} = \frac{1}{3}\pi r^2 h$$

$$\textit{Volume of Small Cone} = \frac{1}{3} \times \pi \times 4^2 \times 5 = 83.8\ cm^3$$

The volume of the Frustum = **670.3 – 83.8 = <u>586.5 cm³</u>.**

(ii) The total surface area of the Frustum;

The Total surface area = **Difference in curve surface area + area of Big circle + area of Small Circle.**

The big ***Slant*** length is given by;

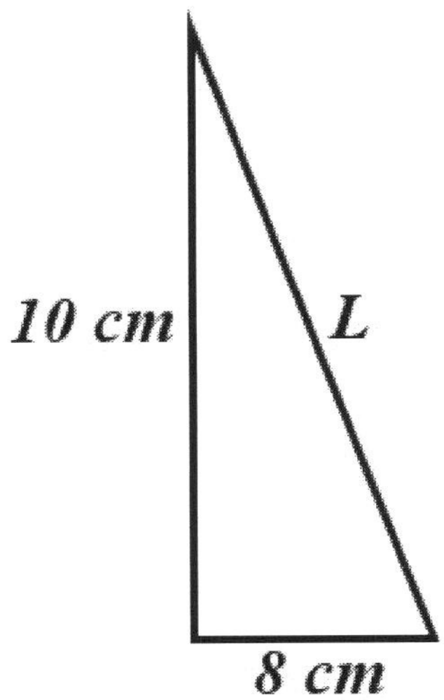

- SQUARE $= 10^2 = 100$
- SQUARE $= 8^2 = 64$
- **ADD** $= 100 + 64 = 164$
- SQUARE ROOT $= \sqrt{164} = 12.8$

→ It means $L = 12.8$ cm

The Small ***Slant*** length is given by;

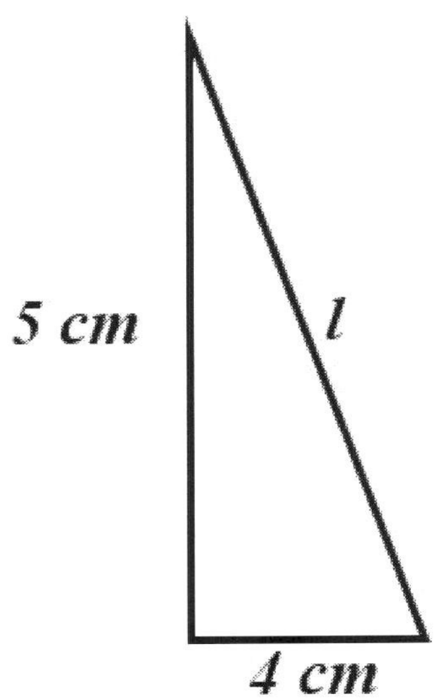

- SQUARE $= 5^2 = 25$
- SQUARE $= 4^2 = 16$
- **ADD** $= 25 + 16 = 41$
- SQUARE ROOT $= \sqrt{41} = 6.4$

→ It means, $l = 6.4$ cm

Or using the scale factor of 2 = 12.8 ÷2 = **6.4 cm.**

$$Difference\ in\ curve\ surface\ area = \pi RL - \pi rl$$

$$= \pi(RL - rl)$$

$$= \pi(8 \times 12.8 - 4 \times 6.4)$$

$$= 241.3\ cm^2$$

Therefore, the total surface area = **241.3** + $\pi R^2 + \pi r^2$.

Therefore, the total surface area = **241.3** + $\pi \times 8^2 + \pi \times 4^2$.

The total surface area of the Frustum = **<u>492.6 cm²</u>**.

Q2. The diagram below shows a cone which has been cut into a small Cone and Frustum. Calculate the volume and total surface area of the Frustum.
Note: *diagram not drawn to scale.*

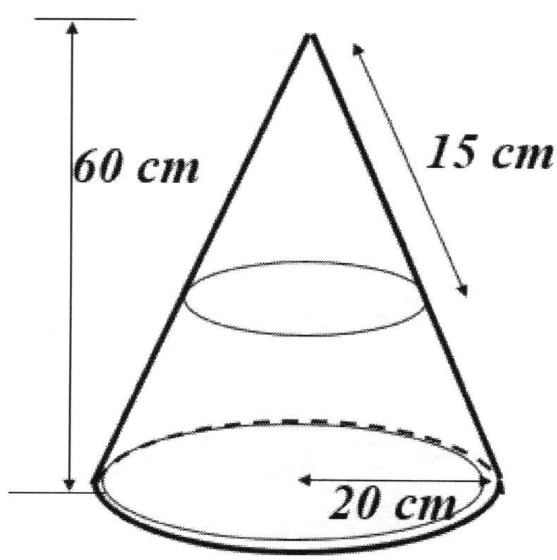

Solution:

(i) The volume of the Frustum;

The volume of the Frustum = **Volume of Big Cone – Volume of Small Cone.**
Scale factor:

The Big slant height (***L***), the small height (***h***), and the small radius (***r***) are needed. In order to get those values, a ***SCALE FACTOR*** is needed.

To find the scale factor, the Big *slant* height (***L***) needs to be calculated and must be compared with the small slant height (***l***);

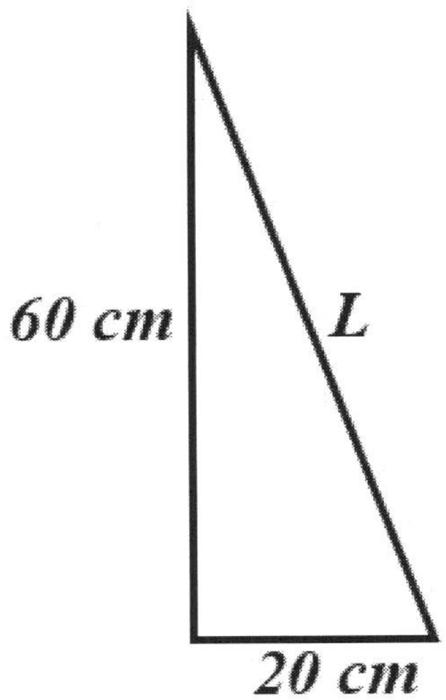

- SQUARE $= 60^2 = 3600$
- SQUARE $= 20^2 = 400$
- **ADD** $= 3600 + 400 = 4000$
- SQUARE ROOT $= \sqrt{4000} = 63.3$

→ It means, $L = 63.3$ cm

$$\text{Hence, Scale factor} = \frac{63.3}{15} = \mathbf{4.2}$$

Therefore;

$$\textbf{Height of Small Cone } (h)\textbf{: } \frac{60}{4.2} = \mathbf{14.3}\ cm$$

$$\textbf{Radius of Small Cone } (r)\textbf{: } \frac{20}{4.2} = \mathbf{4.8}\ cm$$

$$\boldsymbol{Volume\ of\ Big\ Cone} = \frac{1}{3}\pi R^2 H$$

$$\boldsymbol{Volume\ of\ Big\ Cone} = \frac{1}{3} \times \pi \times 20^2 \times 60 = \mathbf{25132.7}\ cm^3$$

$$\boldsymbol{Volume\ of\ Small\ Cone} = \frac{1}{3}\pi r^2 h$$

$$\boldsymbol{Volume\ of\ Small\ Cone} = \frac{1}{3} \times \pi \times 4.8^2 \times 14.3 = \mathbf{345}\ cm^3$$

The volume of the Frustum = **25132.7 – 345 =** **<u>24,787.7 cm³</u>.**

(ii) The total surface area of the Frustum;

The Total surface area = **Difference in curve surface area + area of Big circle + area of Small Circle.**

Therefore, the total surface area = $(\pi RL - \pi rl) + \pi R^2 + \pi r^2$.

$$= \pi \times 20 \times 63.3 - \pi \times 4.8 \times 15 + \pi \times 20^2 + \pi \times 4.8^2.$$

The total surface area of the Frustum = **5080.1 cm^2.**

Q3. The diagram below shows a cone which has been cut into a small Cone and Frustum. Calculate the volume and total surface area of the Frustum.

Note: *diagram not drawn to scale.*

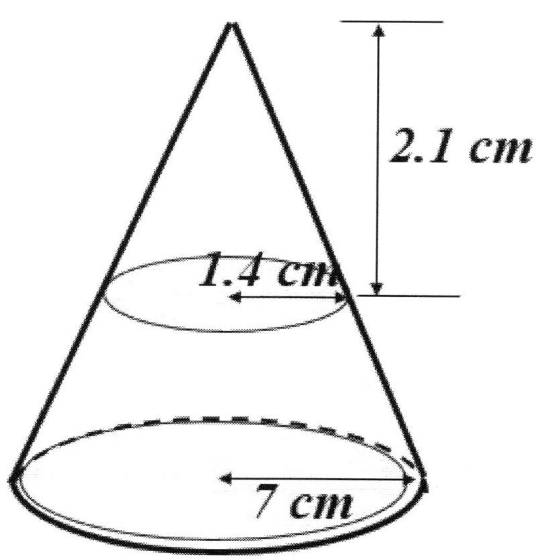

<u>Solution:</u>

(i) The volume of the Frustum;
The volume of the Frustum = **Volume of Big Cone – Volume of Small Cone.**

Scale factor:

$$\textbf{The Scale factor} = \frac{7}{1.4} = 5$$

The big height (***H***), the big (***L***) and small slant height (***l***) need to be calculated.

$$\text{The Big height } (H) = 5 \times 2.1 = 10.5\ cm$$

The Big (*L*) and small *slant* height (*l*);

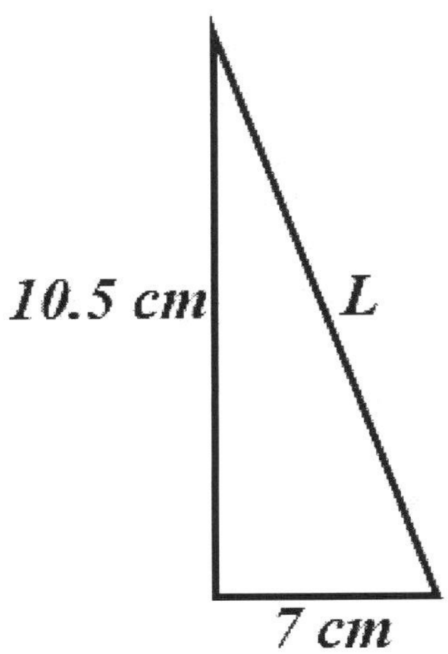

- SQUARE $= 10.5^2 = 110.25$
- SQUARE $= 7^2 = 49$
- **ADD** $= 110.25 + 49 = 159.25$
- SQUARE ROOT $= \sqrt{159.25} = 12.6$

→ It means, $L = 12.6$ cm

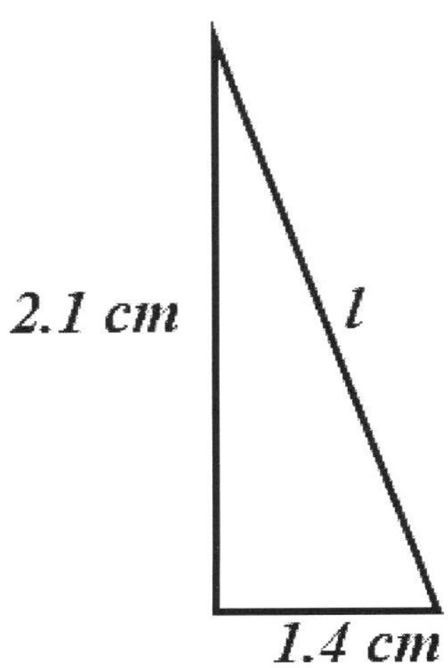

- SQUARE $= 2.1^2 = 4.41$
- SQUARE $= 1.4^2 = 1.96$
- **ADD** $= 4.41 + 1.96 = 6.37$
- SQUARE ROOT $= \sqrt{6.37} = 2.5$

→ It means, $l = 2.5$ cm

Therefore;

$$Volume\ of\ Frustum = \frac{1}{3}\pi R^2 H - \frac{1}{3}\pi r^2 h$$

$$Volume\ of\ Frustum = \frac{1}{3}\pi(R^2 H - r^2 h)$$

$$Volume\ of\ Frustum = \frac{1}{3}\pi(7^2 \times 10.5 - 1.4^2 \times 2.1)$$

The volume of the Frustum = **534.5 cm^3.**

(ii) The total surface area of the Frustum;

The Total surface area = **Difference in curve surface area + area of Big circle + area of Small Circle.**

Therefore, the total surface area = $(\pi RL - \pi rl) + \pi R^2 + \pi r^2$.

$$= (\pi \times 7 \times 12.6 - \pi \times 1.4 \times 2.5) + \pi \times 7^2 + \pi \times 1.4^2.$$

The total surface area of the Frustum = **426.2 cm^2.**

Q4. Calculate the volume and total surface area of the Frustum below.
Note: *diagram not drawn to scale.*

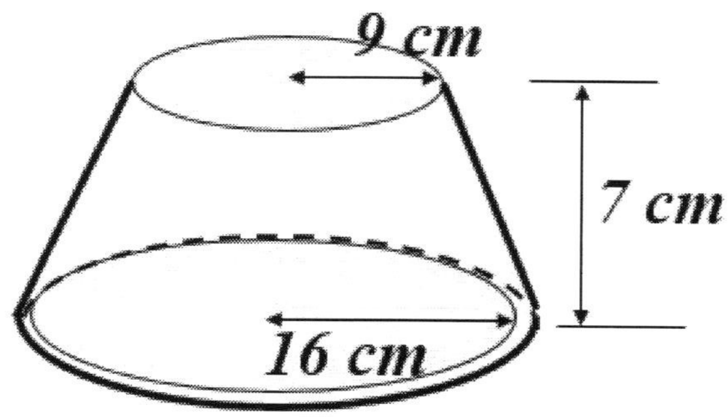

Solution:

(i) The volume of the Frustum;
The volume of the Frustum = **Volume of Big Cone – Volume of Small Cone.**

It is always difficult to calculate the volume of the Frustum alone.
Hence, an imaginary full cone needs to be constructed and H, L calculated.

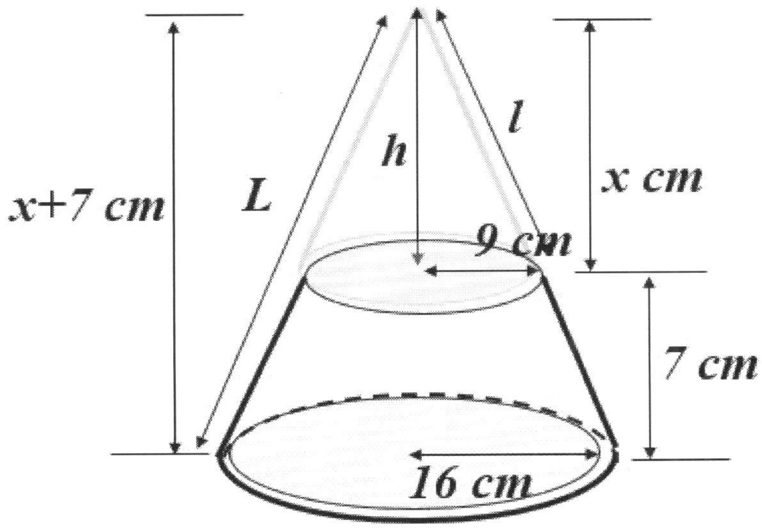

Scale factor:
Comparing the scale factors between heights and radii;

$$\frac{x}{x+7} = \frac{9}{16}$$

$$16x = 9(x+7)$$

$$16x - 9x = 63$$

$$7x = 63$$

$$x = 9\ cm$$

Hence, $\boldsymbol{H = 9 + 7 = 16\ cm}$.

Therefore, imaginary, $\boldsymbol{L}$ and l can be obtained by;

The Big (*L*) and small *slant* height (*l*);
Note that all diagrams not drawn to scale.

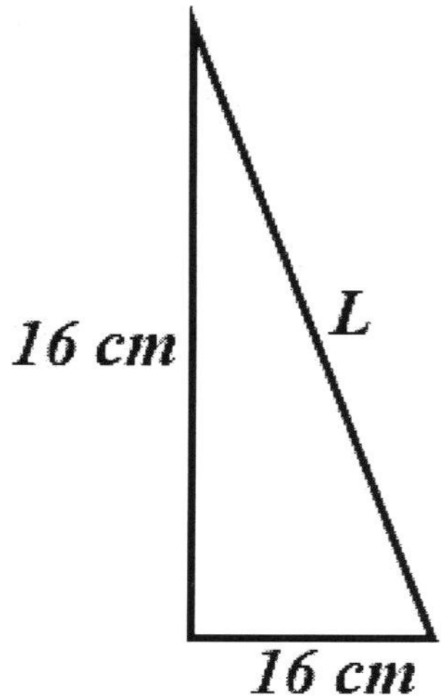

- SQUARE $= 16^2 = 256$
- SQUARE $= 16^2 = 256$
- **ADD** $= 256 + 256 = 512$
- SQUARE ROOT $= \sqrt{512} = 22.6$

→ It means, $L = 22.6$ cm

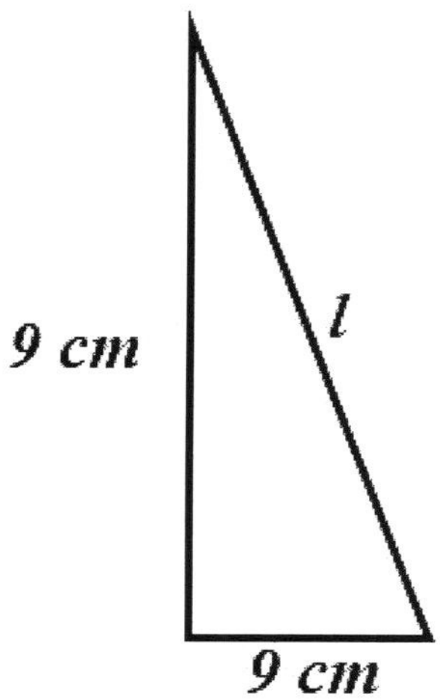

- SQUARE $= 9^2 = 81$
- SQUARE $= 9^2 = 81$
- **ADD** $= 81 + 81 = 162$
- SQUARE ROOT $= \sqrt{162} = 12.7$

→ It means, $l = 12.7$ cm

Therefore;

$$\textbf{\textit{Volume of Frustum}} = \frac{1}{3}\pi R^2 H - \frac{1}{3}\pi r^2 h$$

$$\textbf{\textit{Volume of Frustum}} = \frac{1}{3}\pi(R^2 H - r^2 h)$$

$$\textbf{\textit{Volume of Frustum}} = \frac{1}{3}\pi(16^2 \times 16 - 9^2 \times 9)$$

The volume of the Frustum = **<u>3525.9 cm³</u>.**

(ii) The total surface area of the Frustum;

The Total surface area = **Difference in curve surface area + area of Big circle + area of Small Circle.**

Therefore, the total surface area = $(\pi RL - \pi rl) + \pi R^2 + \pi r^2$.

$$= (\pi \times 16 \times 22.6 - \pi \times 9 \times 12.7) + \pi \times 16^2 + \pi \times 9^2.$$

The total surface area of the Frustum = **1835.6 cm²**.

Q5. Calculate the volume and total surface area of the Frustum below.
Note: *diagram not drawn to scale.*

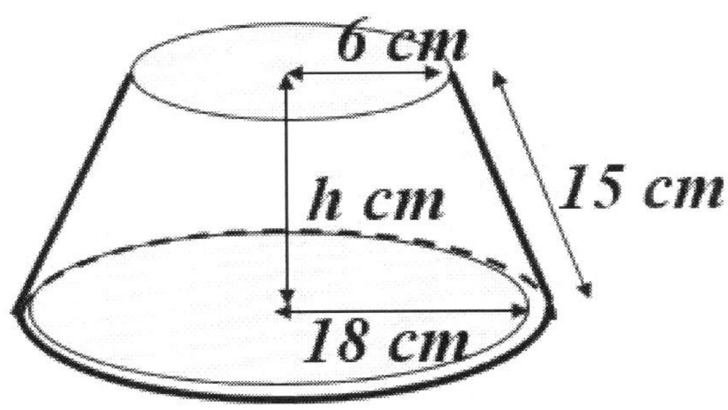

Solution:

(i) The volume of the Frustum;

The volume of the Frustum = **Volume of Big Cone – Volume of Small Cone.**

First of all, the height of the Frustum can be obtained by Pythagoras;

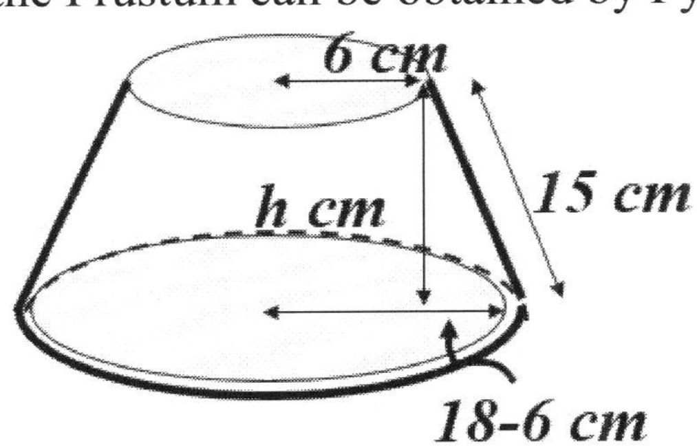

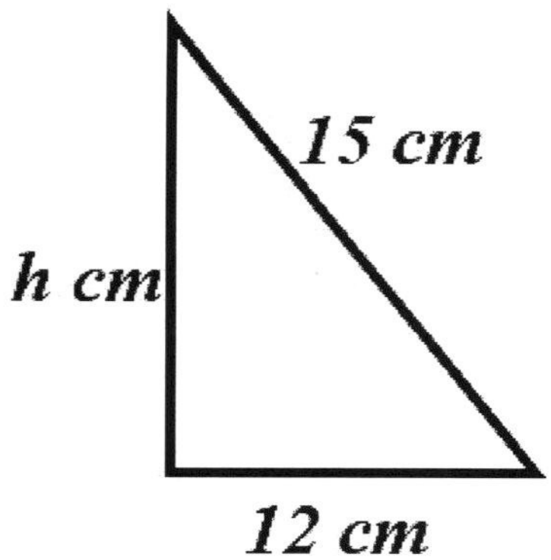

- SQUARE = $15^2 = 225$
- SQUARE = $12^2 = 144$
- **SUBTRACT** = $225 + 144 = 369$
- SQUARE ROOT = $\sqrt{369} = 19.2$

→ It means, $h = 19.2$ cm

An imaginary full cone needs to be constructed and *H*, *L* calculated.

That is;

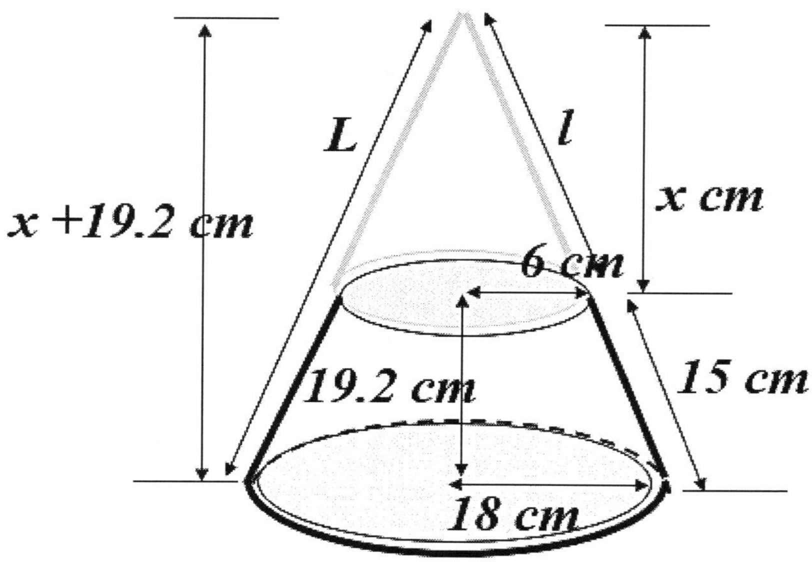

Scale factor:

Comparing the scale factors between heights and radii;

$$\frac{x}{x + 19.2} = \frac{6}{18}$$

$$18x = 6(x + 19.2)$$

$$18x - 6x = 115.2$$

$$12x = 115.2$$

$$x = 9.6\ cm$$

Hence, $\boldsymbol{H = 9.6 + 19.2 = 28.8\ cm}$.

Therefore, the imaginary, $\boldsymbol{L}$ can be obtained by;

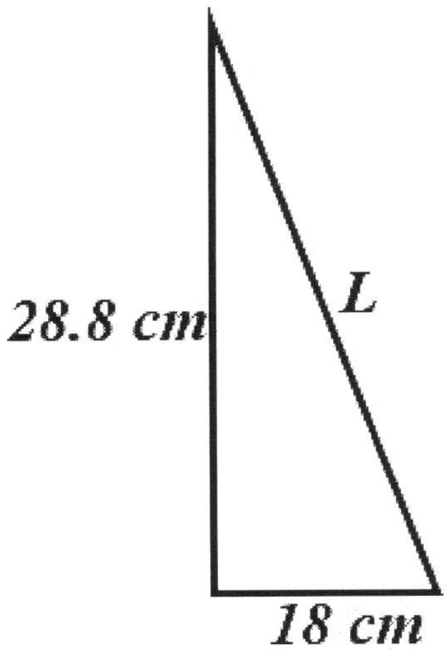

- SQUARE $= 28.8^2 = 829.44$
- SQUARE $= 18^2 = 324$
- **ADD** $= 829.44 + 324 = 1153.44$
- SQUARE ROOT $= \sqrt{1153.44} \approx 33.96$

→ It means, $L = 33.96$ cm

Meaning the *slant* height, $\boldsymbol{l = 33.96 - 15 = 18.96\ cm}$.

Therefore;

$$\boldsymbol{Volume\ of\ Frustum = \frac{1}{3}\pi R^2 H - \frac{1}{3}\pi r^2 h}$$

$$\boldsymbol{Volume\ of\ Frustum = \frac{1}{3}\pi (R^2 H - r^2 h)}$$

$$\boldsymbol{Volume\ of\ Frustum = \frac{1}{3}\pi (18^2 \times 28.8 - 6^2 \times 9.6)}$$

The volume of the Frustum = **<u>9409.7 cm^3</u>.**

(ii) The total surface area of the Frustum;

The Total surface area = **Difference in curve surface area + area of Big circle + area of Small Circle.**

Therefore, the total surface area = $(\pi RL - \pi rl) + \pi R^2 + \pi r^2$.

$$= (\pi \times 18 \times 33.96 - \pi \times 6 \times 18.96) + \pi \times 18^2 + \pi \times 6^2.$$

The total surface area of the Frustum ≈ **2694 cm²**.

C. Using Linear, Area & Volume ratios for a SIMILAR CONE

I. The Linear ratio (i.e. Scale Factor) needs to be calculated first.
II. Then the Area and Volume ratio calculated.

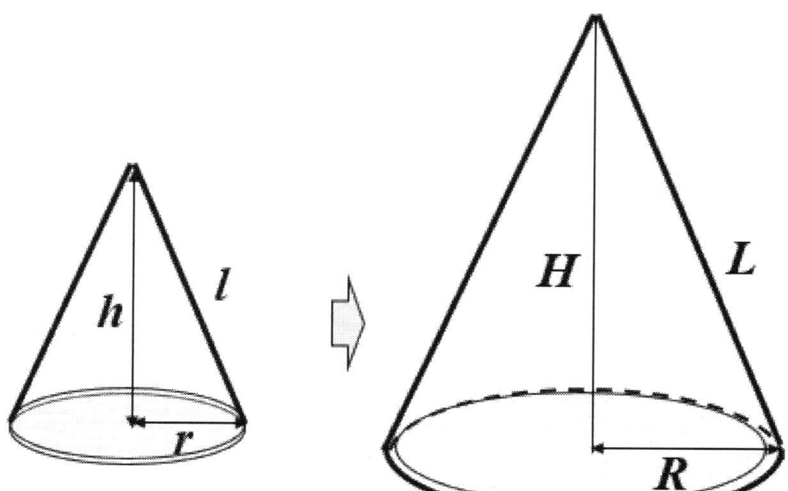

Linear ratio (1: *n*)

$$\textbf{Linear ratio} = \frac{R}{r} = \frac{H}{h} = \frac{L}{l}$$

$$\textbf{Linear ratio} = (r{:}R) \, or \, (h{:}H) \, or (l : L)$$

Once the linear ratio identified, then a ***UNIT ratio*** needs to be created by dividing with the smaller unit (i.e. ***r***, ***h*** or ***l***);

$$\textbf{Linear ratio} = \left[\frac{r}{r}:\frac{R}{r}\right] or \left[\frac{h}{h}:\frac{H}{h}\right] or \left[\frac{l}{l}:\frac{L}{l}\right]$$

$$\textbf{Linear ratio} = \left[1:\frac{R}{r}\right] or \left[1:\frac{H}{h}\right] or \left[1:\frac{L}{l}\right]$$

Hence, the ***Linear Ratio*** can be written as: $[1 : n]$

Area ratio $(1 : n^2)$

To find the ***Area ratio***, the ***Linear ratio*** needs to be **SQUARED**.

Area ratio $= [1^2 : n^2]$

Area ratio $= [1 : n^2]$

Volume ratio $(1 : n^3)$

To find the ***Volume ratio***, the ***Linear ratio*** needs to be **CUBED**.

Volume ratio $= [1^3 : n^3]$

Volume ratio $= [1 : n^3]$

Questions

Q1. The cones A and B are similar. If the volume of shape A is 83.8 cm^3,

i. calculate the volume of shape B,

ii. calculate the total surface area of A if the total surface area of B is 517.7 cm^2.

Note: *diagram not drawn to scale.*

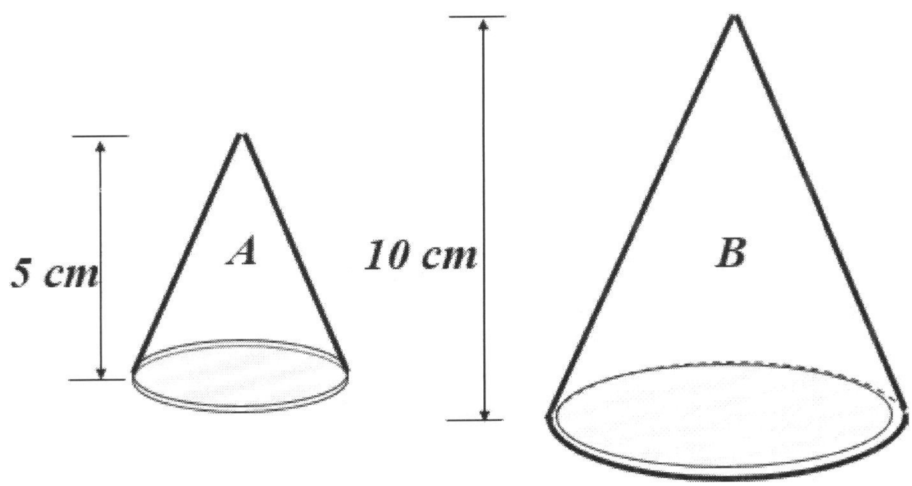

Solution:

(i) To solve the above question, you first need the linear scale factor.

$$\textbf{Linear ratio} = \left[\frac{h}{h} : \frac{H}{h}\right]$$

$$\begin{array}{c} \underline{A} : \underline{B} \end{array}$$

$$\textbf{Linear ratio} = \left[\frac{5}{5} : \frac{10}{5}\right]$$

$$\textbf{Linear ratio} = [1 : 2]$$

Volume ratio is given by;

$$\textbf{\textit{Volume} ratio} = [1^3 : 2^3] = [1 : 8]$$

Therefore, if $A = 83.8$ cm^3, B will be;

$$\underline{A} : \underline{B}$$

$$\textbf{\textit{Volume} ratio} = [1 : 8]$$

$$83.8 : 8 \times 83.8$$

$$\textbf{\textit{New Volumes are}} = [83.8 : 670.4]$$

Hence, the volume of B = **670.4 cm^3**.

ii. The total surface areas of A and B can be obtained by comparing their linear ratios;

From **Linear ratio** $= [1 : 2]$

Area ratio is given by;

$$\textit{Area}\ \textbf{ratio} = [1^2 : 2^2] = [1 : 4]$$

Therefore, if $B = 517.7$ cm^2, A will be;

$$\underline{A} : \underline{B}$$

$$\textit{Area}\ \textbf{ratio} = [1 : 4]$$

$$4 \div \downarrow \quad \downarrow \div 4$$

$$\frac{1}{4} : \frac{4}{4}$$

$$517.7 \times \downarrow \quad \downarrow \times 517.7$$

$$517.7 \times \frac{1}{4} : 517.7$$

$$\textit{New Areas are} = [129.4 : 517.7]$$

The total surface area of shape A is **<u>129.4 cm^2</u>.**

Q2. The cones A and B are similar. If the volume of shape B is 25132.7 cm^3,

i. calculate the volume of shape A,
ii. calculate the total surface area of B if the total surface area of A is 298.6 cm^2.

Note: *diagram not drawn to scale.*

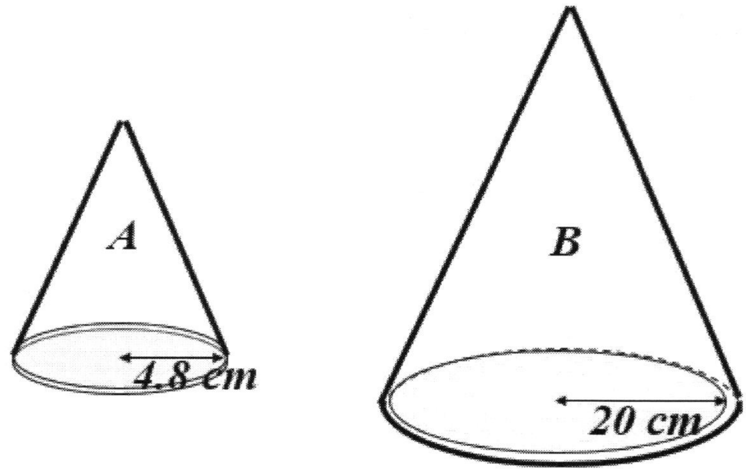

Solution:

(i) To solve the above question, you first need the linear scale factor.

$$\textbf{Linear ratio} = \left[\frac{r}{r} : \frac{R}{r}\right]$$

$$\underline{A} : \underline{B}$$

$$\textbf{Linear ratio} = \left[\frac{4.8}{4.8} : \frac{20}{4.8}\right]$$

$$\textbf{Linear ratio} = [1 : 4.2]$$

Volume ratio is given by;

$$\textbf{\textit{Volume} ratio} = [1^3 : 4.2^3] = [1 : 74.088]$$

Therefore, if $B = 25132.7\text{ cm}^3$, A will be;

$$\underline{A} : \underline{B}$$

$$\textit{Volume}\ \textbf{ratio} = [\mathbf{1} : \mathbf{74.088}]$$

$$74.088 \div \downarrow \quad \downarrow \div 74.088$$

$$\frac{\mathbf{1}}{\mathbf{74.088}} : \frac{\mathbf{74.088}}{\mathbf{74.088}}$$

$$74.088 \times \downarrow \quad \downarrow \times 25132.7$$

$$25132.7 \times \frac{\mathbf{1}}{\mathbf{74.088}} : \mathbf{25132.7}$$

$$\textit{New Volumes are} = [\mathbf{339.2} : \mathbf{25132.7}]$$

Hence, the volume of A = **339.2 cm³**.

(ii) The total surface areas of A and B can be obtained by comparing their linear ratios;

$$\text{From }\ \textbf{Linear ratio} = [\mathbf{1} : \mathbf{4.2}]$$

Area ratio is given by;

$$\textit{Area}\ \textbf{ratio} = [\mathbf{1^2} : \mathbf{4.2^2}] = [\mathbf{1} : \mathbf{17.64}]$$

Therefore, if $A = 298.6\text{ cm}^2$, B will be;

$$\underline{A} : \underline{B}$$

$$\textit{Area}\ \textbf{ratio} = [\mathbf{1} : \mathbf{17.64}]$$

$$\downarrow \quad \downarrow$$

$$\mathbf{298.6} : \mathbf{17.64 \times 298.6}$$

$$\textit{New Areas are} = [\mathbf{298.6} : \mathbf{5267.3}]$$

The total surface area of shape B is <u>**5267.3 cm²**</u>**.**

Q3. The cones *A* and *B* are similar. If the volume of shape *A* is 5394.7 cm^3,

i. calculate the volume of shape *B,*
ii. calculate the total surface area of *A* if the total surface area of *B* is 263.9 cm^2.

Note: *diagram not drawn to scale.*

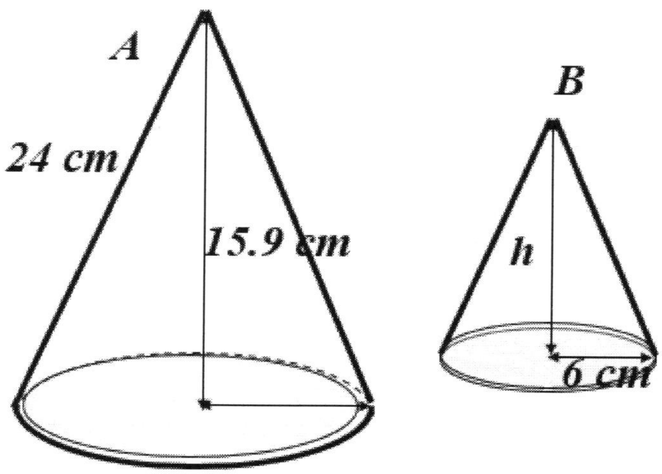

Solution:

(i) To solve the above question, you first need the linear scale factor. But to find the linear ratio, SAME dimensions needed for comparison.

It is appropriate to find the radius of shape A.

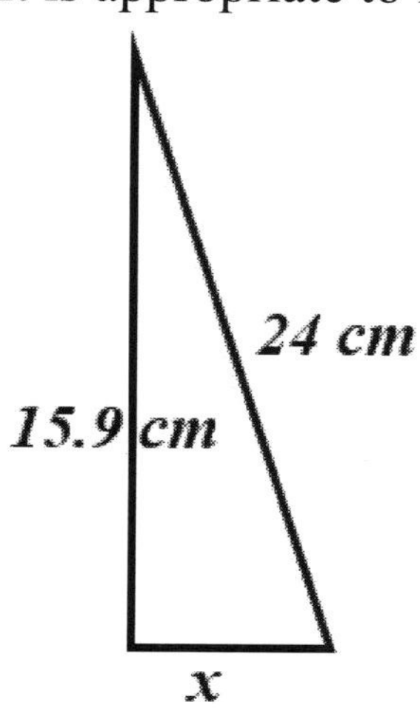

- SQUARE $= 24^2 = 576$
- SQUARE $= 15.9^2 = 252.81$
- **SUBTRACT** $= 576 - 252.81 = 323.19$
- SQUARE ROOT $= \sqrt{323.19} \approx 18$

$\rightarrow$ It means, $R = 18$ cm

Therefore;

$$\textbf{Linear ratio} = \left[\frac{r}{r} : \frac{R}{r}\right]$$

$$\underline{B} : \underline{A}$$

$$\textbf{Linear ratio} = \left[\frac{6}{6} : \frac{18}{6}\right]$$

$$\textbf{Linear ratio} = [1 : 3]$$

Volume ratio is given by;

$$\textit{Volume}\ \textbf{ratio} = [1^3 : 3^3] = [1 : 27]$$

Therefore, if $A = 5394.7$ cm^3, B will be;

$$\underline{B} : \underline{A}$$

$$\textit{Volume}\ \textbf{ratio} = [1 : 27]$$

$$27 \div \quad\quad \div 27$$

$$\frac{1}{27} : \frac{27}{27}$$

$$27 \times \quad\quad \times 5394.7$$

$$5394.7 \times \frac{1}{27} : 5394.7$$

$$\textit{New Volumes are} = [199.8 : 5394.7]$$

Hence, the volume of B = **199.8 cm^3**.

(ii) The total surface areas of A and B can be obtained by comparing their linear ratios;

From **Linear ratio** $= [\mathbf{1} : \mathbf{3}]$

Area ratio is given by;

$$\textbf{\textit{Area}}\ \textbf{ratio} = [\mathbf{1^2} : \mathbf{3^2}] = [\mathbf{1} : \mathbf{9}]$$

Therefore, if $B = 263.9$ cm^2, A will be;

$$\underline{\boldsymbol{B}} : \underline{\boldsymbol{A}}$$

$$\textbf{\textit{Area}}\ \textbf{ratio} = [\mathbf{1} : \mathbf{9}]$$

$$\mathbf{263.9 : 9 \times 263.9}$$

$$\textbf{\textit{New Areas are}} = [\mathbf{263.9 : 2375.1}]$$

The total surface area of shape A is **<u>2375.1 cm^2</u>.**

Q4. The cones A and B are similar. If the areas of shape A and B are 613.6 cm^2 and 1918.1 cm^2, respectively,

i. calculate the volume of shape A, if the volume of B is 4289.3 cm^3.
ii. calculate the radius of shape A if the radius of B is 16 cm.

Note: *diagram not drawn to scale.*

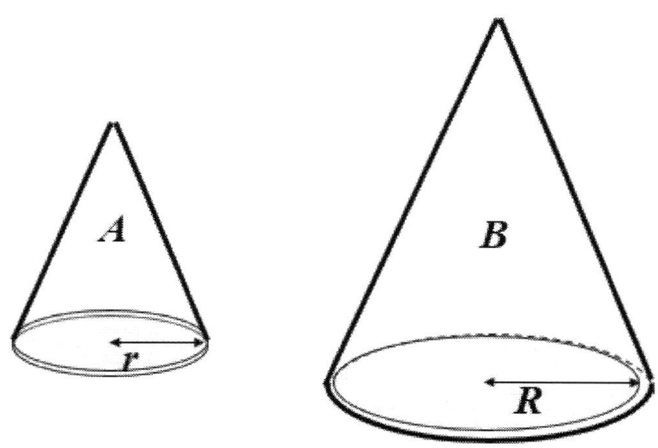

<u>Solution:</u>

(i) To solve the above question, the linear scale factor (i.e. the linear ratio) needs to be calculated.

This can be obtained from the area ratios given.

$$\underline{A} \quad : \quad \underline{B}$$

$$\textit{Area}\ \textbf{ratio} = \left[\frac{613.6}{613.6} \quad : \quad \frac{1918.1}{613.6}\right]$$

$$\textit{Area}\ \textbf{ratio} = [1 \quad : \quad 3.13]$$

Linear ratio can be obtained by square rooting the area ratios

$$\textit{Linear}\ \textbf{ratio} = [\sqrt{1} \quad : \quad \sqrt{3.13}]$$

$$\textbf{Linear ratio} = [1 : 1.77]$$

Volume ratio is given by;

$$\textit{Volume}\ \textbf{ratio} = [1^3 : 1.77^3] = [1 : 5.55]$$

Therefore, if $B = 4289.3\ \text{cm}^3$, A will be;

$$\underline{A} : \underline{B}$$

$$\textit{Volume}\ \textbf{ratio} = [1 \quad : \quad 5.55]$$

$$5.55 \div \downarrow \qquad \downarrow \div 5.55$$

$$\frac{1}{5.55} : \frac{5.55}{5.55}$$

$$4289.3 \times \downarrow \qquad \downarrow \times 4289.3$$

$$4289.3 \times \frac{1}{5.55} : 4289.3$$

$$\textit{New Volumes are} = [772.9 : \quad 4289.3]$$

Hence, the volume of A = **772.9 cm³**.

(ii) To find the radius A, compare the radius of B with the linear ratio since the radii are linear dimensions;

If radius of $B = 16$ cm , A will be;

$$\begin{array}{rccc} & \underline{A} & : & \underline{B} \\ \textit{Radius}\ \text{ratio} = & [1 & : & 1.77] \\ 5.55 \div & \downarrow & & \downarrow \div 1.77 \\ & \dfrac{1}{1.77} & : & \dfrac{1.77}{1.77} \\ 16 \times & \downarrow & & \downarrow \times 16 \\ & 16 \times \dfrac{1}{1.77} & : & 16 \\ \textit{New radii are} = & [9 & : & 16] \end{array}$$

The radius of shape A is **9 cm.**

Q5. The cones A and B are similar. If the volume of shape A and B are 361.9 cm^3 and 9771.6 cm^3, respectively,

i. calculate the area of shape B, if the area of A is 470.5 cm^2.
ii. calculate the radius of shape B if the radius of A is 6 cm.

Note: *diagram not drawn to scale.*

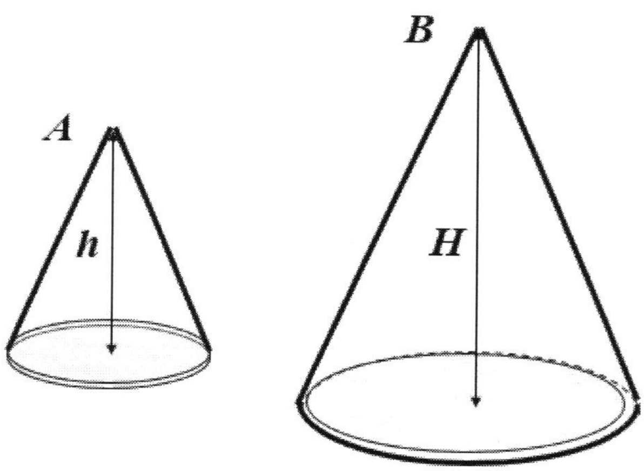

Solution:

(i) To solve the above question, the linear scale factor (i.e. the linear ratio) needs to be calculated.

This can be obtained from the volume ratios given.

$$\begin{array}{ccc} \underline{A} & : & \underline{B} \end{array}$$

$$\textit{Volume}\ \textbf{ratio} = \left[\frac{361.9}{361.9} \quad : \quad \frac{9771.6}{361.9}\right]$$

$$\textit{Volume}\ \textbf{ratio} = [1 \quad : \quad 27]$$

Linear ratio can be obtained by cube rooting the volume ratios

$$\textit{Linear}\ \textbf{ratio} = \left[\sqrt[3]{1} \quad : \quad \sqrt[3]{27}\right]$$

$$\textbf{Linear ratio} = \quad [1 \ : 3]$$

Area ratio is given by;

$$\textit{Area}\ \textbf{ratio} = \quad \left[1^2 \ : 3^2\right] = \quad [1 \ : 9]$$

Therefore, if $A = 470.5\ \text{cm}^2$, B will be;

$$\begin{array}{ccc} \underline{A} & : & \underline{B} \end{array}$$

$$\textit{Area}\ \textbf{ratio} = \quad [1 \quad : \quad 9]$$

↓ ↓

$$470.5 : \ 9 \times 470.5$$

$$\textit{New Areas are} = \quad [470.5 : \quad 4234.5]$$

Hence, the area of $B = \mathbf{4234.5\ cm^2}$.

(ii) To find the radius B, compare the radius of A with the linear ratio since the radii are linear dimensions;

From the linear ratios;

$$\textit{Linear}\ \textbf{ratio} = \quad [1 \quad : \quad 3]$$

If radius of $A = 6$ cm , B will be;

$$\underline{A} : \underline{B}$$

$$\textit{Radius}\ \text{ratio} = [1 : 3]$$

$$6 : 3 \times 6$$

$$\textit{New Areas are} = [6 : 18]$$

The radius of shape *B* is **18 cm.**

Note: Once the volumes and surface areas for the similar cones are calculated,

- The volumes of the Frustums can be determined by subtracting small cones from the big cones.
- The total surface areas of the Frustums can be obtained by resolving the curve surface areas of the *Big* and *Small* cones plus the area of the *big circles*.

4. Vectors

A vector is a quantity that has magnitude and direction. That means it describes the direction and length of a movement.
While the magnitude tells you the size the displacement tells you the direction.
A displacement vector can be displayed on a co-ordinate grid as a directed line segment.
Vectors are denoted by a bold letter and a column pair = $(\boldsymbol{x}, \boldsymbol{y})$.
There are lots of key factors to consider when working with vectors;

A. **Position vectors of (*x*, *y*) from the origin O can be written as;**

$$= \begin{pmatrix} x \\ y \end{pmatrix}$$

B. **MULTIPLYING a vector by SCALER;**

If a vector $\boldsymbol{t} = \begin{bmatrix} x \\ y \end{bmatrix}$, then **k*t*** can be written as;

$$\boldsymbol{kt} = \boldsymbol{k}\begin{bmatrix} x \\ y \end{bmatrix} = \begin{bmatrix} \boldsymbol{kx} \\ \boldsymbol{ky} \end{bmatrix}$$

C. **Finding a PARALLEL vector;**

When two vectors are ***PARALLEL***, one of them is scaler MULTIPLE of the other.

Example, if a vector $\overrightarrow{\boldsymbol{CD}} = \begin{bmatrix} x \\ y \end{bmatrix}$ and $\overrightarrow{\boldsymbol{WR}} = \begin{bmatrix} \boldsymbol{kx} \\ \boldsymbol{ky} \end{bmatrix}$ then **they** can be written as;

$$\overrightarrow{\boldsymbol{CD}} = \boldsymbol{k}\overrightarrow{\boldsymbol{WR}}$$

$$\overrightarrow{\boldsymbol{CD}} \text{ and } \overrightarrow{\boldsymbol{WR}} \text{ are PARALLEL}$$

D. The displacement vector from A to B is written as $\overrightarrow{AB}$;

If $A = (5, 9)$ and $B = (3, 4)$. The displacement vector will be;

$$\overset{12}{\overrightarrow{AB}} = \overset{2}{\vec{B}} - \overset{1}{\vec{A}}$$

Remember: its ***B***(position ***2***) minus ***A***(position ***1***).

E. Displacement vector can be obtained by Pythagoras.

Example: A displacement of (4, 3) can be written;

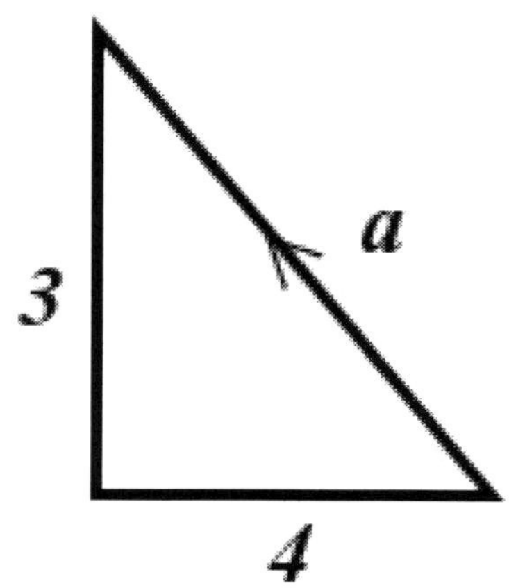

And can be calculated as.

$$a = \sqrt{3^2 + 4^2} = 5$$

F. **Finding Position vectors from the origin O;**

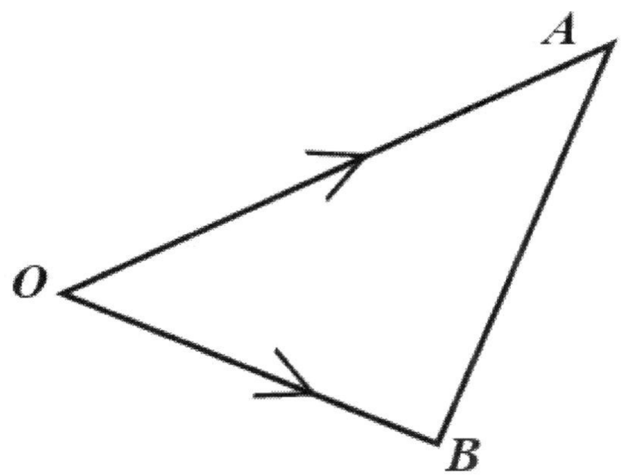

And the vector $\overrightarrow{AB}$ is given by;

$$\overrightarrow{\boldsymbol{AB}} = \overrightarrow{\boldsymbol{OB}} - \overrightarrow{\boldsymbol{OA}}$$

G. **Finding EQUAL vectors;**

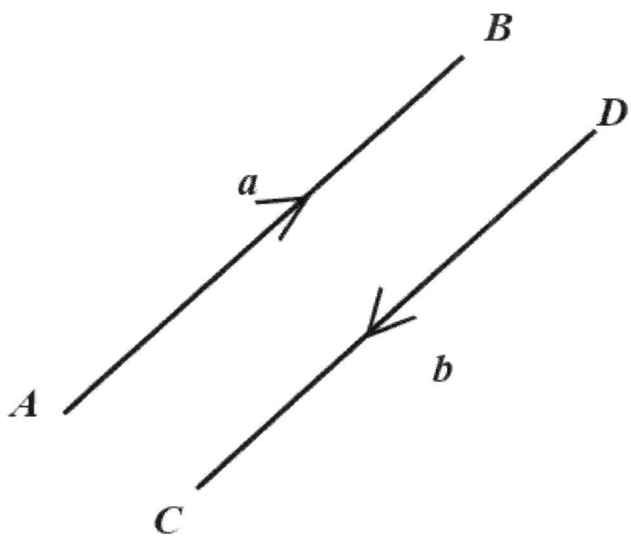

Vectors can be equal but opposite;

$$\overrightarrow{\boldsymbol{AB}} = \boldsymbol{a} \text{ and } \overrightarrow{\boldsymbol{DC}} = \boldsymbol{b}$$

This can also be written as;

$$\overrightarrow{\boldsymbol{AB}} = -\boldsymbol{b}$$

Hence,

$$\overrightarrow{\boldsymbol{AB}} = -\overrightarrow{\boldsymbol{DC}}$$

H. **ADDING and SUBTRACTING vectors;**

To add or subtract vectors, the triangle law is used.

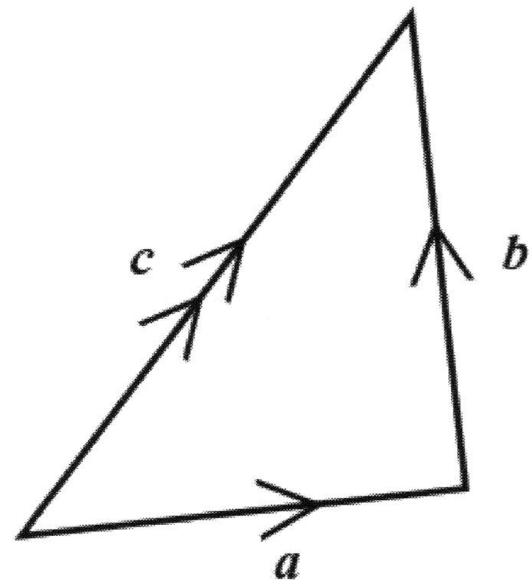

This means the vector $\boldsymbol{c}$ can be obtained by moving a distance of $\boldsymbol{a}$ and $\boldsymbol{b}$.

$$\boldsymbol{c} = \boldsymbol{a} + \boldsymbol{b} \quad \text{or} \quad \boldsymbol{a} + \boldsymbol{b} = \boldsymbol{c}$$

I. You must know all the basic rules surrounding *Triangle*, *Trapezium*, *Rhombus* and *Parallelogram*;

In vectors, this is simple as **walking around** a fence to get to your destination but you must follow the rules of vectors such as the **direction** of the ***displacement vector***.

When you walk opposite to the **direction** of the displacement vector, the value begins **negatively**.

Example 1: To find $\overrightarrow{AM}$ from the diagram below;

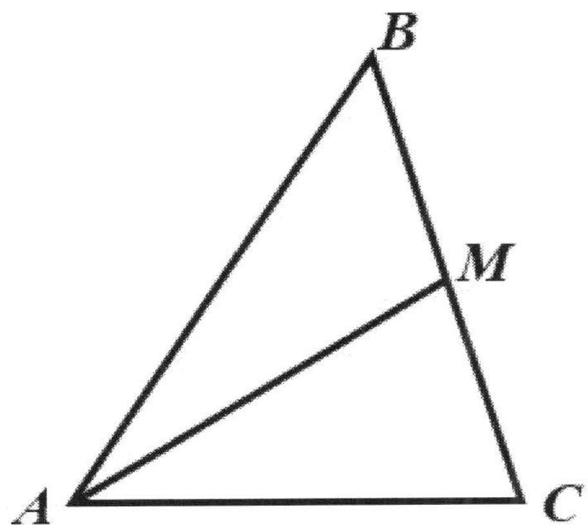

You must find the direction to go ROUND from $\boldsymbol{A}$ and get to $\boldsymbol{M}$. It does not matter which path you take. So far as you add the appropriate magnitudes along that path.

Method 1: go from $\boldsymbol{A} \rightarrow \boldsymbol{B} \rightarrow \boldsymbol{M}$

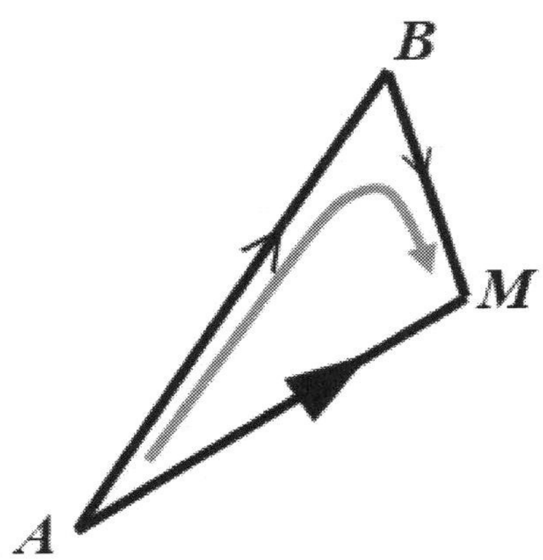

$$\overrightarrow{\boldsymbol{AM}} = \overrightarrow{\boldsymbol{AB}} + \overrightarrow{\boldsymbol{BM}}$$

Or

Method 2: go from $\boldsymbol{A} \rightarrow \boldsymbol{C} \rightarrow \boldsymbol{M}$

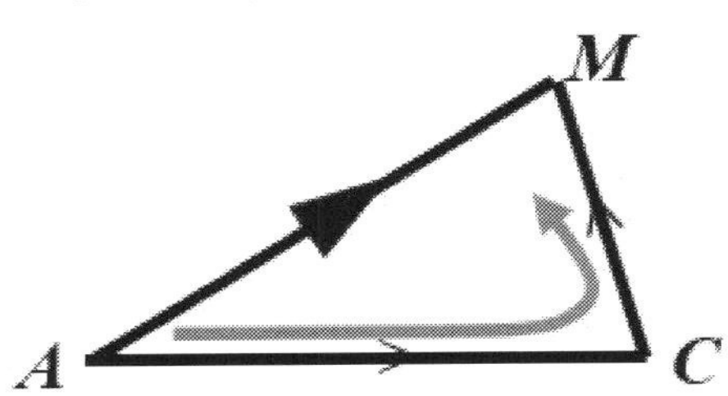

$$\overrightarrow{\boldsymbol{AM}} = \overrightarrow{\boldsymbol{AC}} + \overrightarrow{\boldsymbol{CM}}$$

Example 2: To find vector $\overrightarrow{\boldsymbol{AE}}$ from the diagram below;

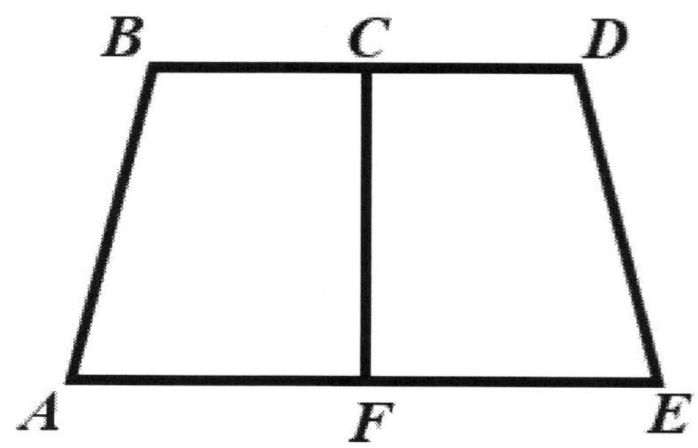

There are ***THREE*** ways to move from ***A*** to ***E*** as illustrated below.

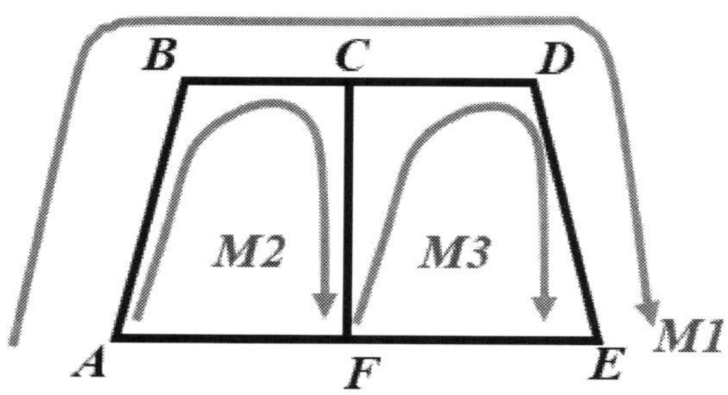

Method 1 → M1

$$\overrightarrow{AE} = \overrightarrow{AB} + \overrightarrow{BC} + \overrightarrow{CD} + \overrightarrow{DE}$$

Method 2 → M2

$$\overrightarrow{AE} = 2\overrightarrow{AF} = 2[\overrightarrow{AB} + \overrightarrow{BC} + \overrightarrow{CF}]$$

Method 3 → M3

$$\overrightarrow{AE} = 2\overrightarrow{FE} = 2[\overrightarrow{FC} + \overrightarrow{CD} + \overrightarrow{DE}]$$

J. **Changing BEARINGS information into Vector Components;**

The following information can be resolved as follows;

Moving from ***A*** to ***B*** at a bearing of $\boldsymbol{\theta}$ (i.e. 0 < 90°) for ***R*** distance;

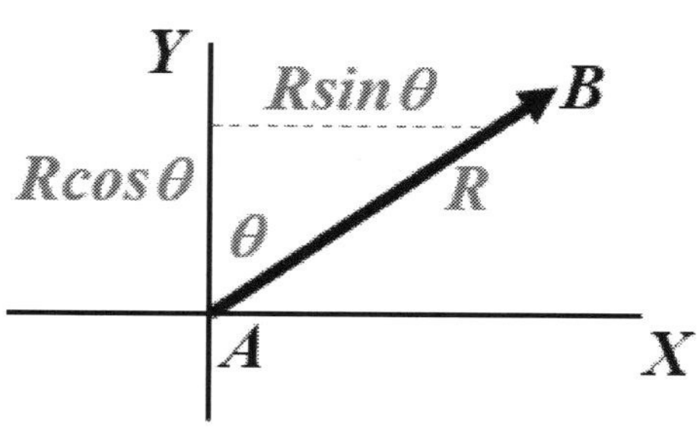

The vector $\overrightarrow{AB}$ is then given by;

$$\overrightarrow{AB} = \begin{bmatrix} R\sin\theta \\ R\cos\theta \end{bmatrix}$$

Moving from ***A*** to ***B*** at a bearing of ***θ*** (i.e. $0 < \theta < 180°$) for ***R*** distance;

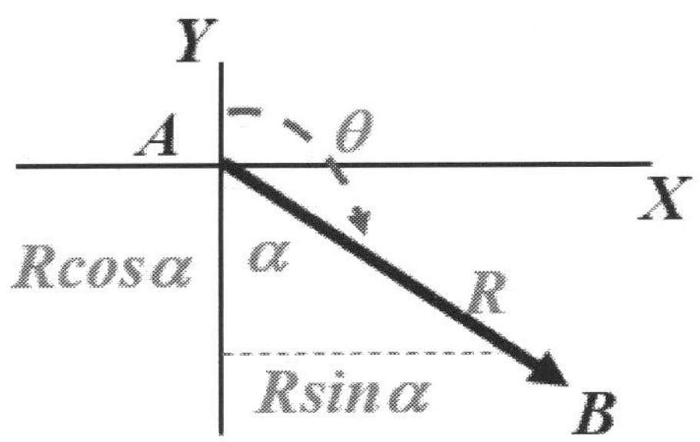

Note: *180 - θ = α*

The vector $\overrightarrow{AB}$ is then given by;

$$\Rightarrow \quad \overrightarrow{AB} = \begin{bmatrix} R\sin\alpha \\ R\cos\alpha \end{bmatrix}$$

Questions

Q1. Vector ***R*** and ***S*** are depicted in the diagram below;

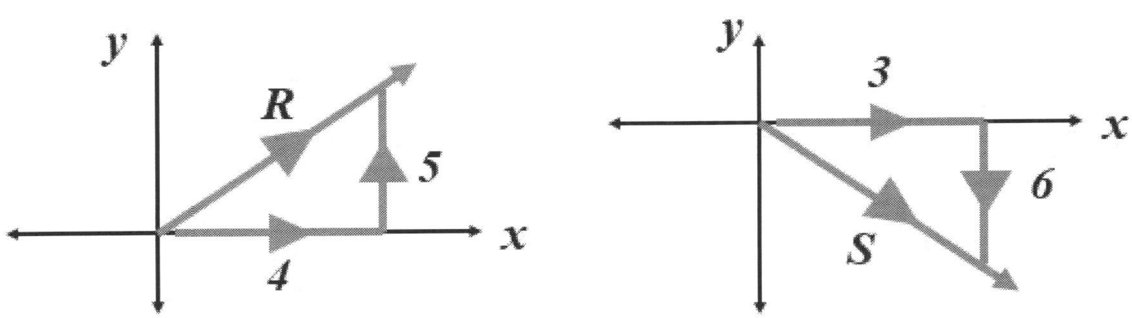

Note: *diagram not drawn to scale.*

Use the graphs to answer the following questions;

i. Write the two vectors as column vectors,

ii. Find (*a*) ***R+S***, (*b*) ***S-R***, and (*c*) ***7R-4S***.

iii. Find $\overrightarrow{RS}$ and $|RS|$.

Solution:

(i) The column vectors are given by;

$$R = \begin{bmatrix} 3 \\ -6 \end{bmatrix} \text{ and } S = \begin{bmatrix} 4 \\ 5 \end{bmatrix}$$

(ii) These are additions and subtractions of vectors as well as the finding the magnitude of vectors.

$$\text{(a) } R + S = \begin{bmatrix} 3 \\ -6 \end{bmatrix} + \begin{bmatrix} 4 \\ 5 \end{bmatrix} = \begin{bmatrix} 3+4 \\ -6+5 \end{bmatrix} = \begin{bmatrix} 7 \\ -1 \end{bmatrix}$$

$$\text{(b) } S - R = \begin{bmatrix} 4 \\ 5 \end{bmatrix} - \begin{bmatrix} 3 \\ -6 \end{bmatrix} = \begin{bmatrix} 4-3 \\ 5--6 \end{bmatrix} = \begin{bmatrix} 1 \\ 11 \end{bmatrix}$$

$$\text{(c) } 7R - 4S = 7\begin{bmatrix} 3 \\ -6 \end{bmatrix} - 4\begin{bmatrix} 4 \\ 5 \end{bmatrix} = \begin{bmatrix} 21 \\ -42 \end{bmatrix} - \begin{bmatrix} 16 \\ 20 \end{bmatrix}$$

$$= \begin{bmatrix} 21-16 \\ -42-20 \end{bmatrix} = \begin{bmatrix} 5 \\ -62 \end{bmatrix}$$

(iii)

$$\overrightarrow{RS} = S - R = \begin{bmatrix} 4 \\ 5 \end{bmatrix} - \begin{bmatrix} 3 \\ -6 \end{bmatrix} = \begin{bmatrix} 1 \\ 11 \end{bmatrix}$$

$$|RS| = \sqrt{x^2 + y^2} = \sqrt{1^2 + 11^2} = 11.1 \text{ units}$$

Q2. If the coordinates of ***M*** from the origin is (8, 3) and that of ***N*** is (5, 5)

i. Write the M and N as position vectors,

ii. Find the displacement vectors $\overrightarrow{MN}$ and $\overrightarrow{NM}$.

iii. Find the magnitudes of $\overrightarrow{MN}$ (i.e. $|MN|$) and $\overrightarrow{NM}$ (i.e. $|NM|$)

Solution:

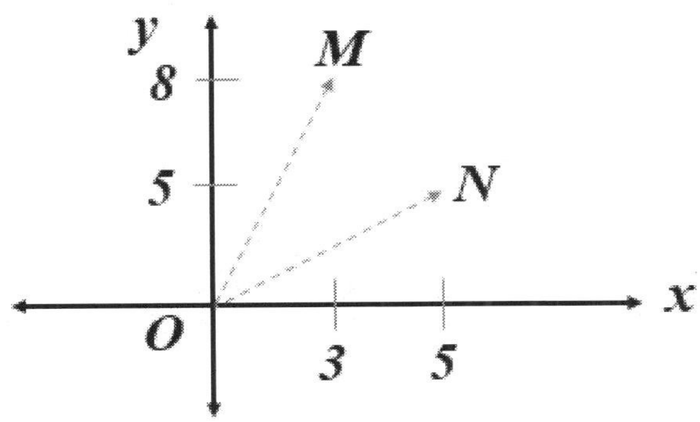

(i) The column vectors are given by;

$$\overrightarrow{OM} = \begin{bmatrix} 8 \\ 3 \end{bmatrix} \text{ and } \overrightarrow{ON} = \begin{bmatrix} 5 \\ 5 \end{bmatrix}$$

(ii)

$$\overrightarrow{MN} = N - M = \begin{bmatrix} 5 \\ 5 \end{bmatrix} - \begin{bmatrix} 8 \\ 3 \end{bmatrix} = \begin{bmatrix} 5-8 \\ 5-3 \end{bmatrix} = \begin{bmatrix} -3 \\ 2 \end{bmatrix}$$

$$\overrightarrow{NM} = M - N = \begin{bmatrix} 8 \\ 3 \end{bmatrix} - \begin{bmatrix} 5 \\ 5 \end{bmatrix} = \begin{bmatrix} 8-5 \\ 3-5 \end{bmatrix} = \begin{bmatrix} 3 \\ -2 \end{bmatrix}$$

(iii)

$$|MN| = \sqrt{x^2 + y^2} = \sqrt{(-3)^2 + 2^2} = 3.6\ units$$

$$|MN| = \sqrt{x^2 + y^2} = \sqrt{9^2 + (-2)^2} = 3.6\ units$$

Q3. Find the column vectors of the following bearings

i. $\overrightarrow{CD} = [7\ km,\ 046°]$,

ii. $\overrightarrow{DA} = [13\ km,\ 157°]$.

<u>Solution:</u>

The bearings can be resolved as follows;

(i) $\overrightarrow{CD} = [7\ km,\ 046°]$,

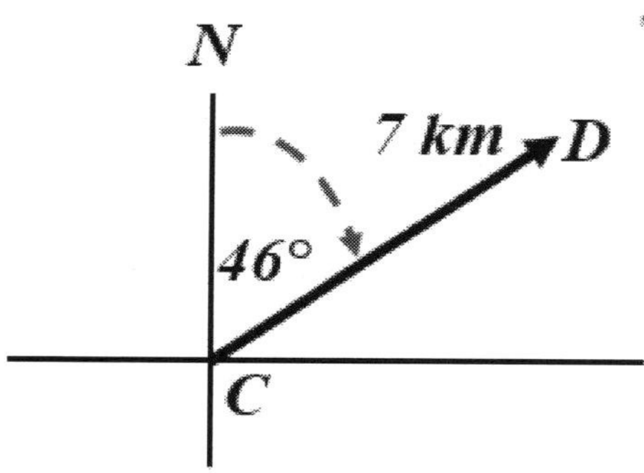

The column vector $\overrightarrow{CD}$ is given by;

$$\Rightarrow \quad \overrightarrow{CD} = \begin{bmatrix} 7\sin 46 \\ 7\cos 46 \end{bmatrix}$$

$$\overrightarrow{CD} = \begin{bmatrix} 5 \\ 4.9 \end{bmatrix}$$

(ii) $\overrightarrow{DA} = [13\ km,\ 157°]$.

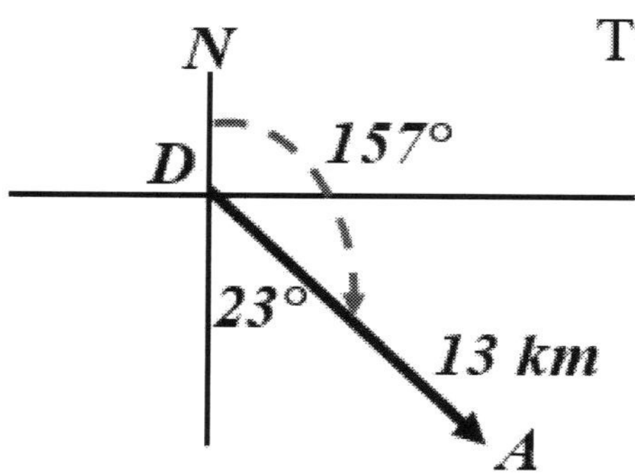

The column vector $\overrightarrow{DA}$ is given by;

$$\Rightarrow \quad \overrightarrow{DA} = \begin{bmatrix} 13\sin 23 \\ -13\cos 23 \end{bmatrix}$$

$$\overrightarrow{DA} = \begin{bmatrix} 5.1 \\ -12 \end{bmatrix}$$

The ***y*-vector** is ***NEGATIVE*** because it is moving down.

Q4. The shape $QRST$ below is a trapezium with the vector $\overrightarrow{QR} = a$, $\overrightarrow{RS} = b$ and $\overrightarrow{QM} = c$. M is the mid-point of $\overrightarrow{ST}$. Find;

i. the vector $\overrightarrow{MS}$,

ii. the vector $\overrightarrow{MT}$, and

iii. the vector $\overrightarrow{QT}$.

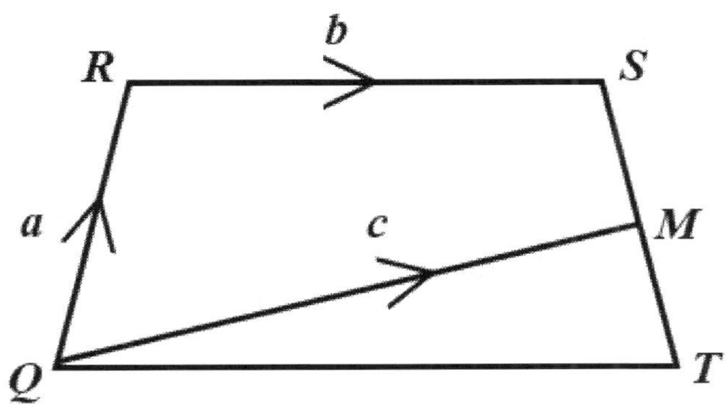

Solution:

(i) The vector can be obtained by going round from;

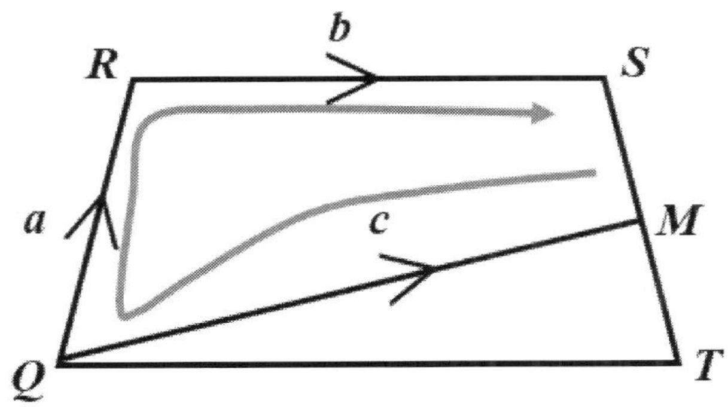

$$\boldsymbol{M \rightarrow Q \rightarrow R \rightarrow S}$$

That is;

$$\overrightarrow{\boldsymbol{MS}} = \overrightarrow{\boldsymbol{MQ}} + \overrightarrow{\boldsymbol{QR}} + \overrightarrow{\boldsymbol{RS}}$$

<u>**Note**</u> that we are moving opposite to $\overrightarrow{QM} = c$. Hence $\overrightarrow{MQ} = -c$.

Therefore;

$$\overrightarrow{\boldsymbol{MS}} = -\boldsymbol{c} + \boldsymbol{a} + \boldsymbol{b}$$

$$\underline{\overrightarrow{MS} = a + b - c}$$

(ii) The vector $\overrightarrow{MT}$ is **EQUAL** but **OPPOSITE** to $\overrightarrow{MS}$,;

That is;

$$\overrightarrow{MT} = -\overrightarrow{MS}$$

$$\overrightarrow{MT} = -(a + b - c)$$

Therefore;

$$\underline{\overrightarrow{MT} = (c - a - b)}$$

(iii) The vector can be obtained in two ways;

Method 1; we go from $Q \rightarrow M \rightarrow T$;

$$\overrightarrow{QT} = \overrightarrow{QM} + \overrightarrow{MT}$$

$$\overrightarrow{QT} = c + (c - a - b)$$

$$\underline{\overrightarrow{QT} = 2c - a - b}$$

Method 2; we go from $Q \rightarrow M \rightarrow T$;

$$\overrightarrow{QT} = \overrightarrow{QR} + \overrightarrow{RS} + \overrightarrow{ST}$$

But;

$$\overrightarrow{ST} = 2\overrightarrow{MT}$$

$$\overrightarrow{QT} = a + b + 2(c - a - b)$$

$$\overrightarrow{QT} = a + b + 2c - 2a - 2b$$

$$\underline{\overrightarrow{QT} = 2c - a - b}$$

Q5. The shape *MNOPQRST* below is an octagon having a vector $\overrightarrow{TO}$ parallel to $\overrightarrow{SP}$.

Find;

i. the vector $\overrightarrow{TO}$, and

ii. the vector $\overrightarrow{PS}$.

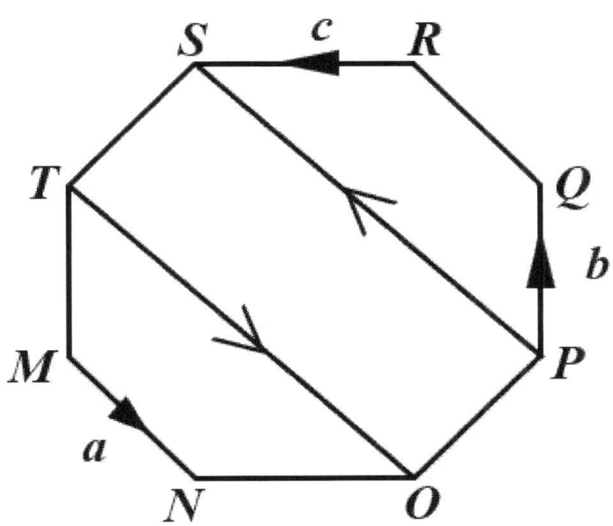

Solution:

(i) Note that the vector $\overrightarrow{\boldsymbol{NO}}$ is the same, **PARALLEL** but ***OPPOSITE*** to $\overrightarrow{\boldsymbol{SR}}$. Hence,

$$\overrightarrow{NO} = -c$$

Also, the vector $\overrightarrow{\boldsymbol{TM}}$ is the same, **PARALLEL** but ***OPPOSITE*** to $\overrightarrow{\boldsymbol{QP}}$. Hence,

$$\overrightarrow{TM} = -b$$

It means that the diagram can be drawn as;

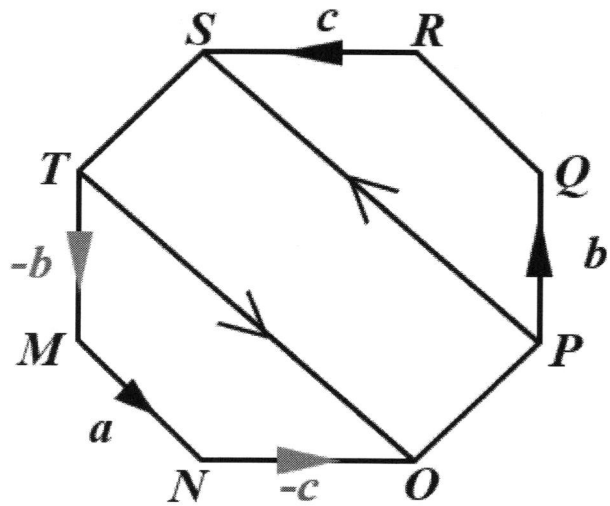

Therefore,

$$\overrightarrow{TO} = \overrightarrow{TM} + \overrightarrow{MN} + \overrightarrow{NO}$$

$$\overrightarrow{TO} = -\boldsymbol{b} + \boldsymbol{a} + -\boldsymbol{c}$$

$$\overrightarrow{TO} = \boldsymbol{a} - \boldsymbol{b} - \boldsymbol{c}$$

(ii) $\overrightarrow{PS}$ is PARALLEL, Equal but ***OPPOSITE*** to $\overrightarrow{TO}$.

Hence,

$$\overrightarrow{PS} = -\overrightarrow{TO}$$
$$\overrightarrow{PS} = -[\boldsymbol{a} - \boldsymbol{b} - \boldsymbol{c}]$$
$$\underline{\overrightarrow{PS} = \boldsymbol{b} + \boldsymbol{c} - \boldsymbol{a}}$$

Q6. The shape below is a triangle *XYZ* such that *Xt* : *tY* is in a ratio of 3: 5. Find;

i. the vector $\overrightarrow{XY}$, in terms of ***a*** and ***b***.

ii. the vector $\overrightarrow{tZ}$. In terms of ***a*** and ***b***.

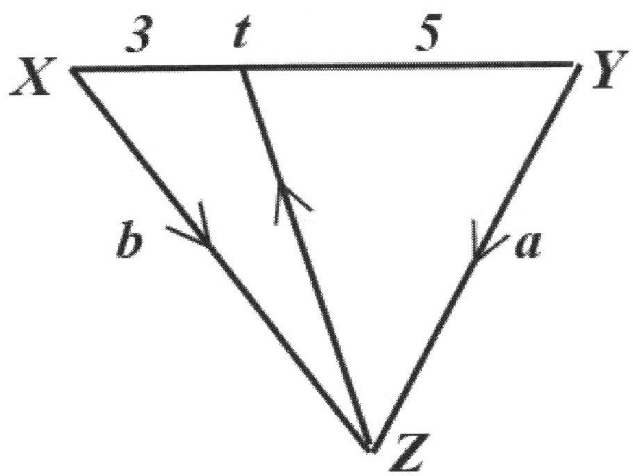

Solution:

1. To find $\overrightarrow{XY}$ go from X to Z then to Y.

Therefore;

$$\overrightarrow{XY} = \overrightarrow{XZ} + \overrightarrow{ZY}$$

$$\overrightarrow{XY} = \boldsymbol{b} + -\boldsymbol{a}$$

$$\overrightarrow{XY} = \boldsymbol{b} - \boldsymbol{a}$$

2. To find $\overrightarrow{tZ}$ go from t to X then to Z.

Therefore;

$$\overrightarrow{tZ} = \overrightarrow{tX} + \overrightarrow{XZ}$$

But

$$\overrightarrow{tX} = \frac{3}{8}\overrightarrow{YX}$$

This leads to;

$$\overrightarrow{tX} = \frac{3}{8}\left(-\overrightarrow{XY}\right)$$

$$\overrightarrow{tX} = \frac{3}{8}[-(b-a)]$$

$$\overrightarrow{tX} = \frac{3}{8}[a-b]$$

The answer for $\overrightarrow{tZ}$ **is;**

$$\overrightarrow{tZ} = \overrightarrow{tX} + \overrightarrow{XZ} = \frac{3}{8}[a-b] + b$$

$$\overrightarrow{tZ} = \frac{3}{8}[a-b] + b$$

$$\overrightarrow{tZ} = \frac{3}{8}a - \frac{3}{8}b + b$$

$$\overrightarrow{tZ} = \frac{3}{8}a + b - \frac{3}{8}b$$

$$\overrightarrow{tZ} = \frac{3}{8}a + \frac{5}{8}b$$

$$\overrightarrow{tZ} = \frac{1}{8}[3a + 5b]$$

5. Circles – Equation & Geometry

Strategy:

A. Equation of a Circle

Note: The focus will be on the GCSE curriculum although the content can be applied to other curriculums.

I. Equation having a centre at point (a, b)

In general, if $\boldsymbol{Q}(x, y)$ is a point on a circle whose centre $\boldsymbol{C}(a, b)$ and radius, $\boldsymbol{r}$, then this can be represented as illustrated below;

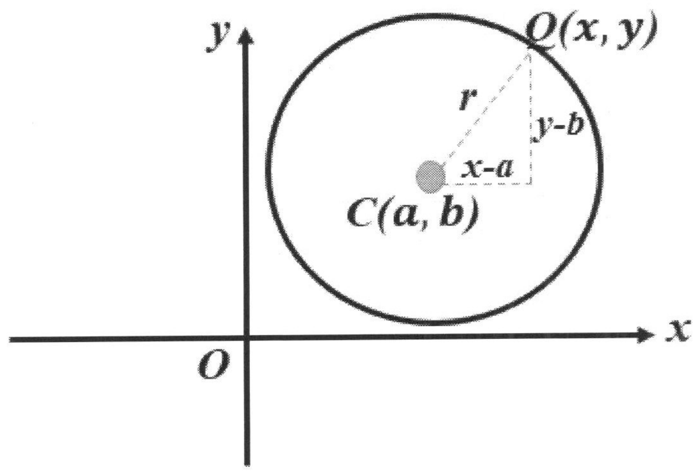

Using Pythagoras theorem,

$$(x-a)^2 + (y-b)^2 = r^2$$

II. Equation having centre at the origin $(0, 0)$

If $\boldsymbol{Q}(x, y)$ is a point on a circle whose centre is at the origin $\boldsymbol{C}(0, 0)$ and radius, $\boldsymbol{r}$, then this can be represented as illustrated below;

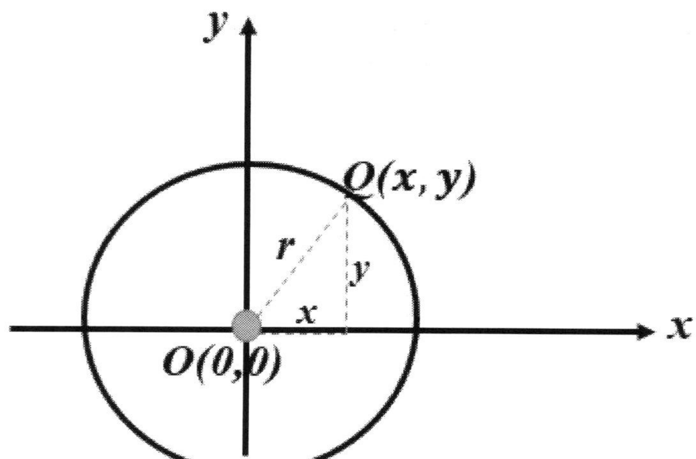

Using Pythagoras theorem,

$$(x-0)^2+(y-0)^2=r^2$$

$$x^2+y^2=r^2$$

B. Perpendicular lines within and around the circles

In general, when **two straight lines** meet at an angle of ***90°*** or when two straight lines cross **perpendicularly**, the ***PRODUCT*** of their gradients must be equal to ***-1***.

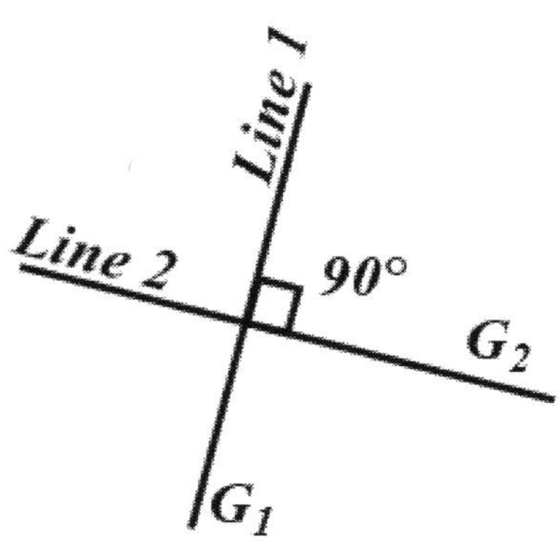

If gradient of line 1 is G_1.
and that of line 2 is G_2.

$$G_1 \times G_2 = -1$$

It implies that;

$$G_1 = \frac{-1}{G_2}$$

It simply means that the ***Gradient*** of one straight line is ***EQUAL*** to the ***RECIPROCAL*** of the second straight line **MINUS ONE**.

I. Perpendicular lines within Circles

The diagram below illustrated perpendicular lines within a circle.

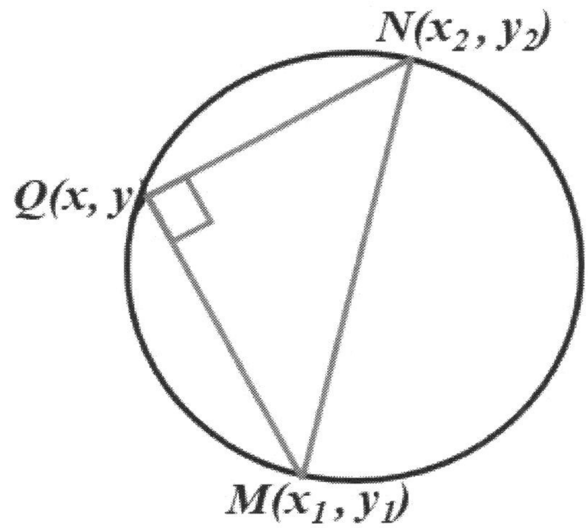

Using the above Principle, the ***product*** of the gradient of ***QM*** (i.e. G_{QM}) and the gradient of ***QN*** (i.e. G_{QN}) must be equal to **-1**.

This means that;

$$[G_{QM}] \times [G_{QN}] = -1$$

$$\left[\frac{y - y_1}{x - x_1}\right] \times \left[\frac{y - y_2}{x - x_2}\right] = -1$$

The *equation above* can be used to prove that the TWO lines are PERPENDICULAR.

II. Perpendicular lines around the Circles: Tangents

Note: Focus will be limited to circles having the centre at the origin as shown in the diagram below;

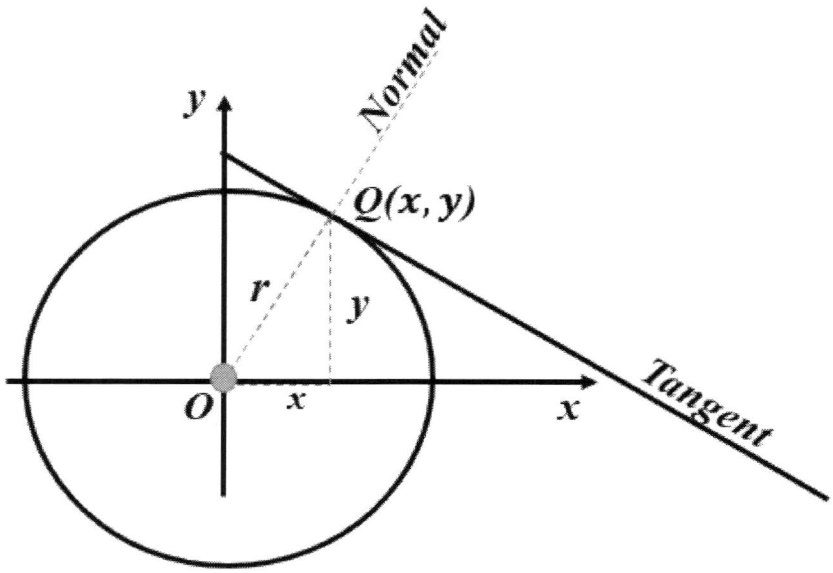

In this case, the ***Normal*** and the ***Tangent*** are at **RIGHT Angle**. It means that the product of their gradient must be equal to -1.

$$[Normal] \times [Tangent] = -1$$

This means that, when the Gradient of the **NORMAL** is known, the Gradient of the **TANGENT** can be obtained.

The gradient of the Normal can be obtained by;

$$Gradient\ of\ the\ Normal = \frac{y-0}{x-0} = \frac{y}{x}$$

Then the gradient of the Tangent obtained by;

$$[Tangent] = -\frac{1}{[Normal]}$$

The *equation of the Tangent* can be obtained using the above equation.
Just use the gradient of the Tangent in the equation of the straight line.
The equation of the straight line is given by;

$$y = mx + c$$

Questions

Q1. A circle has its centre at the origin.
Find;

i. the radius of the circle if the equation is given by

$$x^2 + y^2 = 13$$

ii. the equation of the circle if its radius is $4\sqrt{3}$.

iii. the radius of the circle if its equation is given by

$$5x^2 + 5y^2 = \left(2\sqrt{15}\right)^2$$

Leave your answer as a surd.

Solution:

i. The general equation of a circle is given by

$$x^2 + y^2 = r^2$$

And when compared with the given equation, the value 13 must be changed into a square number $= \left(\sqrt{13}\right)^2$

This means that;

$$x^2 + y^2 = r^2$$

$$x^2 + y^2 = \left(\sqrt{13}\right)^2$$

Hence, the radius is $= \sqrt{13}$.

ii. The general equation of a circle is given by

$$x^2 + y^2 = r^2$$

To place the radius into the equation, it must be squared.

That is $= \left(4\sqrt{3}\right)^2$

This means that;

$$x^2 + y^2 = (4\sqrt{3})^2$$

$$x^2 + y^2 = (4\sqrt{3}) \times (4\sqrt{3})$$

$$x^2 + y^2 = 4 \times 4 \times \sqrt{3} \times \sqrt{3}$$

$$x^2 + y^2 = 16 \times \sqrt{3 \times 3}$$

$$x^2 + y^2 = 16 \times \sqrt{9}$$

$$x^2 + y^2 = 16 \times 3$$

$$\underline{x^2 + y^2 = 48}$$

iii. The equation needs to be rearranged as follows;

$$5x^2 + 5y^2 = (2\sqrt{15})^2$$

$$5(x^2 + y^2) = (2 \times \sqrt{5} \times \sqrt{3})^2$$

$$5(x^2 + y^2) = (\sqrt{5})^2 \times (2\sqrt{3})^2$$

$$5(x^2 + y^2) = 5 \times (2\sqrt{3})^2$$

Then all the 5's cancels out.

$$x^2 + y^2 = (2\sqrt{3})^2$$

The radius is $2\sqrt{3}$.

Q2. The circle below has its centre at the origin as shown.

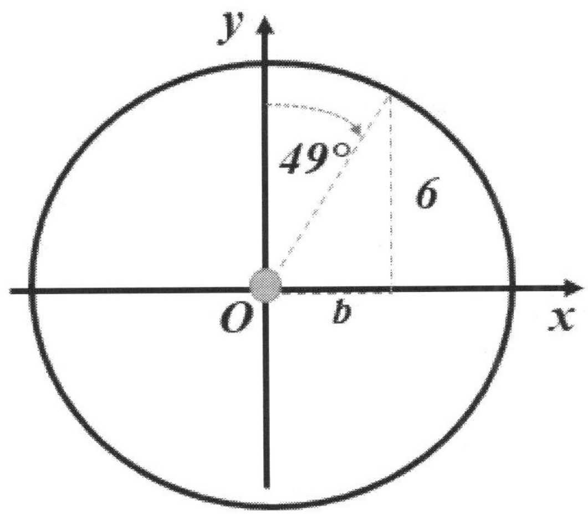

Find;

i. the equation of the circle.

ii. The value of ***b***.

Solution:

i. The general equation of a circle is given by

$$x^2 + y^2 = r^2$$

The radius of the circle can be calculated as the hypotenuse of the triangle within the circle; That is;

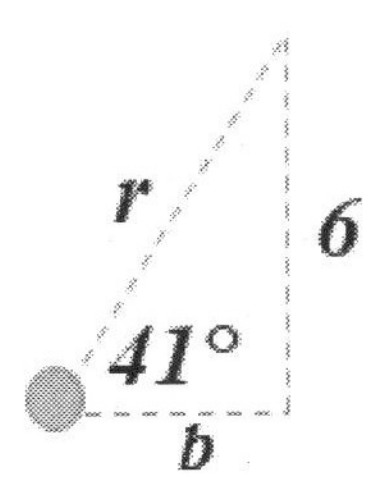

Note: that the angle within the triangle = **90° - 49° = 41°.**

$$\sin\theta = \frac{O}{H} = \frac{6}{r}$$

$$r = \frac{6}{\sin 41} = 9.1 \approx 9\, units$$

Hence, the equation of the circle is given by

$$x^2 + y^2 = 9^2$$

ii. The value of ***b*** can be calculated by taking the Tan of the angle; That is;

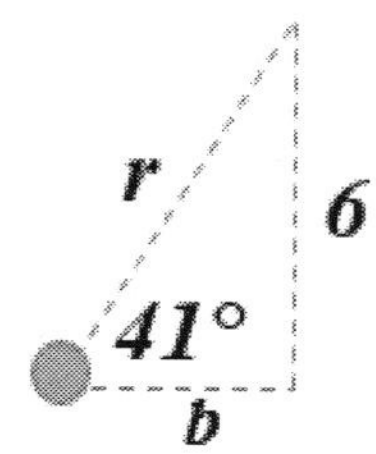

$$\tan\theta = \frac{O}{A} = \frac{6}{b}$$

$$b = \frac{6}{\tan 41} = 6.9 \approx 7\ units$$

Q3. The circle below has its centre at the origin as shown in the diagram below;

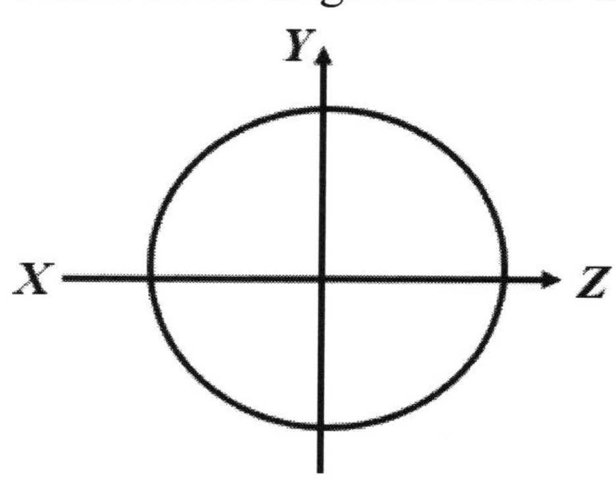

If the equation of the circle is $x^2 + y^2 = 8$.

Show that the line *XY* is perpendicular to the line *YZ*.

Solution:

The general equation of a circle is given by

$$x^2 + y^2 = r^2$$

The equation $x^2 + y^2 = 8$ can be written as $x^2 + y^2 = (\sqrt{8})^2$

The radius can be deduced as $\sqrt{8}$.

This means that the diagram shown can be illustrated as;

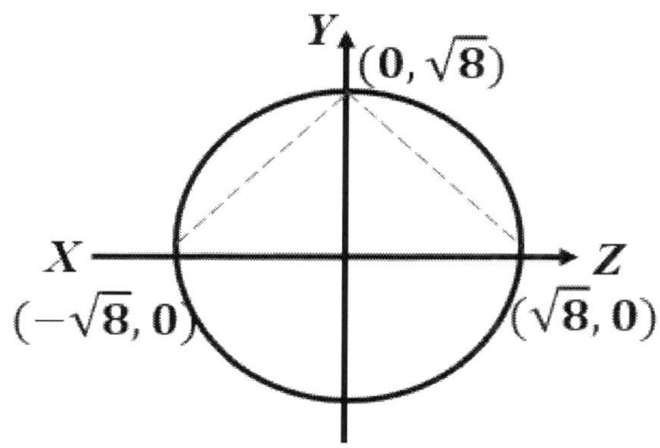

For perpendicular lines,

$$[Gradient\ of\ XY] \times [Gradient\ of\ YZ] = -1$$

Therefore;

$$[Gradient\ of\ XY] = \frac{\sqrt{8} - 0}{0 - -\sqrt{8}} = \frac{\sqrt{8}}{\sqrt{8}} = 1$$

$$[Gradient\ of\ YZ] = \frac{\sqrt{8} - 0}{0 - \sqrt{8}} = \frac{\sqrt{8}}{-\sqrt{8}} = -1$$

$$[Gradient\ of\ XY] \times [Gradient\ of\ YZ] = 1 \times -1 = -1$$

Hence, line *XY* and *YZ* are perpendicular.

Q4. A circle has its origin at the centre at the origin. The equation of the circle is

$$x^2 + y^2 = 17.$$

A line $y = 2x + 3$ crosses the circle at two points.

Find the coordinates of the two points.

Solution:

The above question can be solved by either simultaneous equation or by graphical means.

The simultaneous method will be employed here.

Let;

$$x^2 + y^2 = 17 \quad \ldots\ldots (1)$$

$$y = 2x + 3 \ldots\ldots (2)$$

Substitute (2) in (1). That is put $y = 2x + 3$ in equation (1).

$$x^2 + (2x + 3)^2 = 17$$

Expanding the bracket gives

$$x^2 + 4x^2 + 12x + 9 = 17$$

$$5x^2 + 12x - 8 = 0$$

Using the quadratic equation;

$$x_{1,2} = \frac{-b \pm \sqrt{b^2 - 4 \times a \times c}}{2 \times a}$$

From the above;

$$a = 5, b = 12, c = -8$$

Hence,

$$x_{1,2} = \frac{-12 \pm \sqrt{12^2 - 4 \times 5 \times -8}}{2 \times 5}$$

$$x_{1,2} = \frac{-12 \pm \sqrt{304}}{10}$$

Therefore, either

$$x_1 = \frac{-12 + \sqrt{304}}{10} = 0.5$$

Or

$$x_2 = \frac{-12 - \sqrt{304}}{10} = -3$$

Using the two $\boldsymbol{x}$ values, $\boldsymbol{y} = \mathbf{2}\boldsymbol{x} + \mathbf{3}$**,** the y values can be calculated as follows;

For $x_1 = 0.5$,

$$y_1 = 2(0.5) + 3 = 4$$

For $x_1 = -3$,

$$y_2 = 2(-3) + 3 = -3$$

Hence, the two coordinates are $(\mathbf{0.5}, \mathbf{4})$ and$(-\mathbf{3}, -\mathbf{3})$.

Q5. The circle below has its centre at the origin as shown. A tangent touches the circle at (-*4*, ***6***) and crosses the x-axis at (***k***, ***0***).

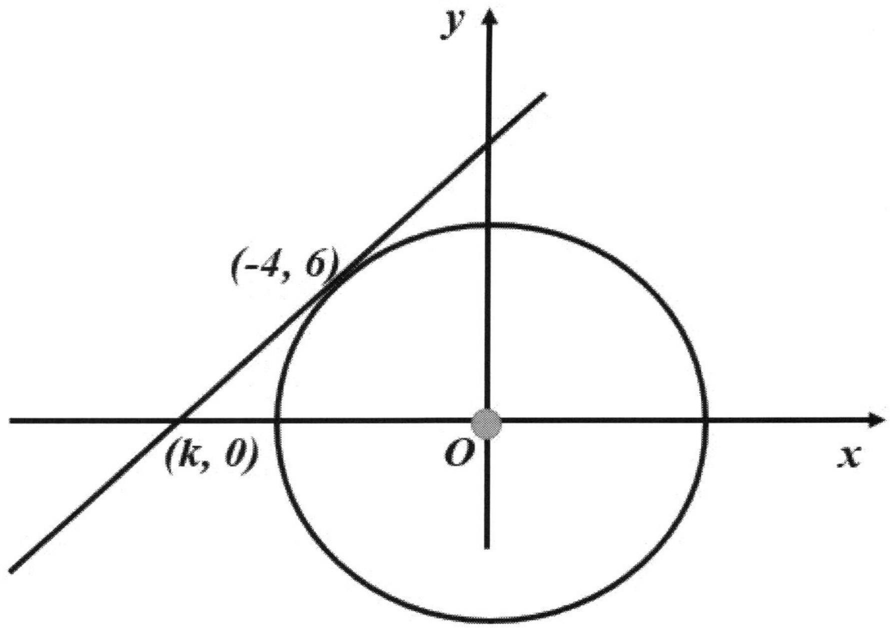

Find;

i. the equation of the tangent.

ii. the value of ***k***.

Solution:

i. The gradient of the ***Normal*** can be obtained by;

$$\textit{Gradient of the Normal} = \frac{6-0}{-4-0} = \frac{6}{-4} = \frac{3}{-2}$$

Then the gradient of the ***Tangent*** obtained by;

$$[Tangent] = -\frac{1}{[Normal]} = -\frac{-2}{3} = \frac{2}{3}$$

The equation of the ***Tangent*** can be obtained from the straight line equation by.

$$y = mx + c$$

Since the gradient is $\frac{2}{3}$,

This becomes;

$$y = \frac{2}{3}x + c$$

To find the intercept, ***c***, use the same coordinates (*-4*, ***6***) given: It means when ***x*** = -4, ***y*** = 6; This means,

$$6 = -\frac{8}{3} + c$$

$$6 + \frac{8}{3} = c$$

$$\frac{26}{3} = c$$

Hence, the equation of the tangent is given by;

$$y = \frac{2}{3}x + \frac{26}{3}$$

ii. Every point on the tangent (*straight line*) MUST obey equation of the tangent. Therefore, using the straight-line equation of the tangent, ***b*** can be calculated. At the point that the line crosses the *x*-axis, the ***y*** = 0.
Therefore;

$$0 = \frac{2}{3}x + \frac{26}{3}$$

$$\frac{2}{3}x = -\frac{26}{3}$$

$$2x = -26$$

$$x = -13$$

Hence, ***b*** = -13.

Q6. The circle below has its centre at the origin as shown below. A tangent having the equation, $\boldsymbol{y = -\frac{5}{7}x + 11}$, touches the circle at $(\boldsymbol{x, y})$. Find the coordinates $(\boldsymbol{x, y})$ where the tangent meets the circle.

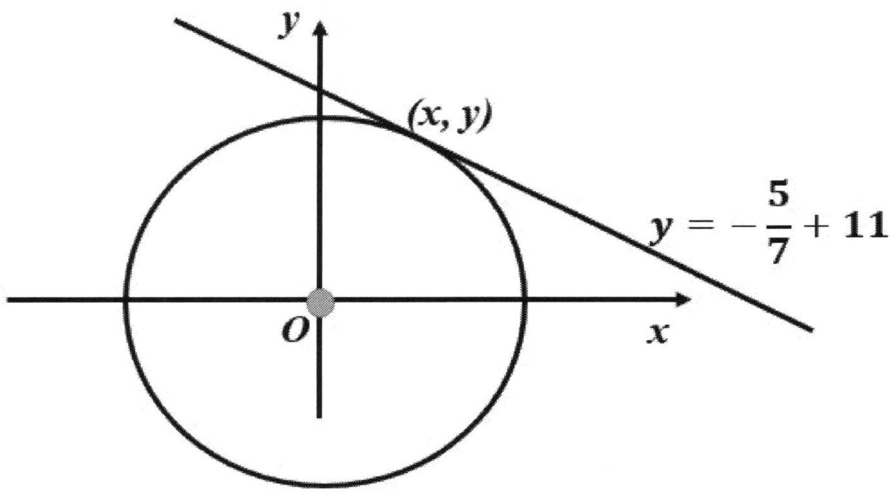

Solution:

Note that since the circle's centre is at the origin, the gradient of the Normal can ***ONLY*** be given by the coordinates at $(\boldsymbol{x, y})$.

That is:

$$\boldsymbol{Gradient\ of\ the\ Normal = \frac{y-0}{x-0} = \frac{y}{x}}$$

But the gradient of the ***Normal*** obtained by;

$$\boldsymbol{[Normal] = -\frac{1}{[Tangent]}}$$

From the equation of the tangent;

$$\boldsymbol{y = -\frac{5}{7}x + 11}$$

The gradient of the tangent $= -\frac{5}{7}$

Hence, the gradient of the ***Normal*** is;

$$[Normal] = -\frac{1}{[Tangent]} = -\,-\frac{7}{5} = \frac{7}{5}$$

But;

$$Gradient\ of\ the\ Normal = \frac{y}{x} = \frac{7}{5}$$

Therefore, the coordinates of (***x***, ***y***) are **(5, 7).**

6. Circle Theorem

Strategy:

There are ***EIGHT*** (***8***) Principles that can be employed in resolving any Circle Theorem problems.
The Eight Principles are

I. Angles at the centre:

This principle proposes that, on any given circles, the angle at the **centre** is ***TWICE*** the angle at the **circumference**.

Examples are:

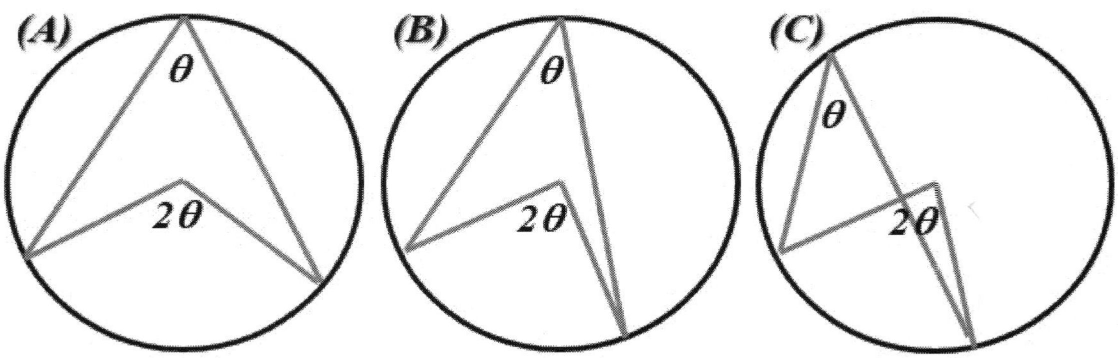

Meaning:

$$Centre = 2\theta$$

$$Circumference = \theta$$

II. Angles in a semicircle:

This principle proposes that, in any semicircle, the angle at the **circumference** is ***ALWAYS*** **90°**.

Examples are:

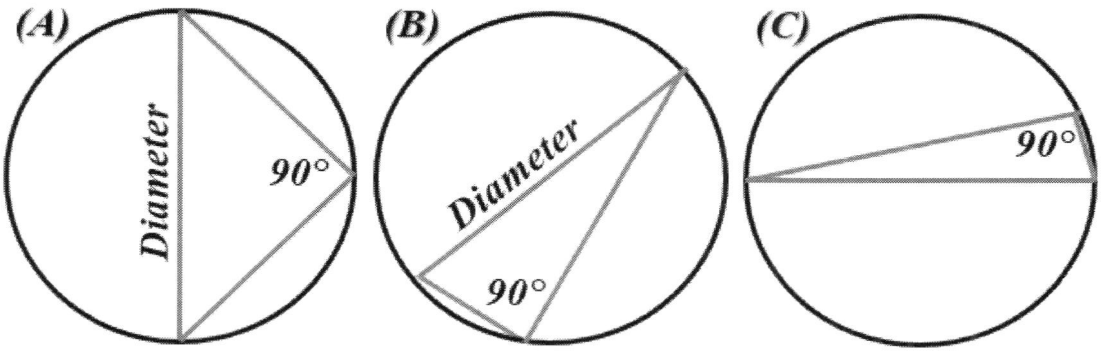

Meaning:

$\boldsymbol{Angle\ at\ the\ circumference\ = 90°}$

$\boldsymbol{The\ other\ two\ angles\ must\ add\ up\ to\ = 90°}$

III. <u>Angles in the same segment:</u>

This principle proposes that the angles at the **circumference** from the same segment are ***EQUAL.***

Examples are:

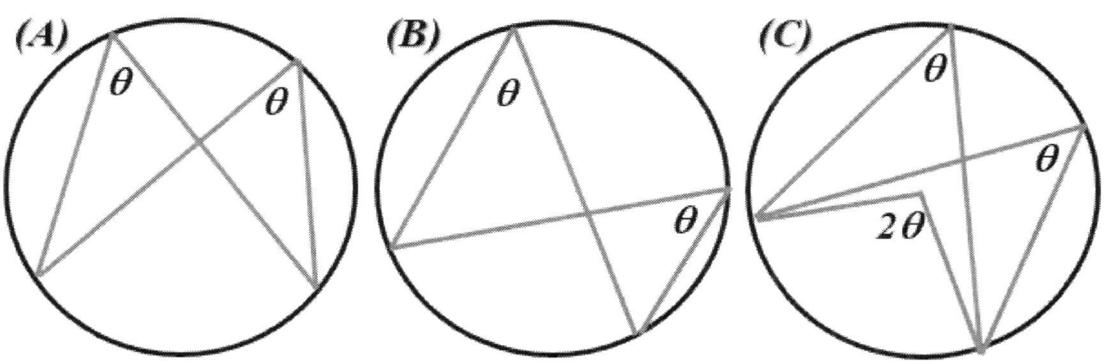

Meaning:

$$\boldsymbol{Angle\ at\ the\ circumference\ = EQUAL}$$

$$\textbf{\textit{Angles within a traingle add up to}} = 180°$$

IV. Cyclic quadrilateral:

This principle proposes that OPPOSITE angles in a **cyclic quadrilateral** add up to ***180°.***

Examples are:

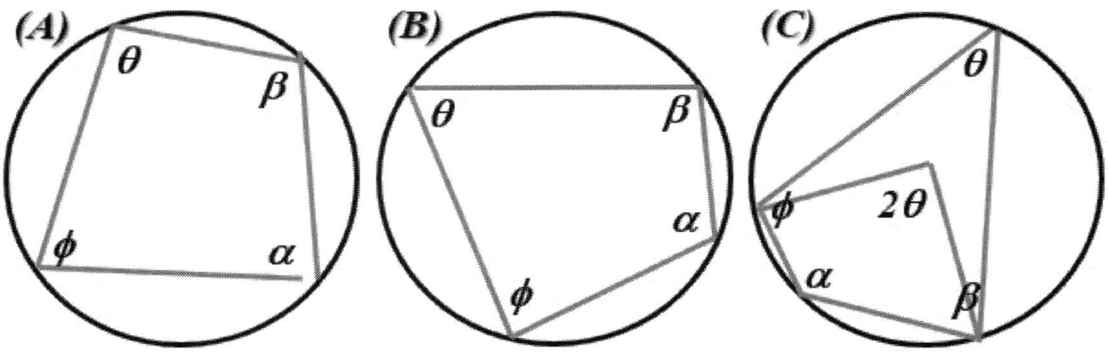

Meaning:

$$\textbf{\textit{Angles}}, \theta + \alpha = 180°$$

$$\textbf{\textit{Angles}}, \beta + \emptyset = 180°$$

$$\textbf{\textit{All angles within the cyclic quadrilaterals add up to}} = 360°$$

V. The angle between a tangent and radius:

This principle proposes that all tangents make a ***right-angle*** to all **radii (i.e. *90°*)**

Examples are:

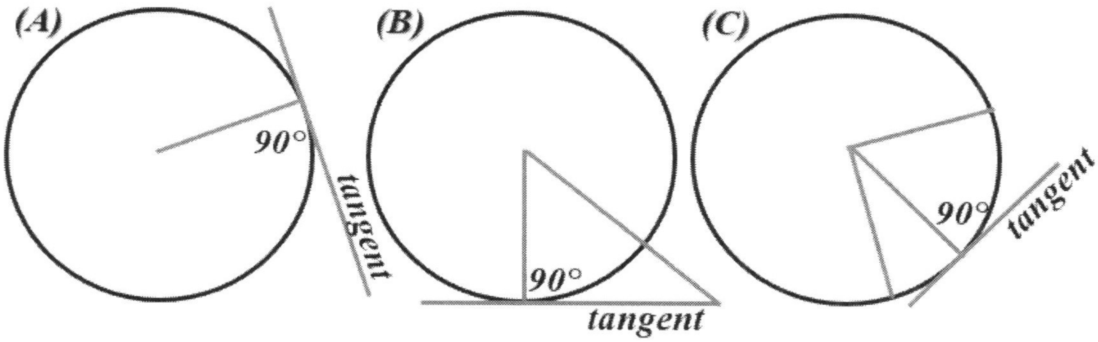

Meaning:

$$\textit{Tangent meet the all radii at } 90^\circ$$

VI. **<u>Angles in the alternate segment:</u>**

This principle proposes that, in any circle, the angle between a ***tangent*** and a ***chord*** through at one endpoints of the chord is **equal** to the ***angle*** in the **alternate segment**.

Examples are:

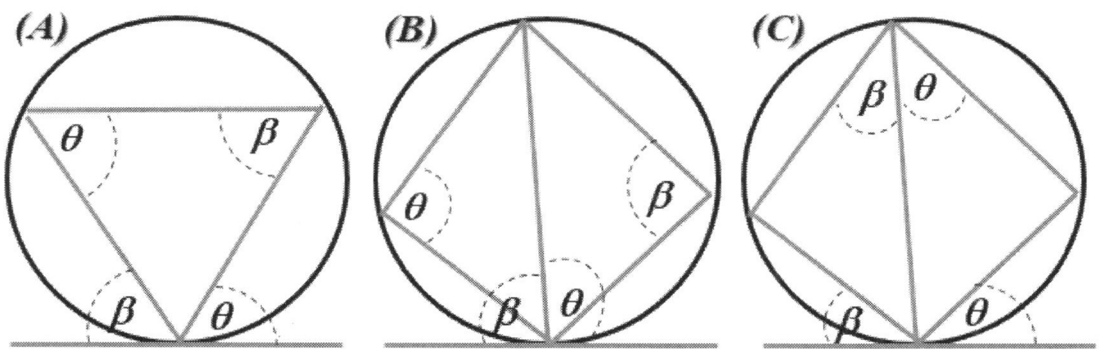

Meaning:

$$\textit{Angles at the tangent}, \beta = \beta, \textit{at the alternate segment}$$

$$\textit{Angles at the tangent}, \theta . = \theta, \textit{at the alternate segment}$$

VII. Two tangents from an external point:

This principle proposes that, in any circle, the ***tangents*** from the **SAME** external point have ***EQUAL*** length. It is also known that they make ***right angles*** to the **radii**.

Examples are:

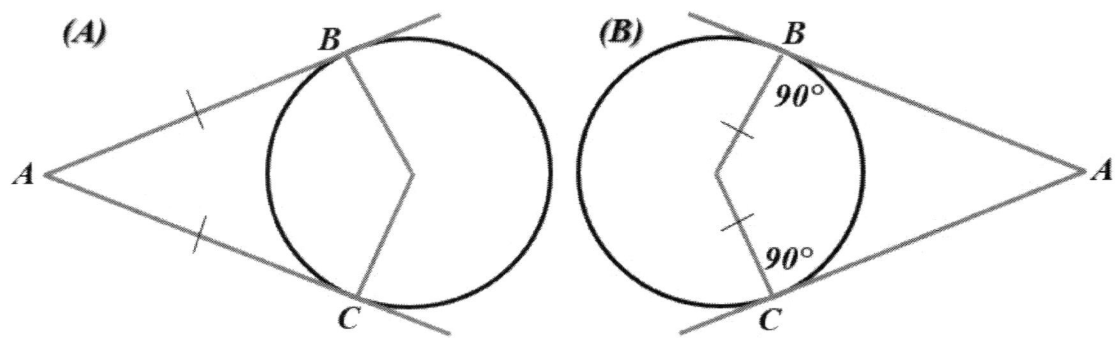

Meaning:

$$\boldsymbol{Length, AB = Length, AC}$$

$$\boldsymbol{Angle, ABC = Angle, ACB}$$

VIII. Chord bisector:

This principle proposes that, in any circle, a **perpendicular** line (i.e. radius or diameter) to a chord divides it into TWO HALVES.

Examples are:

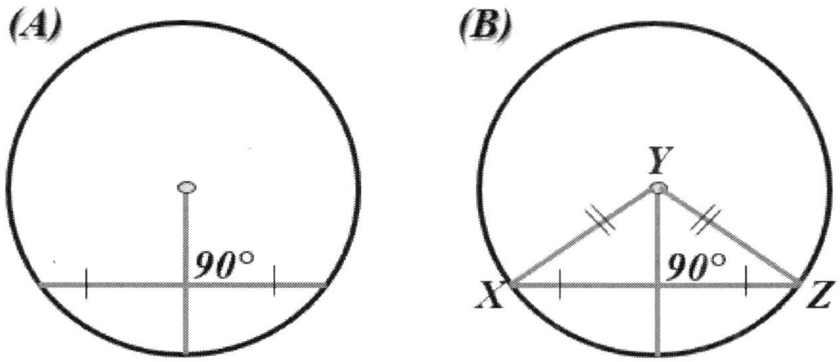

Meaning:

Perpendicular lines divides chord equally

Angle XYZ is ISOSCELES

Length, XY = Length, YZ

Questions

Q1. Find the missing angles in the following circles.

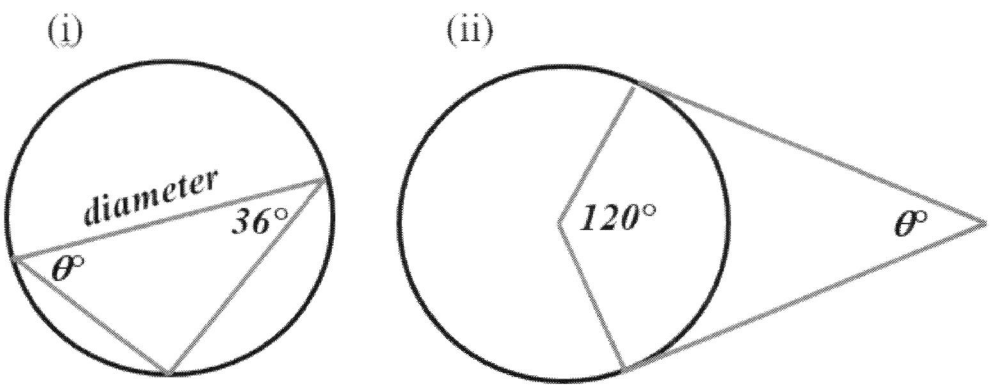

Solution:

i. This is an angle within the ***same semicircle***.

The angle at the circumference is **90°**.

Hence, the remaining two angles must add up to $\mathbf{90°}$.

Therefore, the missing angle, $\theta° = 90 - 36 = \mathbf{54°}$.

ii. This is two tangents meeting at a point.

They all make an angle of $\mathbf{90°}$ to the radius.

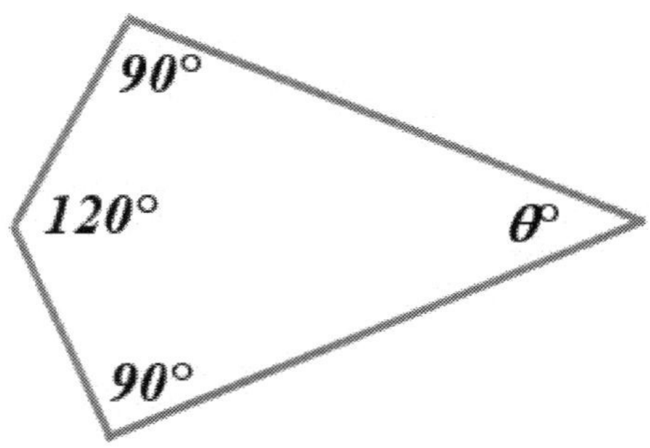

Therefore, the missing angle, $\theta° = 180 - 120 = \mathbf{60°}$.

Q2. Find the missing angles in the following circles.

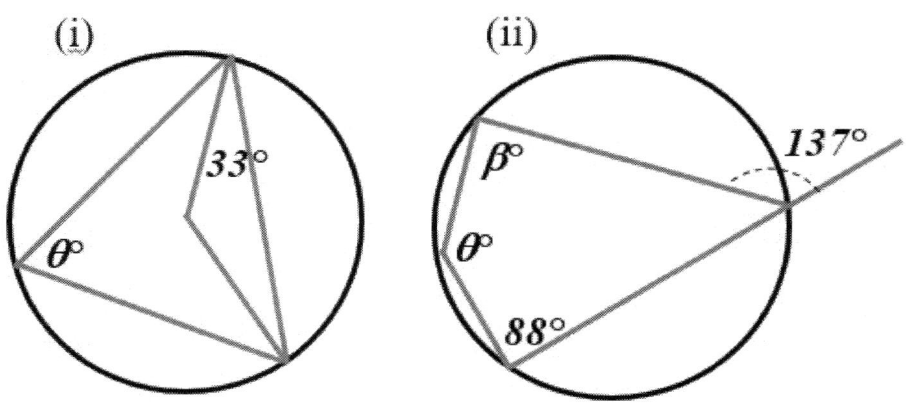

Solution:

i. The first point to consider is that angle $\mathbf{33}°$ makes an isosceles triangle having two radii on both sides.

Hence, the angle at the centre can be calculated as

$$\theta° = 180 - (33 + 33) = \mathbf{114}°.$$

This can be seen as illustrated below;

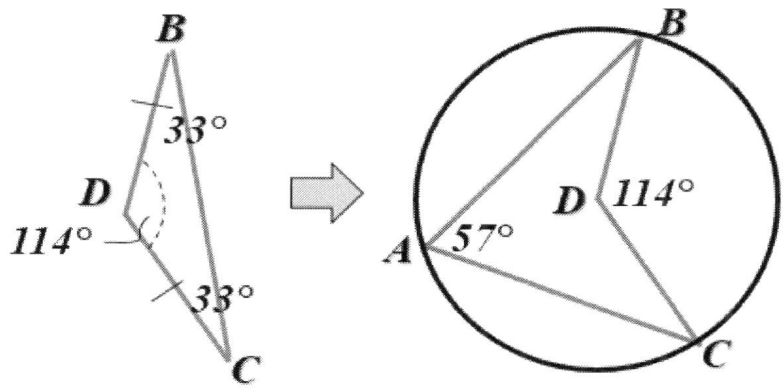

The second point is that the angle at the centre is twice the angle at the circumference.

Therefore, the angle at the circumference, $\theta° = \frac{114}{2} = \mathbf{57}°$.

The first point to consider is that angles on a straight line add up to $\mathbf{180}°$.

Hence the internal angle on the other side of $\mathbf{137}°$ is $180 - 137 = \mathbf{43}°$.

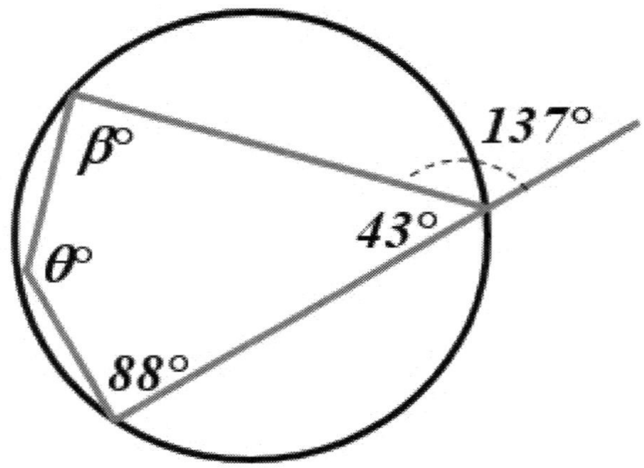

Using cyclic quadrilateral;

(a) $\theta^{\circ} + 43 = \mathbf{180^{\circ}}$ **and** $\theta^{\circ} = \mathbf{137^{\circ}}$

(b) $\beta^{\circ} + 88 = \mathbf{180^{\circ}}$ **and** $\beta^{\circ} = \mathbf{92^{\circ}}$

Q3. The circle below has a triangle *BDE* drawn within it and a tangent *AC* touching the triangle at the lower end of the triangle. If angle $\angle ABE = \mathbf{4x - 70}$ and $\angle BDE = \mathbf{175 - 3x}$,

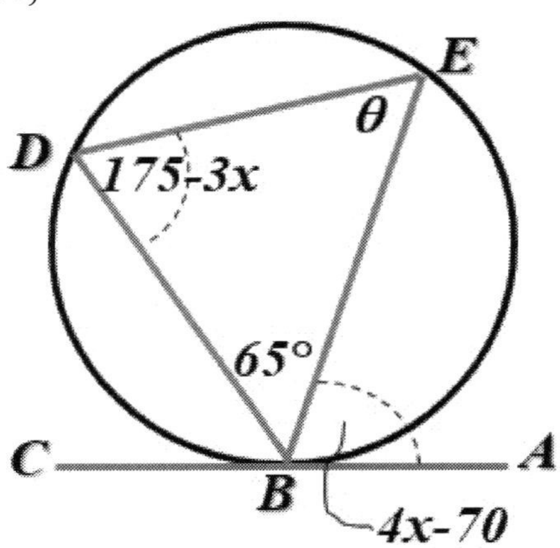

Find;

i. the value of *x*.

ii. the angle *θ*.

Solution:

i. The first point to consider is that, the angle ∠ABE and ∠BDE are angles in the alternate segment, hence they are ***EQUAL***.
Therefore;

$$4x - 70 = 175 - 3x$$

$$4x + 3x = 175 + 70$$

$$7x = 245$$

$$x = 35$$

ii. From (*i*), it can be deduced that the ∠ABE and ∠BDE = **70°**.
The angle ∠CBD and ∠CBD are angles in the alternate segment, hence they are equal.

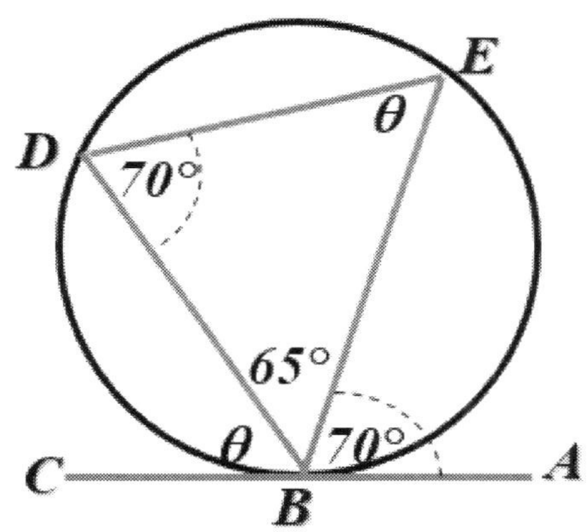

On the straight line,

$$\theta° + 65° + 70° = \mathbf{180°} \text{ and}$$

$$\theta° = \mathbf{45°}$$

Q4. The circle below has two tangents *AF* and *AB* attached to it. *CF* is the diameter of the circle. Tangent *AB* is at an angle of $\theta°$ to the horizontal and the angle subtended at the circumference ∠CDB is 32°. If its radius is 6 cm,

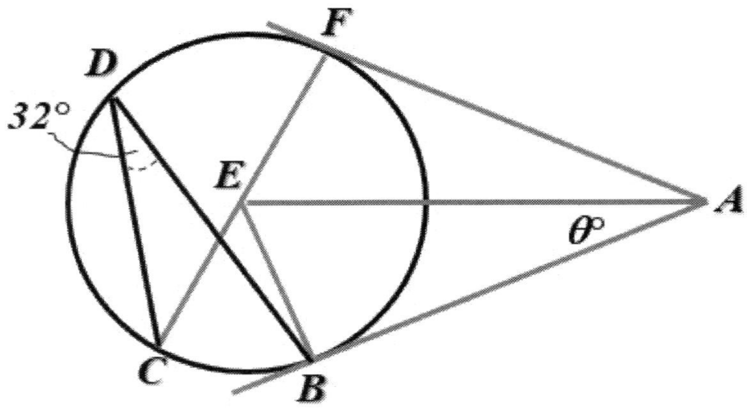

find;

i. the angle θ.

ii. the length AF.

Solution:

i. The first point to consider is that the angle at the circumference is twice the angle at the centre.

Hence, $\angle CEB = \mathbf{2 \times 32 = 64°}$.

The second point is that the two tangents must have ***Equal*** lengths, hence

$$\angle CEB = \angle FEA = \mathbf{64°}.$$

That is;

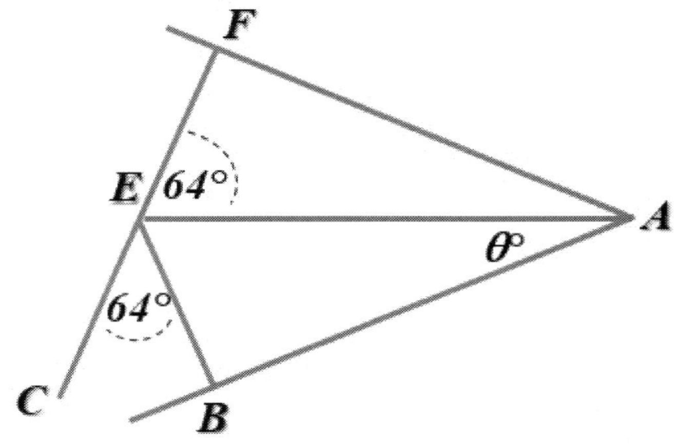

On a straight line, angle $\angle BEA = 180° - (64° + 64°) = \mathbf{52°}$.

The angle at the tangent is **90°**

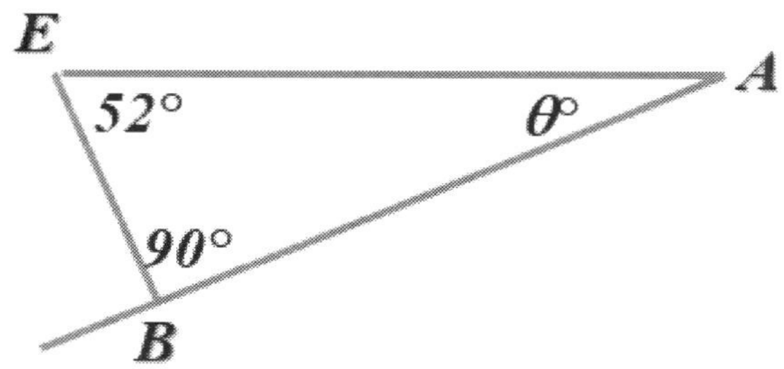

Therefore,

$$\theta° + 52° + 90° = \mathbf{180°} \text{ and}$$

$$\theta° = \mathbf{38°}$$

ii. The length $AF = AB$.

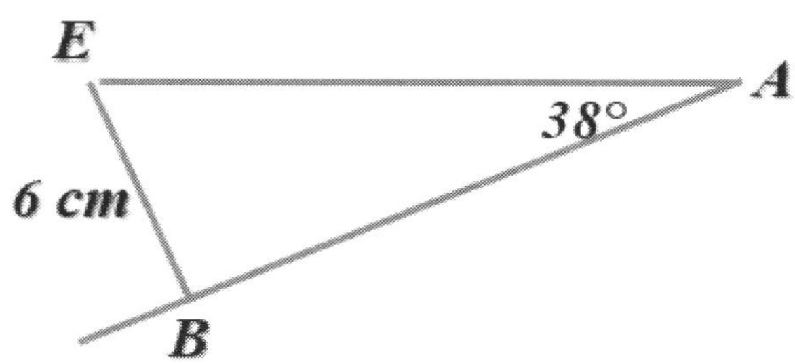

From the triangle above;

$$\tan 38 = \frac{EB}{AB}$$

$$\text{AB} = \frac{6}{\tan 38} = 7.7\ cm$$

Hence the length $AF =$ **7.7 cm**.

Q5. The circle below has a quadrilateral *WXYZ* inscribed in it. Prove that the opposite angles within the quadrilateral add up to 180°.

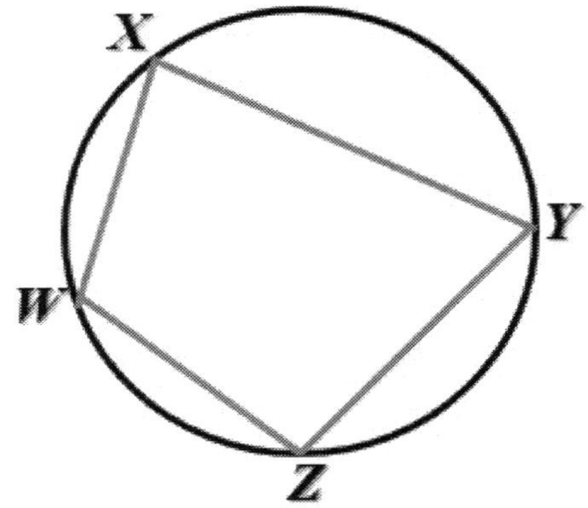

Solution:

Let angle $\angle ZWX = \theta^{\circ}$ and $\angle ZYX = \beta^{\circ}$.

Note that the Angle at the circumference = Twice the angle at the Centre.

Hence,

$$\text{If } \textbf{\textit{circumference}} = \theta^{\circ};\ \textbf{\textit{centre}} = 2\theta^{\circ} \text{ and}$$

$$\text{If } \textbf{\textit{circumference}} = \beta^{\circ};\ \textbf{\textit{centre}} = 2\beta^{\circ}$$

That is;

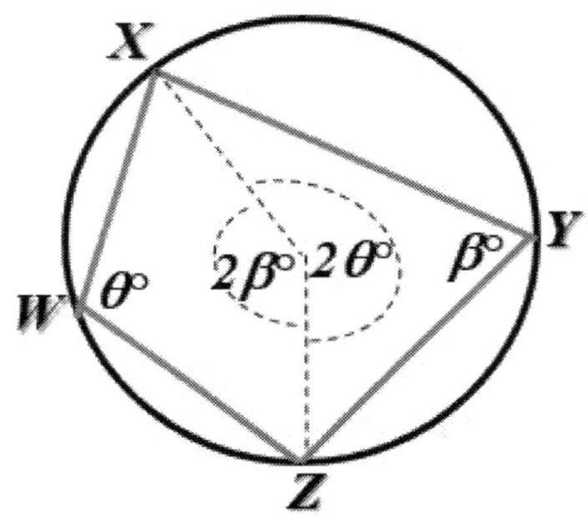

At the centre and resolving the angles around a point, it means that;

$$\mathbf{2\theta + 2\beta = 360^{\circ}}$$

Dividing through by 2 gives

$$\boldsymbol{\theta + \beta = 180^{\circ}}$$

Hence, the opposite angles add up to 180°.

7. Inequality Region

Strategy:

I. The strategies of plotting certain graphs need to be known.

II. Then, strategies of plotting straight lines from straight-line equations such as

$$y = mx + c, \text{ need to be known.}$$

III. Inequality equations such as

$$y > mx + c \rightarrow must\ be\ shaded\ upwards$$

$$y < mx + c \rightarrow must\ be\ shaded\ downwards$$

Note the inequality signs.

Below are examples of the three strategies;

I. Examples of standard plots:

Some of the standard plots can be seen below.

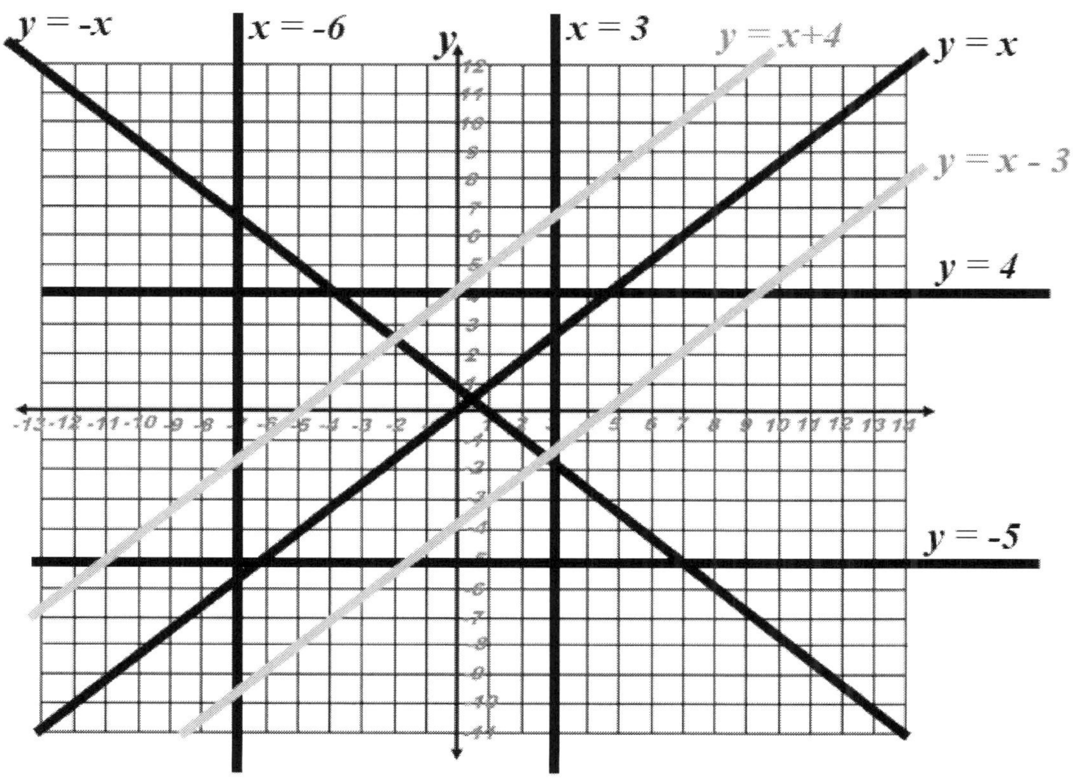

Explanation:

i. $\boldsymbol{y = 4} \rightarrow$ Go to where $y = 4$, then plot a straight line across the number.

ii. $\boldsymbol{y = -5} \rightarrow$ Go to where $y = -5$, then plot a straight line across the number.

iii. $\boldsymbol{x = 3} \rightarrow$ Go to where $x = 3$, then plot a straight line across the number.

iv. $\boldsymbol{x = -6} \rightarrow$ Go to where $x = -5$, then plot a straight line across the number.

v. $\boldsymbol{y = x} \rightarrow$ This means that, ***when x = 0, y = 0***; ***when x = 1, y = 1; when x = -1, y = -1; when x = 3, y = 3 etc.*** There will be a complete POSITIVE diagonal line.

vi. $\boldsymbol{y = -x} \rightarrow$ This means that, ***when x = 0, y = 0***; but ***when x = 1, y = -1; when x = -1, y = 1; when x = 3, y = -3 etc.*** There will be a complete NEGATIVE diagonal line.

vii. $\boldsymbol{y = x + 4} \rightarrow$ This means that the ***value 4*** has been added to the line $\boldsymbol{y = x}$.

Meaning, the line $\boldsymbol{y = x}$ has been raised upwards by 4.

$$\boldsymbol{y = x}$$

$$\rightarrow \boldsymbol{y = x + 4}$$

The is why the line $\boldsymbol{y = x + 4}$ is **4 points** above $\boldsymbol{y = x}$.

viii. $\boldsymbol{y = x - 3} \rightarrow$ Similar to (g), ***value 3*** has been subtracted from the line $\boldsymbol{y = x}$.

Meaning, the line $\boldsymbol{y = x}$ has been pushed downwards by 3.

The is why the line $\boldsymbol{y = x - 3}$ is **3 points** below $\boldsymbol{y = x}$.

II. Plotting straight line graphs from $y = mx + c$;

Let us plot.

(i) $y = \mathbf{2}x + \mathbf{1}$ and

(ii) $y = -\mathbf{3}x - \mathbf{4}$

Note: You will need only two coordinate points to plot a straight line graph.

i. $y = \mathbf{2}x + \mathbf{1}$

This is how you can get the two coordinates points;

Choose any value for ***x*** and find the corresponding ***y*** value.

Remember: Do not choose a bigger number.

When x = 1, $y = \mathbf{2(1) + 1 = 3}$. Hence, the first coordinate is (***1, 3***).

When x = -1, $y = \mathbf{2(-1) + 1 = -1}$.

Hence, second coordinate is (***-1, -1***).

Therefore the coordinates to the plot are (***1, 3***) and (***-1, -1***).

ii. $y = -\mathbf{3}x - \mathbf{4}$

Similar to the above, choose any value for ***x*** and find the corresponding ***y*** value.

When x = 1, $y = \mathbf{-3(1) - 4 = -7}$.

Hence, the first coordinate is (***1, -7***).

When x = -1, $y = \mathbf{-3(-1) - 4 = -1}$.

Hence, second coordinate is (***-1, -1***).

Therefore the coordinates to the plot are (***1, -7***) and (***-1, -1***).

The two straight lines can be seen below.

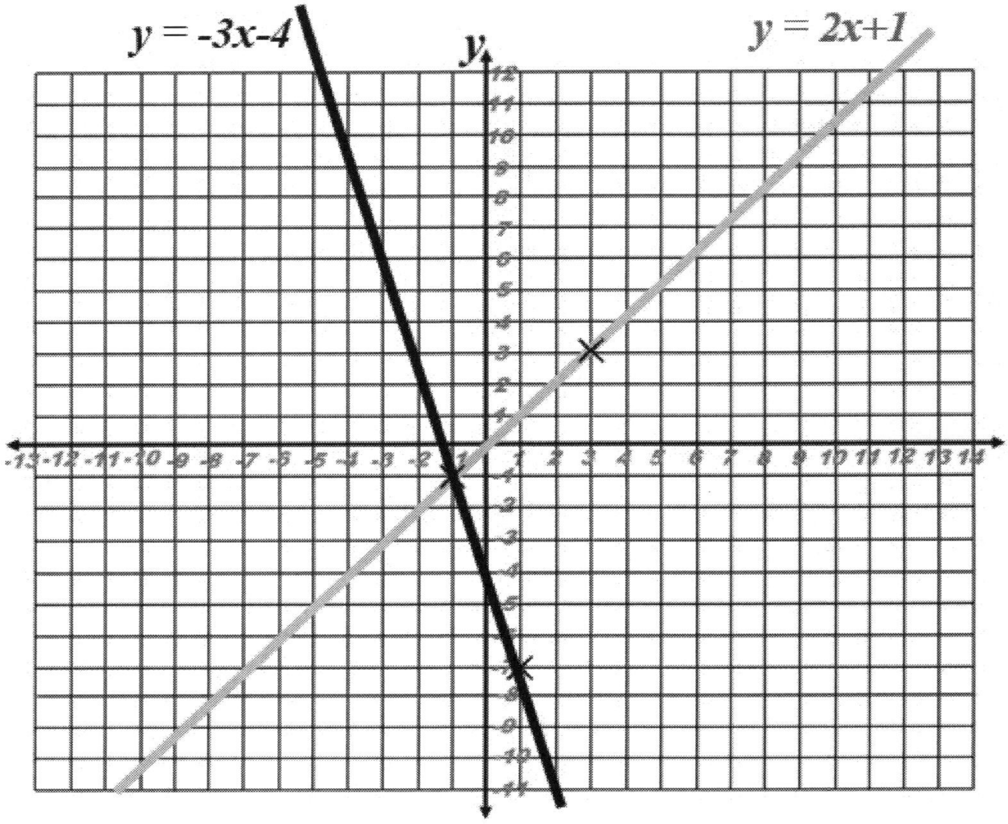

III. Plotting the inequality graphs from $y < mx + c$ and $y > mx + c$

Let us plot.

i. $y < \mathbf{2x + 1}$ *and*

ii. $y > \mathbf{-3x - 4}$

Note:

1. You will still need two coordinate points to plot a straight line graph.
2. Then, when ***y*** is ***GREATER THAN*** (i.e. ***y*** >…..), shade the graph ***UPWARDS***.
3. Then, when ***y*** is ***LESS THAN*** (i.e. ***y*** <…..), shade the graph ***DOWNWARDS***.

i. $y<2x+1$

From (II), the equation $y<2x+1$ can be plotted using the coordinates (*1, 3*) and (-*1*, -*1*).

→but since, $y <$, we shade downwards.

ii. $y > -3x - 4$

From (II), the equation $y > -3x - 4$ can be plotted using the coordinates (*1*, -*7*) and (-*1*, -*1*).

→but since, $y >$, we shade upwards.

The plots and the shading can be seen below;

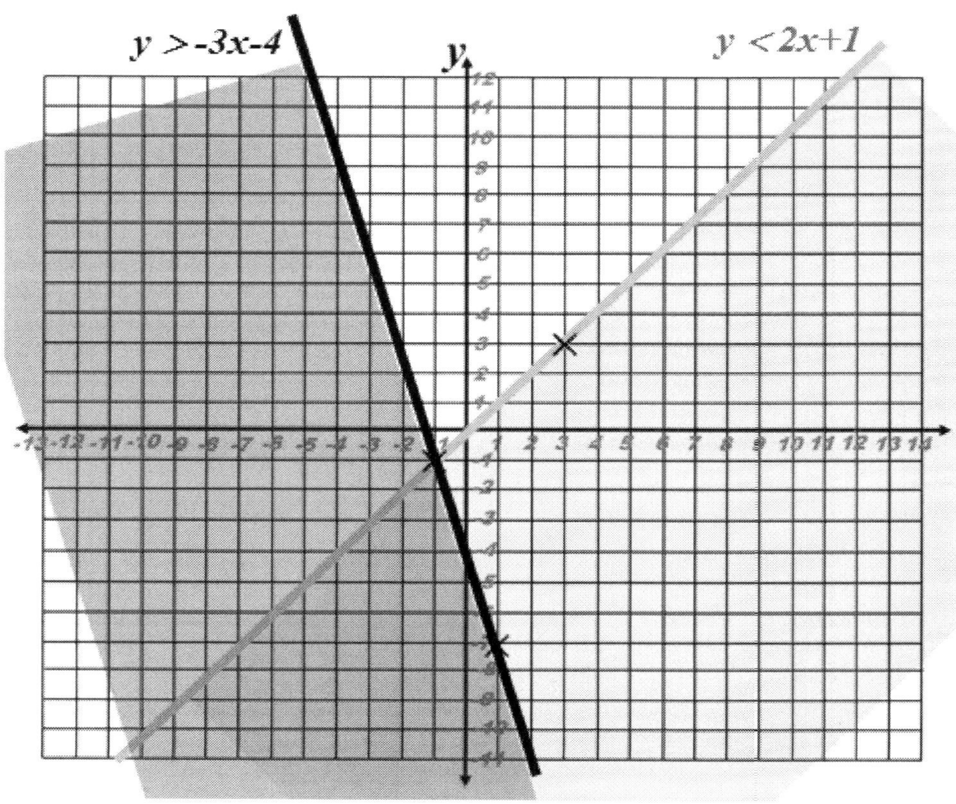

Questions

Q1. Plot the following inequalities and find the region, ***Q***, that satisfy the three equations.

$$x < 5, \; y > -6 \text{ and } y < x + 2$$

Solution:

(a) To plot $\underline{< 5}$, go to the line $x = 5$ and draw a **perpendicular** line across the number. After that, since $\underline{< 5}$, ***shade all the spaces*** on the left-hand side of the line where $x < 5$.

(b) To plot > -6, go to the line $y = -6$ and draw a **parallel** line across the number. After that, since $y > -6$, ***shade all the spaces*** above the line where $y > -6$.

(c) To plot $\underline{< x + 2}$, we must generate two coordinates to plot a straight line.

Note: You can choose any smaller number:

When $x = 0$, $y = (0) + 2 = 2$. Hence, the first coordinate is (*0, 2*).

When $y = 0$, $\rightarrow 0 = x + 2, x = -2$.
Hence, second coordinate is (*-2, 0*).
Therefore the coordinates to the plot are (*0, 2*) and (*-2, 0*). ***Lastly, shade all spaces below this line since y <***

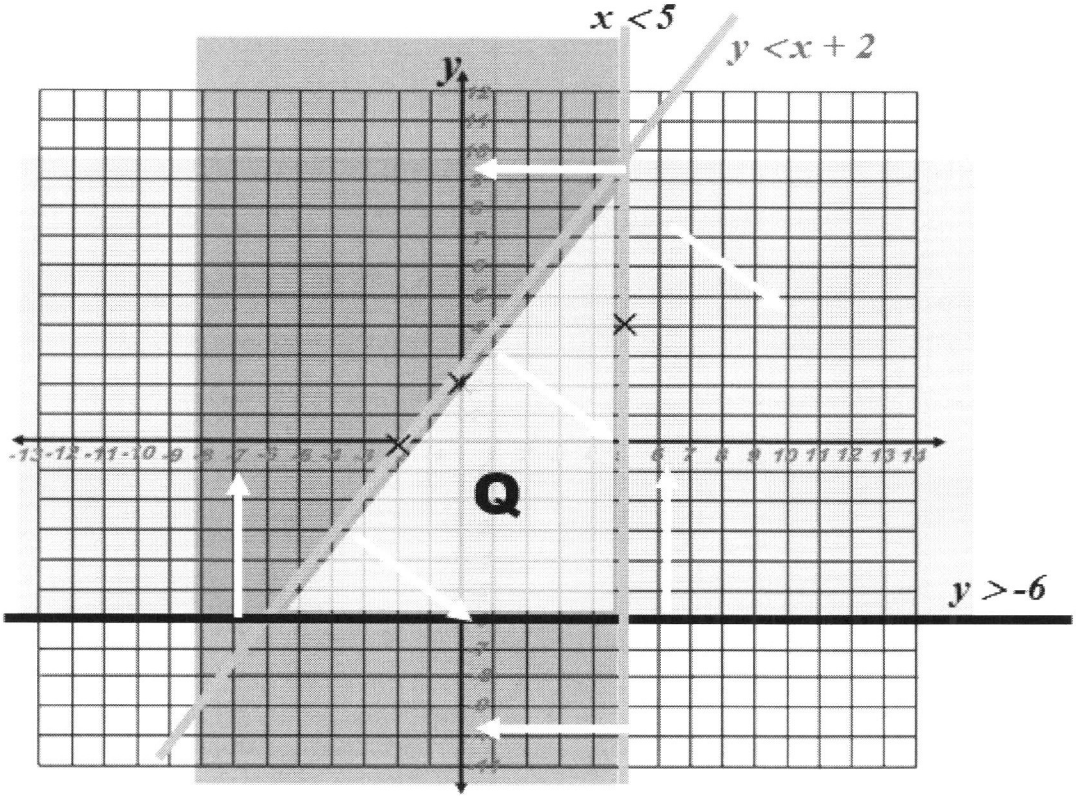
x < 5
y < x + 2
y
Q
y > -6

Q2. Plot the following inequalities and find the region, ***Q,*** that satisfy the three equations.

$$y > -6, \ \ y < -2x + 4 \text{ and } y < x + 2$$

<u>Solution:</u>

(a) To plot > -6, go to the line $y = -6$ and draw a **<u>parallel</u>** line across the number. After that, since **$y > -6$, *shade all the spaces*** above the line where $y > -6$.

(b) To plot $< -2x + 4$, two coordinates must be generated.

When $x = 0$, $y = -2(0) + 4 = 4$. Hence, the first coordinate is (*0, 4*).

When $y = 0$, $\rightarrow 0 = -2x + 4, \ x = 2$.

Hence, the second coordinate is (*2, 0*).

Therefore the coordinates to the plot are (*2, 0*) and (*0, 4*). ***Lastly, shade all spaces below this line since y <***

(c) To plot $\underline{< x + 2}$, two coordinates must be generated.

When $x = -8$, $y = (-8) + 2 = -6$. Hence, the first coordinate is (*-8, -6*).

When $x = 2$, $\rightarrow y = 2 + 2, \ y = 4$.

Hence, the second coordinate is (*2, 4*).

Therefore the coordinates to the plot are (*-8, -6*) and (*2, 4*). ***Lastly, shade all spaces below this line since y <***

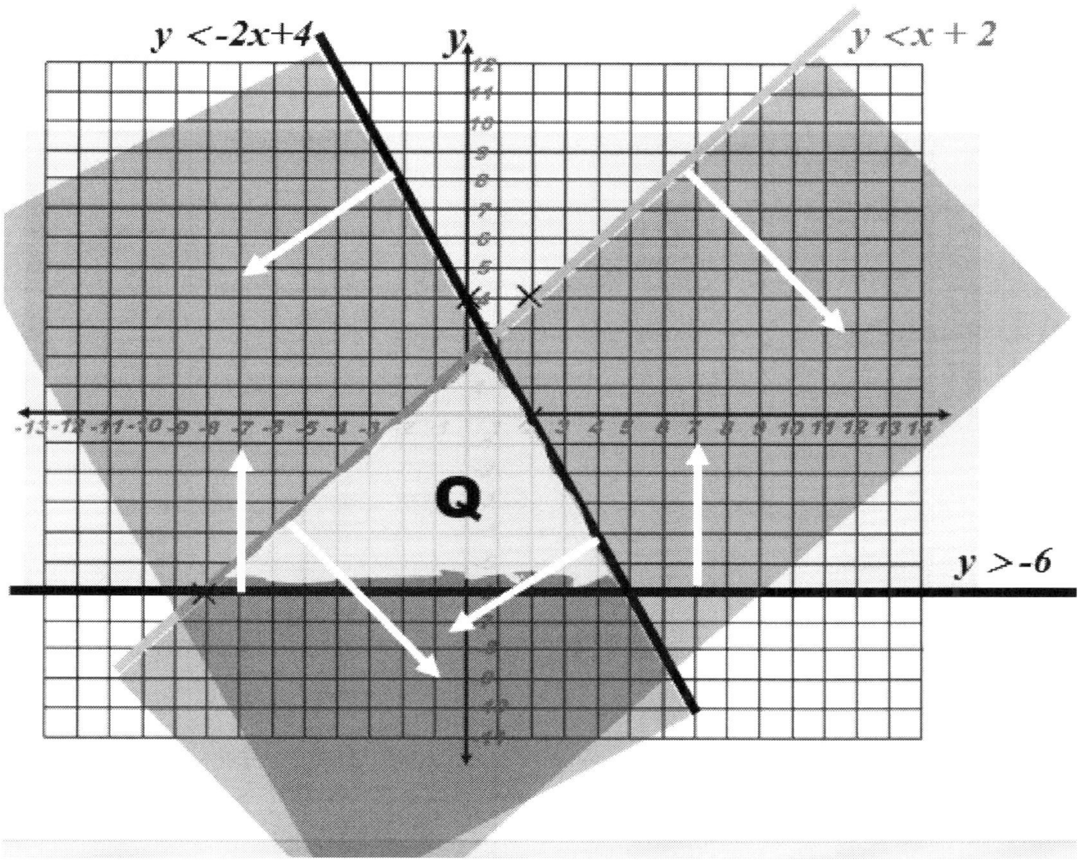

y < -2x+4
y
y < x + 2
Q
y > -6

Q3. Plot the following inequalities and find the region, ***Q***, that satisfy the three equations.

$$x < 5, \quad y > -2x + 4 \text{ and } y < x + 2$$

Solution:

(a) To plot $\underline{< 5}$, go to the line $x = 5$ and draw a **perpendicular** line across the number. After that, since $\underline{< 5}$, ***shade all the spaces*** on the left-hand side of the line where $x < 5$.

(b) To plot $> -2x + 4$, two coordinates must be generated.

When $x = 0$, $y = -2(0) + 4 = 4$. Hence, the first coordinate is (*0, 4*).

When $y = 0$, $\rightarrow 0 = -2x + 4$, $x = 2$.

Hence, the second coordinate is (*2, 0*).

Therefore the coordinates to the plot are (*2, 0*) and (*0, 4*). ***Lastly, shade all spaces above this line since y >.***

(c) To plot $\underline{< x + 2}$, two coordinates must be generated.

When $x = -8$, $y = (-8) + 2 = -6$. Hence, the first coordinate is (*-8, -6*).

When $x = 2$, $\rightarrow y = 2 + 2$, $y = 4$.

Hence, the second coordinate is (*2, 4*).

Therefore the coordinates to the plot are (*-8, -6*) and (*2, 4*). ***Lastly, shade all spaces below this line since y <***

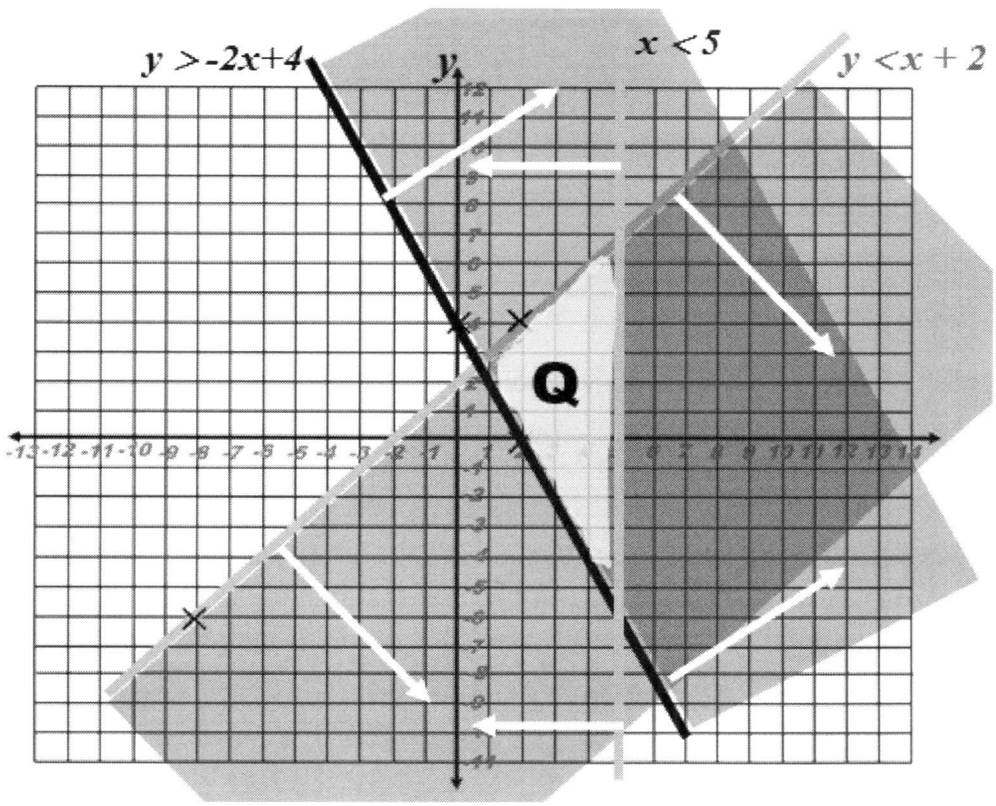

y > -2x+4
x < 5
y < x + 2
y
Q

Q4. Plot the following inequalities and find the region, ***Q,*** that satisfy the three equations.

$$y > -2x - 6, \ \ y > 2x - 4 \text{ and } \ y < x + 2$$

Solution:

(a) To plot $y > -2x - 6$, two coordinates must be generated.

When x = -7, $y = -2(-7) - 6 = 8$. Hence, the first coordinate is **(*-7, 8*)**.

When x = -1, $\rightarrow y = -2(-1) - 6, \ y = -4$.

Hence, the second coordinate is (***-1, -4***).

Therefore the coordinates to the plot are (-*7, 8*) and (-1, ***-4***). ***Lastly, shade all spaces above this line since y >.***

(b) To plot $> 2x - 4$, two coordinates must be generated.

When x = -3, $y = 2(-3) - 4 = -10$, Hence, first coordinate is (***-3, -10***).

When x = 5, $\rightarrow y = 2(5) - 4, \ y = 6$.

Hence, the second coordinate is (***5, 6***).

Therefore the coordinates to the plot are (***-3, -10***) and (***5, 6***). ***Lastly, shade all spaces above this line since y >.***

(c) To plot $\underline{< x + 2}$, two coordinates must be generated.

When x = -8, $y = (-8) + 2 = -6$. Hence, the first coordinate is (***-8, -6***).

When x = 2, $\rightarrow y = 2 + 2, \ y = 4$.

Hence, the second coordinate is (***2, 4***).

Therefore the coordinates to the plot are (***-8, -6***) and (***2, 4***). ***Lastly, shade all spaces below this line since y <***

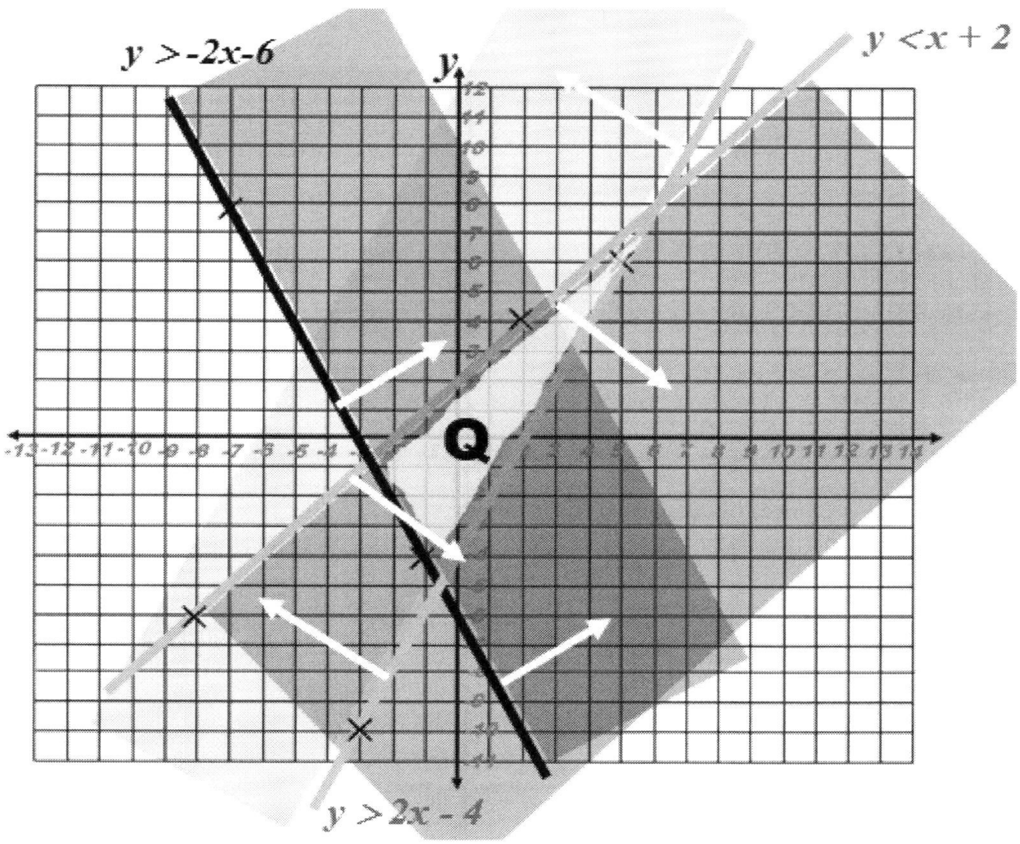

Q5. Plot the following inequalities and find the region, ***Q,*** that satisfy the three equations.

$$y > -0.5x - 2,\ y > 2x - 4 \text{ and } y < 0.3x + 5.$$

Solution:

(a) To plot $y > -0.5x - 2$, two coordinates must be generated.

When $x = 2$, $y = -0.5(2) - 2 = -3$. Hence, the first coordinate is (*2, -3*).

When $x = -4$, $\rightarrow y = -0.5(-4) - 2,\ y = 0$.

Hence, the second coordinate is (*-4, 0*).

Therefore the coordinates to the plot are (*2, -3*) and *(-4, 0*). ***Lastly, shade all spaces above this line since y >.***

(b) To plot $> 2x - 4$, two coordinates must be generated.

When $x = -3$, $y = 2(-3) - 4 = -10$, Hence, first coordinate is (*-3, -10*).

When $x = 5$, $\rightarrow y = 2(5) - 4,\ y = 6$.

Hence, the second coordinate is (*5, 6*).

Therefore the coordinates to the plot are (*-3, -10*) and (*5, 6*). ***Lastly, shade all spaces above this line since y >.***

(c) To plot $\underline{< 0.3x + 5}$, two coordinates must be generated.

When $x = 1$, $y = 0.3(1) + 5 = 5.3$. Hence, the first coordinate is (*1, 5.3*).

When $x = -4$, $\rightarrow y = 0.3(-4) + 5,\ y = 3.8$.

Hence, the second coordinate is (*-4, 3.8*).

Therefore the coordinates to the plot are (***1, 5.3***) and (***-4, 3.8***). ***Lastly, shade all spaces below this line since y <***

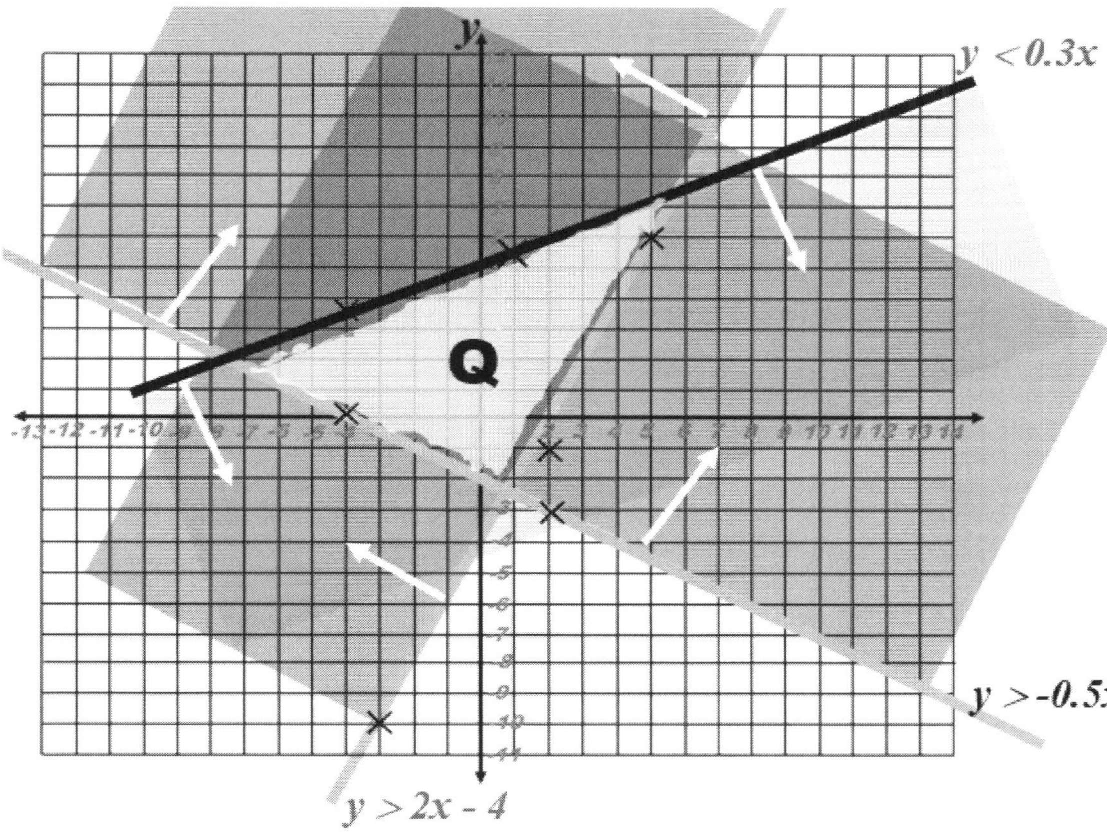

8. Exponential Graphs

Strategy:

I. Explanation of Graphs

(a) The ***POSITIVE*** form of exponential decay is what is termed as ***Growth***. It grows exponentially;

This is given by the equation;

$$y = k \times b^x$$

This can be illustrated as;

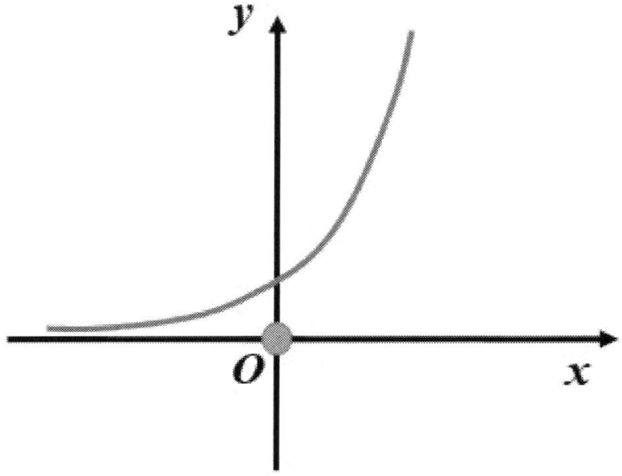

It means, as x increases, y increases exponentially and grows upwards.

This can also be represented by the cumulative percentage increase as;

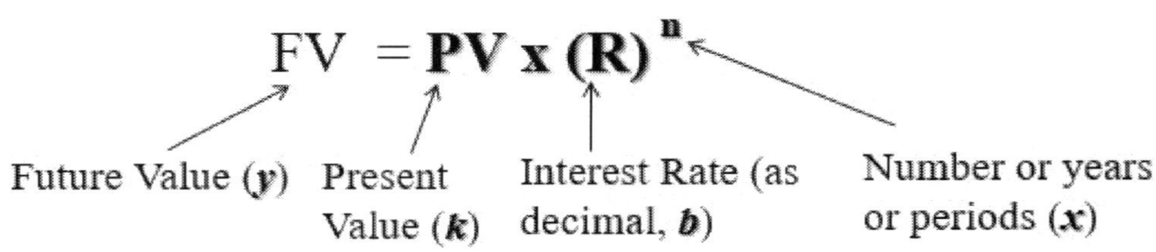

Note: From the general POSITIVE formula;

$$y = k \times b^x$$

If $x = 0$, then,

$$y = k \times b^0$$

Any power raised to the power 0, 1

$$y = k \times 1$$

$$y = k$$

This can be illustrated as;

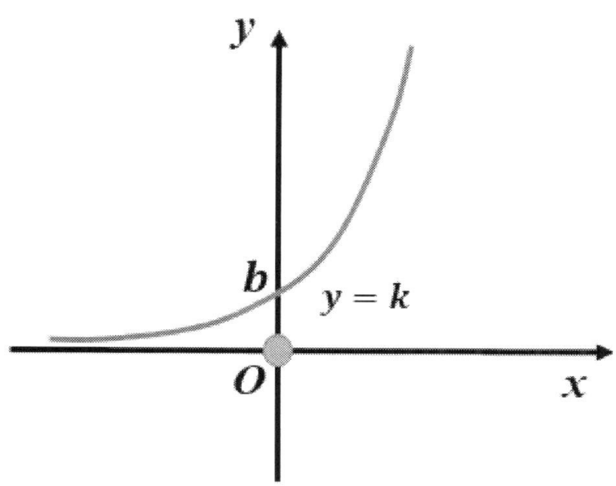

(b) The ***NEGATIVE*** form of exponential decay is what is termed as ***Decay***. It decays exponentially;

This is given by the equation;

$$y = k \times b^{-x}$$

This can be illustrated as;

$$y = k \times \left(\frac{1}{b}\right)^x$$

The graphs can be illustrated as;

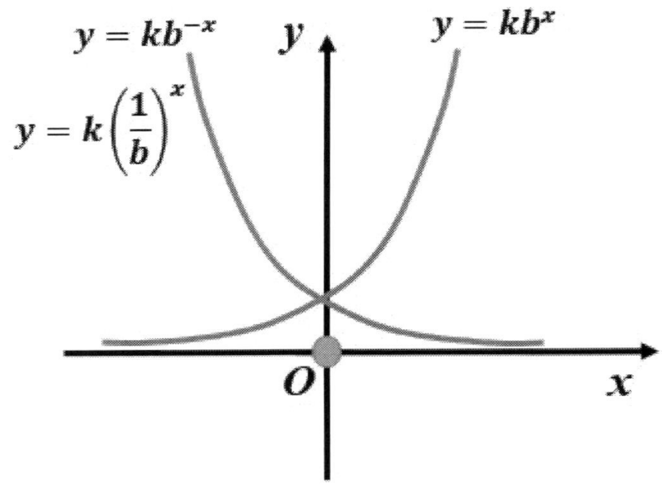

It means, as $\boldsymbol{x}$ increases, $\boldsymbol{y}$ decreases exponentially and decays downwards.

Questions

Q1. The coordinates (**2**, **50**) and (**9**, **2560**) are points on the curve. Find the value of $\boldsymbol{a}$ if (3, $\boldsymbol{a}$) lies on the curve.

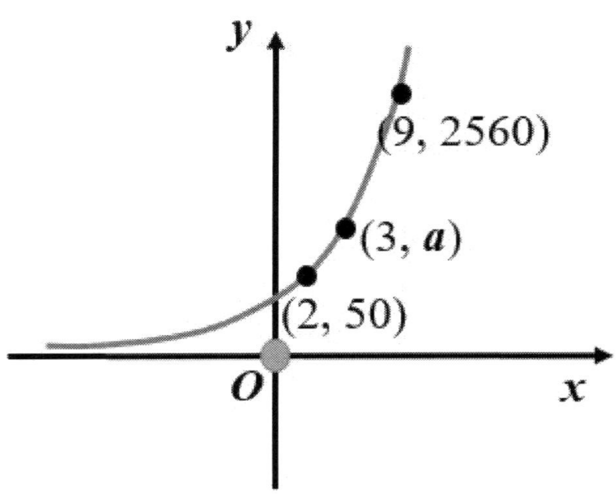

Solution:

The equation of the curve is;

$$y = k \times b^x$$

The constants of $\boldsymbol{k}$ and $\boldsymbol{b}$ need to be determined.
When $x = 2$, $y = 50$. This means;

$$50 = k \times b^2 \qquad \textbf{(1)}$$

When $x = 9$, $y = 2560$. This means;

$$2560 = k \times b^9 \qquad \textbf{(2)}$$

This is two equations and two unknowns. Divide equation (*2*) by equation (*1*).

$$\frac{2560}{50} = \frac{kb^9}{kb^2}$$

The $\boldsymbol{k}$'s cancels out and the $\boldsymbol{b}$'s are resolved by indices.

$$51.2 = b^7$$

Taking the seventh route on both sides gives;

$$b = 1.76$$

Put $\boldsymbol{b} = 1.76$ into (*1*) and that gives;

$$50 = k \times 1.76^2$$

$$k = 16$$

Hence the full equation is;

$$y = 16 \times 1.76^x$$

Hence, when $\boldsymbol{x} = \mathbf{3}$, y is given by;

$$y = 16 \times 1.76^3$$

$$y = 87.2$$

Q2. The coordinates (**3**, **512**) and (**5**, **8192**) are points on the curve. The equation is given by $y = \boldsymbol{k} \times \boldsymbol{b}^x$. Find the value of $\boldsymbol{k}$ and $\boldsymbol{b}$.

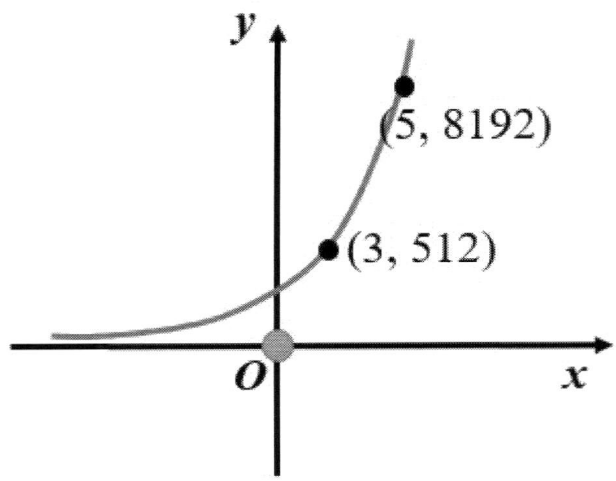

Solution:
The equation of the curve is;

$$y = k \times b^x$$

When $x = 3$, $y = 512$. This means;

$$512 = k \times b^3 \qquad (1)$$

When $x = 5$, $y = 8192$. This means;

$$8192 = k \times b^5 \qquad (2)$$

This is two equations and two unknowns. Divide equation (*2*) by equation (*1*).

$$\frac{8192}{512} = \frac{kb^5}{kb^3}$$

The ***k***'s cancels out and the ***b***'s are resolved by indices.

$$16 = b^2$$

Taking the square route on both sides gives;

$$b = 4$$

Put ***b*** = 4 into (*1*) and that gives;

$$512 = k \times 4^3$$

$$k = 8$$

Hence the full equation is;

$$y = 8 \times 4^x$$

Q3. The coordinates (**1**, **70**) and (**5**, **43750**) are points on the curve. The equation is given by $y = k \times b^x$. Find the value of k and b.

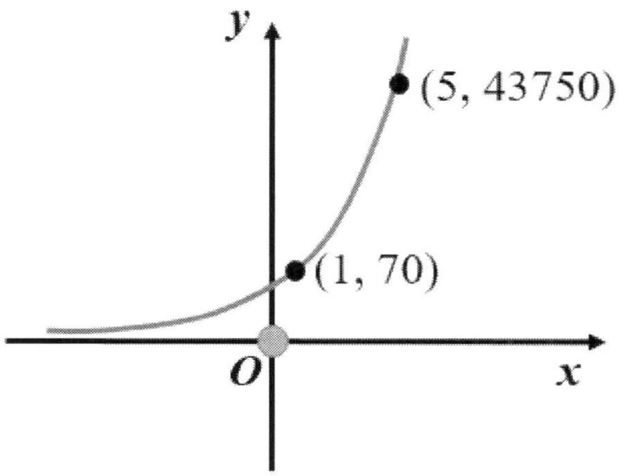

Solution:
The equation of the curve is;

$$y = k \times b^x$$

When $x = 1, y = 70$. This means;

$$70 = k \times b^1 \qquad (1)$$

When $x = 5, y = 43750$. This means;

$$43750 = k \times b^5 \qquad (2)$$

This is two equations and two unknowns. Divide equation (*2*) by equation (*1*).

$$\frac{43750}{70} = \frac{kb^5}{kb^1}$$

The k's cancels out and the b's are resolved by indices.

$$625 = b^4$$

Taking the fouth route on both sides gives;

$$b = 5$$

Put $\boldsymbol{b} = 5$ into (*1*) and that gives;

$$\mathbf{70} = \boldsymbol{k} \times \mathbf{5^1}$$

$$\boldsymbol{k} = \mathbf{14}$$

Hence the full equation is;

$$\boldsymbol{y} = \mathbf{14} \times \mathbf{5^x}$$

Q4. The coordinates **(2, 0.12)** and **(5, 9.6 x 10^{-4})** are points on the curve. The equation is given by $y = \boldsymbol{k} \times \left(\frac{1}{b}\right)^x$. Find the value of ***k*** and ***b***.

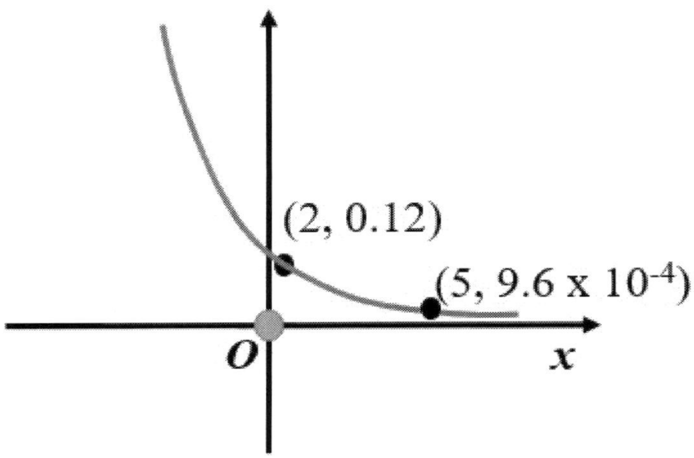

Solution:
The equation of the curve is;

$$\boldsymbol{y} = \boldsymbol{k} \times \left(\frac{1}{b}\right)^x.$$

When $x = 2$, $y = 0.12$. This means;

$$\mathbf{0.12} = \boldsymbol{k} \times \left(\frac{1}{b}\right)^2 \qquad \textbf{(1)}$$

$$\mathbf{0.12} = \boldsymbol{k} \times \boldsymbol{b}^{-2} \qquad \textbf{(1)}$$

When $x = 5$, $y = 9.6 \text{ x } 10^{-4}$. This means;

$$\mathbf{9.6 \text{ x } 10^{-4}} = \boldsymbol{k} \times \left(\frac{1}{b}\right)^5 \qquad \textbf{(2)}$$

$$9.6 \text{ x } 10^{-4} = k \times b^{-5} \qquad \textbf{(2)}$$

This is two equations and two unknowns. Divide equation (*2*) by equation (*1*).

$$\frac{0.12}{9.6 \text{ x } 10^{-4}} = \frac{kb^{-2}}{kb^{-5}}$$

The ***k***'s cancels out and the ***b***'s are resolved by indices.

$$125 = b^{-2--5}$$

$$125 = b^3$$

Taking the square route on both sides gives;

$$b = 5$$

Put ***b*** = 5 into (*1*) and that gives;

$$0.12 = k \times \left(\frac{1}{5}\right)^2$$

$$k = 3$$

Hence the full equation is;

$$y = 3 \times \left(\frac{1}{5}\right)^x$$

Q5. The coordinates (**1**, **0.8**) and (**3**, **0.032**) are points on the curve. The equation is given by $y = k \times \left(\frac{1}{b}\right)^x$. Find the value of ***k*** and ***b***.

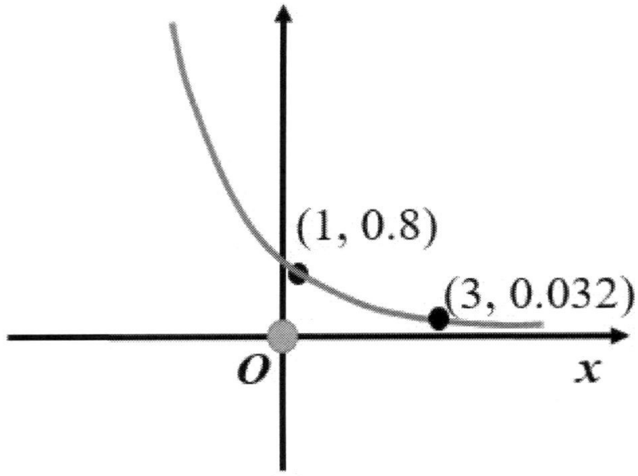

<u>Solution:</u>

The equation of the curve is;

$y = k \times \left(\frac{1}{b}\right)^x$.

When $x = 1$, $y = 0.8$. This means;

$$0.8 = k \times \left(\frac{1}{b}\right)^1 \qquad (1)$$

$$0.8 = k \times b^{-1} \qquad (1)$$

When $x = 3$, $y = 0.032$. This means;

$$0.032 = k \times \left(\frac{1}{b}\right)^3 \qquad (2)$$

$$0.032 = k \times b^{-3} \qquad (2)$$

This is two equations and two unknowns. Divide equation (*2*) by equation (*1*).

$$\frac{0.8}{0.032} = \frac{kb^{-1}}{kb^{-3}}$$

The ***k***'s cancels out and the ***b***'s are resolved by indices.

$$25 = b^{-1--3}$$

$$125 = b^2$$

Taking the square route on both sides gives;

$$\boldsymbol{b = 5}$$

Put $\boldsymbol{b} = 5$ into (*1*) and that gives;

$$\mathbf{0.8} = \boldsymbol{k} \times \left(\frac{\mathbf{1}}{\mathbf{5}}\right)^{\mathbf{1}}$$

$$\boldsymbol{k} = \mathbf{4}$$

Hence the full equation is;

$$\boldsymbol{y} = \mathbf{4} \times \left(\frac{\mathbf{1}}{\mathbf{5}}\right)^{\boldsymbol{x}}$$

9. Algebraic Fraction

FOUR main areas need to be understood. All four areas use normal basic algebraic skills to solve or resolve the problems.

Strategy:

I. Simplifying algebraic fractions

The main point is to make the equation ***simple.***

Example:

(a) Simple factorizing;

$$\frac{4x+12}{6x^2}$$

Simplify 4 at the numerator

$$\frac{4(x+3)}{6x^2}$$

And 2 at the denominator

$$\frac{4(x+3)}{2(3x^2)}$$

That gives a simplified version when 2 divides the 4 at the numerator.

$$\frac{2(x+3)}{3x^2}$$

(b) Factorizing quadratics;

$$\frac{2x^2+5x+3}{2x+2}$$

Simplify the numerator into expressions: Find factor pairs of ***6*** *that will give you 5 when added. (i.e. 2 and 3).*

$$\frac{2x^2+2x+3x+3}{2x+2}$$

This will give;

$$\frac{2x(x+1)+3(x+1)}{2x+2}$$

$$\frac{(2x+3)(x+1)}{2x+2}$$

The denominator can be simplified into 2 and x+1.

$$\frac{(2x+3)(x+1)}{2(x+1)}$$

x +1 then cancels out as;

$$\frac{2x+3}{2}$$

(c) Using the difference of two squares;

*It simply states that if **a** and **b** are integers, then*

$$a^2 - b^2 = (a+b)(a-b)$$

If a =15 and b = 13, then.

$$15^2 - 13^2 = 225 - 169 = 56$$

And

$$(15+13)(15-13) = (28)(2) = 56$$

It means that;

$$a^2 - b^2 = (a+b)(a-b)$$

Example question:

$$\frac{4x^2 - 9}{6x^2 + 9x}$$

The numerator can be resolved using the difference of two squares;

$$\frac{(2x)^2 - 3^2}{6x^2 + 9x} = \frac{(2x+3)(2x-3)}{6x^2 + 9x}$$

The denominator can be simplified into 3x and 2x+3.

$$\frac{(2x+3)(2x-3)}{3x(2x+3)}$$

2x +3 then cancels out as;

$$\frac{2x-3}{3x}$$

II. Adding and Subtracting algebraic fractions

This is the same as adding or subtracting ***fractions.***

Example:

(a) Adding;

$$\frac{3x}{4x+1} + \frac{7}{x+1}$$

Add them as a normal fraction. Find the common denominator;

$$\frac{3x(x+1) + 7(4x+1)}{(4x+1)(x+1)}$$

Expanding the brackets gives;

$$\frac{3x^2 + 3x + 28x + 7}{4x^2 + 4x + x + 1}$$

Finally, the numerator and the denominator can be simplified as;

$$\frac{3x^2 + 31x + 7}{4x^2 + 5x + 1}$$

(b) Subtracting;

$$\frac{4x}{9x^2 - 25} - \frac{3}{3x - 5}$$

Find the common denominator by resolving the difference of two squares;

$$\frac{4x}{(3x)^2 - 5^2} - \frac{3}{3x - 5}$$

This gives;

$$\frac{4x}{(3x - 5)(3x + 5)} - \frac{3}{3x - 5}$$

Using normal fraction;

$$\frac{4x - 3(3x + 5)}{(3x - 5)(3x + 5)}$$

Expanding the bracket on the numerator gives;

$$\frac{4x - 9x - 15}{(3x - 5)(3x + 5)}$$

The numerator can be simplified as;

$$\frac{-5x - 15}{(3x - 5)(3x + 5)}$$

The denominator can be simplified and reversed back as;

$$\frac{-5x - 15}{(3x)^2 - 5^2}$$

III. Multiplying and dividing algebraic fractions

This is the same as adding or subtracting ***fractions.***

Example:

(a) Multiplying;

i. When no cancellations needed;

$$\frac{3x}{4x+1}\times\frac{7}{x+1}$$

If there is no cancellation to be done, then the expressions can simplify be multiplied as;

$$\frac{3x\times 7}{(4x+1)(x+1)}$$

And this gives;

$$\frac{21x}{4x^2+4x+x+1}$$

Finally, the numerator and the denominator can be simplified as;

$$\frac{21x}{4x^2+5x+1}$$

ii. When cancellations needed;

$$\frac{15x}{14x+7}\times\frac{7}{5x}$$

The numerators and the denominators can be simplified, rearranged and cancelled before multiplying;

$$\frac{15x}{5x} \times \frac{7}{14x + 7}$$

And this gives;

$$\frac{15x}{5x} \times \frac{7}{7(2x + 1)}$$

15x and 5x will cancel as well as the 7s;

$$3 \times \frac{1}{(2x + 1)}$$

The final answer is;

$$\frac{3}{2x + 1}$$

(b) Dividing;

i. When no cancellations needed;

$$\frac{3x}{4x + 1} \div \frac{7}{x + 1}$$

If there is no cancellation to be done, then the expressions can simplify be DIVIDED; the method is KEEP, FLIP, CHANGE (KFC). The division sign changes to multiplication.

$$\frac{3x}{4x + 1} \times \frac{x + 1}{7}$$

And this gives;

$$\frac{3x(x + 1)}{7(4x + 1)}$$

Finally, the numerator and the denominator can be simplified as;

$$\frac{3x^2}{28x+7}$$

ii. When cancellations needed;

$$\frac{4x}{9x^2-25} \div \frac{3}{3x-5}$$

Find the common denominator by resolving the difference of two squares;

$$\frac{4x}{(3x)^2-5^2} \div \frac{3}{3x-5}$$

This gives;

$$\frac{4x}{(3x-5)(3x+5)} \div \frac{3}{3x-5}$$

The expressions can simplify be DIVIDED; the method is to KEEP, FLIP, CHANGE (KFC). The division sign changes to multiplication.

$$\frac{4x}{(3x-5)(3x+5)} \times \frac{3x-5}{3}$$

And this gives;

$$\frac{4x\,(3x-5)}{3(3x-5)(3x+5)}$$

The 3x-5 cancels out;

$$\frac{4x}{3(3x+5)}$$

IV. Solving equations with algebraic fractions

The same strategies used for adding or subtracting of ***fractions*** can be employed here;

Example:

$$\frac{3}{2x+1}+\frac{x}{x+1}=1$$

The first point is to find a common denominator;

$$\frac{3(x+1)+x(2x+1)}{(2x+1)(x+1)}=1$$

And this gives;

$$\frac{3x+3+2x^2+x}{2x^2+2x+x+1}=1$$

$$\frac{2x^2+4x+3}{2x^2+3x+1}=1$$

Then multiply both sides by the denominator to cancel the denominator.

$$(2x^2+3x+1)\times\frac{2x^2+4x+3}{2x^2+3x+1}=1(2x^2+3x+1)$$

This becomes;

$$2x^2+4x+3=2x^2+3x+1$$

Move all the x's and numbers to one side;

$$4x-3x=1-3$$

$$x=-2$$

Questions

Q1. Simplify the following fractions.

i.

$$\frac{28x^2 + 7x}{14x}$$

ii.

$$\frac{24}{9x} - \frac{9}{27x}$$

Solution:

i. *The first point is to simplify the numerator and the denominator;*

$$\frac{28x^2 + 7x}{14x} = \frac{7x(4x + 1)}{7x(2)}$$

The 7's can cancel out to;

$$\frac{4x + 1}{2}$$

ii.

$$\frac{24}{9x} - \frac{9}{27x}$$

Find a common denominator;

$$\frac{24(3) - 9(1)}{27x}$$

Simplify the numerator;

$$\frac{63}{27x}$$

Divide the numerator and the denominator by 9;

$$\frac{7}{3x}$$

Q2. Simplify the following fractions.

i.

$$\frac{3x+2}{9x^2-4} \times \frac{3x}{2}$$

ii.

$$\frac{4x+1}{8x^2+6x+1} \div \frac{8x+2}{2x+1}$$

Solution:

i. The first point is to simplify the difference of two squares at the denominator;

$$\frac{3x+2}{9x^2-4} \times \frac{3x}{2} = \frac{3x+2}{(3x)^2-2^2} \times \frac{3x}{2}$$

$$\frac{3x+2}{(3x-2)(3x+2)} \times \frac{3x}{2}$$

The 3x-2 at the numerator and the denominator will cancel out as;

$$\frac{1}{(3x-2)} \times \frac{3x}{2}$$

Simplifying that gives;

$$\frac{3x}{2(3x-2)}$$

ii.

$$\frac{4x+1}{8x^2+6x+1} \div \frac{8x+2}{2x+1}$$

From the above, the quadratic equation at the denominator can be factorized as;

$$8x^2+6x+1 = 8x^2+4x+2x+1$$

Then;

$$8x^2+4x+2x+1 = 4x(2x+1)+1(2x+1)$$

This gives;

$$4x(2x+1)+1(2x+1) = (4x+1)(2x+1)$$

It implies that;

$$\frac{4x+1}{(4x+1)(2x+1)} \div \frac{8x+2}{2x+1}$$

The 4x+1 at the numerator and the denominator will cancel out;

$$\frac{1}{(2x+1)} \div \frac{8x+2}{2x+1}$$

The expressions can simplify be DIVIDED; the method is to KEEP, FLIP, CHANGE (KFC). The division sign changes to multiplication.

$$\frac{1}{(2x+1)} \times \frac{2x+1}{8x+2}$$

This gives;

$$\frac{2x+1}{(2x+1)(8x+2)}$$

Finally, the 2x+1 cancels out;

$$\frac{1}{(8x+2)}$$

This can also be written as;

$$\frac{1}{2(4x+1)}$$

Q3. Solve the algebraic fraction below.

$$\frac{3x+1}{3}+\frac{4x+3}{4}=1$$

Solution:

The first point is to multiply through by the common denominator (i.e. 12) to remove the denominators;

$$(12)\times\frac{3x+1}{3}+(12)\times\frac{4x+3}{4}=1\times(12)$$

The denominators cancel the common denominator out and give

$$4\times(3x+1)+3\times(4x+3)=1\times(12)$$

By expanding the brackets, the equations give;

$$12x+4+12x+9=12$$

Simplifying that gives;

$$24x=12-13$$

$$24x=-1$$

And the final answer is;

$$x=\frac{-1}{24}$$

Q4. Solve the algebraic fraction below.

$$\frac{5}{3x-1} - \frac{2x}{x+1} = 2$$

Solution:

The first point is to multiply through by the common denominator [i.e. (3x+1)(4x+1)] to remove the denominators;

$$(3x-1)(x+1)\left[\frac{5}{3x-1} - \frac{2x}{x+1}\right] = 2 \times (3x-1)(x+1)$$

The denominators cancel the common denominator out and give

$$5(x+1) - 2x(3x-1) = 2(3x-1)(x+1)$$

By expanding the brackets, the equations give;

$$5x + 5 - 6x^2 + 2x = 2(3x^2 + 2x - 1)$$

This gives;

$$5x + 5 - 6x^2 + 2x = 6x^2 + 4x - 2$$

The equations can be simplified and rearranged on one side as;

$$-6x^2 - 6x^2 + 5x + 2x - 4x + 5 + 2 = 0$$

Resulting in;

$$-12x^2 - 3x + 7 = 0$$

This equation can be multiplied through by -1 as;

$$12x^2 + 3x - 7 = 0$$

This equation can be solved by the quadratic formula;

$$x_{1,2} = \frac{-b \pm \sqrt{b^2 - 4 \times a \times c}}{2 \times a}$$

Where;

a = 12, b = 3 and c = -7

Therefore;

$$x_{1,2} = \frac{-3 \pm \sqrt{3^2 - 4 \times 12 \times -7}}{2 \times 12}$$

$$x_{1,2} = \frac{-3 \pm \sqrt{345}}{24}$$

The two values of x are;

$$x_1 = \frac{-3 + 18.6}{24} = 0.65$$

and

$$x_2 = \frac{-3 - 18.6}{24} = -0.9$$

Q5. Solve the algebraic fraction below.

$$\frac{3x}{5x+2} + \frac{3x-2}{2x+1} = 3$$

Solution:

The first step is to multiply through by the common denominator [i.e. (5x+2)(2x+1)] to remove the denominators;

$$(5x+2)(2x+1)\left[\frac{3x}{5x+2} + \frac{3x-2}{2x+1}\right] = 3 \times (5x+2)(2x+1)$$

The denominators cancel the common denominator out and give

$$3x(2x+1)+(3x-2)(5x+2)=3(5x+2)(2x+1)$$

By expanding the brackets, the equations give;

$$6x^2+3x+15x^2+6x-10x-4=3(10x^2+5x+4x+2)$$

This gives;

$$21x^2-x-4=30x^2+27x+6$$

The equations can be simplified and rearranged on one side as;

$$-9x^2-28x^2-10=0$$

This equation can be multiplied through by -1 as;

$$9x^2+28x+10=0$$

This equation can be solved by the quadratic formula;

$$x_{1,2}=\frac{-b\pm\sqrt{b^2-4\times a\times c}}{2\times a}$$

Where;

a = 9, b = 28 and c = 10

Therefore;

$$x_{1,2}=\frac{-28\pm\sqrt{28^2-4\times 9\times 10}}{2\times 9}$$

$$x_{1,2}=\frac{-28\pm\sqrt{424}}{18}$$

The two values of x are;

$$x_1=\frac{-28+20.6}{18}=-0.4$$

and

$$x_2 = \frac{-28 - 20.6}{18} = -2.7$$

10. Iterations

Iterations are used to find approximations to certain simple and complex equations that cannot be solved by basic mathematical methods.

It involves the ***creation of a formula*** from the ***equation*** and the use of the ***formula to generate sequences***.

- When the sequences move closer and closer to a definite limit, the solution can be obtained and it is called ***Converging***.
- When the sequence does not have a finite limit it is called a ***Diverging***.

This chapter will ***focus on Converging sequences*** to find solutions to equations.

Strategy (FOCUS ON CONVERGING):

I. Rearrangement or Change of Subjects

There should be massive skills in rearranging equations. In some cases, the change of subject is used.

Example:

Rearrange to make x the subject of the equation $x^3 + 4x - 120 = 0$

Solution:

$$x^3 + 4x - 120 = 0$$

It can be rearranged as;

$$x^3 = 120 - 4x$$

And finally;

$$x = \sqrt[3]{120 - 4x}$$

II. Setting the iterative rule

The subject (x) must be written in such a way that it is always the next future value of x (i.e. x_{n+1}) while the x value inside the formula represents the current x (i.e. x_n) number.

Example:

The equation;

$$x = \sqrt[3]{120 - 4x}$$

can be written as;

$$x_{n+1} = \sqrt[3]{120 - 4x_n}$$

III. **Checking where the value of x converges**

The change in the x **values minimizes** when it gets close to the solution and any further calculations to generate ***further terms of the sequences*** will result in a tiny change from the previous values.

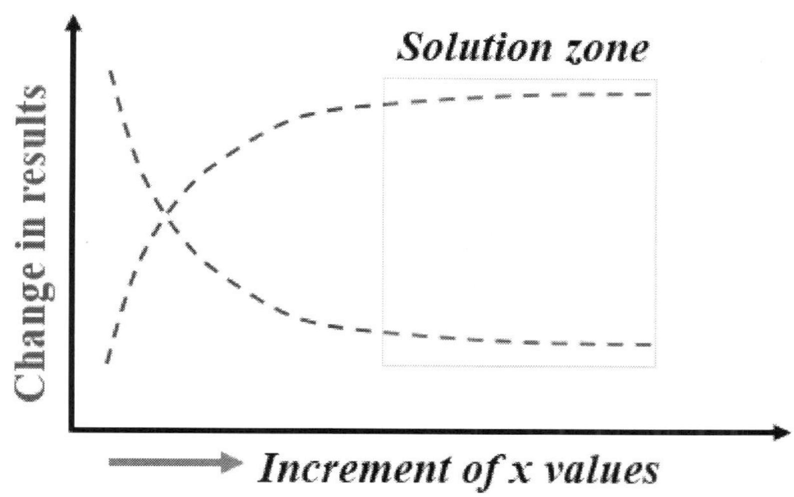

Example question and solution:

(a) Show that the following equation $x^2 - 10x + 21 = 0$ can be rearranged to give $x = \sqrt{10x - 21}$.

(b) Find an approximate solution to the equation $x^2 - 10x + 21 = 0$ using an iteration process with a starting value $x_0 = 4$.

Solution:

(a) From,

$$x^2 - 10x + 21 = 0$$

It can be rearranged as;

$$x^2 = 10x - 21$$

And finally, taking the square root on both sides of the equation gives;

$$x = \sqrt{10x - 21}$$

(b) The rearranged formula created in (*a*) can be used to create the solution sequences of *x*.

From;

$$x = \sqrt{10x - 21}$$

It can be changed into;

$$x_{n+1} = \sqrt{10x_n - 21}$$

The solution can be expressed as;

x values	$x_{n+1} = \sqrt{10x_n - 21}$
x_0	4
x_1	4.358898944
x_2	4.752787544
x_3	5.150521861
x_4	5.523152959
x_5	5.850771709

x_6	6.124354422
x_7	6.343779963
x_8	6.514430108
x_9	6.644117780
x_{10}	6.741007180
x_{11}	6.812493802
x_{12}	6.864760595
x_{13}	6.902724531
x_{14}	6.930169212
x_{15}	6.949941879
x_{16}	6.964152410
x_{17}	6.974347575
x_{18}	6.981652795

The approximate solution is 6.98 at 2 decimal places. It started converging at $\boldsymbol{x}_{12}$.

Note: All the answers from $\boldsymbol{x}_{12}$ **to** $\boldsymbol{x}_{18}$ are CORRECT.

Questions

Q1.

i. Show that the following equation $\boldsymbol{x^2 - 3x - 10 = 0}$ can be rearranged to give $\boldsymbol{x = \sqrt{3x + 10}}$.

ii. Use the iteration formula from $\boldsymbol{x = \sqrt{3x + 10}}$ to find $\boldsymbol{x_3}$ to 3 decimal places, starting with $x_0 = 2$.

iii. Find an approximate solution to the equation $\boldsymbol{x^2 - 3x - 10 = 0}$ using an iteration process with a starting value $x_0 = 2$.

Solution:

i. From;

$$\boldsymbol{x^2 - 3x - 10 = 0}$$

It can be rearranged as;

$$\boldsymbol{x^2 = 3x + 10}$$

And finally, taking the square root on both sides of the equation gives;

$$\boldsymbol{x = \sqrt{3x + 10}}$$

ii. The rearranged formula given in (*i*) can be used to create the solution sequences of *x*.

From;

$$\boldsymbol{x = \sqrt{3x + 10}}$$

It can be changed into;

$$\boldsymbol{x_{n+1} = \sqrt{3x_n + 10}}$$

The solution for x_3 can be expressed as;

x values	$x_{n+1} = \sqrt{3x_n + 10}$
x_0	2
x_1	4
x_2	4.69041576
x_3	4.90624574

Hence, the value for x_3 is **4.906**.

iii. The approximate solution for x can be obtained using

$$x_{n+1} = \sqrt{3x_n + 10}$$

The solution can be expressed as;

x values	$x_{n+1} = \sqrt{3x_n + 10}$
x_0	2
x_1	4
x_2	4.69041576
x_3	4.90624574
x_4	4.97179416
x_5	4.99153108
x_6	4.99745868

x_7	4.99992300

The approximate solution is **4.999923 ≈ 5**. It started converging at x_5.

Q2.

i. Show that the following equation $2x^2 - 3x - 9 = 0$ can be rearranged to give

$x = \sqrt{\frac{3x+9}{2}}$.

ii. Use the iteration formula from $x = \sqrt{\frac{3x+9}{2}}$ to find x_3 to 3 decimal places, starting with $x_0 = 4.9$.

iii. Find an approximate solution to the equation $2x^2 - 3x - 9 = 0$ using an iteration process with a starting value $x_0 = 4.9$.

Solution:

i. From;

$$2x^2 - 3x - 9 = 0$$

It can be rearranged as;

$$2x^2 = 3x + 9$$

And finally, taking the square root on both sides of the equation gives;

$$x = \sqrt{\frac{3x+9}{2}}$$

ii. The rearranged formula given in (*i*) can be used to create the solution sequences of x.

From;

$$x = \sqrt{\frac{3x+9}{2}}$$

It can be changed into;

$$x_{n+1} = \sqrt{\frac{3x_n+9}{2}}$$

The solution for x_3 can be expressed as;

x values	$x_{n+1} = \sqrt{\frac{3x_n+9}{2}}$
x_0	4.9
x_1	3.442382896
x_2	3.108629013
x_3	3.027035434

Hence, the value for x_3 is **3.027**.

iii. The approximate solution for x can be obtained using

$$x_{n+1} = \sqrt{\frac{3x_n+9}{2}}$$

The solution can be expressed as;

x values	$x_{n+1} = \sqrt{\frac{3x_n+9}{2}}$
x_0	4.9
x_1	3.442382896
x_2	3.108629013
x_3	3.027035434
x_4	3.006751262
x_5	3.001687341
x_6	3.000421806
x_7	3.000105450

The approximate solution is **3.0001** $\approx$ **3**. It started converging at $\boldsymbol{x}_4$.

Q3.

i. Show that the following equation $2x^2 - 4x - 126 = 0$ can be rearranged to give $x = \sqrt{\frac{4x+126}{2}}$.

ii. Use the iteration formula from $x = \sqrt{\frac{4x+126}{2}}$ to find x_3 to 3 decimal places, starting with $x_0 = 2$.

iii. Find an approximate solution to the equation $2x^2 - 4x - 126 = 0$ using an iteration process with a starting value $x_0 = 2$.

Solution:

i. From;

$$2x^2 - 4x - 126 = 0$$

It can be rearranged as;

$$2x^2 = 4x + 126$$

And finally, taking the square root on both sides of the equation gives;

$$x = \sqrt{\frac{4x + 126}{2}}$$

ii. The rearranged formula given in (*i*) can be used to create the solution sequences of *x*.

From;

$$x = \sqrt{\frac{4x + 126}{2}}$$

It can be changed into;

$$x_{n+1} = \sqrt{\frac{4x_n + 126}{2}}$$

The solution for x_3 can be expressed as;

x values	$x_{n+1} = \sqrt{\frac{4x_n+126}{2}}$
x_0	2
x_1	8.185352772
x_2	8.909023827
x_3	8.989885853

Hence, the value for x_3 is **8.990**.

iii. The approximate solution for x can be obtained using

$$x_{n+1} = \sqrt{\frac{4x_n + 126}{2}}$$

The solution can be expressed as;

x values	$x_{n+1} = \sqrt{\frac{4x_n+126}{2}}$

x_0	2
x_1	8.185352772
x_2	8.909023827
x_3	8.989885853
x_4	8.998876136
x_5	8.999875125
x_6	8.999986125
x_7	8.999998458

The approximate solution is **8.999998** $\approx$ **9**. It started converging at $\boldsymbol{x}_3$.

Q4.

i. Show that the following equation $\boldsymbol{x^3 - 2x + 1 = 0}$ can be rearranged to give $\boldsymbol{x = \sqrt[3]{2x - 1}}$.

ii. Use the iteration formula from $\boldsymbol{x = \sqrt[3]{2x - 1}}$ to find $\boldsymbol{x_4}$ to 3 decimal places, starting with $x_0 = 3$.

iii. Find an approximate solution to the equation $\boldsymbol{x^3 - 2x + 1 = 0}$ using an iteration process with a starting value $x_0 = 3$.

Solution:

i. From;

$$\boldsymbol{x^3 - 2x + 1 = 0}$$

It can be rearranged as;

$$x^3 = 2x - 1$$

And finally, taking the cube root on both sides of the equation gives;

$$x = \sqrt[3]{2x - 1}$$

ii. The rearranged formula given in (*i*) can be used to create the solution sequences of x.

From;

$$x = \sqrt[3]{2x - 1}$$

It can be changed into;

$$x_{n+1} = \sqrt[3]{2x_n - 1}$$

The solution for x_4 can be expressed as;

x values	$x_{n+1} = \sqrt[3]{2x_n - 1}$
x_0	3
x_1	1.709975947
x_2	1.342565793
x_3	1.189993547

Hence, the value for x_3 is **1.190**.

iii. The approximate solution for x can be obtained using

$$x_{n+1} = \sqrt[3]{2x_n - 1}$$

The solution can be expressed as;

x values	$x_{n+1} = \sqrt[3]{2x_n - 1}$
x_0	3
x_1	1.709975947
x_2	1.342565793
x_3	1.189993547
x_4	1.113332811
x_5	1.070472212
x_6	1.044932323
x_7	1.029099866
x_8	1.019035270
x_9	1.012532461

The approximate solution is **1.0125** ≈ **1**. It started converging at x_7.

Q5.

i. Show that the following equation $x^2 + 11x + 30 = 0$ can be rearranged to give $x = \frac{-x^2-30}{11}$.

ii. Use the iteration formula from $x = \frac{-x^2-30}{11}$ to find x_4 to 3 decimal places, starting with $x_0 = 2$.

iii. Find an approximate solution to the equation $\boldsymbol{x^2 + 11x + 30} = \mathbf{0}$ using an iteration process with a starting value $x_0 = 2$.

Solution:

i. From;

$$\boldsymbol{x^2 + 11x + 30 = 0}$$

It can be rearranged as;

$$\boldsymbol{11x = -\,x^2 - 30}$$

And finally, dividing both sides of the equation by 11 gives;

$$\boldsymbol{x = \frac{-x^2 - 30}{11}}$$

ii. The rearranged formula given in (*i*) can be used to create the solution sequences of *x*.

From;

$$\boldsymbol{x = \frac{-x^2 - 30}{11}}$$

It can be changed into;

$$\boldsymbol{x_{n+1} = \frac{-x_n{}^2 - 30}{11}}$$

The solution for x_4 can be expressed as;

x values	$x_{n+1} = \frac{-x_n{}^2-30}{11}$
x_0	2
x_1	-3.090909090

x_2	-3.595792637
x_3	-3.902702244

Hence, the value for x_3 is **1.190**.

iii. The approximate solution for x can be obtained using

$$x_{n+1} = \sqrt[3]{2x_n - 1}$$

The solution can be expressed as;

x values	$x_{n+1} = \frac{-x_n^2 - 30}{11}$
x_0	2
x_1	-3.090909090
x_2	-3.595792637
x_3	-3.902702244
x_4	-4.111916801
x_5	-4.264350889
x_6	-4.380426228
x_7	-4.471648540
x_8	-4.545058242
x_9	-4.605232220

x_{10}	-4.655287618
x_{11}	-4.697427528
x_{12}	-4.733256853
x_{13}	-4.763974585
x_{14}	-4.790495804
x_{15}	-4.813531823
x_{16}	-4.833644419
x_{17}	-4.851283488
x_{18}	-4.866813771
x_{19}	-4.880534208
x_{20}	-4.892692196
x_{21}	-4.903494265
x_{22}	-4.913114183
x_{23}	-4.921699179
x_{24}	-4.929374801
x_{25}	-4.936248721
x_{26}	-4.942413767
x_{27}	-4.947950349

The approximate solution is **-4.94795** ≈ **-5**. It started converging at $\boldsymbol{x}_{20}$.

11. Functions

A function is a formula that converts one value into another. It acts as a relation between the two values.

Example, if, $y = 3x + 2$ then any value of x can be multiplied by 3 and added by 2. It means, when $x = 2, y = 8$.

The relation between y (called the ***Range***) and x (called the ***Domain***) is called **Mapping**. The formula to change the ***domain*** to the ***range*** is called the **Rule**.

There are three (3) main mapping relations.

(a) ***One-to-one***: Each domain value gives you exactly one value of the range. Example, $y = 2x + 2$.

(b) ***Many-to-one***: Many domain values can give you the same range number. Example, $y = (x)^2$. Meaning, $-1 \times -1 = 1$ and $+1 \times +1 = 1$.

(c) ***One-to-Many***: One domain value can give many range numbers. Example, $y = \pm\sqrt{x}$. Meaning, $\pm\sqrt{4} = +2$ **or** -2. (***Note***: this is not a function).

(d) ***Many-to-Many***: Many domain values can be mapped to many range numbers. Example, $y = factors\ of\ 6$ and $y = factors\ of\ 12$. Meaning, 1, 2 and 3 are all factors 6 and 12.

The main focus is on how to solve problems involving functions.

Strategies for Solving Functions:

I. Using the Rule or Inserting Values

The main point is the skills of substituting values in formulas. Sometimes, it is also required to solve the equation by a certain rule.
The symbols for functions must be learnt.

Symbols;

- $y = 2x + 2$ can be written as $f(x) = 2x + 2$ or $f: x = 2x + 2$.
- $g = x - 3$ can be written as $g(x) = 2x + 2$ or $g: x = 2x + 2$.

Example question 1:

If $f(x) = 3x - 1$, find
(i) $f(3)$ and
(ii) $f(-4)$.

Solution:

i. The value, *3*, must substitute x in the formula. It must be put in any place where the x can be found.

$$f(3) = 3(3) - 1 = 8$$

ii. The value, *-4*, must substitute x in the formula. It must be put in any place where the x can be found.

$$f(-4) = 3(-4) - 1 = -13$$

Example question 2:

If $g(x) = 7x - 24$, **solve**
(i) $g(x) = 4$ and
(ii) $g(x) = -3$.

Solution:

i. Note that the question says ***SOLVE***. The value of x must be calculated. The formula must be equated to 4.

$$g(x) = 7x - 24 = 4$$

It means that;

$$7x - 24 = 4$$

By rearranging, this becomes;

$$7x = 4 + 24$$

$$7x = 28$$

The value of x is;

$$x = \frac{28}{7} = 4$$

ii. The value of x must be calculated. The formula must be equated to **-3**.

$$g(x) = 7x - 24 = -3$$

It means that;

$$7x - 24 = -3$$

By rearranging, this becomes;

$$7x = -3 + 24$$

$$7x = 21$$

The value of x is;

$$x = \frac{21}{7} = 3$$

II. Finding inverse functions

Note that there are several ways of finding the inverse but the symbol remains the same.

The inverse function of the function $f(x) = 3x - 1$ can be written as

$$f^{-1}(x) = \frac{x+1}{3}$$

Steps in finding the inverse function:

Step 1:

If

$$f(x) = 3x - 1$$

Let ***f(x) = y***

$$y = 3x - 1$$

Step 2:

Then make ***x*** *the subject;*

$$y = 3x - 1$$

$$y + 1 = 3x$$

$$\frac{y + 1}{3} = x$$

Meaning;

$$x = \frac{y + 1}{3}$$

Step 3:

Write the inverse of the function by interchanging the ***y*** *with* ***x*** *as;*

$$f^{-1}(x) = \frac{x + 1}{3}$$

<u>Example question:</u>

If

$$g(x) = \frac{4x - 7}{3}$$

Solution:

Again, the steps above must be followed.

Step 1:

If

$$g(x) = \frac{4x - 7}{3}$$

Let ***g(x) = y***

$$y = \frac{4x - 7}{3}$$

Step 2:

Then make **x** *the subject;*

$$y = \frac{4x - 7}{3}$$

$$3y = 4x - 7$$

$$3y + 7 = 4x$$

$$\frac{3y + 7}{4} = x$$

Meaning;

$$x = \frac{3y + 7}{4}$$

Step 3:

Write the inverse of the function by interchanging the **y** *with* **x** *as;*

$$f^{-1}(x) = \frac{3x + 7}{4}$$

III. <u>Finding Composite Functions</u>

This is simply by inserting one function into the other.

Note: The symbols used for composite functions.

- If the function of ***f*** is ***f***(x) and the function of **g** is **g**(x);

  Placing the function **g**(x) into ***f***(x) can be written as;

  $$g(f(x)) \text{ or } (g \circ f) \text{ or } gf \text{ or } gf(x)$$

- The inverse function of ***f*** which is f^{1}(x) can also be put into the function of **g** (i.e. **g**(x) by writing;

  $$g\left(f^{-1}(x)\right) \text{ or } (g \circ f^{-1}) \text{ or } gf^{-1} \text{ or } gf^{-1}(x)$$

- A number (e.g. 4) can be placed into the function ***f*** (i.e. f(4)) before placing it into the function of ***g***. This can be written as;

$$g(f(4)) \text{ or } (g \circ f(4)) \text{ or } gf(4) \text{ or } gf(4)$$

- The function ***f***, can be placed into itself (i.e. *f*(*f*(x)) before placing it into the function of ***g***. This can be written as;

$$g(ff(x)) \text{ or } (g \circ ff(x)) \text{ or } gff(x) \text{ or } gff(x)$$

- Multiplication of function ***f*** and function ***g*** can be written as;

$$g(x).f(x) \quad or \quad f.g$$

Example question and solution:

If

$$f(x) = 3x - 1$$

and

$$g(x) = \frac{4x - 7}{3}$$

Find;

i. $gf(x)$.

ii. $gf^{-1}(x)$.

iii. $gf(2)$

iv. $gff(x)$

v. $g(x).f(x)$

Solution:

i. Put function ***f*** into **g**. It means, where ever you see ***x*** in function **g**, put all the function ***f*(x)** there and resolve the resulting equation as follows;

$$gf(x) = \frac{4(fx) - 7}{3}$$

This gives;

$$gf(x) = \frac{4(3x - 1) - 7}{3}$$

Resolving it gives;

$$gf(x) = \frac{12x - 4 - 7}{3}$$

And finally;

$$gf(x) = \frac{12x - 11}{3}$$

ii. Put the inverse function ***f*** into **g**. It means, where ever you see ***x*** in function **g**, put all the $f^{1}(x)$ there and resolve the resulting equation as follows;

$$gf^{-1}(x) = \frac{4(f^{-1}(x)) - 7}{3}$$

But $f^{-1}(x)$ *is already known from the previous sub-chapter above. Otherwise, it must be solved first.*

$$f^{-1}(x) = \frac{x + 1}{3}$$

This gives;

$$gf^{-1}(x) = \frac{4(\frac{x + 1}{3}) - 7}{3}$$

Resolving it gives;

$$gf^{-1}(x) = \frac{\frac{4x + 4}{3} - 7}{3}$$

It becomes;

$$gf^{-1}(x) = \frac{\frac{4x + 4 - 21}{3}}{3}$$

and;

$$gf^{-1}(x) = \frac{4x - 17}{3} \div 3$$

That results in;

$$gf^{-1}(x) = \frac{4x - 17}{3} \times \frac{1}{3}$$

And finally;

$$gf^{-1}(x) = \frac{4x - 17}{9}$$

iii. Put 2 in place of x in the function f and place the results in g. It means, where ever you see x in function g, put the results there and resolve the resulting equation as follows;

$$f(2) = 3(2) - 1 = 5$$

Therefore;

$$gf(2) = \frac{4(f(2)) - 7}{3}$$

Gives;

$$gf(2) = \frac{4(5) - 7}{3}$$

Resolving it gives;

$$gf(2) = \frac{13}{3}$$

iv. This can be resolved by putting function f into itself (i.e. put the function f in place of x in function f. Then put the results in function g as follows.

Step 1: Putting function f into itself.

$$f(x) = 3x - 1$$

Hence,

$$ff(x) = 3(3x - 1) - 1$$

Resolving it gives,

$$ff(x) = 9x - 3 - 1$$

$$ff(x) = 9x - 4$$

The answer for ***ff*(x)** can now replace ***x*** in function ***g*** as follows;

$$gff(x) = \frac{4(ff(x)) - 7}{3}$$

This gives;

$$gff(x) = \frac{4(9x - 4) - 7}{3}$$

Resolving it gives;

$$gff(x) = \frac{36x - 16 - 7}{3}$$

And finally;

$$gff(x) = \frac{36x - 23}{3}$$

v. This is simply by multiplying the two functions.

This means,

$$g(x).f(x) = \frac{4x - 7}{3} \times 3x - 1$$

Resolving it gives,

$$g(x).f(x) = \frac{(4x - 7)(3x - 1)}{3}$$

Expanding the bracket gives;

$$g(x).f(x) = \frac{12x^2 - 4x - 21x + 7}{3}$$

And finally;

$$g(x).f(x) = \frac{12x^2 - 25x + 7}{3}$$

Questions

Q1. The function of *h* is such that;

$$h(x) = \frac{11 - 2x^2}{3}$$

i. Find $h(2)$

ii. Find $h^{-1}(x)$

iii. Solve $h(x) = 1$

Solution:

i.

$$h(2) = \frac{11 - 2(2)^2}{3} = \frac{3}{3} = 1$$

ii. Let ***h(x) = y***

This means;

$$y = \frac{11 - 2x^2}{3}$$

This becomes;

$$3y = \mathbf{11 - 2x^2}$$

This gives;

$$3y - 11 = \mathbf{-2x^2}$$

Multiplying through by -1 gives;

$$11 - 3y = \mathbf{2x^2}$$

$$\frac{11 - 3y}{2} = \boldsymbol{x^2}$$

Taking the square root of both sides gives;

$$x = \sqrt{\frac{11 - 3y}{2}}$$

Hence, the ***h^{-1}(x)*** *is;*

$$\boldsymbol{h}^{-1}(\boldsymbol{x}) = \sqrt{\frac{11 - 3x}{2}}$$

iii. The function ***h*(x)** must be equated to 1.

$$h(x) = \frac{\mathbf{11 - 2x^2}}{\mathbf{3}} = \mathbf{1}$$

This means;

$$\frac{\mathbf{11 - 2x^2}}{\mathbf{3}} = \mathbf{1}$$

Resolving it gives;

$$\mathbf{11 - 2x^2 = 3}$$

This becomes;

$$\mathbf{11 - 3 = 2x^2}$$

This gives;

$$\mathbf{8 = 2x^2}$$

And finally;

$$x = 2$$

Q2. The function of *f* is such that;

$$f(x) = \frac{x+2}{x+1}$$

i. Find $f(3)$

ii. Find $f^{-1}(x)$

iii. Solve $f(x) = 5$

Solution:

i.

$$f(3) = \frac{3+2}{3+1} = \frac{5}{4} = 1.25$$

ii. Let ***f(x) = y***

This means;

$$y = \frac{x+2}{x+1}$$

This becomes;

$$y(x+1) = x+2$$

This gives;

$$xy - y = x + 2$$

Rearranging gives;

$$xy - x = 2 + y$$

Factorizing x out gives;

$$x(y-1) = 2 + y$$

Making x the subject gives;

$$x = \frac{2 + y}{y - 1}$$

Hence, the $f^{1}(x)$ is;

$$f^{-1}(x) = \frac{2 + x}{x - 1}$$

iii. The function $f(x)$ must be equated to 5.

$$f(x) = \frac{x + 2}{x + 1} = 5$$

This means;

$$\frac{x + 2}{x + 1} = 5$$

Resolving it gives;

$$x + 2 = 5(x + 1)$$

Expanding the bracket gives;

$$x + 2 = 5x + 5$$

Rearranging gives;

$$2 - 5 = 5x - x$$

This becomes;

$$-3 = 4x$$

And finally;

$$x = -\frac{3}{4} = -.0.75$$

Q3. The function *f* and *g* are given as;

$$f(x) = 2x + 1$$

and

$$g(x) = \frac{2x}{x + 1}$$

i. Find $gf(x)$

ii. Find $fg(2)$

Solution:

i. This is done by placing the function ***f*** at every ***x*** positions in function ***g***.

$$gf(x) = \frac{2(f(x))}{f(x) + 1}$$

This means;

$$gf(x) = \frac{2(2x + 1)}{(2x + 1) + 1}$$

Resolving it gives;

$$gf(x) = \frac{4x + 2}{2x + 2}$$

It can be simplified by factorizing 2 out;

$$gf(x) = \frac{2(2x + 1)}{2(x + 1)} = \frac{2x + 1}{x + 1}$$

ii. This is done by solving ***g***(2) and placing the results in function ***f***. That is placing the results at the position of ***x*** in function ***f***.
This means;

$$g(2) = \frac{2(2)}{(2) + 1}$$

This becomes;

$$g(2) = \frac{4}{3}$$

Then;

$$fg(2) = 2\left(\frac{4}{3}\right) + 1$$

Resolving it gives;

$$fg(2) = \frac{8}{3} + 1 = \frac{11}{3}$$

Q4. The function *h* and g are given as;

$$h(x) = 3x - 2$$

and

$$g(x) = \frac{x-2}{3-x}$$

i. Find $gh(x)$

ii. Find $gh^{-1}(x)$

Solution:

i. This is done by placing the function *h* at every ***x*** positions in function ***g***.

$$gh(x) = \frac{(h(x)) - 2}{3 - (h(x))}$$

This means;

$$gh(x) = \frac{(3x - 2) - 2}{3 - (3x - 2)}$$

Resolving it gives;

$$gh(x) = \frac{3x - 4}{3 - 3x + 2}$$

It can be simplified as;

$$gh(x) = \frac{3x - 4}{5 - 3x}$$

ii. This is done by placing the inverse function of *h* (i.e. $h^{-1}(x)$) at every ***x*** positions in function ***g***.

$$gh^{-1}(x) = \frac{(h^{-1}(x)) - 2}{3 - (h^{-1}(x))}$$

But $h^{-1}(x)$ can be resolved by letting $h(x) = y$;

$$g(2) = \frac{4}{3}$$

This means;

$$y = 3x - 2$$

Making x the subject becomes;

$$x = \frac{y+2}{3}$$

Hence $\boldsymbol{h^{-1}}(\mathbf{x})$ is given by*;*

$$h^{-1}(x) = \frac{x+2}{3}$$

This means that;

$$gh^{-1}(x) = \frac{(h^{-1}(x)) - 2}{3 - (h^{-1}(x))}$$

Becomes;

$$gh^{-1}(x) = \frac{\left(\frac{x+2}{3}\right) - 2}{3 - \left(\frac{x+2}{3}\right)}$$

Resolving that gives;

$$gh^{-1}(x) = \frac{\left(\frac{x+2-6}{3}\right)}{\left(\frac{9-x+2}{3}\right)}$$

$$gh^{-1}(x) = \frac{\left(\frac{x-4}{3}\right)}{\left(\frac{11-x}{3}\right)}$$

This can now be resolved as;

$$gh^{-1}(x) = \frac{x-4}{3} \div \frac{11-x}{3}$$

That gives;

$$gh^{-1}(x) = \frac{x-4}{3} \times \frac{3}{11-x}$$

Finally;

$$gh^{-1}(x) = \frac{3(x-4)}{3(11-x)} = \frac{x-4}{11-x}$$

Q5. The function *f* and g are given as;

$$f(x) = \frac{x+2}{x+1}$$

and

$$g(x) = \frac{x-2}{3-x}$$

Solve $f(x) = g(x)$.

<u>Solution:</u>

This is calculated by equating the function ***f*** to the function **g** and the value of ***x*** is solved as follows.

$$f(x) = g(x)$$

$$\frac{x+2}{x+1} = \frac{x-2}{3-x}$$

This is resolved by cross-multiplication using the denominators;

$$\frac{x+2}{x+1} \quad \frac{x-2}{3-x}$$

Resolving it gives;

$$(3-x)(x+2) = (x-2)(x+1)$$

Expanding the brackets gives;

$$3x + 6 - x^2 - 2x = x^2 + x - 2x - 2$$

Rearranging gives;

$$0 = x^2 + x^2 + x - 2x + 2x - 3x - 2 - 6$$

The equation now becomes;

$$0 = 2x^2 - 2x - 8$$

$$2x^2 - 2x - 8 = 0$$

The equation can be divided by 2 since the constants are factors of 2;

$$x^2 - x - 4 = 0$$

The above equation can be solved by the quadratic formula;

$$x = \frac{-b \pm \sqrt{b^2 - 4ac}}{2a}$$

From the equation, ***a*** = 1, ***b*** = -1 and ***c*** = -4.

Using the formula,

$$x = \frac{- - 4 \pm \sqrt{-1^2 - 4 \times 1 \times -4}}{2 \times 1}$$

Resolving it becomes;

$$x = \frac{1 \pm \sqrt{17}}{2}$$

Therefore x values can be obtained by;

$$x = \frac{1 \pm 4.12}{2}$$

This means that x can be either;

$$x = \frac{1 + 4.12}{2} = 2.56$$

or

$$x = \frac{1 - 4.12}{2} = -1.56$$

Therefore is either 2.56 and x = -1.56.

<u>**Note:**</u> The positive value is normally required.

12. Solving Index Laws Equations

Index forms are special ways of writing numbers with a base and an index as illustrated below.

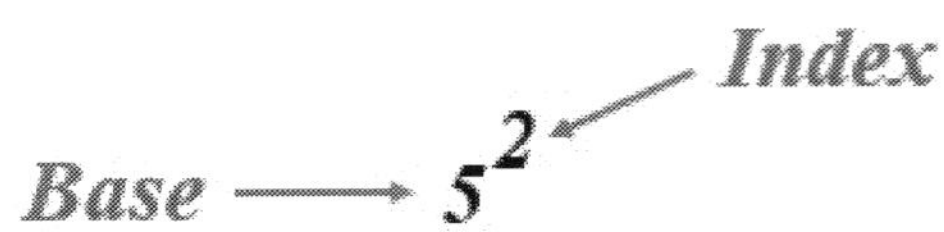

The focus of this chapter is ***how to solve equations in index forms***. However, the **basic six laws of indices** will be explained to enable us to solve the equations.

Laws of indices

1. ***Law 1*- Multiplication rule**:

$$a^m \times a^n = a^{m+n}$$

Example: $(5 \times 5 \times 5) \times (5 \times 5) = 5^3 \times 5^2 = 5^{3+2} = 5^5$

2. ***Law 2*- Division rule**:

$$a^m \div a^n = a^{m-n}$$

Example:

$$\frac{(5 \times 5 \times 5 \times 5 \times 5)}{(5 \times 5)} = 5^5 \div 5^2 = 5^{5-2} = 5^3$$

3. ***Law 3*- Power rule**:

$$(a^m)^n = a^{mn}$$

Example: $(5^3)^2 = 5^{3 \times 2} = 5^6$

4. ***Law 4*- Zero Power rule**:

$$a^0 = 1$$

Example: $5^0 = 1$

5. ***Law 5*- Negative index rule**:

$$a^{-n} = \frac{1}{a^n}$$

Example:

$$5^{-3} = \frac{1}{5^3} = \frac{1}{5 \times 5 \times 5} = \frac{1}{125}$$

6. ***Law 6*- Fractional index rule**:

There are two parts for this rule which are important to this chapter;

Part 1:

$$a^{\frac{1}{n}} = \sqrt[n]{a}$$

Meaning:

The denominator of the ***fractional*** index is the number of the ***ROOT***.

Examples:

1. $125^{\frac{1}{3}} = \sqrt[3]{125} = 5$

2. $25^{\frac{1}{2}} = \sqrt[2]{25} = 5$

Part 2:

$$a^{\frac{m}{n}} = \left(\sqrt[n]{a}\right)^m$$

Meaning:

The ***numerator*** and the ***denominator*** of the ***fractional*** index need to be **separated**. Then the ***denominator*** of the fractional index becomes the ***number*** of the ***ROOT*** whiles the ***numerator*** remains the **power**.

Examples:

1. $125^{\frac{2}{3}} = 125^{\frac{1}{3}\times 2} = \left(125^{\frac{1}{3}}\right)^2 = (\sqrt[3]{125})^2 = 5^2 = 25$

2. $25^{\frac{3}{2}} = 25^{\frac{1}{2}\times 3} = \left(25^{\frac{1}{2}}\right)^3 = (\sqrt[2]{25})^3 = 5^3 = 125$

Strategies for Solving Equations:

I. Multiplying or Dividing Numbers and Same Letters

When multiplying numbers and letters,

- Multiply the ***numbers normally***.
- Multiply the ***letters*** by applying ***laws of indices.***

Examples:

1. $6b \times 7b^2 \times 3b = (6 \times 7 \times 3) \times (b \times b^2 \times b)$
$= 126b^{1+2+1}$
$= 126b^3$

2. $2a^7 \times 12a^2 \div 3a^3 = (2 \times 12 \div 3) \times (a^7 \times a^2 \div a^3)$
$= (24 \div 3)a^{7+2-3}$
$= 8a^6$

II. Separating Powers in Multiplication

When two or more index numbers (i.e. multiplying) are raised by the same power, they can be separated having the same power.

Examples:

1. $(a^2b^3)^3 = (a^2)^3 \times (b^3)^3$
$= a^{2\times 3} \times b^{3\times 3}$
$= a^6 \times b^9$
$= a^6b^9$

2. $(3x^2y^3)^{-3} = (3)^{-3} \times (x^2)^{-3} \times (y^3)^{-3}$

$$= \frac{1}{3^3} \times x^{2\times -3} \times y^{3\times -3}$$

$$= \frac{1}{9} \times x^{-6} \times y^{-9}$$

$$= \frac{1}{27x^6y^9}$$

III. <u>Separating Powers in Division</u>

When two or more index numbers (i.e. Dividing) are raised by the same power, they can be separated having the same power.

Part 1:

$$\left(\frac{x}{y}\right)^n = \frac{x^n}{y^n}$$

Examples:

$$\left(\frac{4}{5}\right)^3 = \frac{4^3}{5^3} = \frac{64}{125}$$

Part 2: In a **<u>negative</u>** power, it must be changed to a **<u>positive</u>** power by reciprocating.

$$\left(\frac{x}{y}\right)^{-n} = \left(\frac{y}{x}\right)^n = \frac{y^n}{x^n}$$

Examples 1:

$$\left(\frac{4}{3}\right)^{-2} = \left(\frac{3}{4}\right)^2 = \frac{3^2}{4^2} = \frac{9}{16}$$

Examples 2:

$$\left(\frac{125}{1000}\right)^{-\frac{1}{3}} = \left(\frac{1000}{125}\right)^{\frac{1}{3}} = \frac{\sqrt[3]{1000}}{\sqrt[3]{125}} = \frac{10}{5} = 5$$

IV. Solving equations

When solving equations involving index numbers, the must be resolved to have the same base. After that, the indices can be equated.

Part 1:

$$x^m = x^n$$

Meaning, ***m*** = ***n***

Example:

$$16^x = 64$$

This can be expressed as;

$$(4^2)^x = 4^3$$

This can be expressed as;

$$4^{2x} = 4^3$$

Since the bases are the same, it means;

$$2x = 3$$

And x is;

$$x = \frac{3}{2} = 1.5$$

Part 2:

$$x^{2m-3} = x^n$$

Meaning, ***2m - 3*** = ***n***

Example:

$$3^{2x-9} = 27$$

This can be expressed with the SAME BASE;

$$3^{2x-9} = 3^3$$

Since it is the same base the index numbers must equate;

$$2x - 9 = 3$$

And that becomes;

$$2x = 12$$

Finally;

$$x = 6$$

Questions

Q1. Simplify the following;

i. $7x^5y^{-2} \times 5x^3y^{-3}$

ii. $(3ab^7)^3$

iii. $\frac{6x^2 \times 4x^7}{3x^5}$

Solution:

i.

$$7x^5y^{-2} \times 5x^3y^{-3}$$

$$= (7 \times 5) \times (x^5 \times x^3) \times (y^{-2} \times y^{-3})$$

$$= 35 \times (x^{5+3}) \times (y^{-2+-3})$$

$$= 35x^8y^{-5}$$

ii.

$$(3ab^7)^3 = 3^3 \times a^3 \times b^{7\times3}$$

$$= 27a^3b^{21}$$

iii.

$$\frac{6x^2 \times 4x^7}{3x^5}$$

This can be resolved to separating the numbers from the letters and resolving the numbers as index numbers.

$$= (6 \times 4 \div 3) \times (x^2 \times x^7 \div x^5)$$

Resolving it gives;

$$= 8x^{2+7-5}$$

This becomes;

$$= \mathbf{8x^4}$$

Q2. Evaluate the following;

i. $\mathbf{8^{\frac{2}{3}}}$

ii. $\mathbf{27^{\frac{4}{3}}}$

iii. $\mathbf{\frac{27^2 \times 9^3}{81}}$

Solution:

i.

$$\mathbf{8^{\frac{2}{3}} = 8^{\frac{1}{3}\times 2} = \left(\sqrt[3]{8}\right)^2 = 2^2 = 4}$$

ii.

$$\mathbf{27^{\frac{4}{3}} = 27^{\frac{1}{3}\times 4} = \left(\sqrt[3]{27}\right)^4 = 3^4 = 81}$$

iii.

$$\mathbf{\frac{27^2 \times 9^3}{81}}$$

This can be resolved to have the same base (i.e. base 3) as follows

$$\mathbf{\frac{(3^3)^2 \times (3^2)^3}{3^4}}$$

Resolving it gives;

$$\mathbf{\frac{3^6 \times 3^6}{3^4}}$$

This becomes;

$$3^6 \times 3^6 \div 3^4$$

This gives;

$$3^{6+6-4}$$

And finally;

$$3^8 = 6561$$

Q3. Work out following;

i. $\left(\frac{256}{81}\right)^{-\frac{3}{4}}$

ii. $243^{\frac{1}{5}}\left(27341^0 \times 256^{-\frac{1}{4}}\right)$

iii. $(0.125)^{-\frac{1}{3}}$

Solution:

i.

$$\left(\frac{256}{81}\right)^{-\frac{3}{4}}$$

The negative fractional index must be turned into a positive one by reciprocating as follows;

$$\left(\frac{81}{256}\right)^{\frac{3}{4}}$$

This becomes;

$$\left(\frac{81^{\frac{1}{4}}}{256^{\frac{1}{4}}}\right)^3 = \left(\frac{\sqrt[4]{81}}{\sqrt[4]{256}}\right)^3 = \left(\frac{3}{4}\right)^3 = \frac{3^3}{4^3}$$

$$= \frac{27}{64}$$

ii.

$$243^{\frac{1}{5}}\left(27341^{0} \times 256^{-\frac{1}{4}}\right)$$

This can be resolved as (Note: any number raised to power zero =1);

$$= \sqrt[5]{243} \times 1 \times \left[\frac{1}{256}\right]^{\frac{1}{4}}$$

This now becomes;

$$= 3 \times 1 \times \frac{1}{256^{\frac{1}{4}}}$$

$$= 3 \times 1 \times \frac{1}{\sqrt[4]{256}}$$

$$= 3 \times \frac{1}{4} = \frac{3}{4}$$

iii.

$$(0.125)^{-\frac{1}{3}}$$

This can be resolved by changing the decimals to fractions as follows

$$\left(\frac{125}{1000}\right)^{-\frac{1}{3}}$$

The negative of the fractional index can be removed by reciprocating as follows;

$$\left(\frac{1000}{125}\right)^{\frac{1}{3}}$$

This becomes;

$$\frac{\sqrt[3]{1000}}{\sqrt[3]{125}}$$

This gives;

$$\frac{10}{5}$$

And finally;

$$2$$

Q4. Solve the following equations;

i. $\left(\frac{1}{5}\right)^x = 125$

ii. $4^{x^2} = 256^{\frac{1}{2}}$

iii. $(3^2)^{x-1} = 27^{x-2}$

Solution:

i.

$$\left(\frac{1}{5}\right)^x = 125$$

This can be transformed into;

$$(5^{-1})^x = 5^3$$

This becomes;

$$5^{-1\times x} = 5^3$$

$$5^{-x} = 5^3$$

Since the bases are the same, the indices are also the same;

$$-x = 3$$

And finally;

$$x = -3$$

ii.

$$4^{x^2} = 256^{\frac{1}{2}}$$

This can be resolved to have the same bases;

$$4^{x^2} = \sqrt{256} = 16$$

This now becomes;

$$4^{x^2} = 4^2$$

Since the bases are the same, the index numbers are the same;

$$x^2 = 2$$

And finally;

$$x = \sqrt{2}$$

iii.

$$(3^2)^{x-1} = 27^{x-2}$$

This can be resolved by changing the equation to have the same base;

$$3^{2x-2} = (3^3)^{x-2}$$

Resolving that gives;

$$3^{2x-2} = 3^{3x-6}$$

This becomes;

$$2x - 2 = 3x - 6$$

Rearranging and solving gives;

$$-2 + 6 = 3x - 2x$$

And finally;

$$4 = x$$

$$x = 4$$

Q5. Solve the following equation giving the two possible values of x that satisfy the equation.

$$3^{x(x-3)} = 9^{(3-x)}$$

Solution:

This can be transformed to have the same bases on both sides;

$$3^{x(x-3)} = 3^{2(3-x)}$$

Since we have the same bases, it means the in;

$$x(x-3) = 2(3-x)$$

This becomes;

$$x^2 - 3x = 6 - 2x$$

This can be resolved into a quadratic equation by;

$$x^2 - 3x + 2x - 6 = 0$$

$$x^2 - x - 6 = 0$$

*Solving by factorization method, the **factor pairs** of -6 (i.e. c) that when you added can give you **b** are ; (-3 and 2). Refer to the quadratic equation chapter.*

Hence, the solution is given by;

$$(x-3)(x+2) = 0$$

This means that either;

$$(x-3) = 0 \text{ and } x = 3.$$

Or;

$$(x+2) = 0 \text{ and } x = -2.$$

*Therefore the **two** possible values for x are; 3 and x= -2.*

13. Recurring Decimals to Fractions

Recurring decimal is a decimal that repeats its digits at regular intervals without ending.

Examples are $\mathbf{0.\dot{7}}$, $\mathbf{0.\dot{3}\dot{2}}$, $\mathbf{0.\dot{3}\dot{2}\dot{2}}$ **etc.**

The focus of this chapter is ***to show how to convert a recurring fraction into a normal fraction.***

Strategies for converting to Fractions:

I. Part 1: Same SINGLE numbers after decimal point

This is when there are ***single repeating*** numbers after the decimal point.

Note: *It must be multiplied by* **10** *to get remove the first decimal.*

Example 1;
If there is ***0.3333333333…..***

Solution:

Let, $x = 0.33333333333\ .....$

$\rightarrow \quad 10x = 3.33333333333\ .....$

Subtracting, $10x - x = 3$

This gives, $9x = 3$

And, $x = \frac{3}{9}$

Example 2;
If there is ***0.7777777777777…..***

Solution:

Let, $x = 0.77777777777\ .....$

$\rightarrow \quad 10x = 7.77777777777\ .....$

Subtracting, $10x - x = 7$

This gives, $9x = 7$

And, $x = \frac{7}{9}$

→**Rules**: if there is a single repeat number, $\mathbf{0}.\boldsymbol{aaaaaaaaaa} \ldots \ldots$

$$\boldsymbol{The\ fraction} = \frac{\boldsymbol{a}}{\mathbf{9}}$$

II. Same repeated DOUBLE Digits after decimal point

This is when there is a ***Double-digit*** repeating pattern after the decimal point.

Note: *It must be multiplied by* **100** *to remove the decimal point from the first two digits.*

Example 1;
If there is ***0.454545454545…..***

Solution:

Let, $x = \mathbf{0.454545454545\ldots}$

→ $100x = \mathbf{45.4545454545} \ldots\ldots$

Subtracting, $100x - x = \mathbf{45}$

This gives, $99x = \mathbf{45}$

And, $x = \frac{\mathbf{45}}{\mathbf{99}}$

Example 2;
If there is ***0.737373737373…..***

Solution:

Let, $x = \mathbf{0.737373737373} \ldots\ldots$

→ $100x = \mathbf{73.7373737373} \ldots\ldots$

Subtracting, $100x - x = \mathbf{73}$

This gives, $99x = \mathbf{73}$

And, $x = \frac{\mathbf{73}}{\mathbf{99}}$

→**Rules**: if there is a single repeat number, $\mathbf{0.abababababab\ldots\ldots}$

$$The\ fraction = \frac{ab}{99}$$

III. Same repeated TRIPLE Digits after decimal point

This is when there is a ***TRIPLE digit*** repeating pattern after the decimal point.

Note: *It must be multiplied by* **1000** *to remove the decimal point from the first three digits.*

Example 1;
If there is ***0.452452452452452452.....***

Solution:

Let, $x = 0.452452452452452452\ldots$

$\rightarrow$ $1000x = 452.452452452452452\ldots\ldots$

Subtracting, $1000x - x = 452$

This gives, $999x = 452$

And, $x = \frac{452}{999}$

Example 2;
If there is ***0.736736736736736736.....***

Solution:

Let, $x = 0.736736736736736736\ldots\ldots$

$\rightarrow$ $1000x = 736.736736736736736\ldots\ldots$

Subtracting, $1000x - x = 736$

This gives, $999x = 736$

And, $x = \frac{736}{999}$

→**Rules**: if there is a single repeat number, $\mathbf{0.}\,\boldsymbol{abcabcabcabcabcabc}$...

$$\boldsymbol{The\ fraction} = \frac{\boldsymbol{abc}}{\mathbf{999}}$$

IV. <u>When recurring numbers divided by 10</u>

This is when there is a ***ZERO starting*** the repeating pattern after the decimal point.

<u>**Note**</u>**: Two steps needed;**

- *First, multiply by* **<u>10</u>** *to remove the* ***<u>ZERO</u>*** *after the decimal point.*
- *Secondly, apply the necessary steps as described above.*

Example 1;
If there is ***0.03333333333…..***

Solution:

First step: *Let,* $x = \mathbf{0.033333333333}\ \ldots..$

Second step: $\rightarrow\ \mathbf{10}x = \mathbf{0.33333333333}\ \ldots..$

Appropriate step: $\rightarrow\ \mathbf{100}x = \mathbf{3.33333333333}\ \ldots..$

Subtracting, $\mathbf{100}x - \mathbf{10}x = \mathbf{3}$

This gives, $\mathbf{90}x = \mathbf{3}$

And, $x = \frac{3}{90}$

<u>**Note**</u>**:** Compared to the previous answer

$$\mathbf{0.3333333333}\ \ldots. = \frac{\mathbf{3}}{\mathbf{9}}$$

When divided by **10;**

$$\mathbf{0.03333333333}\ \ldots = \frac{\mathbf{3}}{\mathbf{9}} \times \frac{\mathbf{1}}{\mathbf{10}} = \frac{\mathbf{3}}{\mathbf{90}}$$

Example 2;
If there is ***0.0454545454545…..***

Solution:

First step: *Let,* $x = \mathbf{0.0454545454545} \ldots..$

Second step: $\rightarrow\ 10x = \mathbf{0.454545454545} \ldots..$

Appropriate step: $\rightarrow\ 1000x = \mathbf{45.4545454545} \ldots..$

Subtracting, $\mathbf{1000x - 10x = 45}$

This gives, $\mathbf{990x = 45}$

And, $x = \frac{45}{990}$

<u>**Note**</u>**:** Compared to the previous answer;

$$\mathbf{0.454545454545} \ldots. = \frac{\mathbf{45}}{\mathbf{99}}$$

When divided by **10;**

$$\mathbf{0.045454545}\ldots = \frac{\mathbf{45}}{\mathbf{99}} \times \frac{\mathbf{1}}{\mathbf{10}} = \frac{\mathbf{45}}{\mathbf{990}}$$

Example 3;
If there is ***0.0736736736736736736…..***

Solution:

First step: *Let,* $x = \mathbf{0.0736736736736} \ldots..$

Second step: $\rightarrow\ 10x = \mathbf{0.736736736736} \ldots..$

Appropriate step: $\rightarrow\ 1000x = \mathbf{736.736736736} \ldots..$

Subtracting, $\mathbf{10000x - 10x = 736}$

This gives, $\mathbf{9990x = 736}$

And, $x = \frac{736}{9990}$

<u>**Note**</u>**:** Compared to the previous answer;

$$0.736736736736\ldots = \frac{736}{999}$$

When divided by **10;**

$$0.0736736736736\ldots = \frac{736}{999} \times \frac{1}{10} = \frac{736}{9990}$$

Note: Apply the same rule when divided by ***100***, ***1000***, ***etc***.

V. When the recurring number does not start from the decimal point

This is when ***Non-recurring number or Numbers start*** before the recurring numbers.

Note: Three steps needed;

- **Separate** *the* **ordinary decimal number** *from the* ***recurring decimals****.*
- *Change the* **ordinary decimal number** *to fraction using a* **basic approach**.
- *Apply* **appropriate method** *to change* ***recurring decimal*** *to fractions as described above.*
- *Lastly,* **ADD** *the two* ***resulting fractions****.*

Example 1;
If there is ***0.53333333333…..***

Solution:

***Step 1*: Separate:** $0.533333333\ldots. = 0.5 + 0.033333333\ldots.$

Part 1

$$0.5 = \frac{5}{10}$$

Part 2

$0.033333333\ldots.$

Let, $x = 0.033333333333\ldots..$

$$\rightarrow \quad 10x = 0.33333333333 \ldots..$$

$$\rightarrow \quad 100x = 3.33333333333 \ldots..$$

Subtracting, $100x - 10x = 3$

This gives, $90x = 3$

And, $x = \frac{3}{90}$

Step 2: **ADD**:

$$0.533333333 \ldots. = \frac{5}{10} + \frac{3}{90}$$

Change the fraction $\frac{5}{10}$ *to equivalent fraction that has the same denominator by multiplying both numerator and denominator by 9*$\left(i.e. \frac{45}{90}\right)$

This is done so that the fractions will have the same denominator for easy addition.

It means that;

$$= \frac{45}{90} + \frac{3}{90}$$

$$= \frac{48}{90}$$

Example 2;
If there is ***0.8454545454545…..***

Solution:

Step 1: **Separate:** $0.845454545\ldots = 0.8 + 0.0454545 \ldots.$

Part 1

$$0.8 = \frac{8}{10}$$

Part 2

$\mathbf{0.04545454545}$ ....

$$\text{Let,} \quad x = 0.04545454545 \ldots..$$

$$\rightarrow \quad 10x = 0.4545454545 \ldots..$$

$$\rightarrow \quad 1000x = 45.45454545 \ldots..$$

$$\text{Subtracting,} \quad 1000x - 10x = 45$$

$$\text{This gives,} \quad 990x = 45$$

$$\text{And,} \quad x = \frac{45}{990}$$

***Step 2*: ADD**:

$$0.845454545\ldots.. = \frac{8}{10} + \frac{45}{990}$$

Change the fraction $\frac{8}{10}$ to equivalent fraction that has the same denominator by multiplying both numerator and denominator by 99 $\left(i.e. \frac{792}{990}\right)$

It means that;

$$= \frac{792}{990} + \frac{45}{990}$$

$$= \frac{837}{990}$$

Example 3;
If there is ***0.4736736736736736736…..***

Solution:

***Step 1*: Separate**: $\mathbf{0.4736736736\ldots = 0.4 + 0.0736736736}$ ....

Part 1

$$0.4 = \frac{4}{10}$$

Part 2

0.0736736736736 ....

$$Let, \quad x = 0.0736736736736 \ldots..$$

$$\rightarrow \quad 10x = 0.736736736736 \ldots..$$

$$\rightarrow \quad 10000x = 736.736736736736 \ldots..$$

$$Subtracting, \quad 10000x - 10x = 736$$

$$This\ gives, \quad 9990x = 736$$

$$And, \quad x = \frac{736}{9990}$$

***Step 2*: ADD**:

$$0.4736736736736. \ldots. = \frac{4}{10} + \frac{736}{9990}$$

Change the fraction $\frac{4}{10}$ *to equivalent fraction that has the same denominator by multiplying both numerator and denominator by 999* $\left(i.e. \frac{3996}{9990}\right)$

It means that;

$$= \frac{3996}{9990} + \frac{736}{9990}$$

$$= \frac{4732}{9990}$$

Hence;

$$0.4\dot{7}3\dot{6} = \frac{4732}{9990} = \frac{2366}{4995}$$

Note: Sometimes, you are required to simplify the resulting fraction to the lowest numbers possible.

Summary on recurring number to fractions:

	Pattern	Results	Remarks
Dividing by 10, 100, 1000 etc.			
1	0.33333333333 …..	$\frac{3}{9}$	When the questions are divided by ***10***, ***100*** or ***1000***, divide the answer by the same amount.
2	0.033333333333 …..	$\frac{3}{90}$	
3	0.0033333333333 …..	$\frac{3}{900}$	
Single, Double and Triple recurring numbers.			
1	0.33333333333 …..	$\frac{3}{9}$	The denominator (*9*), ***doubles*** in double digits and ***triples*** in triple digits recurring numbers.
2	0.454545454545…	$\frac{45}{99}$	
3	0.452452452452…..	$\frac{452}{999}$	
Having non-recurring numbers before the recurring numbers.			
1	0.533333333 …..	$\frac{5}{10} + 0.0\dot{3}$	Always separate the ***non-recurring*** fractions from the ***recurring fractions*** before
2	0.845454545…	$\frac{8}{10} + 0.0\dot{4}\dot{5}$	

3	$\mathbf{0.4736736736.\ldots}$	$\frac{4}{10} + 0.0\dot{7}3\dot{6}$	solving.

Questions

Q1. Convert the following recurring numbers to fractions.

i. $\mathbf{0.\dot{5}}$

ii. $\mathbf{0.\dot{7}}$

Solution:

i.

Let, $\boldsymbol{x} = \mathbf{0.55555555555\ldots}$

$\rightarrow 10\boldsymbol{x} = \mathbf{5.55555555555\ldots}$

Subtracting, $10\boldsymbol{x} - \boldsymbol{x} = \mathbf{5}$

This gives, $9\boldsymbol{x} = \mathbf{5}$

And, $\boldsymbol{x} = \frac{\mathbf{5}}{\mathbf{9}}$

ii.

Let, $\boldsymbol{x} = \mathbf{0.77777777777\ldots}$

$\rightarrow 10\boldsymbol{x} = \mathbf{7.77777777777\ldots}$

Subtracting, $10\boldsymbol{x} - \boldsymbol{x} = \mathbf{7}$

This gives, $9\boldsymbol{x} = \mathbf{7}$

And, $x = \frac{7}{9}$

Q2. Convert the following recurring numbers to fractions.

i. $0.\dot{4}\dot{7}$

ii. $0.4\dot{6}8\dot{3}$

<u>Solution:</u>

i.

Let, $x = 0.474747474747....$

$\rightarrow$ $100x = 47.4747474747 .....$

Subtracting, $100x - x = 47$

This gives, $99x = 47$

And, $x = \frac{47}{99}$

ii.

***Step 1*: Separate**: $0.4683683683... = 0.4 + 0.0683683683 ....$

Part 1

$$0.4 = \frac{4}{10}$$

Part 2

$$0.0683683683683 ....$$

Let, $x = 0.0683683683683 .....$

$$\rightarrow \quad 10x = 0.683683683683 \ldots..$$

$$\rightarrow \quad 10000x = 683.683683683683 \ldots..$$

Subtracting, $\quad 10000x - 10x = 683$

This gives, $\quad 9990x = 683$

And, $\quad x = \frac{683}{9990}$

***Step 2*: ADD:**

$$0.4683683683683\ldots.. = \frac{4}{10} + \frac{683}{9990}$$

Change the fraction $\frac{4}{10}$ *to an equivalent fraction that has the same denominator by multiplying both numerator and denominator by 999* $\left(i.e. \frac{3996}{9990}\right)$

It means that;

$$= \frac{3996}{9990} + \frac{683}{9990}$$

$$= \frac{4679}{9990}$$

Q3. Convert the following recurring numbers to fractions.

i. $\quad 0.3\dot{2}\dot{5}$

ii. $\quad 3.1\dot{6}$

Solution:

i.

***Step 1*: Separate:** $0.325252525\ldots = 0.3 + 0.025252525\ldots.$

Part 1

$$0.3 = \frac{3}{10}$$

Part 2

$\mathbf{0.0252525252525}$ ....

Let, $x = \mathbf{0.02525252525}$ .....

$\rightarrow$ $\mathbf{10}x = \mathbf{0.252525252525}$ .....

$\rightarrow$ $\mathbf{1000}x = \mathbf{25.252525252525}$ .....

Subtracting, $\mathbf{1000}x - \mathbf{10}x = \mathbf{25}$

This gives, $\mathbf{990}x = \mathbf{25}$

And, $x = \frac{25}{990}$

***Step 2*: ADD**:

$$\mathbf{0.32525252525.} \ldots = \frac{3}{10} + \frac{25}{990}$$

Change the fraction $\frac{3}{10}$ *to an equivalent fraction that has the same denominator by multiplying both numerator and denominator by 99* $\left(i.e. \frac{297}{990}\right)$

It means that;

$$= \frac{297}{990} + \frac{25}{990}$$

$$= \frac{322}{990}$$

Divide both numerator and denominator by 2.

$$= \frac{161}{495}$$

ii.

***Step 1*: Separate:** $3.166666666... = 3.1 + 0.066666666 ....$

Part 1

$$3.1 = \frac{31}{10}$$

Part 2

$0.066666666 ....$

Let, $x = 0.066666666666 .....$

$\rightarrow \quad 10x = 0.666666666666 .....$

$\rightarrow \quad 100x = 6.66666666666 .....$

Subtracting, $100x - 10x = 6$

This gives, $90x = 6$

And, $x = \frac{6}{90}$

***Step 2*: ADD**:

$$3.16666666666. .... = \frac{31}{10} + \frac{6}{90}$$

Change the fraction $\frac{31}{10}$ *to equivalent fraction that has the same denominator by multiplying both numerator and denominator by 9* $\left(i.e. \frac{279}{90}\right)$

It means that;

$$= \frac{279}{90} + \frac{6}{90}$$

$$= \frac{285}{90}$$

Divide both numerator and denominator by 15. Note that you can do that step by step before arriving at the final answer.

$$= \frac{19}{6}$$

Q4. The following recurring decimals have been changed into fractions. Show how the results were obtained.

i. $0.\dot{a}\dot{b} = \frac{ab}{99}$

ii. $0.\dot{a}b\dot{c} = \frac{abc}{999}$

Solution:

i.

Let, $x = 0.abababababab\ldots$

$\rightarrow \quad 100x = ab.abababab\ldots$

Subtracting, $100x - x = ab$

This gives, $99x = ab$

And, $x = \frac{ab}{99}$

ii.

Let, $x = 0.abcabcabcabcabcabc\ldots$

$\rightarrow \quad 1000x = abc.abcabcabcabcabc\ldots$

Subtracting, $1000x - x = abc$

This gives, $999x = abc$

And, $x = \frac{abc}{999}$

Q5. Prove that the recurring decimal;

i. $0.\dot{3}0\dot{9} = \frac{103}{333}$

ii. $0.5\dot{6}\dot{9} = \frac{94}{165}$

Solution:

i.

Let, $x = 0.309309309309309....$

$\rightarrow \quad 1000x = 309.309309309309 .....$

Subtracting, $1000x - x = 309$

This gives, $999x = 309$

And, $x = \frac{309}{999}$

Divide both numerator and denominator by 3.

$$x = \frac{103}{333}$$

ii.

***Step 1*: Separate:** $0.569696969... = 0.5 + 0.069696969 ....$

Part 1

$$0.5 = \frac{5}{10}$$

Part 2

$0.06969696969 ....$

Let, $x = 0.06969696969 .....$

$\rightarrow \quad 10x = 0.6969696969 .....$

$$\rightarrow \quad 1000x = 69.6969696969\ldots..$$

Subtracting, $1000x - 10x = 69$

This gives, $990x = 69$

And, $x = \frac{69}{990}$

***Step 2*: ADD**:

$$0.32525252525\ldots.. = \frac{5}{10} + \frac{69}{990}$$

Change the fraction $\frac{5}{10}$ *to equivalent fraction that has the same denominator by multiplying both numerator and denominator by 99* $\left(i.e. \frac{495}{990}\right)$

It means that;

$$= \frac{495}{990} + \frac{69}{990}$$

$$= \frac{564}{990}$$

Divide both numerator and denominator by 6.

$$= \frac{161}{495}$$

14. Sequences

Sequences are numbers that obey a certain rule or pattern.

Examples are:

- $1, 2, 3, 4, 5, 6$ .....etc. (i.e. adding 1)
- $10, 8, 6, 4, 2$ ....etc. (i.e. subtracting 2)

Each term (i.e. each number) is defined by the position number which is denoted by the letter ***n***.(i.e. $n = 2$, means position number 2).

The **first term** every sequence is denoted by the letter, ***a***, and the **common difference** by the letter, ***d*** (i.e. the constant adding or subtracting number).

The **n^{th}-term** represent the rule or formula behind each term in a sequence at the position ***n***.

A series is when the terms with the sequences are added (e.g. $10 + 8 + 6 + 4 + 2$ ... and it can be ***finite*** (i.e. stops at a certain number terms) or ***infinite*** that continues without end.

The focus of this chapter is ***to show how to find the nth terms in Arithmetic, Quadratic, Geometric and Fibonacci sequences.***

Strategies for finding n^{th}- term:

I. Arithmetic Sequence

This is sometimes called a ***linear sequence*** that can be described as a sequence with a constant difference between consecutive terms. When there is an increase by a constant number, it called the ***arithmetic sequence***.

(a) Finding the nth-term of an arithmetic sequence

To find the ***n^{th}-term***, the steps are;

1. find the common difference (***d***),
2. generate a ***new*** sequence by multiplying the ***d*** and ***n*** (i.e. ***dn***).
3. Subtract the first term of the new sequence (***dx1 = d***) from the first term of the given sequence $(\boldsymbol{a - d})$.
4. The ***n^{th}-term*** $= \boldsymbol{dn + (a - d) = a + dn - d = a + (n - 1)d}$.

   Hence, this is normally written as $\boldsymbol{n^{th} = a + (n - 1)d}$

Example 1;
Find the nth term of the arithmetic sequence, ***3, 9, 15, 21, 27…..***

Solution:

	3,	**9,**	**15,**	**21,**	**27**
Difference (***d***)		6	6	6	6

n	1	2	3	4	5
Original	*3*	*9*	*15*	*21*	*27*
$\boldsymbol{d \times n = 6n}$	6	12	18	24	30
Subtract $(\boldsymbol{a - d})$	*-3*				
$n^{th} = dn + (a - d) =$	*3*	*9*	*15*	*21*	*27*
$\boldsymbol{n^{th} = 6n - 3}$					

Example 2;
Find the nth term of the arithmetic sequence, ***4, 1, -2, -5, -8…..***

Solution:

	4,	**1,**	**-2,**	**-5,**	**-8**
Difference (***d***)	-3	-3	-3	-3	

n	1	2	3	4	5
Original	*4*	*1*	*-2*	*-5*	*-8*
$\mathbf{d \times n = -3n}$	-3	-6	-9	-12	-15
Subtract $(\mathbf{a} - \mathbf{d})$	*7*				
$\mathbf{n^{th}} = dn + (a - d) =$	*4*	*1*	*-2*	*-5*	*-8*
$\mathbf{n^{th} = -3n + 7}$					

(b) Verifying terms within arithmetic sequence

To check whether a particular number is part of a sequence, the ***n***-value must be calculated from the ***nth-term*** formula.

This is done by ***equating*** the number to the $\boldsymbol{n^{th}}$***-term*** formula.

Note:

1. The number is ***part of the sequence*** if the calculated ***n*** is a whole number.
2. The number is **NOT** ***part of the sequence*** if the calculated ***n*** is a *fraction* or *decimal*.

Example 1;

Verify whether 146 is part of the arithmetic sequence ***6, 11, 16, 21, 26…..***

Solution:

	6,	**11,**	**16,**	**21,**	**26**
Difference (***d***)	5	5	5	5	

n	1	2	3	4	5
Original	*6*	*11*	*16*	*21*	*26*
$\mathbf{d \times n = 5n}$	5	10	15	20	25

Subtract $(\mathbf{a}-\mathbf{d})$	*1*				
$n^{th} = dn + (a-d) =$	*6*	*11*	*16*	*21*	*26*
$n^{th} = 5n + 1$					

To verify whether the number is part of the sequence,

$$n^{th} = 5n + 1 = 146$$

$$5n + 1 = 146$$

$$5n = 146 - 1$$

$$n = \frac{145}{5}$$

$$n = 29$$

Hence, since $\underline{n} = \mathbf{29}$, the number is part of the sequence and it is at the **29th position**.

Example 2;
Verify whether -225 is part of the arithmetic sequence ***5, -2, -9, -16, -23…..***

Solution:

5, -2, -9, -16, -23

Difference (***d***) -7 -7 -7 -7

n	1	2	3	4	5
Original	*5*	*-2*	*-9*	*-16*	*-23*
$\mathbf{d \times n = -7n}$	-7	-14	-21	-28	-35
Subtract $(\mathbf{a}-\mathbf{d})$	*12*				
$n^{th} = dn + (a-d) =$	*5*	*-2*	*-9*	*-16*	*-23*
$n^{th} = -7n + 12$					

To verify whether the number is part of the sequence,

$$n^{th} = -7n + 12 = -225$$

$$-7n + 12 = -225$$

$$-7n = -225 - 12$$

$$n = \frac{-237}{-7}$$

$$n = 33.9$$

Hence, since **n** = **33.9**, the number is ***NOT*** part of the sequence.

II. Quadratic Sequence

This is a ***sequence*** that has a constant on any two consecutive terms during the second difference. It means a sequence can only be a ***quadratic sequence*** when the ***second difference*** becomes a constant.

(a) Finding the nth-term of a quadratic sequence

To find the ***n^{th}-term***, the steps are;

1. find the ***first*** and ***second*** difference. You must have a ***constant number*** after the second difference to ensure it is a *quadratic sequence.*
2. generate a ***new*** sequence by using ***HALF*** of the ***second common difference*** multiplied by n^2 $\left(i.e. \frac{d}{2}n^2\right)$.
3. ***Subtract*** the new sequence $(\frac{d}{2}n^2)$ from the Original sequence (***O***). The results will be a ***LINEAR Sequence***.
4. Find the ***n^{th} term*** of the ***linear sequence*** as described before.

5. The ***Overall*** n^{th}***-term*** is the addition of the ***First new sequence*** plus ***the linear sequence.*** That is;

$$n^{th} = \frac{d}{2}n^2 + n^{th}\ term\ of\ linear\ sequence$$

Example 1;
Find the nth term of the quadratic sequence, ***7, 12, 21, 34, 51…..***

Solution:

Step 1:

	7,		**12,**		**21,**		**34,**		**51**
First difference		5		9		13		17	
Second difference			4		4		4		

Step 2:
Start a new sequence with half of the second difference **multiply** *by* n^2.

$$\frac{4}{2}n^2 = 2n^2$$

n	1	2	3	4	5
Original (O)	*7*	*12*	*21*	*34*	*51*
$\frac{4}{2} \times n^2 = 2n^2$	2	8	18	32	50
Subtract $(O - 2n^2)$	*5*	*4*	*3*	*2*	*1*

The result is a ***linear sequence***, **5, 4, 3, 2, 1,……….**

Step 3:
Find the nth *term of the linear sequence.*

	5,		**4,**		**3,**		**2,**		**1**
Difference (***d***)		-1		-1		-1		-1	

n	1	2	3	4	5
Original	*5*	*4*	*3*	*2*	*1*
$\mathbf{d \times n = -1n}$	-1	-2	-3	-4	-5
Subtract $(\mathbf{a} - \mathbf{d})$	*6*				
$n^{th} = dn + (a - d) =$	*6*	*11*	*16*	*21*	*26*
$\mathbf{n^{th} = -1n + 6}$					

Step 4:
*The nth term of the overall sequence (***add first** *and* **second n^th^ term***) is;*

$$= \mathbf{2n^2 - 1n + 6}$$

Example 2;
Find the $\boldsymbol{n}^{th}$ term of the quadratic sequence, ***-2, 3, 14, 31, 54…..***

Solution:

Step 1:

	-2,		**3,**		**14,**		**31,**		**54**
First difference		5		11		17		23	
Second difference			6		6		6		

Step 2:
Start a new sequence with half of the second difference **multiply** *by* $\boldsymbol{n^2}$.

$$\frac{6}{2}\boldsymbol{n^2} = \mathbf{3}\boldsymbol{n^2}$$

n	1	2	3	4	5
Original (***O***)	***-2***	*3*	*14*	*31*	*54*
$\frac{6}{2} \times \boldsymbol{n^2} = \mathbf{3}\boldsymbol{n^2}$	3	12	27	48	75
Subtract $(\boldsymbol{O} - \mathbf{3}\boldsymbol{n^2})$	***-5***	*-9*	*-13*	*-17*	*-21*

The result is a ***linear sequence***, **-5, -9, -13, -17, -21,……….**

Step 3:
Find the nth *term of the linear sequence.*

	-5,	**-9,**	**-13,**	**-17,**	**-21**
Difference ($\boldsymbol{d}$)	-4	-4	-4	-4	

n	1	2	3	4	5
Original	***-5***	***-9***	***-13***	***-17***	***-21***
$\boldsymbol{d \times n = -4n}$	-1	-8	-12	-16	-20
Subtract ($\boldsymbol{a - d}$)	*-4*				
$\boldsymbol{n^{th}} = dn + (a - d) =$	*-5*	*-9*	*-13*	*-17*	*-21*
$\boldsymbol{n^{th} = -4n - 4}$					

Step 4:
*The nth term of the overall sequence (***add first*** and* **second n^th term***) is;*

$$= \boldsymbol{3n^2 - 4n - 4}$$

III. <u>Geometric Sequence</u>

Geometric sequence, also called a ***geometric progression***, is a sequence where there is a common ratio (***r***) that is normally used to multiply and change the terms in the sequence to the next terms.

That is; if the terms are

$$\boldsymbol{a, a \times r, a \times r \times r, a \times r \times r \times r \ldots\ldots}$$

$$\rightarrow \boldsymbol{a, ar, ar^2, ar^3} \ldots\ldots$$

The common ratio is given by;

$$\boldsymbol{r = \frac{ar}{a} = \frac{ar^2}{ar} = \frac{ar^3}{ar^2}} \ldots\ldots\ldots$$

The **n^{th} term** of a geometric sequence is given by;

$$\boldsymbol{n^{th} = ar^{n-1}}$$

This equation can be used to resolve any geometric sequence problems.

(a) Finding the nth-term of geometric sequence

To find the ***n^{th}-term***, the steps are;

1. find the common ratio (***r***),
2. identify the first term, (***a***).
3. put the values in the formula to find the ***n***th-term.

$$n^{th} = ar^{n-1}$$

Example 1;

Find the nth term and the 8th term of the geometric sequence, ***2, 6, 18, 54, 162…..***

Solution:

2, 6, 18, 54, 164

Step 1:

*Common ratio (**r**),*

$$r = \frac{6}{2} = \frac{18}{6} = 3$$

*First term (**a**) = 2*

Hence, the nth term is;

$$n^{th} = ar^{n-1}$$

$$n^{th} = 2 \times 3^{n-1}$$

Therefore, the 8th term is;

$$8^{th} = 2 \times 3^{8-1}$$

$$8^{th} = 2 \times 3^{7}$$

$$8^{th} = 4374$$

Example 2;

Find the nth term and the 7th term of the geometric sequence, ***1024, 256, 64, 16, 4…..***

Solution:

1024, 256, 64, 16, 4 ……

Step 1:

*Common ratio (**r**),*

$$r = \frac{256}{1024} = \frac{64}{256} = \frac{1}{4}$$

*First term (**a**) = **1024***

*Hence, the **n**th term is;*

$$n^{th} = ar^{n-1}$$

$$n^{th} = 1024 \times \left(\frac{1}{4}\right)^{n-1}$$

Therefore, the 7th term is;

$$7^{th} = 1024 \times \left(\frac{1}{4}\right)^{7-1}$$

$$7^{th} = 1024 \times \left(\frac{1}{4}\right)^{6}$$

$$7^{th} = 0.25$$

IV. Fibonacci Sequence

Fibonacci sequence is a special sequence such that the ***next term*** in the sequence is the ***sum*** of the ***two previous*** terms.

That is;

if

$$First\ term\ (a) = x$$

and

$$second\ term\ (a) = y$$

It means that the;

$$\textit{third term} = x + y$$

Example of a Fibonacci sequence is;

$$\underbrace{4,\quad 7,}_{}\quad \overset{4+7}{11},\quad \overset{7+11}{18},\quad \overset{11+18}{29},\quad \overset{18+29}{47}\ \ldots\ldots\ldots$$

Example question 1;
Fin the next 5 terms of the Fibonacci sequence, -3, 2 **.....**

Solution:

n	*1*	2	*3*	*4*	*5*	*6*	*7*
Rule			*-3+2*	*2+-1*	*-1+1*	*1+0*	*0+1*
Sequences	*-3*	*2*	*-1*	*1*	*0*	*1*	*1*

Example 2;
Find the sixth term of a Fibonacci sequence if the first term is ***x*** and the second term is ***y***.

Solution:

n	*1*	*2*	*3*	*4*	*5*	*6*
Rule				y + $x+y$	$x+y$ + $x+2y$	$x+2y$ + $2x+3y$
Sequences	x	y	$x+y$	$x+2y$	$2x+3y$	$3x+5y$

Questions

Q1. Find the nth term of the arithmetic sequence, $\frac{1}{4}, \frac{13}{4}, \frac{25}{4}, \frac{37}{4}, \frac{49}{4}$ .....

Solution:

Note *that the common difference* $= \frac{13}{4} - \frac{1}{4} = \frac{12}{4} = 3$

$$\frac{1}{4}, \quad \frac{13}{4}, \quad \frac{25}{4}, \quad \frac{37}{4}, \quad \frac{49}{4} \ldots..$$

Difference (***d***) 3 3 3 3

n	1	2	3	4	5
Original	$\frac{1}{4}$	$\frac{13}{4}$	$\frac{25}{4}$	$\frac{37}{4}$	$\frac{49}{4}$
$\boldsymbol{d \times n = 3n}$	3	6	9	12	15
Subtract $(\boldsymbol{a} - \boldsymbol{d})$	$\frac{-11}{4}$				
$n^{th} = dn + (a - d) =$	*3*	*9*	*15*	*21*	*27*
$n^{th} = 3n - \frac{11}{4}$					

Q2. Verify whether 1556 is part of the arithmetic sequence ***9, 16, 23, 30, 37…..***

Solution:

To verify whether a particular number is part of a sequence, the $\mathbf{n^{th}}$ **term** must be determined first.

9, 16, 23, 30, 37

Difference (***d***) 7 7 7 7

n	1	2	3	4	5
Original	*9*	*16*	*23*	*30*	*37*
$\mathbf{d \times n = 7n}$	7	14	21	28	35
Subtract $(\mathbf{a - d})$	*2*				
$n^{th} = dn + (a - d) =$	*9*	*16*	*23*	*30*	*27*
$\mathbf{n^{th} = 7n + 2}$					

To verify whether the number is part of the sequence,

$$\mathbf{n^{th} = 7n + 2 = 1556}$$

$$\mathbf{7n + 2 = 1556}$$

$$\mathbf{7n = 1556 - 2}$$

$$\mathbf{n = \frac{1554}{7}}$$

$$\mathbf{n = 222}$$

Hence, since $\underline{\boldsymbol{n}}$ = **222**, the number is part of the sequence and it is at the **222th position**.

Q3. Find the $\boldsymbol{n}^{th}$ term of the quadratic sequence, ***28, 39, 44, 43, 36…..***

Solution:

Step 1:

	28,		**39,**		**44,**		**43,**		**36**
First difference		11		5		-1		-7	
Second difference			-6		-6		-6		

Step 2:
Start a new sequence with half of the second difference **multiply** *by* $\boldsymbol{n^2}$.

$$\frac{-6}{2}n^2 = -3n^2$$

n	1	2	3	4	5
Original (O)	***28***	***39***	***44***	***43***	***36***
$\frac{-6}{2} \times n^2 = -3n^2$	-3	-12	-27	-48	-75
Subtract $(\boldsymbol{O - 3n^2})$	***31***	***51***	***71***	***91***	***111***

The result is a ***linear sequence***, **31, 51, 71, 91, 111, ……**

Step 3:
Find the nth *term of the linear sequence.*

	31,		**51,**		**71,**		**91,**		**111**
Difference (***d***)		20		20		20		20	

n	1	2	3	4	5
Original	***31***	***51***	***71***	***91***	***111***
$\boldsymbol{d \times n = 20n}$	20	40	60	80	100
Subtract $(\boldsymbol{a - d})$	***11***				
$n^{th} = dn + (a - d) =$	***31***	***51***	***71***	***91***	***111***
$n^{th} = 20n + 11$					

Step 4:
The ***n***[th] ***term*** *of the overall sequence (***add first*** and* ***second n***[th] ***term****) is;*

$$= -3n^2 + 20n + 11$$

Q4. Find the nth term of the quadratic sequence, ***2, 9, 19, 32, 48…..***

Solution:

Step 1:

	2,		**9,**		**19,**		**32,**		**48**
First difference		7		10		13		16	
Second difference			3		3		3		

Step 2:

Start new sequence with half of the second difference,

$$\frac{3}{2}n^2$$

n	1	2	3	4	5
Original (O)	*2*	*9*	*19*	*32*	*48*
$\frac{3}{2} \times n^2 = 1.5n^2$	1.5	6	13.5	24	37.5
Subtract $(O - 1.5n^2)$	***0.5***	***3***	***5.5***	***8***	***10.5***

The result is a ***linear sequence***, **0.5, 3, 5.5, 8, 10.5, ……….**

Step 3:

Find the nth term of the linear sequence.

	0.5,		**3,**		**5.5,**		**8,**		**10.5**
Difference (d)		2.5		2.5		2.5		2.5	

n	1	2	3	4	5
Original	***0.5***	***3***	***5.5***	***8***	***10.5***
$d \times n = 2.5n$	2.5	5	7.5	10	12.5
Subtract $(a - d)$	**-2**				
$n^{th} = dn + (a - d) =$	***0.5***	***3***	***5.5***	***8***	***10.5***
$n^{th} = 2.5n - 2$					

Step 4:

*The nth term of the overall sequence (***add first** *and* **second n**[th] **term***) is;*

$$= 1.5n^2 + 2.5n - 2$$

Q5. The 4th term of a geometric sequence is 194.4 and the 6th term is 6998.4. Find the common ratio and the first term.

Solution:

The nth term of a geometric sequence is given by;

$$n^{th} = ar^{n-1}$$

The 4th term is given by;

$$4^{th} = ar^{4-1} = 194.4$$

This implies that;

$$ar^3 = 194.4 \quad (1)$$

Also, the 8th term is given by;

$$6^{th} = ar^{6-1} = 6998.4$$

This implies that;

$$ar^5 = 6998.4 \quad (2)$$

Dividing equation (2) by (1) gives;

$$\frac{ar^5}{ar^3} = \frac{6998.4}{194.4}$$

Note: the ***a****'s cancels out and the common ratio, (***r***), is solved by indices (i.e.* $r^5 \div r^3 = r^{5-3} = r^2$*) and the numbers are divided normally.*

$$r^2 = 36$$

Hence, r is given by;

$$r = 6$$

Using (1), a can be calculated as;

$$a \times 6^3 = 194.4$$

$$\rightarrow a \times 216 = 194.4$$

$$\rightarrow a = \frac{194.4}{216} = 0.9$$

Therefore, the first term is **0.9**.

Q6. A positive geometric sequence has **5**, ***x***, ***x*** + **30**, as the first three terms of the sequence. Calculate the 7th term of the sequence.

Solution:
This can be resolved by comparing the common ratios;

$$\frac{x}{5} = \frac{x+30}{x}$$

Using cross-multiplication described under algebraic expressions gives;

$$x \times x = 5 \times (x + 150)$$

This gives;

$$x^2 = 5x + 150$$

This implies that;

$$x^2 - 5x - 150 = 0$$

Using the factorization method described under Quadratic equations gives factor pairs of ***-15*** *and* ***10*** *(i.e. Factor pairs of* ***-150*** = ***-15*** ×***10****);*

This implies that;

$$(x - 15)(x + 10) = 0$$

This means that either;

$$(x - 15) = 0 \text{ and } x = 15.$$

Or;

$$(x + 10) = 0 \text{ and } x = -19.$$

But since we are dealing with positive sequence, $x = 15$.

Hence, the common ratio is given by;

$$r = \frac{15}{5} = 3$$

The nth term of a geometric sequence is given by;

$$n^{th} = ar^{n-1}$$

Since $a = 5$ *and* $r = 3$; *the required* n^{th} *term is given by;*

$$n^{th} = 5 \times 3^{n-1}$$

Therefore, the 7th *term is given by;*

$$7^{th} = 5 \times 3^{7-1}$$

$$= 3645$$

Q7. If the third term of a Fibonacci sequence is 22 and the fifth term 56, find the first term of the sequence.

Solution:

Let

$$first\ term = x$$

$$second\ term = y$$

It means the table can be filled as follows;

n	1	2	3	4	5	6
Rule				y + $x+y$	$x+y$ + $x+2y$	$x+2y$ + $2x+3y$
Sequences	x	y	$x+y$	$x+2y$	$2x+3y$	$3x+5y$
n^{th}			22		56	

It implies that;

$$x + y = 22 \quad (1)$$

$$2x + 3y = 56 \quad (2)$$

Using simultaneous equation;

Multiply (1) x2

$$2x + 2y = 44 \quad (3)$$

$$2x + 3y = 56 \quad (2)$$

Subtract; (3) – (2)

$$0 + -y = -12$$

$$y = 12$$

Since; $x + y = 22$

$$x + 12 = 22$$

Hence;

$$x = 22 - 12$$

$$x = 10$$

Therefore the first term is **10**.

Q8. If the 4th term of a Fibonacci sequence is -1 and the 8th term -14, find the first term of the sequence.

Solution:

Let

$$first\ term = x$$

$$second\ term = y$$

It means the table can be filled as follows;

n	1	2	3	4	5	6	7	8
Rule				y + $x+y$	$x+y$ + $x+2y$	$x+2y$ + $2x+3y$	$2x+3y$ + $3x+5y$	$3x+5y$ + $5x+8y$
Sequences	x	y	$x+y$	$x+2y$	$2x+3y$	$3x+5y$	$5x+8y$	$8x+13y$
n^{th}				-1				-14

It implies that;

$$x + 2y = -1 \quad (1)$$

$$8x + 13y = -14 \quad (2)$$

Using simultaneous equation;

Multiply (1) $x8$

$$8x + 16y = -8 \quad (3)$$

$$8x + 13y = -14 \quad (2)$$

Subtract; $(3) - (2)$

$$0 + 3y = 6$$

$$y = 2$$

Since; $x + 2y = -1$

$$x + 4 = -1$$

Hence;

$$x = -1 - 4$$

$$x = -5$$

Therefore the first term is **-5**.

15. Direct and Inverse Proportion

Proportions are the relationships between quantities which are governed by rules. They can be ***direct*** or ***inverse*** proportions.

Direct Proportion. This is when there is a positive linear relation between two values and a multiple of one will give the other.

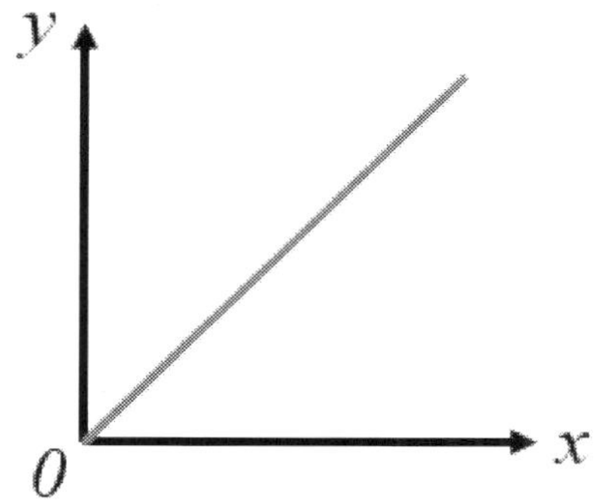

This can be described as the graph of $\boldsymbol{y = kx}$ is a straight line that passes through the origin.

Inverse Proportion. This is when there is a negative relationship between two values such that when one value increases, the other decreases.

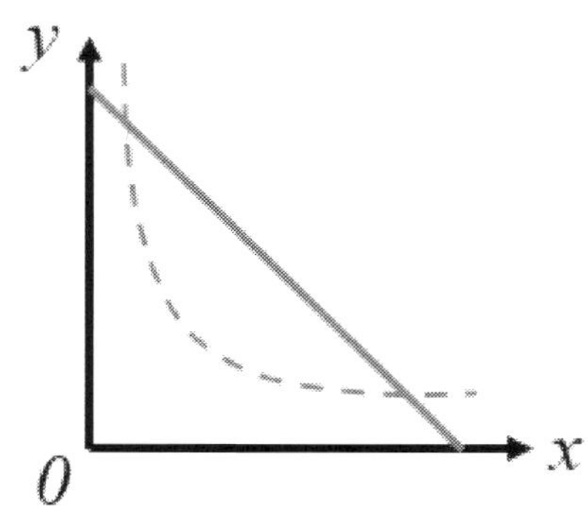

This can be described as the graph of $\boldsymbol{y = k\frac{1}{x}}$ is a reciprocal graph.

<u>Strategies for solving direct and inverse proportion:</u>

To resolve ***direct and inverse problems***, the steps are;

1. Write the relation between the two values using ***proportional sign*** ($\propto$),
2. Change the ***proportional sign*** ($\propto$) to ***equal sign*** (=) and **proportionality constant** (***k***).
3. Find the value of ***k*** and insert it back into the equation.

   <u>Note</u>: Two values are always given to solve the value of ***k***.
4. Use the established ***equation*** to solve the rest of the questions.

I. <u>Direct Proportion</u>

Example 1;
The amount of marks (***m***) obtained in GCSE exams is directly proportional to the hours of learning (***h***). A student studies for 150 hours and received 60 marks.

i. Find the relationship between ***m*** and ***h***.
ii. Find how long a student must study to obtain 70 marks.
iii. A student studies for 200 *h*. What will be his marks?

Solution:

i. Finding a relationship.

This can be solved by the following steps;

Step 1:
Write the relation;

$$m \propto h$$

Step 2:
Change the proportional sign into (=) and constant (<u>k</u>).

$$m = kh$$

Step 3:

Find k.

$$k = \frac{m}{h}$$

When $\boldsymbol{h}$ = 150 h, $\boldsymbol{m}$ = 60

It means that;

$$k = \frac{60}{150} = \frac{2}{5}$$

Therefore the equation is;

$$m = \frac{2}{5}h$$

Step 4:
Use the equation to solve the remaining questions;

ii. Find how long a student must study to obtain 70 marks.

If $\boldsymbol{m}$ = 70,

$$70 = \frac{2}{5}h$$

This can be resolved as;

$$h = \frac{70 \times 5}{2} = 175h$$

Hence, the student must study for 175h to achieve 70 marks;

iii. A student studies for 200 h. What will be his marks?

If $\boldsymbol{h}$ = 200,

$$m = \frac{2}{5}(200)$$

This can be resolved as;

$$m = \frac{2 \times 200}{5} = 80\ marks$$

Hence, the will achieve 80 marks;

Example 2;

The distance covered (***x***) in a race (i.e. *metres*) is proportional to the ***square*** of the time (***t***) in seconds. When $x = 12$, $t = 4$.

i. Find the relationship between ***x*** and ***t***.
ii. Find ***x*** when $t = 7$.
iii. Find ***t*** when $x = 27$.

Solution:

i. Finding a relationship.

This can be solved by the following steps;

Step 1:
Write the relation;

$$x \propto t^2$$

Step 2:
*Change the proportional sign into (=) and constant (**k**).*

$$x = kt^2$$

Step 3:
Find k.

$$k = \frac{x}{t^2}$$

When $x = 12$, $t = 4$

It means that;

$$k = \frac{12}{4^2} = \frac{12}{16}$$

Therefore the equation is;

$$x = \frac{3}{4}t^2$$

Step 4:
Use the equation to solve the remaining questions;

ii. Find $\boldsymbol{x}$ when $\boldsymbol{t} = 7$.

If $\boldsymbol{t} = 7$,

$$x = \frac{3}{4}(7)^2$$

This can be resolved as;

$$x = \frac{3 \times 49}{4} = 36.75$$

Hence, the distance covered is 36.8 metres.

iii. Find $\boldsymbol{t}$ when $\boldsymbol{x} = 19$.

If $\boldsymbol{x} = 27$,

$$27 = \frac{3}{4}t^2$$

This can be resolved as;

$$t^2 = \frac{27 \times 4}{3}$$

It means;

$$t = \sqrt{\frac{27 \times 4}{3}} = 6$$

Hence, time is 6 seconds.

II. Inverse Proportion

Example 1;

The pressure (***P***) of a gas is inversely proportional to its volume (***V***). When the volume is 10 m^3, the pressure is 700 N/m^2.

i. Find the relationship between ***P*** and ***V***.
ii. Find the pressure when the volume is 7 m^3.
iii. Find the volume of the gas when the pressure is 1100 N/m^2.

Solution:

i. Finding a relationship.

This can be solved by the following steps;

Step 1:
Write the relation;

$$P \propto \frac{1}{V}$$

Step 2:
*Change the proportional sign into (=) and constant (**k**).*

$$P = \frac{k}{V}$$

Step 3:
Find k.

$$k = PV$$

When ***P*** = 700 N/m^2, ***V*** = 10 m^3.

It means that;

$$k = 700 \times 10 = 7000$$

Therefore the equation is;

$$P = \frac{7000}{V}$$

Step 4:
Use the equation to solve the remaining questions;

ii. Find the pressure when the volume is 7 m³.

If ***V*** = 7,

$$P = \frac{7000}{7}$$

This can be resolved as;

$$P = 1000$$

Hence, the pressure is 1000 N/m².

iii. Find the volume of the gas when the pressure is 1100 N/m².

If ***P*** = 1100,

$$980 = \frac{7000}{V}$$

This can be resolved as;

$$V = \frac{7000}{1100} = 6.4$$

Hence, the volume is 6.4 m³.

Example 2;

The value (***y***) inversely is proportional to the ***square-root*** of the value (***x***). When ***x*** = 16, ***y*** = 3.

i. Find the relationship between ***y*** and ***x***.
ii. Find ***x*** when ***y*** = 5.
iii. Find ***y*** when ***x*** = 49.

Solution:
i. Finding a relationship.

This can be solved by the following steps;

Step 1:
Write the relation;

$$y \propto \frac{1}{\sqrt{x}}$$

Step 2:
*Change the proportional sign into (=) and constant (**k**).*

$$y = \frac{k}{\sqrt{x}}$$

Step 3:
Find k.

$$k = y \times \sqrt{x}$$

When $x = 16$, $y = 3$

It means that;

$$k = 3 \times \sqrt{16} = 12$$

Therefore the equation is;

$$y = \frac{12}{\sqrt{x}}$$

Step 4:
Use the equation to solve the remaining questions;

ii. Find x when $y = 5$.

If $y = 5$,

$$5 = \frac{12}{\sqrt{x}}$$

This can be resolved as;

$$\sqrt{x} = \frac{12}{5}$$

The value x will be;

$$x = \left(\frac{12}{5}\right)^2 = 5.8$$

Hence, x is 5.8.

iii. Find $\boldsymbol{y}$ when $\boldsymbol{x} = 49$.

If $\boldsymbol{x} = 49$,

$$y = \frac{12}{\sqrt{49}}$$

This can be resolved as;

$$y = \frac{12}{7} = 1.7$$

Hence, y is 1.7.

Questions

Q1. The power (***P in watts***) of an engine is directly proportional to the volume of fuel (***V***) it consumes. If the volume of 25 litres gives 700 watts power,

i. Find the relationship between ***P*** and ***V***.
ii. Find the power when the volume is 70 litres.
iii. Find the volume of fuel used when the power is 450 watts.

Solution:

i. Finding a relationship.

This can be solved by the following steps;

Step 1:
Write the relation;

$$P \propto V$$

Step 2:
*Change the proportional sign into (=) and constant (**k**).*

$$P = kV$$

Step 3:
Find k.

$$k = \frac{P}{V}$$

When $P = 700$ N/m^2, $V = 25$ litres.

It means that;

$$k = \frac{700}{25} = 28$$

Therefore the equation is;

$$P = 28V$$

Step 4:
Use the equation to solve the remaining questions;

ii. Find the power when the volume is 70 litres.

If $V = 70$,

$$P = 28 \times 70$$

This can be resolved as;

$$P = 784$$

Hence, the power is **784 Watts**.

iii. Find the volume of fuel used when the power is 450 watts.

If $P = 450$ watts,

$$450 = 28V$$

This can be resolved as;

$$V = \frac{450}{28} = 16.1$$

Hence, the volume is 16.1 litres.

Q2. The sale (***S***) of jackets is inversely proportional to the environmental temperature (***T***). At 5 °C, the sale was £500.

i. Find the relationship between ***S*** and ***T***.
ii. Find the possible sales amount when the temperature is 12 °C.
iii. What will the temperature be if sales amounted to £1200?

Solution:

i. Finding a relationship.

This can be solved by the following steps;

Step 1:
Write the relation;

$$S \propto \frac{1}{T}$$

Step 2:
*Change the proportional sign into (=) and constant (**k**).*

$$S = \frac{k}{T}$$

Step 3:
Find k.

$$k = ST$$

When $S = £500$, $T = 5$ °C.

It means that;

$$k = 500 \times 5 = 2500$$

Therefore the equation is;

$$S = \frac{2500}{T}$$

Step 4:
Use the equation to solve the remaining questions;

ii. Find the possible sales amount when the temperature is 12 °C.

If $T = 12$ °C,

$$S = \frac{2500}{12}$$

This can be resolved as;

$$S = 208.33$$

Hence, the possible sales will be £208.33.

iii. What will the temperature be if sales amounted to £1200?

If $S = 1200$,

$$1200 = \frac{2500}{T}$$

This can be resolved as;

$$T = \frac{2500}{1200} = 2.1$$

Hence, the temperature will be is approximately 2°C.

Q3. In a tensile test experiment of a polymer, the stress (***S***) of the polymer is found to be directly proportional to the strain (ε) within the elastic region. A strain of about 250 % was obtained at a stress of 40 MPa.

i. Find the relationship between $\boldsymbol{S}$ and ε.
ii. Find Stress when the strain is about 150 %.
iii. What is the strain if the stress reaches 49 MPa within the elastic region?

Solution:

i. Finding a relationship.

This can be solved by the following steps;

Step 1:
Write the relation;

$$S \propto \varepsilon$$

Step 2:
Change the proportional sign into (=) and constant (k).

$$S = k\varepsilon$$

Step 3:
Find k.

$$k = \frac{S}{\varepsilon}$$

When $\boldsymbol{S} = 40$ MPa, $\varepsilon = 250$ %.

It means that;

$$k = \frac{40}{250} = \frac{4}{25}$$

Therefore the equation is;

$$S = \frac{4}{25}\varepsilon$$

Step 4:
Use the equation to solve the remaining questions;

ii. Find Stress when the strain is about 150 %.

If $\varepsilon = 150$,

$$S = \frac{4}{25} \times 150$$

This can be resolved as;

$$S = 24$$

Hence, the stress will be **24 MPa**.

iii. What is the strain if the stress reaches 49 MPa within the elastic region?

If $S = 49$ watts,

$$49 = \frac{4}{25}\varepsilon$$

This can be resolved as;

$$\varepsilon = \frac{49 \times 25}{4} = 306.25$$

Hence, the strain will be 306.3 %.

Q4. The value y is directly proportional to the cube of x. Fill in the table below.

x	2	3	4	5	6
y			288		

Solution:

In other to fill in the table, a relationship between x and y needs to be established. The equation can then be used to find the y values.

This can be solved by the following steps;

Step 1:

Write the relation;

$$y \propto x^3$$

Step 2:
*Change the proportional sign into (=) and constant (**k**).*

$$y = kx^3$$

Step 3:
Find k.

$$k = \frac{y}{x^3}$$

From the table, it can be seen that when $x = 4$, $y = 288$.

It means that;

$$k = \frac{288}{4^3} = 4.5$$

Therefore the equation is;

$$y = 4.5x^3$$

Step 4:
Use the equation to solve find the remaining y-values;

When x = 2;

$$y = 4.5 \times 2^3 = 36$$

When x = 3;

$$y = 4.5 \times 3^3 = 121.5$$

When x = 5;

$$y = 4.5 \times 5^3 = 562.5$$

When x = 6;

$$y = 4.5 \times 6^3 = 972$$

Hence, the full table is;

x	2	3	4	5	6
y	36	121.5	288	562.5	972

Q5. The value y is inversely proportional to the cube root of x. Fill in the table below.

x	1	8	27	64	125
y				25	

Solution:

In other to fill in the table, a relationship between x and y needs to be established. The equation can then be used to find the y values.

This can be solved by the following steps;

Step 1:
Write the relation;

$$y \propto \frac{1}{\sqrt[3]{x}}$$

Step 2:
*Change the proportional sign into (=) and constant (**k**).*

$$y = \frac{k}{\sqrt[3]{x}}$$

Step 3:
Find k.

$$k = y \times \sqrt[3]{x}$$

From the table, it can be seen that when $x = 64$, $y = 25$.

It means that;

$$k = 25 \times \sqrt[3]{64} = 100$$

Therefore the equation is;

$$y = \frac{100}{\sqrt[3]{x}}$$

Step 4:
Use the equation to solve find the remaining y-values;

When x = 1;

$$y = \frac{100}{\sqrt[3]{x1}} = 100$$

When x = 8;

$$y = \frac{100}{\sqrt[3]{8}} = 50$$

When x = 27;

$$y = \frac{100}{\sqrt[3]{27}} = 33.3$$

When x = 125;

$$y = \frac{100}{\sqrt[3]{125}} = 20$$

Hence, the full table is;

x	1	8	27	64	125
y	100	50	33.3	25	20

Summary:

In all cases, the relationship between the variables given must be found even if the question does not ask for it. The resulting equation can be used to answer any further questions.

Printed in Great Britain
by Amazon

62110477R00196